Mastering Pro Tools® Effects:
Getting the Most Out of Pro Tools' Effects Processors

Jeremy Krug

Course Technology PTR
A part of Cengage Learning

COURSE TECHNOLOGY
CENGAGE Learning®

Australia • Brazil • ⌐ ...dom • United States

COURSE TECHNOLOGY
CENGAGE Learning

**Mastering Pro Tools® Effects:
Getting the Most Out of Pro Tools'
Effects Processors
Jeremy Krug**

Publisher and General Manager, Course
Technology PTR: Stacy L. Hiquet

Associate Director of Marketing:
Sarah Panella

Manager of Editorial Services:
Heather Talbot

Senior Marketing Manager: Mark Hughes

Acquisitions Editor: Orren Merton

Project Editor: Dan Foster, Scribe Tribe

Copy Editor: Donna Poehner

Interior Layout Tech: MPS Limited, a
Macmillan Company

Cover Designer: Luke Fletcher

Indexer: Larry Sweazy

Proofreader: Mike Beady

For product information and technology assistance, contact us at
Cengage Learning Customer & Sales Support, 1-800-354-9706

For permission to use material from this text or product,
submit all requests online at **www.cengage.com/permissions**

Further permissions questions can be emailed to
permissionrequest@cengage.com

Avid and Pro Tools are registered trademarks of Avid Technology, Inc., in the
United States. All other trademarks are the property of their respective owners.

All images © Cengage Learning unless otherwise noted.

Library of Congress Control Number: 2011920274

ISBN-13: 978-1-4354-5678-5

ISBN-10: 1-4354-5678-5

Course Technology, a part of Cengage Learning

20 Channel Center Street

Boston, MA 02210

USA

Cengage Learning is a leading provider of customized learning solutions with
office locations around the globe, including Singapore, the United Kingdom,
Australia, Mexico, Brazil, and Japan. Locate your local office at: **international.
cengage.com/region**

Cengage Learning products are represented in Canada by Nelson Education, Ltd.

For your lifelong learning solutions, visit **courseptr.com**

Visit our corporate website at **cengage.com**

Printed in the United States of America
1 2 3 4 5 6 7 14 13 12

For Dr. Fuzz...
and the rest of my family

Acknowledgments

A very special thanks must go out to Orren Merton and Dan Foster for their immeasurable patience and assistance in helping me get this book written.

Thanks must also go to the Washington State University School of Music, especially Dr. Gerald Berthiaume and Dr. Gregory Yasinitsky for their support and encouragement. And a big thanks to my student employees (and friends) John T. Baunsgard and Josué Schneegans who helped keep things flowing at the studio through all the distractions.

Big thanks also go to all the friends and family who helped to push me along, especially Michelle Boese who worked hardest to keep me going, along with Zoriah Wieth and Eric Engerbretson who both kept asking if I was done yet, everyone in the Palouse Board Gamers club for keeping me thoroughly distracted, and all my family in Colorado who told me to hurry up and come visit.

Thanks as well to my photo models, Eric Engerbretson (www.eric-e.com), Krista Penney (www.kristapenney.com), Charles Scott Benson III, and Josué Schneegans for lending your time and faces to brighten up the pages.

About the Author

Jeremy Krug, engineer and producer, has more than 15 years of experience in location and studio recording, and describes himself as drawing from many sources. Jeremy studied Music Performance as an undergraduate student at The Harid Conservatory in Boca Raton, FL, and at the University of Colorado at Boulder, where he also studied composition, electronic music, film, and radio production. Later, Jeremy studied Audio Engineering at the University of Colorado at Denver, served as sound designer for several productions with the National Theatre Conservatory, and started his own location recording business serving schools, community ensembles, and individual artists in Colorado, Washington, and Idaho.

In December of 2002, Jeremy joined the staff of Washington State University to serve as the Audio Engineer for the School of Music. He began his work there by designing, purchasing, and installing the electronics package to complete the 1.5-million-dollar WSU Recording Studio. Since then he has run the studio and produced nearly 1,000 recording projects. The projects span every genre of music and include work for film and television, live theatre, and even the entomology department. Jeremy also introduced and began teaching recording courses for the School of Music in 2006 while serving as the staff advisor for both the WSU chapter of MEISA and the WSU Electronic Music Association.

In November of 2011, Jeremy took on a new position with Solid State Logic that will see him touring the United States with their latest broadcast mixing consoles. Jeremy lives somewhere between Washington State, Los Angeles, and New York City, and can be found online at LinkedIn.com.

Contents

Chapter 4
Equalizers

73

Chapter 8
Dither, Sound Field, and Other Plug-Ins

331

Introduction

While the subject of this book, the plug-in audio effects suite included with Pro Tools software, seems a simple enough subject at first glance, the content is intentionally in-depth and can be a lot to consume if not approached in the right way. A quick read through this introduction will help give you an idea of how best to begin based on what you are hoping to do with Pro Tools.

Why This Book Was Written

Many books attempt to describe the use of Pro Tools software in its entirety or describe individual uses and functions of the software such as editing or mixing. But the intention here is to explore, in-depth, the plug-in effects processors available within Pro Tools. Of course, to truly explore this aspect of the software means more than simply rehashing the manual or creating a list of all of the plug-ins available. Exploring means understanding what each plug-in can do and how it might be applied during various stages of music and audio production from the very starting point of composition or songwriting, through the recording, editing, and mixing process, all the way through to mastering.

Who This Book Is For

Let's face it: Every author likes to think that simply everyone needs to read his book. But as it happens there really is something in here for just about everyone who uses Pro Tools on a regular basis, whether you are just getting started or are a fairly seasoned professional. It is probably best to take a moment and talk about some of the different Pro Tools users and what each type can expect to learn.

The Musician, Composer, or Home Studio User

This is the person who may or may not have a lot of recording experience, but who is interested in being able to use Pro Tools for songwriting, musical composition, basic demo recording, or more. If you are among this group and are reading this book, you have probably already set up your home studio and probably have done some recording already. If you are truly just getting started, much of the material here may be a little advanced, but every effort has been made to include refreshers on basic concepts and references to other resources for learning the basics. However, all users of this group will find benefit in learning to use the wealth of tools available within Pro Tools to enhance their musical and composing creativity, and to expand their sonic creativity.

The Audio Student

Audio students are the only readers likely to approach this book from cover to cover, especially if they are using it as a text in class, or if they are studying on their own and trying to ingest all of the possibilities available within the Pro Tools plug-in suite. As an aspiring professional audio engineer, learning about all of the many ways audio can be manipulated, repaired, enhanced, or demolished should be an essential part of your studies. Of course, while you are still a student it is very difficult to predict what kind of career you might later find within the larger audio industry. You might find a place as a recording engineer involved in music production, but you might just as likely find a career in audio for film and television, or maybe sound design for theatre, film, or video games, or you might even find yourself working as a mastering engineer. You will find that while each individual plug-in may not include a specific usage example for every professional field, each family of processors will have examples that cover a broad range of possible applications. So having a good sense of all of the possibilities will help you later when you do land in your audio career.

The Emerging Professional or New Pro Tools Convert

You might be someone fresh out of recording school, just starting your career, or someone with some experience putting together your first commercial studio, or possibly a somewhat seasoned veteran who is taking the plunge by finally putting that old tape machine into the mothball fleet and embracing digital. Every effort has been made to not seem pedantic or condescending to any level of reader, least of all this group. This group most likely already knows what it is they would like to do with the effects processor plug-ins, but simply needs a handy guidebook for how to get around and how to make the most of the tools available to them. But be open-minded, because you may also find some new ideas on how to apply tools in ways you hadn't previously considered. And you might even find some tools you didn't know existed.

Anyone Else Involved in Audio Production

It's important to remember that there is more to the field of audio engineering than simply music production. Anyone using Pro Tools for sound design in theatre, video, film, video games, or multimedia design will find this book a resourceful guide to adding effects to the sound they are creating. Likewise, those involved in radio production, voice-overs, post-production, and other similar fields will benefit. Audio is audio, whether the source is a bass drum, a voice, a car door, or a thunderstorm; we still record, edit, mix, and master the material in much the same way. While most of the usage examples may well be music related, some are more specifically geared to other fields as well. And you will find that subjects like making a voice or instrument sound brighter, or making something stand out in a mix or seem to be in another space, are just as applicable to almost any kind of audio production.

Those Not Even Using Pro Tools for Studio Production

This is admittedly an unusual group to consider, but there may be something here for non-Pro Tools users as well. Avid also produces the very popular VENUE live-sound mixing console, and there may be users who want to know more about the plug-in effects in Pro Tools that are also available on the console. And, of course, this is as much a book about how to use effects processors in general. Yes, the plug-in processors described here are specific to Pro Tools, but when you think about it, learning creative ways to use one equalizer or dynamics processor means learning creative ways to use almost any equalizer or dynamics processor.

A Master Class on When and How to Use Plug-Ins

Just as the plug-in suite is applicable to many different types of users, it is also useful in all aspects of music and audio production to varying degrees. Of course, not all plug-ins are useful in every stage of the game, and some are downright dangerous to use in the wrong places, but some can be used in places and ways that aren't immediately obvious—which is why it is helpful to see some examples outside your regular work environment and comfort zone.

The Role of Plug-Ins in the Music Production Process

Let's face it: Most Pro Tools users are likely to be involved in some aspect of music production. So we will explore what kinds of plug-ins can help during the songwriting and composition process, during basic recording and overdubbing, and then during editing, through mixing, and all the way to mastering. The differences between these various stages of production will be discussed later, and the usage examples given for various plug-ins will usually mention whether the particular technique being described is more applicable to one stage than another. For example, we will explore how using effects such as reverb during vocal overdubs might help a performance, but can be tricky if there is too much delay caused by the processing involved.

The Role of Plug-Ins in Other Kinds of Audio Production

We will also look at some plug-ins that can be particularly useful for other kinds of audio production beyond just music. Is compressing the sound of a rim shot for a rock song really that much different from compressing the sound of a gunshot for a film soundtrack? Maybe not, but there are some production techniques particular to sound design, voice-over, and other audio production work that can be a little more specialized.

The goal is not to simply list a bunch of processors, show a few screenshots, and explain how to save some presets. Instead, you will see how to connect creative ideas to a variety of possible technical solutions. That's not to say that we can "teach" creativity; it just doesn't work that way. But in learning about connecting problems to solutions, creative concepts to technical details, and common requests to common solutions, you will develop a set of tools that will allow you to more easily express your creative ideas when it is time.

Getting Around

So hopefully the question at the front of your mind at this point is, "Where do I fit in to this book?" Of course, that is something you have to answer yourself, but you will have some help.

This book is arranged so that every reader would do well to read through Chapter 1, "Establishing a Baseline." There's a reason for that choice of chapter title. Chapter 1 will try to explain how you might proceed through the rest of the book based on your knowledge base and experience.

After that, Chapter 2, "Fundamentals of Recording," tries to cover some of the basic concepts involved in getting good material from the start. While the plug-in suite within Pro Tools is a very powerful set of tools for manipulating audio, there are some things that simply cannot be "fixed in the mix." Readers already well versed in good recording practice might find themselves skipping this chapter, but it is included to make sure some basic ideas are covered for those who need them.

Chapter 3 explores the different "stages" of the recording process and provides a better explanation of when you are involved in each different task. When does the editing stage stop and the mixing stage begin? This is important for all readers since these stages will be mentioned throughout the rest of the book. Chapter 3 explains the thought process behind the various descriptions.

After these introductory chapters, the real learning begins. Chapters 4–8 explore all of the most essential plug-ins included with Pro Tools. These are the tools you'll want to know best, because they are the ones you'll tend to reach for every day. At the beginning of each of these chapters, you'll find a refresher section that explains some of the basic technical concepts you should know to better understand the plug-ins described in the chapter.

Simply trying to work through all the plug-in chapters in order could work if you are approaching each chapter as a series of exercises meant to help you explore each new tool, but, practically speaking, we tend to think in terms of creative ideas, and those ideas might have many different ways of being accomplished. It's more likely that you will jump directly to a particular chapter or even to a specific plug-in. I've tried to include references to other plug-ins and information that can help you in this approach as well. In either case, the goal is to help you learn to get the most out of the Pro Tools plug-in suite.

1 Establishing a Baseline

We all have to start somewhere.

In a book of this style it isn't really possible to meet all readers at their level of experience with the plug-in effects processors, with Pro Tools software in general, and with general audio engineering skills. Regardless of your level of experience, start by reading through this first chapter. Since the rest of this book is written with the expectation that you already have a fair grasp of the basics of audio, recording, and Pro Tools in general, this chapter is included to help you gauge how you might proceed. The first three sections help you establish a starting point, and the last two sections take a look at what these "plug-in" things really are.

The goal is to help you find the tools you need without being weighed down reading about lots of things you might already know. Each chapter dealing with a specific family of processor types will include some relevant refresher material that will be useful to nearly all levels of readers. For example, it's important to understand a little about frequency ranges of instruments, harmonics, and the human range of hearing before trying to figure out what knobs to turn on an equalizer. For now, though, let's get started.

What Pro Tools and Its Plug-In Suite Can (and Cannot) Do for You

While digital audio workstations (DAWs) are very powerful and capable software platforms, there are some features that only need to run on rare occasions, and there are some things the larger platforms simply cannot do...at least not without a little help. This is true of all DAWs, including Pro Tools, and is the reason why plug-ins exist.

The plug-in effects processor suite included with Pro Tools addresses some of the needs that arise during various stages of the recording and audio production process. It's important to realize that these smaller programs are not there because the platform itself isn't up to the task. Rather, they are separated out kind of like the sub-systems in a car. Sure, you want your car to have a heater for the winter, and an air conditioner for the summer, but you aren't likely to run both at the same time. The little motor in the door that raises and lowers the window only needs to be switched on briefly to raise or lower the window. Similarly, the plug-in suite addresses occasional needs. Not every audio clip you record will need to be rendered with the pitch-shift program.

You won't necessarily need to run an equalizer on every single audio channel while you are mixing.

Plug-ins can also provide options, so you can use different kinds of processors at different times. Back to the car analogy again: You probably have the option on your car stereo to choose between AM radio, FM radio, CD playback, and maybe a connection for an MP3 player. Plug-ins can give you the option of using different examples of similar types of audio processors—for example, you might choose one kind of compressor for a bass guitar track and another type for a lead vocal track.

Here's a quick look at some of the advantages of knowing how to use the plug-ins available within Pro Tools.

Improved Flexibility in Recording and Editing

The process of recording seems simple enough: Find a sound, put a microphone in front of it, feed the signal to the computer, and then record it. But as we all learn soon enough, the process becomes much more involved once you actually start working. We run into snags while recording that can use a little help. We can be careful about how we record to avoid more problems down the road. And we can fix little problems that might have crept in along the way.

- When tempo becomes an issue during recording or overdubbing, a click track may be needed to keep the musicians in time.

- A sudden burst of inspiration to add an instrument that isn't available in your home, studio, or even your town can be satisfied with a software synthesizer.

- A little reverb while overdubbing the lead vocal parts can help put the singer at ease and give them a sense of how long to hold out the long notes.

- Watching a correlation meter (e.g., the BF Essential Correlation Meter) while trying to record that wind sound will reassure you that the tracks are in-phase.

- Those one or two out-of-tune notes can be fixed with Pitch Shift during editing to save an otherwise perfect bass track.

- A loud "P" pop on a vocal track can be singled out while editing and fixed by removing the low frequencies with an equalizer.

Of course, those are just a few examples of what can be done to make recording and editing more productive. As you learn more about the tools available and many of the possible ways to use them, you will be more flexible, confident, and creative in how you approach recording, overdubbing, and editing.

A Larger Creative Palette for Mixing or Mastering

Here again, this part of recording seems simple enough: The sounds are there, you adjust the levels, and everything falls into place. But that pesky reality creeps in and you find that the sounds you captured just don't sound as cool as you thought they would, or maybe they don't blend together quite as easily as you had hoped. This is where you see two sides of the tools you have available: the corrective side, and the creative side.

Sometimes an equalizer has to be engaged on a track to fix a particular problem, like removing low-frequency rumble from the traffic outside, or thinning the lower midrange on a muddy rhythm guitar track. Other times that same equalizer might be applied for a creative effect, like creating a telephone effect on a voice or bringing out a little extra shimmer from the wind chimes.

And that's just the tip of the iceberg—just a few uses of one particular kind of plug-in. There is more than one kind of equalizer...and more than just equalizers. When you consider all of the various dynamics processors, reverb processors, pitch, delay, modulation effects, harmonic effects, and more, the sonic palette appears truly immense. Just don't let that seem intimidating.

Yes, the creative palette is huge, staggering even, but you will quickly find that while some tools are used on almost every track in every session, others only come out once in a very rare while—like that ugly sweater in your closet that only comes out when Aunt Edith visits. Indeed, some tools are wrong for entire genres of music. I record a lot of jazz and classical music and hardly ever find a client who enjoys the sound of a flanger on any of their tracks. The point, however, is that once you know a little about what all of these tools can do, you can keep that knowledge on hand and know the tool will be there waiting to go to work when it's needed.

They're Good, but They Can't Fix Everything

The basic Pro Tools software is very powerful, and the plug-in suite expands on that power significantly, but no matter how much time you might spend or how many crayons are in the bucket, there are some things that may still be out of reach.

- Distorted audio cannot easily be "undistorted."

- Noisy rooms can't be easily removed, especially from under quiet sources.

- Reverb can make close-sounding sources seem more distant, but there is no "un-reverb" processor to make distant sources sound closer.

- There is no plug-in for removing the drum sounds that bled into the bass microphone, or vice-versa (Figure 1.1).

- And most importantly, creativity cannot be switched on and plugged in to a track, a song, or a mix. That part is up to you.

So while we are going to explore many of the wonderful possibilities available in the plug-in suite, it's good to keep in mind that there are limitations.

Figure 1.1   There is no plug-in to remove the noise from the fan, traffic, or guitar that is captured by the vocal microphone.

What You Should Know Before Going Further

It is assumed that you have already purchased and installed your Pro Tools software, and that you are already familiar with setting up sessions, recording audio, and doing at least some basic editing. With that said, there are a lot of people who approach Pro Tools from a lot of different directions, and that will be addressed here and a little more in the next section.

If you haven't yet installed or used Pro Tools or any other DAW software, then—as much as I'd love for you to buy my book—it may not be time yet (though feel free to buy it now and have it on the shelf for when you're ready). There are a number of other texts and other media available from Cengage Learning that are better suited to getting you started with Pro Tools or that can give you a great refresher if you're moving to Pro Tools from another DAW platform. Consider the DVD *Pro Tools 8 Course Clips Starter* by Christopher R. Burns (ISBN-10: 1598639897).

If your work will involve the recording of sound (some form of moving air, regardless of what is causing it to move), it's best to have some basic understanding of what is involved in recording those sounds. Chapter 2 will cover just a few basic fundamentals, and there are other "refresher" segments in later chapters that try to make certain that key concepts are covered before they are discussed in the context of particular processors and effects. But with that said, if you are at all in doubt about your experience and understanding of simple acoustics, microphone placement, basic recording, etc., you might consider looking at titles such as:

- *The Ultimate Personal Recording Studio, 1st Edition*, by Gino Robair (ISBN-10: 1598632108)

- *The Recording Engineer's Handbook, 1st Edition*, by Bobby Owsinski (ISBN-10: 1932929002)

Likewise, if editing audio, mixing, and mastering are part of what you plan to do within Pro Tools, but you haven't yet done much of that kind of work, then keep this book ready and take a look at some other more fundamental books on the subjects such as:

■ *The S.M.A.R.T. Guide to Digital Recording, Software, and Plug-Ins*, by Bill Gibson (ISBN-10: 1592006965)

■ *The Mixing Engineer's Handbook, 1st Edition*, by Bobby Owsinski (ISBN-10: 0872887235)

■ *Mastering Music at Home, 1st Edition*, by Mitch Gallagher (ISBN-10: 1598633929)

How Far Can I Skip Ahead?

Of course, if you already have a pretty good grasp of audio production, you can certainly move ahead a little quicker. This book is meant to provide some benefit to everyone from the novice, student, or home-recording musician, to the emerging professional engineer, or even the seasoned industry veteran. Here is how things are laid out in the next few chapters.

Chapter 2, "Fundamentals of Recording" will try to cover precisely that—what it takes to get good quality recordings. You'll find basic recording ideas that are universal and time-tested for getting great results with your finished product. They will keep you from spending hours, days, or weeks trying to fix mistakes that could have been avoided at an earlier stage. This is likely an essential chapter for the novice or the musician looking to start recording themselves at home. For the audio student, it can be a good refresher to pull together all those concepts that were covered in other courses. But for the pro engineers, it's probably something you can skip unless you're only just playing with your first DAW.

Chapter 3, "Compose, Record, Edit, Mix, and Master" will break down the audio production process into five reasonably distinct stages and explain in a general way how plug-ins can help with each of those stages. It will also cover some of the basic handling and manipulation of real-time and audio suite plug-ins. For the novice, musician, or student, the entire chapter is an essential read, but the emerging pro or seasoned veteran might simply skim the first few sections but be sure to catch the parts about managing and organizing the plug-ins.

After that, the fun begins. Chapters 4–8 describe the most essential plug-ins of the Pro Tools suite, the stuff you're likely to use every day, and they are grouped into categories in the same way they appear in the software. Simply trying to absorb all of the information about the various plug-ins and how they might be applied by reading chapters 4–8 straight through is probably not the best approach for most readers. Audio students using this book as a text for class or on their own might do well to work through the book in that way, but most readers are likely to jump to a particular chapter or even to a specific plug-in. With that in mind, each plug-in is described thoroughly on its own with occasional references to other plug-ins or to the refresher sections at the beginning of each chapter. Each plug-in has a usage example of some kind, and at the end of each chapter you'll find extra examples of great techniques to try and terrible mistakes to avoid. So if you jump around to specific plug-ins, be sure to also take a little time to read the beginning and ending sections of each chapter.

So What Are Plug-Ins, Anyway?

It doesn't really make sense to start this exploration of plug-ins until we have at least some general sense of what plug-ins really are. We refer to them as tools and switch them on and off as they are needed. But why aren't they simply set up to run all the time? Why can't Pro Tools manage this stuff on its own? Why are there limitations on how and where we can use plug-ins? This should help make some sense of these things.

The Basic Concept

On its own, Pro Tools is a very powerful software platform for recording, editing, and processing audio. However, there are situations when special tools are required to manipulate audio in a very specific way. These might include something as simple as changing the overall volume level of a piece or audio. Or it might be as complicated as calculating all of the reverberant reflections of various frequencies reflecting from different surfaces in a simulated acoustic space. But whatever the particular task is for any plug-in, it is a smaller program that runs within the larger Pro Tools platform (Figure 1.2).

Figure 1.2 Plug-ins are smaller programs that run within the larger Pro Tools platform.

Why lots of little separate programs? There are several reasons for using smaller programs for these jobs. Some tasks need only be done once and then can be put away, such as the Invert or Reverse functions. Others may only be necessary on certain audio elements, for example, not every track may need a compressor. Others may represent various options for doing the same task, for example, you may only need one equalizer on an audio track, but have several choices available. In the end, it all comes down to managing the processing and memory resources of the computer. If all of the programs were running and ready to go on all of the audio channels at all times, the system would be hopelessly bogged down trying to manage a lot of tools that aren't even in use.

Plug-In Types within Pro Tools

The plug-in suite in Pro Tools is divided into two main categories: real-time processors and non-real-time processors.

Real-Time Processors: RTAS, TDM, and AAX

The real-time processors are the type most users immediately associate with the term "plug-in" for a variety of reasons. One is that they represent the same sort of external processors that were quite literally "plugged in" to a particular analog audio path within a typical recording studio. A signal emerging from a tape machine might be plugged into a compressor whose output is in turn plugged into the mixing console. Another reason is that real-time processors are graphically represented as being placed within an audio channel and so become part of the signal path for that channel.

The real-time processors in Pro Tools come in two primary flavors: RTAS and TDM, and in Pro Tools 10 they are joined by the new AAX format. The Real-Time Audio Suite (RTAS & AAX) plug-ins are "native" processors, meaning they are designed to process audio signals through the host computer's CPU. These are the basic plug-ins included with all levels of earlier Pro Tools LE and Pro Tools M-Powered systems, as well as the current versions of Pro Tools, Pro Tools HD, and Pro Tools HDX. The Time-Division Multiplexing (we'll stick with TDM) plug-ins run on the Core or Accel processing cards within a Pro Tools HD or Pro Tools HDX system.

Some plug-ins, such as the instrument plug-in Xpand! (Figure 1.3), are available only as real-time plug-ins. Once it is added to a track, Xpand! must run and generate the synthesized instrument sounds every time the session is played back.

Non-Real-Time Processors: Audio Suite

While they are indeed still part of the plug-in package, the Audio Suite plug-ins are slightly different in that a single processing program is opened up, used to process selected segments of audio, and then the program is put away. It's like taking a screwdriver from your toolbox, tightening a few screws to mount some flashy new piece of gear in your equipment rack, and then putting the screwdriver away. The Reverse plug-in (Figure 1.4) is a great example, since you can't very well reverse your audio in real-time for what should be the obvious reason that the program needs to start at the end of the file and work backward.

Figure 1.3 The instrument plug-in Xpand! can run only as a real-time processor.

Figure 1.4 The Reverse plug-in takes an audio clip and writes it backward into a new file.

Some of the same plug-ins available as real-time processors are available within the Audio Suite as well. This is also very convenient since it allows a real-time version of a plug-in to be used to listen to and adjust the settings, and then process those tracks into new files so that both the real-time plug-ins can be switched off to reduce stress on the computer's CPU and memory. That concept will be better explained in the "Mixing In the Plug-Ins" section of Chapter 3.

Real-Time versus Audio Suite in Practical Use

As mentioned, the reason for all the different plug-in types is to better manage the memory and processing resources within your Pro Tools system. Real-time plug-ins, especially RTAS and AAX native plug-ins, run continuously and will tax and eventually slow down your system performance. Audio Suite plug-ins process the audio and write it into new files, which means the process is done once and put away. But that also means that changes to the processed tracks involve either bringing back the original files or double-processing the audio. Audio Suite plug-ins will also fill up your hard drive faster since each new process writes a new file, taking up space on the drive. In the end, it's all a game of balancing out all the limited resources inside your machine. But don't worry; this will be covered in better detail throughout Chapter 3.

What Kinds of Tools Are There?

The goal of this book is to take an in-depth look at all of the plug-ins included with Pro Tools software—the ones that most every user will have available. Some of the plug-ins covered may not be included with every version of the software, and premium plug-ins (those that are sold separately, even if they are included in some bundles) are not covered. It shouldn't be too big of a surprise that there are different plug-ins included with different versions of Pro Tools. This is partly because of the differences between the native (RTAS & AAX) and DSP-based (TDM & AAX) processing systems. You can't run TDM or AAX DSP plug-ins without an HD-Core, HD-Accel, or HDX card installed. It's also because extra plug-ins are often included as a premium with different hardware bundles. And, of course, new processors are being developed and added all the time.

If your Pro Tools software is installed and you have worked with it even just a little, then you already have a pretty good idea of at least the names of all the plug-ins included with your particular hardware/software bundle. Most of these will be explored here, and of course the names of all of the processors covered are listed in the Table of Contents. However there are some things you can expect to see in every Pro Tools system:

Real-Time and Audio Suite Processors

The difference between these two types of processors will be explained in more depth in the next chapter, but it is worth mentioning here that this is the basic division between the two types of processors available. Real-time processors (AAX, RTAS, TDM, and HTDM) are engaged for a particular audio channel and run continuously from that point. Some plug-ins can only run in this way. Virtual instruments are a good example, because obviously the instrument needs to be available to be played. On the other hand, Audio Suite plug-ins are engaged for a short period of time, process a selected portion of audio (usually while writing a new file), and then are put away. And again, some plug-ins can only run in this way. The Time Shift plug-in (Figure 1.5) is a great example, since stretching or contracting a piece of audio to fit a longer or shorter period of time is something that can logically happen only when the playback or recording is stopped.

The large majority of plug-in processors are indeed available as both real-time and Audio Suite. We will look at when and why to use each a little later.

Processors by Type

Regardless of the Pro Tools system you're using, it will include a number of different plug-in processors for each of several "family" types. When you open the pull-down menu to select a plug-in, you will likely see them arranged into these groups (Figure 1.6), and they are organized

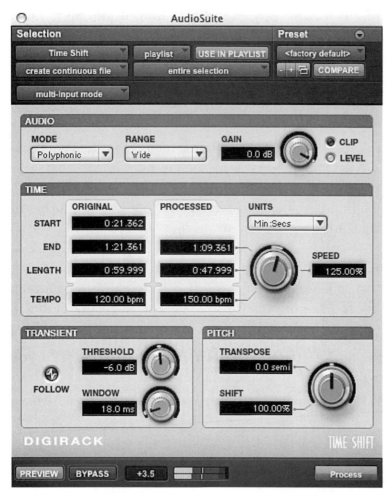

Figure 1.5 The Time Shift plug-in stretches or contracts an audio clip to fit a different length of time.

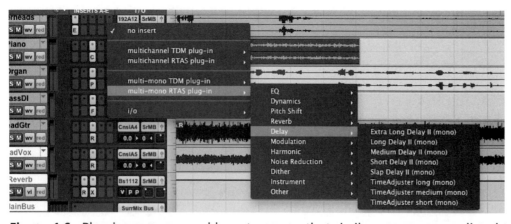

Figure 1.6 Plug-ins are arranged by category so that similar processors are listed together.

similarly in this book. It just makes sense to group all of the equalizers together, and separate from all the dynamics processors, reverb processors, delays, and instruments, etc. You'll find that your system includes several options in all of the various categories. Of course, some plug-ins are a little harder to define and may actually appear in multiple categories. For example, the real-time AIR Frequency Shifter should appear as both a Pitch Shift and a Harmonic processor in the pull-down menu. Although for the sake of organization in this book, plug-ins will only appear in one chapter (you'll find the AIR Frequency Shifter in the Pitch Shift chapter).

At this point it is probably a good idea to take a look through your own Pro Tools system and see what plug-ins are listed there while comparing that listing to the Table of Contents in this book. Open an existing session or start a new one. Take a look at the pull-down menu for the Audio Suite plug-ins first, since that is the easiest to view. Then it's a good idea to select or create both a mono and a stereo track to view the available real-time plug-ins. You should notice just a few differences between the plug-ins available for the different types of tracks, although you'll notice an extra menu separation that will appear for the stereo (and multi-channel) tracks—the option to select between "Multi-Mono" and "Multi-Channel" plug-ins. It is important to notice that some plug-ins will appear in both lists while some appear only in one or the other. Simply stated, some processors process both channels of a stereo track the same, other processors can (if necessary) process each side of the stereo track independently, and some processors can function either way. The differences in use and application of these plug-ins will be explored in more depth in Chapter 3, but it is good to know why some of your processors don't show up in every list.

Hopefully you now have a pretty good idea of how to continue with this book and where you might look for additional help. Next, let's take a look at some of those fundamentals of good audio production practice to make sure we have good materials to work with later. As for those skipping ahead, well, we will meet up again at Chapter 3.

2 Fundamentals of Recording

Breaking the myth of "We'll fix it in the mix."

Great albums are a tower built from great mixes of great recordings, of great performances, and of great material. Each layer builds upon the last, so weakness at any level can unsettle the whole project. Once unsettled, it takes an enormous amount of time and effort to recover, and in the end, it may be too late.

All right, so maybe that sounds a little overly dramatic and severe, but take it in a moment and consider the idea. Since this isn't a book about songwriting, composition, or sound design, we will just assume that the material is great. Likewise, we'll just figure that all the performances are fantastic...or at least that you can edit really well. But if the sound arriving at the microphone isn't as great as it could possibly be, you are likely to spend a lot of time, effort, and energy trying to make it better later.

Yes, of course, that's the entire reason why many of these plug-ins exist in the first place. There may also be times when the quality of the audio you work with may be completely beyond your control. Nonetheless, we will work from the assumption that you are in control of every step in the process and will look at some of the key fundamentals to getting great recordings from the beginning so that the editing, mixing, and mastering stages can be all about creativity...and not recovery.

Outside the Box

Most audio productions will include at least some amount of material generated "outside the box," meaning the sounds are created somewhere outside of the computer. This might include acoustic musical instruments, vocals, spoken voice-overs, sound effects, or any sound that might come into the computer from a microphone or other source. And since much of the sound you will work with inside the computer starts out there, it's the best place to start making sure things sound good.

Start with Great Material

I've already mentioned that the goal here is not to teach you about songwriting, composition, sound design, or whatever other creative endeavor you have planned. The goal is to teach you how and when to use the plug-in suite inside Pro Tools to repair as necessary, enhance the sound of your material, and boost your sonic creativity. But it's still worth mentioning that there is no plug-in for creating more interesting lyrics or a cooler guitar riff or a more intriguing chord progression.

As the recording engineer at a university, I work with many young and aspiring musicians in every genre of music imaginable. One of the most common pieces of advice I give is to find out what strangers think of your material. All proud parents believe their new baby is the cutest baby in the world. And of course, all of their friends and family agree because they are friends and family. It often takes the disconnected honesty of a stranger who can say, "Sure, the baby's cute, but is it supposed to have that third arm sticking out of the middle of its forehead?" There are many great resources out there to help with writing better instrumental parts, writing better lyrics, and more. Depending on the type of material you are creating, consider checking out some works like these:

- *Musicianship in the Digital Age, 1st Edition*, by Brent Edstrom
  (ISBN-10: 1592009832)

- *Music Theory for Computer Musicians, 1st Edition*, by Michael Hewitt
  (ISBN-10: 1598635034)

- *Audio Post-Production in Your Project Studio, 1st Edition*, by Casey Kim
  (ISBN-10: 1598634194)

Make Sure the Instruments Sound Good

Making the instruments sound good can be a much more difficult process than you might first imagine. Not because there is some kind of special magic to making an instrument sound good, but because it takes a while to decide what a "good" sound really is. Of course, there is no single right answer to what makes a "good" sound or even what makes the "right" sound. It is often a balancing act between different concerns, but here are three good starting points to consider.

Personal Sound and Style

Every serious musician tries to develop a tone, a sound, or a style to their playing that is an audible signature of their personality and performance. Some will spend years searching for the "perfect" guitar, or try every kind of string available, or spend hours getting just the right tuning on a snare drum. But that perfect instrument or perfect sound may not always be the *right* sound for every recording project.

If you want a bright "ping" out of the snare drum, you might consider just reaching for an equalizer plug-in during mix-down. But that may not be as effective a choice as reaching for a different drum before the recording even begins. An easy enough choice in principal, but this kind of decision making can be even more complicated if other instruments aren't readily available, or if the musician isn't comfortable playing on some other instrument, or if the musician has a personal dislike for other sounds. Yes, the bright "ping" may be great for the song, but if the drummer hates that kind of sound in general and prefers a deep, dry "thwack" from his snare, that can be a tough sell.

Personal sounds and styles are an important part of making the recorded product your own. But it is important to remember that the two must complement and serve each other. If the performer serves the music and the music serves the performer, then both will be rewarded in the end.

Fit the Genre

This is very closely tied to the previous consideration of personal sound and is often where musicians find themselves at odds with the music...even if they created it. Consider the previous example of the bright "ping" for a snare drum if the overall project is a hard-rock or metal album, but one particular song has a real strong funk groove going. Weighing the difference in genre against the player's personal bias for his sound may help convince him to hear things differently and change it up for that one song.

Sometimes, however, we get lucky and the question of matching an instrument to a song is easily answered. If the project is to record a demo of a folk-style acoustic tune to submit to a few coffeehouses in search of a regular gig, then the thrash-metal guitar is probably not necessary. If the project is to record an audition for a classical pianist hoping to attend a conservatory, finding a place to record a grand piano in a performance space is likely to be a better choice than recording the spinet piano in grandma's living room or the out-of-tune upright in the church basement.

Of course, many musicians are happy to reach out beyond their usual sounds and styles and explore other genres while they work. And while it is possible to record an acoustic guitar and use plug-ins to apply enough distortion, effects, and amplifier modeling to make it sound like a thrash-metal guitar for one song, it would still be a lot easier to simply start with an electric guitar and amplifier in the first place.

Fit with the Other Instruments

If it isn't already hard enough to figure out what sounds good or bad for a single instrument, it is important to consider how all of the various pieces will fit together once the song is assembled. Again, you can reach for a number of plug-ins during mix-down to thicken bass enough to support the band, thin guitars enough to hear the lead vocals, brighten a cymbal crash, or bring out the twang in that piano sound. But some things are just easier to do with the real instruments before they are even recorded.

One of the more frustrating things about understanding how the instruments will eventually fit together is that it can't really be taught so much as it will be learned over time as you record more. And often the most confusing thing we discover is that sometimes an instrument that sounds terrible alone is exactly the right fit when blended with the rest of the band. That's not to say that an out-of-tune or poorly played instrument will suddenly sound in-tune and virtuosic. We are talking about tone quality here, and sometimes a thin, edgy, nasally sounding guitar that sounds terrible on its own may be just the right sound to cut through a dense mix and give a bright new contrast to that final chorus.

It is hard to predict without getting very specific, but there are some general ideas to consider that will be elaborated on in other chapters. For example, remember that not every instrument needs to occupy the entire frequency spectrum, and that within certain bands of spectrum, some instruments should take precedence over others. It is very easy for a distorted guitar sound to dominate most of the audible frequency range, and it may sound great all by itself, but eventually there will be vocals that people want to hear and understand. Also, remember that what works—and for that matter what is sometimes essential in live performances—may not work as well in a recording situation. Sure, those thick, bright, crash cymbals cut through a roaring crowd at the bar like nobody's business, but in the studio they're competing with the top end of an acoustic guitar, so something a little thinner and darker might be a better option.

Make Sure the Room Sounds Good

When the music stops, what do you hear? If your answer is, "Nothing, because my ears are ringing," then you just earned yourself five minutes in time-out. Seriously, though, what is going on in the room? There are two main factors to consider.

Ambient Noise

Sit in your recording space and listen to what sounds you hear when the music is not playing. It doesn't matter if you are in a professional recording studio, a concert stage, your basement, or your bathroom; something is going on in there, and it's good to know what it is. Is there traffic noise coming in from outside, or are there footsteps from the neighbors upstairs? Maybe there is the steady hum of a computer fan or hard drive? Or perhaps there's a vent blowing air into the room? Roommates fighting, dogs barking, kids playing, gnats farting…. Really, it doesn't matter what the specific sound is as long as you start to become aware of it and realize that if you can hear it, your microphones can probably hear it too.

Before the instruments are set, before the microphones are placed, and long before the record button is pressed, it's a good idea to minimize the amount of noise present in your recording space. If moving to a different space is an option (like maybe moving from the basement to the attic), then explore your available rooms and listen to what is going on elsewhere.

Some noises are easier to deal with than others. If the kegerator is too loud, maybe it should be moved out of your bedroom. Maybe some longer cables would allow the computer to live in a closet instead of in the main recording room. Turning off the heat or air-conditioning while recording can help as long as the room doesn't get too uncomfortable. It is impossible to find a completely silent space, but if you start with the quietest space you can find, treat the noise that you can treat, and then dodge the stuff you can't control, you'll be doing all right.

Natural Room Acoustics

After the noise is sorted out as much as possible, listen for what is happening with the acoustics in the room. When we talk, move around, or play instruments in real acoustic spaces, we not only hear the sound travelling directly from the source to our ears (or microphones) but also the sound bouncing off the walls, floors, furniture, and other surfaces. We identify the kinds of rooms we are in by the way our ears hear, and our brains interpret those reflections (see Chapter 6, "Reverberation," for a refresher on this subject). That's why bedrooms sound different than kitchens, which sound different than studios, which sound different than concert halls, which sound different than tunnels.

To get a sense of how your recording space works acoustically, recruit a friend to play an instrument, sing, or just talk to you in your recording space as well as a few other spaces to get a point of reference. Or simply walk around the room talking aloud, clapping your hands, or playing your instrument. (Sorry if you happen to play piano, but were you really going to move it to the bathroom to record anyway?) Then compare that to a space that has many exposed, hard surfaces like a tiled bathroom, and to a space that has many soft and absorbent surfaces like a living room or bedroom that is carpeted and full of furniture. That should give you a point of reference for what is happening in your recording space (but don't get overexcited about how cool things sound in the bathroom with that extra splash of reverb; Figure 2.1).

Figure 2.1 Playing or practicing in the bathroom may sound cool, but there's no removing or "turning down" that reverb once it is recorded.

Again, it is hard to give a simple formula for what is a useful acoustic space and what is not. It is worth saying, however, that it is far easier to add artificial space in the form of reverb than it is to take away the sound of a natural space. But at the same time you can create a more convincing artificial space if you are adding to a foundation of natural ambience. If it seems as though there is no winning, it's only because there is no real "right" answer insomuch as there are simply lots of options that may or may not work for your project. The best solution is to know what is going on in your room through listening and experimenting before you record. If you have to default to something because of time constraints, aim toward less natural room reverberation; it's all but impossible to remove the natural sound of a room, but it's easy to add more artificial reverb.

Keep in mind that although they are related to each other, soundproofing and room acoustics are not the same thing. When we talk about soundproofing and trying to keep sound energy from escaping one room to arrive at the next, we are talking about something that generally has to happen during construction of a room. Acoustic treatment can be placed on top of existing surfaces to change the way sounds move around within a space, but they do very little to keep unwanted sound from entering or escaping. To find out more about soundproofing or acoustic treatments in general, check out *Acoustic Design for the Home Studio,* by Mitch Gallagher (ISBN-10: 159863285X).

Quality on the Way In

The material may be fantastic, the performance inspired, and the instruments sound spectacular in the room, but now the microphone must capture the signal, pass it on through the preamplifier, and into the computer. If this part of the process isn't handled with care, you are likely to spend most of the rest of your time making up for it.

Good Microphones and Careful Placement

Like so many sections in these first few chapters, entire books have been written on this subject alone. Even small commercial recording studios may have upward of 50, 100, or more microphones in their collection. Some manufacturers have almost as many different models and designs available. There are two very good reasons for this. The first is that the choice of microphone has a huge impact on the quality and tone of the captured audio because it is accomplishing a very significant transformation (well, "transduction" really) of one form of energy into another. In the case of a microphone, we are converting acoustic energy (changes in air pressure) into electrical energy (alternating current). The other reason is far simpler to say, though it will get more attention in a moment, and that is no one microphone can possibly handle every task set before it...or at least not particularly well.

Yes, to some people them are fightin' words. But truthfully, no matter how good, bad, cheap, expensive, durable, fragile, popular, or rare a microphone may be, it is not going to be a perfect fit for everything. If that were the case, every studio would own a bunch of those microphones and that would be that. Luckily, it isn't and we get lots of toys, or rather tools, to help us handle specific tasks. Knowing a few basic concepts about microphones in general should help to get your recordings off to a great start.

Dynamic versus Condenser Microphones

Perhaps the most fundamental division of microphone types is the split between dynamic and condenser microphones. This is often oversimplified, even by experienced engineers, as microphones that don't require phantom power versus microphones that do require it. Understanding the fundamental differences in their design will help to make sense of why these two types of microphones act differently in the studio.

A more accurate explanation is that dynamic microphones are, by themselves, little "dynamos," or generators, that generate electricity from acoustic energy. Yes, that means they don't require phantom power, but it isn't just because somebody thought it would be convenient to build a microphone that way. The most common variety for recording or live performance use is the moving-coil dynamic microphone. This type, as illustrated in Figure 2.2, has a thin diaphragm attached to a coil of wire that is in turn suspended within a magnet. As the acoustic energy we call "sound" moves the air back and forth, the microphone diaphragm also moves back and forth, which moves the coil of wire within the magnetic field, which generates alternating current.

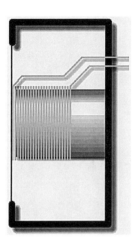

Figure 2.2 A dynamic microphone is a tiny generator that converts sound energy into electricity.

Since the diaphragm in a microphone of this type has to support the weight of the coiled wire, it tends to be thicker and heavier than other microphone designs. That added weight affects how quickly the microphone responds to sounds and its overall frequency response. So while it's a very broad generalization with lots of exceptions, it's still pretty safe to say that in general a typical, general-purpose, dynamic microphone will respond a little slower and have a reduced frequency response compared to a typical, general-purpose, condenser microphone.

Considering their recent rise in availability and popularity, it is probably also worth mentioning a bit about ribbon microphones, which also fall into the dynamic microphone category. In the case of a ribbon microphone, the diaphragm is a thin, corrugated strip of metal suspended within a magnet (Figure 2.3). As the air pressure changes move the ribbon back and forth, it generates an alternating current. It is quite similar in concept to the moving-coil design as far as the physics are concerned. But in practical use, to keep the weight down and increase sensitivity of the microphone means creating a thinner and generally more fragile ribbon which tends to also have a weaker signal output.

Condenser microphones (Figure 2.4) are often oversimplified in their description when explained as a microphone that requires phantom power. It is more accurate, however, to say that they require an external power source. Many condenser microphones can operate with phantom power, but others can be operated with battery power or with stand-alone power supplies. And

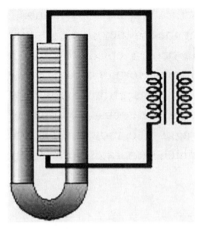

Figure 2.3 A ribbon microphone is a dynamic microphone of a different design.

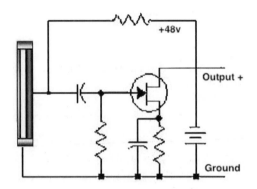

Figure 2.4 The thin diaphragm of a condenser microphone is part of a small amplifier circuit.

either way, this still overlooks a very fundamental difference in the design from a dynamic microphone. In a condenser microphone, the diaphragm is a very thin and light material stretched tightly above a charged back plate, in a way that appears at least somewhat similar to a drumhead. The diaphragm and back plate form a capacitor which is part of an amplifier circuit that is powered by the external supply. The electrical details of the operation of a condenser microphone are a little more complicated than we need to explain here. But the functional difference is that since the diaphragm only needs to support its own weight, it can be considerably thinner and lighter, which in turn can make a microphone that responds much more quickly and has a wider frequency response.

This is a still a very simplified explanation of the differences between these two fundamental types of microphones, and we won't even consider other microphone types such as carbon, crystal, or RF designs. It is more important for where we are headed that you know there are differences; that those differences can affect your recording; and that understanding a little more about how to use these very critical tools can make the rest of the recording process a much better experience.

Microphone Polar Patterns

Careful placement of your microphones means knowing how your microphone works, where it is listening, and where it isn't listening. What we call the polar pattern of a microphone is a description of how the microphone responds to sound arriving from different directions. The charts in Figure 2.5 below show the four most common patterns you will encounter with studio and live-performance microphones. They show the difference in signal output (volume) from the microphone when it is calibrated to a sound arriving "on-axis" at 0° and when that sound source is rotated around the microphone. Keep in mind that these are two-dimensional representations of a three-dimensional effect, so they should be imagined rotated around the 0°–180° axis.

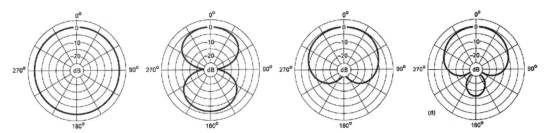

Figure 2.5 Polar pattern charts for omnidirectional, figure-8, cardioid, and hypercardioid microphones.

Don't skim past those patterns too quickly. Take a more careful look at what they are trying to tell you about how the microphone is listening to the things around it. A "cardioid," or "unidirectional," microphone isn't really listening in only one direction; it is really listening in all but one direction. The signal level is lower from all other directions except 0°, but it is only lower by 6dB at 90° off axis. That's something important to keep in mind if you are hoping that aiming the microphone straight down at the snare drum will somehow keep out the sound of the hi-hat.

Similarly, the figure-8 microphone is often looked at with some confusion at first since it is interpreted as being a microphone that "listens" equally in two directions, from the front and the back. If instead you were to view it as a microphone that rejects everything that is 90° off axis, it might suddenly appear much more useful. I often use a figure-8 patterned, ribbon microphone on large floor toms when recording drums as it gives me a great tone from the drum and almost completely ignores the ride cymbal which may be only inches away.

There is, however, one very big catch to the polar responses we expect to get from our microphones: They are not consistent across all frequencies.

This is a pretty serious consideration if you are hoping to use a particular microphone pattern to capture or reject certain sounds. In general, you can expect the patterns to change more toward omnidirectional at lower frequencies and more toward directional patterns (cardioid, hypercardioid) at higher frequencies. Think of it as wider at the low end and narrower at the top. But that actually means the null angles, where the microphone is rejecting the most sound, are changing as well. So if, for example, you are hoping that positioning the bass amp so it faces the drums and using a cardioid microphone for the bass drum will reject the sound of the bass from being picked up as well, you will be unpleasantly surprised.

It seems very complex, but once you know it is happening, this is an easy concept to keep in mind and work around. The best starting place is to experiment a little bit and get familiar with how your microphones perform. This can be as simple as plugging in the microphone and listening to the difference in sound as a friend speaks into it while rotating it from 0° through 90° to 180° and back around. You might even find some interesting and helpful changes in tone as you listen. I had a singer whose voice sounded great on a particular cardioid condenser microphone, but he had a very strong lisp on his "S" sounds. I rotated the microphone 90° and turned up the gain 6dB to compensate for the change. Across the main vocal range, his voice sounded the same, but at the very high frequency where he was hissing, the pattern was closer to a hypercardioid and so the hissing was a bit quieter in the recorded track. After a little extra help from a de-esser plug-in (see Chapter 5) everything sounded great.

Setting Levels and the Myth of Using Every Bit

Equally important to maintaining a high standard of quality on the way into the computer is setting good levels at the microphone preamplifier and any other steps along the path. In the "good old days" of analog recording, the recording medium itself was among the noisiest parts of the signal chain. For that reason, engineers would push the levels of the incoming signal as loud as they could go before distorting to get the highest ratio of wanted signal above the unwanted noise. Today, even the simplest, DAW-based, home recording system has a low enough noise floor that in most cases the noisiest part of your entire signal chain is going to be the room in which you are recording. And in that case, it almost doesn't matter how hard you push the levels heading into your recorder. So not only is it safe to leave some extra room before the tracks hit that funny red light at the top of the meter, but there are a couple really good reasons to avoid that.

The biggest reason to keep levels clear of the little red light is that clipping and distortion sound pretty bad, and there's not really much help for fixing a track after that has occurred. To understand clipping, it is important to understand a little bit about what is going on as an analog audio signal is being converted to digital data. The incoming signal is measured at regular intervals that are flying by really fast (like 44,100 times per second), which we call the sample rate. Each measurement is then represented by a binary number that is usually 16 or 24 bits (digits that can be a 1 or a 0). And the whole system is calibrated so that a particular incoming signal strength will represent the maximum highest and lowest value that can be represented—where all the bits are either 1s, or 0s. If you step on the gas a little too hard and send your signal into the computer at too strong of a level, the system will "clip" off the peaks of the waveforms (Figure 2.6). Quite simply, when the signal strength causes a sample to measure all 1s or 0s, there really is nothing past that...none of the little 1s are going to magically become a 2.

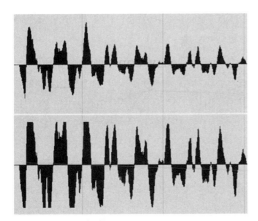

Figure 2.6 Unclipped waveform versus clipped waveform.

The danger that we face with a clipped signal is that it starts to sound different than the original signal we sent into the system. One of the best ways to demonstrate this is by comparing a sine wave to a square wave (Figure 2.7).

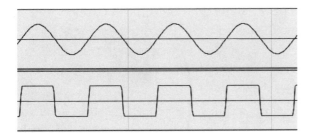

Figure 2.7 Sine wave versus square wave.

The square wave is a pretty severe example, but it's one we can easily listen to with the Signal Generator plug-in shown in Figure 2.8. If you create an Auxiliary Bus track in a Pro Tools session, you can then assign the track to an output you can hear and mute it until you're ready. Then activate a Signal Generator plug-in on that track and set it as shown to a frequency of 110 Hz, an output volume of –20dB, and sine wave. Un-mute the track and adjust your monitor level and you should hear a nice, pure, low A (that's the A at the bottom space of the bass clef for those keeping score).

Figure 2.8 Signal Generator plug-in set to create a 110 Hz sine wave.

Now click the button at the bottom of the Signal Generator plug-in to switch the signal to a square wave and listen to the difference. Yes, it's an extreme example, but it is a worthwhile one. The difference in sound (or more accurately "timbre") is caused by the harmonics that are generated as part of a square wave signal. Harmonics are explained in a little more detail in the refresher section of Chapter 4, but for this example the point is simply to see the relationship of the waveform to the sound you will hear. If you severely clip an audio signal on the way into the computer, what was previously a smoother wave shape will start looking and sounding more like a square wave.

The other big reason to keep levels under control on the way in is that you will eventually need extra room to process and mix your tracks. In a certain way, we can think of it as simple mathematics. One plus one equals two. Record one really great, strong, loud track and it might sound really good. Record another one and it may sound equally good. Put them together and the result may be too loud. Add more tracks and the situation gets worse (Figure 2.9).

Figure 2.9 Meters showing the sum of multiple tracks to one mix bus.

Sure, the tracks can be turned down later on in mixing, and sure enough there is more room to turn them down than there is to turn them up. But leaving a little space for all the layers to add to each other is a pretty good idea from the start.

And let's face it; this is a book about using the plug-in suite in Pro Tools, which means we're thinking about how to use effects! Well, the same consideration should be made. Adding effects may well mean adding strength, and if you are already pushing into the red, you may end up overloading the plug-in processor, clipping the audio as it leaves the track, or overloading the mix bus.

Now, after all those warnings, I don't want you to think all of your audio has to be recorded super quiet either. There is still a noise floor down there in the Pro Tools hardware and software system, and we don't want to turn up the noise while we are trying to bring up the rest of the signal. A good, happy medium is to set your levels so that your average signal peaks are landing around −18dB and so that no individual peaks hit above, say, about −6dB. If the loud peaks get a little too close to going into the red, just back off a little more. In the end, it is much easier to turn up the level than to fix clipped or distorted tracks.

Aim for Good Takes...but Still Keep the Others

Hopefully you are recording all of your audio projects to a secondary hard drive separate from your system drive. (If not, then you should be, so get that going.) Then remember that there's lots of room on that hard drive and quite often it is hard to judge the quality of a take when first hearing it, especially if you are also the one playing.

There are two schools of thought when it comes to keeping extra takes. Some people prefer to toss out the stuff they don't like immediately so it doesn't clutter up the session later or lead to lots of time listening back to bad takes. They tend to figure that making decisions early saves time later, and are probably right about that. Others prefer to keep everything as they go along so other options can be reviewed afterward to see if there might be a hidden gem, or a take that maybe wasn't as bad as they had first thought. I happen to fall into this second category and am quite the packrat when it comes to keeping extra takes. Not only that, but if a group doubts whether a take they just played is good enough and wants to listen back, I will often discourage listening immediately in favor of recording another take while the energy is still there, the hands are still warm, and everyone is still focused on the music. We listen the next day, when ears are fresh, minds are open, and the takes can speak for themselves.

So what does that have to do with using the plug-in suite? Well, many of the tools, particularly those found only in the Audio Suite, are geared toward editing. If the band is listening to three or four takes of a song, it isn't uncommon to decide to take the beginning of one take, cut to the middle of another take, and then use the ending from a third. And that would be a lighter editing session. Some of the tools available allow us to stretch the time a little so a faster take can mate more comfortably with a slower one. Or we can boost the signal level a little on a track if, say, the drummer wasn't playing as loud during one of the takes (as if that might ever happen). Or we can go in and pick out a few notes that were a little flat in a bass solo and shift them up a little so the player doesn't obsess about those weird notes and instead hears it overall as a really great and inspired solo.

There is really no telling what decisions can be made. Who knows what can be changed, fixed, or even mutilated to create a really cool sound that will end up being the perfect effect, or even a signature to the whole project? I couldn't possibly count the number of times an artist has spent hours or even days recording take after take. In the end, they may choose the first take, the tenth, the hundredth, or simply the last take. I even put together an album where the final, fully produced take of a song became track one, while the first take of the same song became a quieter, acoustic reprise at the end of the album. So whenever possible, try to keep every take to review, compare, and rework later. It might only take a little editing or processing to discover the rare gem hidden in that take that was almost thrown away.

3 Compose, Record, Edit, Mix, and Master

Just exactly what do you think you're doing in there?

Regardless of whether you are using Pro Tools as a platform for music creation, music production, radio production, video postproduction, sound-effects design, or any number of other tasks, it is helpful to consider the production process overall as being broken into several key stages. The start-to-finish production of original music will be the framework used to describe useful applications of the plug-in suite throughout this book. So it seems like a good idea to start with a quick look at what these various stages of music production are, and how they might relate to other types of audio production.

Dividing the process into five component stages, and then considering the usefulness (or uselessness) of the various plug-ins for each of those stages can help to give a better idea of the real strengths for each tool available in the suite. At their simplest forms, and with only a brief description to start with, we will look at these five stages as follows:

- The **composition** stage is the start of the creation of the work and may involve music writing, song writing, or similar processes.

- The **recording** stage is when signals are captured from live or synthesized instruments and written into audio files, regions, clips, and tracks.

- The **editing** stage is when recorded material is reviewed, and the best component parts are pulled together to form a complete work.

- The **mixing** stage is when the various audio signals are blended and balanced to a single output signal (whether mono, stereo, or surround) and is when most special effects are added.

- The **mastering** stage is generally where multiple works are brought together into a larger whole (such as individual songs into an album project), and it's the last chance to catch any sonic issues before the recording is sent off into the world.

For most users these stages will overlap. Often, the production process involves going back and forth between tasks. This is especially true within the first three stages, although mixing and mastering engineers still find themselves doing a fair amount of editing. As an example, it's normal to write a part for bass and drums, then record a few takes, and edit those takes into a framework for a song. With that in place you might return to composing a guitar or keyboard part, record several takes of that, edit some more, and then go back to writing and recording lyrics, and so on. There will also be times when the distinction between stages can get a little blurry. Is using an equalizer plug-in to knock out some "P" pops on a vocal track part of the editing or mixing stage? Does it matter?

In the end, the discussion of different stages of the production process is simply intended to serve as a guidepost for when some processors may be more or less effective. Naturally, some plug-ins can be a tremendous value at the right time but can really mess things up at the wrong time. It's impossible to predict how and when you will need to use each tool in your own work, but hopefully this little bit of guidance can help you find your own path.

Use Plug-Ins During the Composition Process

Composition will likely mean different things to different Pro Tools users. It may mean writing notes to be played by musicians playing acoustic or electro-acoustic instruments. Or maybe you will be constructing patterns and textures for electronic music, or beats for rap and hip-hop music. It may mean arranging or adapting someone else's music into your own creation. Or perhaps you are forming ideas about sound effects to accompany a film, a live theatre production, or even a video game. While it's fair to think of plug-ins as tools used primarily during editing, mixing, and mastering, there are a few useful ways that some plug-ins can help in the composition or song-writing process.

Let the Sound Inspire the Song

How many times have you changed something around on an instrument that caused a different sound to emerge, which then inspired you to start playing something that really caught your ear and imagination? Or perhaps that hasn't happened yet. Here are a few ideas that could help get things started. Of course, all the various plug-ins shown in the next few paragraphs are explained in more depth in their respective chapters. For now, let's start by plugging your instrument or microphone into your interface. Then route the input into an audio track and through to an output you can monitor. Then make sure the track is record-enabled so you can hear the signal passing through the system.

If you are a guitarist working on creating a new song, you might consider playing with any of a number of guitar effects plug-ins. Feed the direct-out signal from your electric or acoustic guitar (or even a bass) into the SansAmp amplifier modeler (Figure 3.1) to explore some of the potential character of an electric guitar. Or feed your electric guitar into one of the AIR effects plug-ins to see how the change in sound and texture might influence your playing.

It is impossible to say what kinds of effects might catch your ear, and how they might inspire your creative process. There's no real guarantee this will inspire anything at all. But if you are looking for ideas that don't seem to be coming from your head or instrument "au naturale," then a quick change of character can sometimes help. Pick a plug-in geared toward manipulating your instrument and click through a few presets. Turning a thin acoustic guitar tone into a thick

Figure 3.1 SansAmp amplifier modeler and some of its factory presets.

and crunchy electric guitar tone might suddenly have you picking a different riff and taking your imagination in a whole new direction.

The same holds true for singers and many other instrumentalists as well. We all have a tendency to turn into singers when in the shower or car. And who can resist playing with the mic when the PA system is switched on and the reverb is cranked up? The next time you experiment with a PA system, follow the same method I just described above, except use the D-Verb plug-in (Figure 3.2) and explore a few of the presets available there.

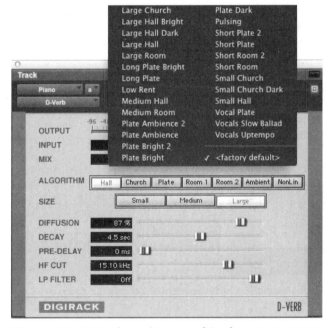

Figure 3.2 D-Verb and some of its factory presets.

In much the same way that the echo off the tiles in the shower makes us feel a little more enthusiastic about stretching our pipes, so too can a quick dose of "large hall" or "small church." That might not be the kind of ambience eventually used in the mix, and might even be a distraction if there is too much going on while actually recording—but, when it comes to getting the song-writing process moving along, a little change of apparent location can sometimes be just like stepping outside for a bit of fresh air.

Using Virtual Instruments While Composing

Although the virtual instrument plug-ins are not discussed in this book about the more fundamental plug-ins and effects, it's still worth understanding how they can fit into the scheme of things. The composition process involves finding instrument sounds that build upon and support each other, so reaching for the virtual instruments available in Pro Tools at this stage of the game should be obvious. Changing up the sound of your own instrument can provide a burst of inspiration, and so can simply switching on and hearing the sound of a software instrument. There's a clear advantage here if you happen to have some skills at piano or keyboard playing, since almost all of the software instruments are built around the musical keyboard as their primary interface. But don't think for a moment that this excludes you when it comes to playing, exploring, getting inspired, or eventually including those sounds in your work.

Opening up a plug-in instrument like the AIR Mini-Grand virtual piano (Figure 3.3) and simply clicking your mouse on the virtual keyboard can start getting new ideas moving in your head. There are only a handful of sounds in that instrument, but it's a great starting point for someone who doesn't normally play keyboard instruments.

Figure 3.3 Mini Grand has seven piano sounds that can help get creativity going while composing.

If you have a MIDI keyboard available to act as a controller, then exploring Mini Grand and some of the other software instruments will be a lot easier. For that matter, if your goal in working with Pro Tools is the creation of original music, then it's a good idea to have at least a basic MIDI keyboard controller available and attached to your system. Even as a professional recording engineer, sound designer, or post production engineer, having a basic MIDI controller is a good idea. Keeping one available for the creative needs of your clients should be an obvious reason. Plus, all the virtual instruments (and many other plug-ins) have the ability to be controlled through such a device, so having a MIDI controller handy can give you more flexibility around the studio beyond simple music composition.

Of course, the keyboard-related instrument plug-ins aren't the only useful ones for music composition. Boom (Figure 3.4) is a virtual drum machine that includes a good selection of percussion instrument sounds along with a pattern sequencer. The plug-in comes equipped with enough presets to get your groove started, and is easy to manipulate. So again, clicking through a few options and finding a cool rhythm pattern can sometimes be exactly the right kind of inspiration to get your creativity flowing.

Figure 3.4 Boom is a virtual drum machine and pattern sequencer.

In the end, the virtual instruments used while composing may well be replaced by physical instruments and live players later. (I'm intentionally calling them "physical" and not "real" instruments, because the simple reality is that if it makes a sound you like, and it ends up in the recording, then it is a real instrument.) Perhaps you are simply writing a piano part that will eventually be played by a live performer on an acoustic piano. A live drummer may adapt a sequenced pattern preset to her own acoustic drum set. But having these virtual instruments available will help when writing new songs and teaching them to the rest of the band.

Using Plug-Ins While Recording and Overdubbing

Before saying anything on this subject, it's worth taking a moment to talk about delay. And yes, the irony is intentional. There are lots of plug-ins available to help get your creativity in motion while writing, composing, brainstorming, or performing whatever other tasks your pre-production process might include. But once you are ready to start recording some of those ideas, it's time to start double-checking how the processing delay, or "latency," might affect the timing of your performance.

This type of delay and how to deal with it is covered in more detail in the last section of this chapter, and also in Chapter 7. For now, it's sufficient to say that processing an audio signal takes time, and if you're not careful about it, that processing delay can mess up your recording. You might record an overdub out of time because you're listening to a track that has some plug-in delay that makes it arrive late to your headphones.

Using Real-Time Plug-Ins While Monitoring

Even so-called "real-time" plug-ins must route audio data through a computer processor to perform calculations and generate new, processed audio data. And any way you slice it, those calculations take some amount of time, sometimes as much as $1/10^{th}$ of a second or more. Trying to record with too much delay will mess up the alignment of your audio tracks and can be more of a headache than an inspiration. Luckily, the amount of time is often short enough that we can't even tell that any time was taken at all, and so there are some ways we can use the real-time plug-ins while recording.

Adding a splash of reverb as mentioned in the previous section can inspire the performance of a vocal take just as much as it can inspire the writing of a vocal track. After all, of the two locations shown in Figure 3.5, what singer would want to perform in the space on the left when they could be in the space on the right?

Figure 3.5 Would you rather sing in the claustrophobic vocal booth or the concert hall?

With experienced singers (or other solo instrumentalists for that matter), including some reverb in the monitors can go beyond simply inspiring the performance, and may also change the delivery. A skilled musician will generally leave a little more space at the end of musical phrases to allow the performance space to do its work, adjusting accordingly if that space is a small room or a large concert hall. In a dry studio environment, they may not leave as much space, which can make a performance seem rushed, especially when a longer reverb is added later on in the mixing stage.

While reverb is a useful tool to add to the monitor feed while tracking, it is not the only trick to have up your sleeve. When trying to record multiple instruments playing together, such as a rock band, it can be difficult to hear some parts clearly in the monitors. Adding a compressor like the Bomb Factory BF76 (Figure 3.6) to the bass guitar track can make it stand out a little clearer in the monitor mix. A simple adjustment like that can get a band focused on the rhythm, which means you record a tighter performance from the beginning.

Figure 3.6 Consider using a compressor like the BF76 on bass guitar during tracking.

Get a Better VU

Just as some plug-ins can help inspire a performance or ensure a better monitoring environment, some measurement plug-ins can help you capture great takes and might save you from extra headaches down the road. There are several tools described in more depth in Chapter 8 that can help to give a better view of the quality of the tracks being recorded. A metering plug-in such as the BF Essential Meter Bridge (Figure 3.7) can give a better view of how close those levels are to hitting that pesky red line.

Figure 3.7 A large meter with a needle provides a different view of your incoming signal levels.

Working with stereo microphone pairs, especially A-B spaced pairs as might be used in front of an acoustic guitar or above a piano can be troublesome if the signals are not reasonably well in-phase with one another. This is a place where using the BF Essential Correlation Meter (Figure 3.8) while

Figure 3.8 When the needle in the BF Essential Correlation Meter swings to the right, your stereo tracks are in-phase.

setting up and recording can help to ensure your stereo tracks are captured in-phase from the beginning.

An out-of-tune instrument is among the most troublesome problems that might creep in while recording or overdubbing. The TL InTune plug-in (Figure 3.9) may not be able to automatically keep your instrument in tune, but having the tool handy while tracking makes it an easy task to retune a guitar, bass, trumpet, flute, or any other solo instrument as often as possible. A quick 30 seconds between takes can save you from hours of editing out-of-tune notes later.

Figure 3.9 Taking a moment to tune up between each take can save lots of editing time.

Recording with Virtual Instruments

If virtual instrument plug-ins were already a part of your composition process, then they are likely to be a part of your recording and overdubbing process as well. If a dark string pad inspired a particular feel for a song, then it is likely to be incorporated directly into the song. Depending on the specific kind of project you are working on, you might include instruments that are played by live musicians through external MIDI controllers. Or maybe it will work better to write the parts into a MIDI track that will play the virtual instrument part while the live musicians play along. The basics of instrument tracks, MIDI inputs, audio outputs, and similar tasks are covered in a little more detail in the "Handling and Implementation of Plug-Ins" section of this chapter.

The same basic warnings about track delay apply to software instruments as well. It takes time to find and play a sample. It takes time to generate a synthesized waveform. It takes time to analyze and route incoming MIDI data. So keep those considerations in mind, watch for tracks that might not line up quite right onscreen, and of course listen to hear that all your parts are lining up as well upon playback as they were during recording.

One catch to using virtual instruments is that they can be very resource intensive, which can slow down your system. If you are running into delay issues, latency, or are overwhelming the system resources with virtual instruments, there can be several causes and cures. Instruments being played by the computer can be "printed" to audio tracks in a manner similar to the description of printing processed tracks described in the "Mixing In the Plug-Ins" section of this chapter. The general idea is to play the MIDI data once into the virtual instrument while recording the instrument output into an audio track. Afterward, the virtual instrument can be disabled to save system resources while the audio track is there for the musicians to hear.

Of course, if the virtual instruments are being played by live players, finding a cure can be a little more difficult. Managing system resources is always a chore, and usually needs to be dealt with on a case-by-case basis. If you find yourself running into trouble here, some possible solutions are to:

- Switch off less-essential plug-ins on other channels. (Maybe the singer can get through a scratch track without reverb on the vocals after all.)

- Turn off special effects within the instrument plug-in itself. (Adding effects, even within the virtual instrument plug-in, still requires more processing power.)

- Make non-essential audio tracks inactive while recording. (Even though those extra guitar tracks are muted, they still consume system resources.)

- Turn off video playback if it is active.

- Close down other software that may be running. (Do you really need to be surfing the Web while recording?)

- Choose a different instrument just for the initial recording. (If there is a lot going on, you could use less complex sound while recording and then replace it later.)

Another very important decision to make when recording any live performance of a virtual instrument (or hardware synthesizer) is whether to record the audio signal, the MIDI data, or both. As a rule of recording live performers, it's always a good idea to record everything you possibly can, so figure on recording both. Sometimes system resources may be running low or the final sound of the virtual instrument may not have been selected. In those cases, record just the data. For as lightweight as MIDI data is when it comes to memory and processing, there's hardly ever a reason not to record and save it. If a keyboard player throws down a fabulous solo that has one or two wrong notes, you may never get as great a performance if he goes back to replay the solo while trying to fix those notes. But it is a snap to find those notes in the MIDI data, move them to the correct pitch, and then fire the data back through the virtual (or hardware) instrument. All of the timing and dynamics of the performance are the same, but the wrong note is fixed.

So with the exception of all those cautions about processing delay and system resources, it's pretty safe to consider using lots of different tools to enhance your recording and overdubbing process. Find some amazing sounds and textures. Inspire some great performances. And make sure the tracks you record are as good as they can be.

Use Plug-Ins During the Editing Process

To put it very simply, here is the place where the Audio Suite plug-ins will really begin to shine. Audio Suite plug-ins operate out of real-time where a portion of the audio timeline, a "clip," is selected, rendered, saved to a new file, and deposited in either the playlist or clip list for further use. By most measures, this is part of the very definition of editing. Something is taken, altered, and returned as something new. The change may be dramatic or subtle, but the original has been edited. Like any other stage of audio production, bouncing back and forth between editing, recording, mixing, or mastering is commonplace. The usefulness of the plug-in suite will become more apparent with a better understanding of what constitutes editing.

When I prepare audition recordings for music students applying to graduate schools, competitions, or music festivals, I include a statement printed directly on the CD or DVD disc. It reads, "Absolutely no digital editing was used to alter the performances recorded on this disc." It is intended to be a very dramatic and authoritative statement and is meant to cast a certain shadow of doubt upon everyone else's audition disc that does not include such a disclaimer. It's a subtle bit of psychological warfare conducted by me on behalf of my music students. But is it true?

To many musicians, music listeners, and engineers, the term "editing" implies a parallel to the plastic surgeon as we reach for our figurative scalpels that are coyly labeled as "Cut," "Copy," and "Paste." By my own measure, if I use those tools to graft the first half of take one onto the second half of take two, then the statement comes off the disc because the *performance* has been edited. However, that clean and simple definition can become a little vague where our plug-in processors are concerned.

Processing a track through an equalizer plug-in to remove a low-frequency rumble caused by the ventilation system can be a less obvious distinction, though most would still consider this an unedited performance. Using that same equalizer to tame the upper mid-range of a somewhat screechy vocalist, however, might certainly feel like something that should be called "editing" a performance. Then again, using a slightly darker-toned microphone, or turning a cardioid microphone 90° off-axis to reduce that same upper mid-range would be passed over as good microphone technique. Where do you draw the line?

Musing about the philosophy of what is a faithful, accurate, or realistic recording can go on for days, and the goal here is to talk about how to utilize the available plug-ins to assist in editing audio. The point really is to take the choice of distinction between what is processing, what is editing, and what is mixing with a healthy and open-minded view. With that said, there are indeed many ways to use plug-ins while editing.

A quick glance down the list of available real-time and Audio Suite plug-ins reveals that many processors are duplicated and available as both types. A few processors, like all of the instrument plug-ins, are available only in the real-time suite. Likewise, several processors are Audio Suite exclusives—mostly those listed under the "Other" category, which are more thoroughly explained in Chapter 8. A processor like Reverse (Figure 3.10) is an excellent example of a plug-in that cannot really be used in real-time. The audio clip to be reversed needs to be recorded and selected so the processor knows what audio to play backward.

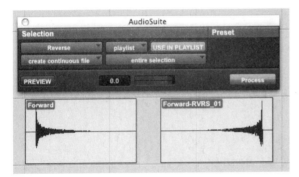

Figure 3.10 The Reverse plug-in and an audio clip that has been reversed.

While the Reverse plug-in may not be a tool needed often, a plug-in like Gain (Figure 3.11) can be very useful when cutting multiple takes into a single composite. When editing vocals, for example, it is natural for singers to move around a little while they are performing multiple takes. A subtle change in distance from the microphone may mean that one take ends up slightly louder than another. If a line from the louder take sounds better, but stands out a bit too much when cut into the quieter take, a quick processing with the Gain plug-in can reduce the level just enough to balance the two takes and make the edit fit into place.

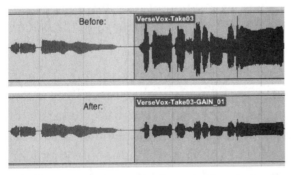

Figure 3.11 Gain can reduce the level of a loud take so it can be smoothly edited into a quieter take.

As already mentioned, most of the plug-ins available within Pro Tools can be used as either real-time or Audio Suite plug-ins depending on how you choose to implement them. An EQ 3 1-Band equalizer, for example, could be switched on for an audio track and used to reduce low-frequency wind noise in room microphones, or "P" pops (called "plosives") on a vocal track. The Audio Suite version of that same equalizer could also be used to process the entire audio clip once, so only the rendered version would remain in the playlist. Or a small segment of audio like the one shown in Figure 3.12 can be selected and rendered to remove a single plosive. This example shows the waveform of the phrase "plosives aren't cool" with a conveniently loud plosive at the beginning that is subsequently removed with an 80 Hz High-Pass filter.

Very low-frequency wave from 'P' pop...

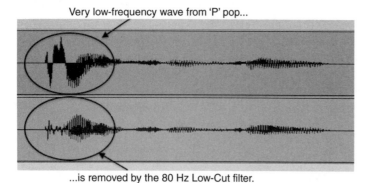

...is removed by the 80 Hz Low-Cut filter.

Figure 3.12 A strong plosive ("P" pop) is removed with the EQ 3 1-Band plug-in.

There are many more ways to use all sorts of plug-ins to enhance your editing capabilities. As always, the only limitations are your time, your familiarity with the tools available, and your imagination and creativity in putting those tools to use.

Mixing In the Plug-Ins

For many people, mixing is the point in the process when they start reaching for special effects plug-ins, and with good reason—this is when timbre and balance problems are fixed, the creative effects get their final adjustments, and the sound of the complete work finally comes together. The distinction of what is corrective versus what is creative may not always be so clear, but in a certain sense, it isn't too important either. Mixing is where all of the audio tracks come together to their final mono, stereo, or multi-channel output format. Although, some adjustments still might need to be made to individual tracks if they are all really going to fit into that final format.

When you are certain you are ready to shift gears from recording and editing to mixing, it's usually a good idea to start with somewhat of a clean slate. That means if you turned on a few effects and processors along the way—such as a compressor to solidify the bass, or a bit of reverb to help the vocalist along—go ahead and bypass all of those plug-ins. Don't close them out completely if you spent a lot of time dialing in a nice setting, but if it was just something temporary, switching it off may not be such a bad idea. It's usually a good idea to set all the channel volume controls back to 0dB as well.

The idea is to reset your ears and give yourself a chance to hear the project with all of the tracks in their natural state. Don't get stuck on a sound or effect that may have just been dropped into place as a quick fix along the way. Instead, open up your imagination to new possibilities for the sound. This kind of reevaluation of your project can help expose little details that should be brought forward in the mix, or maybe little problems that need a bit of correcting.

Switch On the Correctional Devices

There was a time when equalizers were referred to by some engineers and equipment manufacturers as "correctional devices." They saw these as tools designed to fix problems that had been missed, ignored, or unavoidably introduced while recording. And this is a good way to start thinking about how plug-ins can be useful when mixing. It is a kind of bridging step between editing and mixing where a bit of cleanup can set the stage for creativity to take over.

Equalizers are certainly useful as creative tools too, just as they aren't the only type of plug-ins that could be considered "correctional devices." Any number of equalizer, dynamic, delay, or other processors could be considered a corrective or creative measure depending on how they are used. The concept here is more about taking corrective steps before delving into the creative. Sure, it seems like putting off the fun stuff until the practical stuff is done, and yes, that's a good interpretation. Just as getting good sounds and great takes on the way in makes editing easier, doing a little bit of cleanup work before getting too far into the mixing can help as well.

With all of the tracks in place, all of the parts edited, and your mind set on the task of mixing, listen through the rough mix of the whole project and to some or all of the individual tracks with an ear toward getting any odd sounds or levels under control. Think of it as establishing a baseline for the sounds and levels among all the audio tracks. Equalizer plug-ins such as the EQ 3 family (Figure 3.13) are certainly near the top of the list for this task. When listening to individual tracks, try to listen closest to what is going on at the extremities of the high and low frequencies. Often there is sound unrelated to the instrument, like noise from traffic, ventilation, electrical hum, computers, hard drives, or any number of other sources. Applying High-Pass or Low-Pass filters with the 1-Band or 7-Band versions of EQ 3 can reduce or eliminate some unwanted noises before they make it into the mix.

More details on how to apply these kinds of noise filters can be found in Chapter 4, but that's not the only way equalizers can be "correctional devices." Whether the unfortunate sound quality is the fault of the instrument, the room, or the microphone, an equalizer plug-in could also be used to correct and balance the sound before mixing that track in with everything else. For example, a muddy instrument can be thinned by reducing some of the lower mid-range frequencies. Or you might settle down a bright-sounding voice by reducing some of the high frequencies. If the sound of the individual instrument isn't clean and balanced to start with, it isn't at all uncommon to chase the offending sounds while mixing. For example, if the bright vocal track isn't tamed, its overall level might be turned down to compensate, or other instruments might be brought up to match, with the result of a vocal track that gets lost in the depths of the mix.

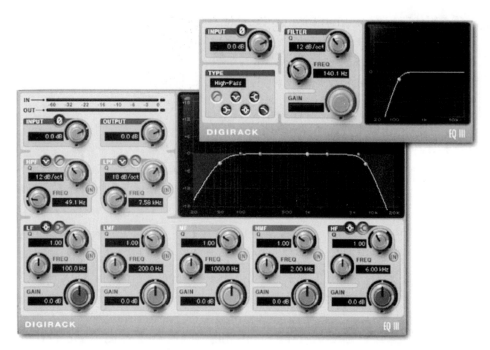

Figure 3.13 A High-Pass or Low-Pass filter can be added with the 1-Band or 7-Band EQ 3 plug-in.

Sometimes, however, the bigger issue at the start of a mix is an imbalance in the average volume level between each of the individual tracks. Setting the channel faders for all of the audio tracks to 0 decibels should reveal whether any tracks are particularly loud or soft compared to others. (Remember here that 0dB means "no change," and check out the "Refresher" section of Chapter 5 for more about the decibel scale.) If a track completely overpowers the others or just seems to be getting lost in the crowd, then some basic level adjusting may be in order. Since many of the real-time plug-ins include an input level control, some basic adjustments can be made to save a step and save resources. But for some tasks, a real-time plug-in like Trim, or the Audio Suite plug-in Gain (Figure 3.14) can be extremely useful for balancing the overall level of a track before getting too deep into mixing.

Certainly, there are other issues related to the volume levels of tracks that could be considered problems in need of correction. The floor tom track from an acoustic drum set recording would likely have run through the entire recording, but the drum itself might only have been played a handful of times. Applying a noise gate to such a track, one that is needed only occasionally in the mix, is a common corrective task that is described in more detail in Chapter 5.

It's also common to encounter tracks that are too low in volume on average, but that still contain loud peaks that push close to the red line on the meters. In those cases, simply setting the level higher might result in clipping the signal at the peaks. It's also just plain frustrating to turn up a track that is too quiet in one part of a project, only to find out it is then too loud elsewhere. In either case, a dynamics processor like the Compressor/Limiter Dyn 3 (Figure 3.15) might be useful. At more conservative and subtle levels, the compressor can act as an automatic volume control that increases the volume of the quietest material on a track but then backs off the level to avoid clipping when louder material comes along.

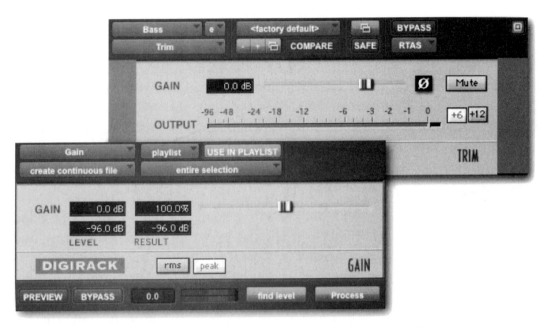

Figure 3.14 The real-time plug-in Trim or the Audio Suite plug-in Gain help to set overall track levels before mixing.

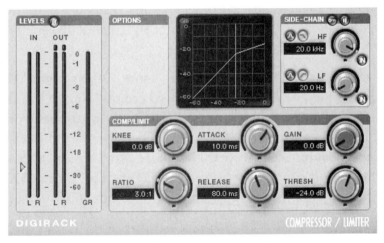

Figure 3.15 The Compress/Limiter Dyn 3 plug-in can even up the level on a track that has too broad of a dynamic range.

Getting the tracks with very broad dynamic ranges under a little better control before mixing can help avoid some headaches. It can also ensure that auxiliary feeds to other effects such as reverb processors are more controlled and predictable. Though here again, level adjustments are not the only potential corrective steps that might be plugged into the tracks before you get to mixing. Adding the Time Adjuster delay plug-in to various drum set microphones can help to time-align the drums before they are added to the mix. (More on that in Chapter 7.) The De-Esser plug-in can help tame hissing "S" sounds on vocal tracks (which is covered in Chapter 4). In other words, if something needs to be fixed while mixing, there is likely a plug-in that can help.

Experiment with Sounds, Textures, and Timbres

Mixing isn't only about repairing problems, balancing levels, and panning tracks across the stereo field. It is also about finding new colors and textures for the sounds. It is about finding creative ways to blend and balance the material. Exploring the possibilities of processors and effects can take a project in a whole new direction or help reveal exactly the voice and character a sound has been waiting for all along. Sometimes simply switching on a processor and flipping through some presets can give new ideas, potential, and possibilities for a sound. There's no exact formula or perfect recipe to create the perfect mix. It takes time. It takes practice. It takes getting to know your tools.

If you aren't sure what a particular kind of plug-in does to the sound or what it might be good for, well, that's part of the reason for this book, but it's also a reason for experimenting and exploring. Every plug-in listed here has at least one usage example to give an idea of how it is applied. Don't let the examples, history, or dogma limit how you explore. There are some plug-ins that are truly utilities, like Trim, Dither, or Time Adjuster, so they may not hold much creative potential. But most of the real-time plug-ins provide enormous creative potential, and there is really no wrong way to use any of them when it comes to being artistic—no rules say how a particular effect can be used. Flangers and phasers may be considered guitar effects, but that's no reason to ignore them as possibilities for other instruments or voices. Some ideas may work and sound fantastic while others may flop. But since switching real-time plug-ins on and off for a track is non-destructive, experimenting with sounds, textures, and timbres is generally pretty safe and can be quite rewarding.

With that said, there are a variety of ways to activate plug-ins and explore some of their potential while mixing. When dealing with real-time plug-ins, the basic decision of where to "plug in" that plug-in usually needs to be addressed first. Plug-ins can be activated directly into instrument or audio tracks but can also be used on auxiliary busses and master faders. Then there's the question of using real-time plug-ins or their Audio Suite counterparts. If you're working on a Pro Tools HD or HDX system there's also the question of whether to use the TDM, RTAS, or AAX versions for your real-time plug-ins. All these questions might seem daunting, but it all comes down to resource management.

Manage Resources by "Printing" Rendered Tracks

Some refer to this as "freezing," "saving," or "printing" the processed tracks, but whatever phrase may be used the concept is the same. There are lots of advantages to using real-time plug-ins, but there is one very distinct disadvantage that is hard to avoid. They consume system resources. The more complicated the effect is, the more processing power is consumed, and software instruments in particular are often the worst offenders.

Once you are certain of the effects that will be applied to a particular track or audio clip, print the rendered audio to a new file and deactivate the real-time plug-in. This is especially true for software instrument plug-ins. Once you are certain of the notes, tempo, dynamics, and other MIDI controls for that instrument, print it and start dealing with it as an audio track instead.

This will free up processing resources, which means more tracks or additional effects can be added. It also has the technical side benefit of making your system run smoother and the psychological side benefit of finalizing decisions to keep a project moving along.

There are, however, some drawbacks to printing rendered tracks. For most engineers, the most critical of these drawbacks is the loss of flexibility described in the previous section. Some processes just can't be undone. A close second for critical audio applications is the layering of noise and distortion that may occur as audio files are processed repeatedly. Processing an audio clip once to adjust the gain, then again with an equalizer, then again with a compressor, then again with a chorus effect, then with reverb, and yet again with another processor, and another, will eventually take its toll. Finally, all of these new audio files will take up space on a hard drive. You can overwrite the original files—although in that case, go back to the first drawback.

But if it has to be done, then it has to be done, and luckily there are many ways of approaching this task. It will depend mostly on how much processing needs to be done and how much audio needs to be processed.

Simply Trading Real-Time for Audio Suite

In many cases, the same plug-in is available in two different versions, such as the EQ 3 1-Band equalizer shown in Figure 3.16. Both versions of the plug-in have the **Preset** section at the top that includes an option in the pull-down menu to copy settings from one copy of the plug-in and paste them to another.

Figure 3.16 Both real-time (left) and Audio Suite (right) versions of plug-ins have the **Preset** section controls.

In this situation, simply copy the settings from the real-time version of the plug-in and paste them into the Audio Suite version. Then select the audio clip (or timeline region around multiple clips) to be processed, render the material once, and deactivate the real-time version of the plug-in for that track. This is the simplest approach for dealing with one or two simple effects that can be applied to a whole track or audio clip. There's more information about real-time versus Audio Suite plug-ins later in the

"Handling and Implementation of Plug-Ins" section of this chapter. This method locks in all plug-in settings and editing decisions for the track, so be sure you're ready for that kind of commitment or consider a different method.

Bussing to Another Audio Track

This approach is necessary for software instruments or other plug-ins that only exist in real-time versions. It's also a more practical method if you have a chain of several plug-ins active on a track. Plus, it allows you to preserve your original audio and plug-in settings. The drawbacks: it takes a real-time pass through the length of the track being rendered, the new file adds more data to the hard drive, and printing mono tracks to stereo-processed tracks may increase your overall track count.

Start by creating a new audio track to record the processed audio. I like to right-click the track name button to open the pull-down menu there (Figure 3.17) to ensure the track I'm working on is selected so the new track will appear below it.

Figure 3.17   Right-click the track name button and select New.

Select New from the pull-down menu to open the New Tracks dialog window. Then create a new mono, stereo, or multichannel audio track, depending on the output of the track being printed (Figure 3.18). Even if the track itself is mono, it may need to be printed to a stereo track if the plug-ins are creating a stereo output or if there is any automated panning.

New Tracks		
Create 1 new	✓ Stereo	Audio Track

Mono
✓ Stereo
LCR
LCRS
Quad
5.0
5.1
6.0
6.1
7.0 SDDS
7.1 SDDS
7.0
7.1

Figure 3.18   Choose the number of channels for your audio track based on the output of the old track.

Reroute the output of the original audio track to an unused bus and select that bus as the input for the new audio track (Figure 3.19). While you're at it, remember that it's always a good idea to name the new track something more meaningful than "Audio 2" since that will also be the name of the new audio file.

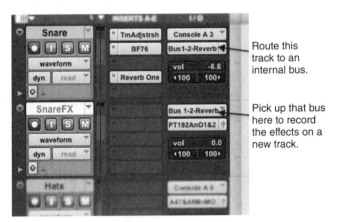

Figure 3.19   Change the output of the original track and the input for the new track to an unused bus.

The last few steps are simple enough. Record-enable the new track and make sure nothing else is record-enabled that might erase something you need. (That's a screw-up not worth learning by experience.) Hit record and let it roll through all of the material on the original track. When it's done, right-click the track name button on the original track and this time select Make Inactive (Figure 3.20).

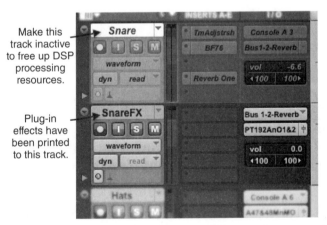

Figure 3.20   Make the original track inactive once the new audio track is "printed."

Remember that to actually save processing power, the original track must be inactive; it can't simply be muted with the plug-ins bypassed. As long as time and hard drive space aren't issues, this method of printing your processed tracks has the benefits of freeing up system resources while still retaining all the flexibility of the original material.

Plug-Ins for Mastering

Some see mastering, the final stage in the recording process, as mysterious, while others tend to oversimplify it. Mastering is the magical point in the process when the music finally comes alive, sounding polished and professional. Equipment manufacturers and software developers are eager to sell one-step processors that promise to give your work that final glow by pushing a single button. The real process of mastering lies somewhere between these two extremes.

Think of mastering as putting on a coat and hat before leaving the house; it's the last line of defense before sending your project off to face the cold, cruel world. A coat and hat may be the last things you put on before leaving but are the first things people see when you step outside. Mastering is your last chance to change, color, or tweak the sound, and the first thing the listeners will hear. That may seem like a strange idea, but overall loudness, timbre, and tone are the first things we notice when hearing something new. Then we start identifying the sounds as instruments, rhythms, melodies, and words.

There's more to mastering than just slapping on another processor or two, so it can't all be covered here. But many of the techniques described above and the tools available for mixing within Pro Tools work just as well for mastering. It's simply a matter of knowing what you are trying to do. The mastering process includes three key component steps: track sequencing, final processing, and level balancing. And sure enough, many plug-ins are available to help with mastering your projects.

Compile Mixes Into a New Session to Layout a CD

Remember, Pro Tools does not include a CD-burning function. That seems odd at first until you consider that CDs are not the only target destination for the projects. The same software may also be used to produce sound effects for a theatre production, dialog for a Webcast, or the soundtrack for a feature film. The software is useful for organizing all of the individual pieces into whatever final form they might take.

Sequencing of songs for an album project is traditionally one of the major components of the mastering process. It's not necessary for every project, but it can be a very helpful step in finishing up, even for a single-song project. Laying out an album is all about comparing each individual final mix to others in the same project. You can use the same method to compare your tracks to commercial releases you are trying to emulate.

The process starts by gathering up all of your finished mixes and pulling them into a new Pro Tools session. Whether the mixes you are mastering come from an external recorder, a mix bus inside Pro Tools, or exported files from some other program, use the highest quality available. Whether the material was tracked and mixed at 16-bit, 44.1 kHz; or 24-bit, 88.2 kHz, simply preserve that quality in the new session.

Once all of the material is pulled together into the new session, it's easier to listen back and forth between songs to hear how one flows into the next. Then you can rearrange the track order as

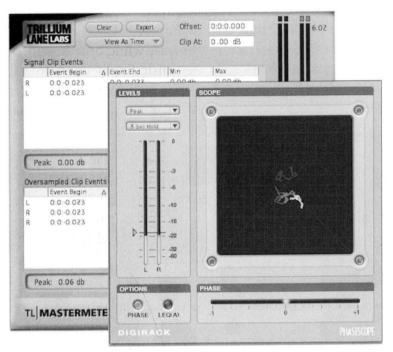

Figure 3.21 Use measurement plug-ins such as Phase Scope or TL Master Meter to get a better look at what is going on.

needed so the individual songs come together to become an album. Here's where the measurement plug-ins (Figure 3.21) give you a better look at what is going on.

There's not really any plug-ins to help make choosing the track order any easier, that's just a matter of taste and understanding the purpose of the recording. (For example, it's usually best to start a four-song demo disc with your strongest material rather than your most experimental stuff.) But as those tracks fall into place, the measurement tools can give you a sense of where to go next. Which tracks are too quiet? Which are too loud? How does the phasing and stereo spread compare between your material and the commercial releases you really like? That kind of listening and observation will tell you what kind of final, overall processing might be needed to polish up each mix.

More Than Just One Last EQ and Compressor

One last pass through a good equalizer and compressor is a common step in mastering, but there's a lot more possible than just that. And, no, that's not just because we forgot about the limiter. Almost any plug-in is fair game at this stage of the recording process, but those are just the more typical ones. Maybe throwing a flanger effect on a string quartet recording isn't a likely scenario, but if the overall stereo mix seems a little too dry, then adding a splash of reverb might be exactly what the track needs.

There are no rules about what plug-ins you should or shouldn't use. As you become more familiar with all of the sounds and capabilities of the many plug-ins available within Pro Tools, you will find new and interesting ways to use them.

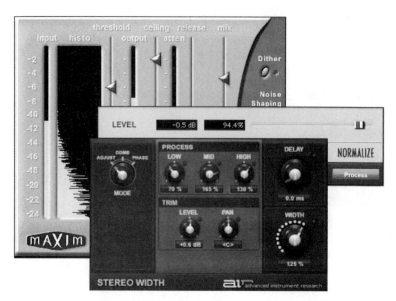

Figure 3.22 AIR Stereo Width, Maxim, and Normalize are just a few of the powerful plug-ins that can help you create a polished master.

Equalizer and compressor plug-ins may indeed be tools you will visit time and again. In addition to measurement plug-ins, other utility plug-ins and processors might see common use in mastering. Tools such as AIR Stereo Width, Maxim, and Normalize (Figure 3.22) help create a polished and professional-sounding final product.

It's impossible to say what kind of treatment any particular song, sound effect, or other audio project might need to sound its best—maybe nothing at all. Whatever the case, remember almost everything is fair game.

Balancing Level, Tone, and Timbre

It seems easy enough to balance the level, tone, and timbre from song to song—until you get in there and start trying to make it happen. Part of the reason mastering seems so mysterious is, just like mixing, there's no exact formula to create the perfect master. It takes time, practice, careful listening, and familiarity with your tools. Listening, watching the meters, and taking notes helps. When you have a song that sounds good, figure out what you need to do to make the others sound similar.

The important thing at this stage is to recognize the similarities and differences between your mixes. How unique should each song sound while still functioning as part of the whole album? This can be especially difficult with very diverse projects or when the individual mixes have been created over several months or years. Applying just one or two processors across all of the mixes is rarely going to get professional-sounding results. Some tracks may need little more than a final limiter and dither, while others might need an equalizer, compressor, some reverb, or some other bit of processing to get the sound to blend better with the other material.

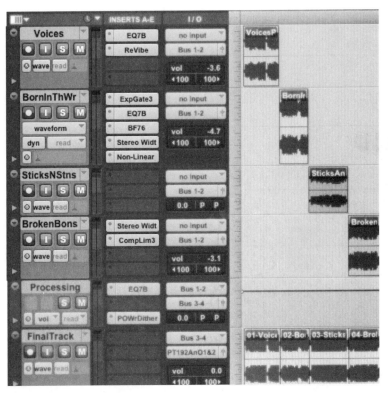

Figure 3.23 A mastering session will balance unique processing for individual tracks with overall processing for the whole album.

The mastering session shown in Figure 3.23 is for a four-song demo assembled for a local band to send to venues to get more gigs. Two of the tracks were recorded in the studio, one was recorded live-to-multitrack at a performance and mixed in the studio, and the other was a board-mix from a show at a local bar.

The demo was made to get more live performances, so the live tracks are the first ones the listener will hear. But being "live" doesn't give them a pass for sounding bad. The live tracks still need to blow away the listener and sound at least somewhat related to the studio tracks. The live-to-multitrack mix was completed in a studio and sounded good. With a little EQ to thin out some muddiness and a tiny bit of shimmery reverb to give a little more space and counteract the heavy compression of the stage mics, the result sounded more like the studio tracks without losing that live feel. The board mix sounded very muddy, dry, narrow, and lacked sparkle, so it required a lot more individual processing. The third song was a studio mix that sounded great and served as the reference point for the others, so it didn't take any individual processing. And the last track was actually a little too light, airy, and spacious for the purpose of the demo, so a stereo width control was used to narrow the image a bit, while a bit of light compression pulled things in a little tighter.

That's just the individual processing for each of the four songs. If you look closely at Figure 3.24, you'll see the tracks are fed through an auxiliary bus for overall processing and sent to an audio track that is catching the final mixes.

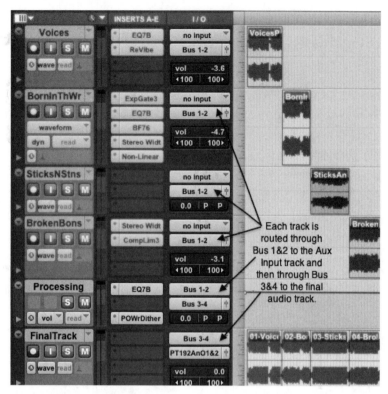

Figure 3.24 Individual tracks can be routed through an auxiliary bus for overall processing of the whole project.

For this particular demo disc project, the overall processing consists of a Low-Cut filter used to control sub-bass frequencies (see Chapter 5) and a dithering processor (see Chapter 13) to prepare the 24-bit tracks for their 16-bit destination.

Throughout the later chapters of this book, usage examples will be given for all of the individual plug-ins, and each chapter will include a description of how various plug-ins might be used for each stage of the recording process. Not every plug-in will make sense for the composition, recording, editing, mixing, and mastering stages. But almost everything is fair game. It's really up to you.

Handling and Implementation of Plug-Ins

All of the power available within Pro Tools and its suite of real-time and Audio Suite plug-ins would be lost without some flexibility in how each tool can be used. Fortunately, there are multiple ways to implement most of the plug-in effects and processors. It's great to have options, of course, but they come with a cost. Does it make more sense to use the real-time or Audio Suite version of a plug-in? What's the difference between an RTAS or TDM version of a real-time plug-in for Pro Tools HD? How does that compare to the AAX Native or DSP options in Pro Tools HDX systems? How is a multichannel plug-in different from multi-mono? It's really all about resource management, so let's start there.

When to Use Real-Time or Audio Suite

Many plug-ins exist in both real-time and Audio Suite formats, so which format should you use for a particular chunk of audio? While it would be wonderful if the answer was a simple formula to use real-time processors in this situation and Audio Suite processors in that situation, that's rarely the case. More often, the decision to use one version of a plug-in over another will raise several key questions:

- Is this plug-in even available in both formats?
- What stage of the mixing and overall production process are you working on?
- How much flexibility is needed for the plug-in?
- How certain are you that the settings are where you want them?
- Will this process need to be undone at some point?
- How much audio actually needs to be processed by a particular plug-in?
- Is the system running low on processing power?

Taking these questions one at a time can help you determine whether to go with a real-time or Audio Suite version of a particular plug-in.

The first question seems straightforward. The processor either shows up on the list of available plug-ins, or it doesn't. But a very simple real-time plug-in such as Trim (Figure 3.25), consists of a gain control, a phase reversal switch, and a mute button. No Trim plug-in is listed among the Audio Suite plug-ins; however, the two primary functions of the plug-in are covered separately by the Gain and Invert plug-ins.

Figure 3.25 Some real-time plug-ins may have Audio Suite counterparts that go by other names.

As you might expect there are no real-time versions of the Gain or Invert plug-ins either. Many tools are available exclusively in either real-time or Audio Suite format, but plenty of others are available as both. Be sure to scan the plug-in lists more closely and consider the functions you are seeking rather than just the plug-in names when deciding if a particular tool is available only in one format.

The next two questions really work together to determine whether to go real-time or not. Are you definitely onto the mixing stage, and if so, how much flexibility will you need for each processor? If you're still at the point of recording new tracks, then it makes more sense to have the flexibility of a real-time processor. If you're editing takes together and making minor adjustments and corrections to smaller pieces of audio, then one-time processing with an Audio Suite plug-in may make more sense. Once you really get to mixing though, it's harder to tell when to go real-time or not.

In general, start with the real-time version of most plug-in processors when you first start to mix your project. At this early point of the process things need to remain flexible, and even with the best of systems, endlessly processing and reprocessing can add noise and distortion. Adjustments to a track that sound just right at first may need to be reworked a bit when other channels are tweaked. Compressing the rhythm guitar to keep it consistent and solid in the mix may sound great on its own, but if adding reverb to the lead guitar solo makes it sound more distant than the "background" instrument, then you might need to revisit those compressor settings.

The next two questions deal with the concept of who might be "in charge" of the production. If you have arrived at a great setting for an effect on one particular track but need to free up some resources, copy the settings from the real-time plug-in over to its Audio Suite counterpart and process the track that way. But consider whether anything (not just the plug-in settings) may need to change later.

If you are engineering a project for a client, there is a possibility someone will listen to your final product and ask for some kind of adjustment. That adjustment may have nothing to do with the plug-in setting, but processing the track may have overwritten the original material. For example, a band might come back a few weeks after receiving their final mixes asking for a longer fade on a chord that was cut a little short. Or perhaps a corporate client may want to change the price of their product or try a different tagline on their radio spot.

With all of those considerations, it seems there is never a time to use the one-time process of an Audio Suite plug-in—until you consider those last two questions. If only a small amount of audio needs to be processed, then using the resources of a real-time plug-in really doesn't make sense. Figure 3.26 shows a fairly typical recording of drums for a rock song including tracks for the bass drum, snare drum, stereo overheads, high tom, and low tom.

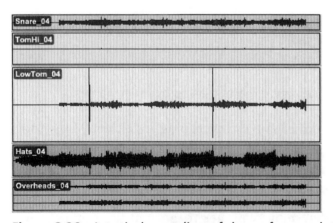

Figure 3.26 A typical recording of drums for a rock tune where the low tom was only played twice.

The two tom tracks were edited so only the places where the drums were actually played are still included in the track. The high tom was played fairly regularly, but the floor tom was only played twice at two dramatic points in the song. So processing those two small clips may make more sense than activating a real-time plug-in for the channel and using valuable system resources.

In the end, the availability of system resources, pure processing power, will have the biggest impact on your decision to use real-time plug-ins. Every Pro Tools system has a finite amount of processing power available, and that power has to run all of the audio channels as well as all of the real-time plug-ins. Older Pro Tools LE and M-Powered systems, as well as the current Pro Tools and Pro Tools HD-Native systems are called "native" workstations because they rely on the memory and processing power of the host computer system to run all aspects of the program. Pro Tools HD and HDX systems have additional digital signal processing (DSP) engines on PCI cards installed within the host system to handle most of the basic audio functions, and they allow the engineer to choose whether real-time plug-ins are processed by the host system or the specialized DSP engines. Click Windows > System Usage to access the System Usage window (Figure 3.27) and see what resources your Pro Tools system has available. The portion of the window labeled "Activity" represents the host system and is present on all Pro Tools systems while the sections labeled "TDM" and "HD Core PCI" will only be present on Pro Tools HD or HDX systems.

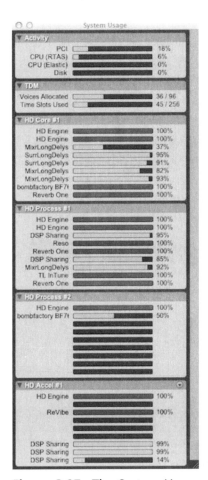

Figure 3.27 The System Usage window shows how heavily the system resources are being taxed.

The graphs in this display show a real-time view of how heavily taxed the system is during recording and playback. Add a few extra tracks and RTAS or AAX-Native plug-ins to see how quickly the resources are consumed. Upgrading to an HD system or using a more powerful host system with more memory and more processing power will allow more tracks to have more real-time processors active, but every system will have an upper limit. When you reach that limit, it's time to do a bit of resource management.

Batch Processing with Audio Suite Plug-Ins   Near the top of the window for every Audio Suite plug-in are two little pull-down menus that allow you to control how the plug-in will deal with multiple audio clips. The right pull-down menu is the Process Mode Selector (Figure 3.28) that lets you specify whether audio is rendered on a "region by region" basis (now labeled "clip by clip" in Pro Tools 10) or as an "entire selection."

Figure 3.28   The Process Mode Selector

For plug-ins like Normalize (Chapter 8) that require measurement of the audio levels before processing, it's important to decide whether every individual clip you've selected should be measured and rendered separately, or processed based on the overall level of the selection. For example, if you were using Normalize on all of the snare drum hits in a rock song, then processing the "entire selection" would bring the loudest strike up to the maximum volume and keep all the others proportional. Selecting "region by region" (clip by clip) would set each strike to the same volume and lose the natural dynamic range of the performance. On the other hand, if you have several finished mixes in a session and want to normalize each one to its own loudest peak, then selecting "clip by clip" allows the system to render each of the mixes individually but all in one batch.

Remember: as the audio clips are processed, new files are being written. Where those files go and what happens to the old ones is determined by the File Mode Selector (Figure 3.29) pull-down menu.

Figure 3.29   The File Mode Selector

This menu allows you to specify how the new files will compare to the original audio clips. Selecting "overwrite files" will destructively overwrite the newly rendered file in place of the old one. The original will be wiped off your hard drive and gone forever, so be careful how you use this option. It's helpful for managing your hard drive space, but there's no going back once the original files are gone.

The other two options are both nondestructive and simply deal with what happens when you are working with multiple audio clips. Selecting "create individual files" will do precisely that and deliver a separate file for each of the audio clips you selected and processed. Watch out though because if you select an audio clip that has a fade-in or a fade-out at either end, then each section will be rendered into separate audio files. Selecting "create continuous file" will write one single file across as much of the audio timeline as you selected, which is handy for keeping things neat and tidy but can eat up hard drive space a lot faster. All of the silence between clips is written into the new file, and it takes the same amount of hard drive space to record silence at 24-bit, 96 kHz as it does to record anything else.

Overall, these functions can be very helpful in keeping things organized. Get to know how these options work for the Audio Suite plug-ins you use most often and they'll help you make more efficient use of time and resources.

Inserts, Auxiliary Busses, and Master Faders

So where exactly do all of these plug-ins actually get "plugged in?" When you start up a new Pro Tools session, the Mix and Edit windows are empty, and there's really not much you can do until you create some tracks. Open up the New Track dialog window (Figure 3.30) and there are five (or more) different options for track types. Four of those track types have a place for real-time plug-ins.

Figure 3.30 The Track Type pull-down menu in the New Track window.

Of the available track types, you can insert plug-ins into an audio track, aux input, master fader, or instrument track. Plug-ins cannot be inserted into a MIDI track, video track, or VCA master track (those are only available in Pro Tools HD). The different options are there so you can use the plug-ins in different ways, have some flexibility in routing, and better manage your resources.

Audio Tracks

Audio tracks are used to record audio to the hard drive and play back audio from the hard drive, but the plug-ins are only active for audio being played back from the hard drive. (See Figure 3.31.) Although the visual display in the Edit window makes it seem like the audio resides in the audio track, it is really being played back from the hard drive and passed through the track. That means you can't add something like a compressor to a track while you are recording it and have the processed signal recorded. You can add the plug-in, and you can hear the plug-in, but it is being applied to the recorded signal as it is played back.

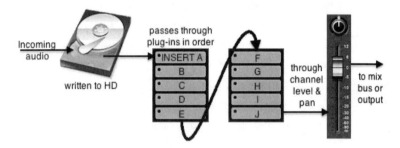

Figure 3.31 Signal flow chart for an audio track.

Keep in mind that with the plug-in insert points appearing after the audio is recorded to the hard drive, instrument plug-ins cannot be placed in an audio track and recorded to that track. You can plug them in there. And you can hear them play back. But if you hit record and play the instrument it won't be recorded to the hard drive. For that you'll need to plug the instrument into an aux input or instrument track, route that to an internal bus, and assign that bus as the input to your audio track. That will be explained in a little more detail in Chapter 12.

Aux Inputs

Auxiliary inputs function in much the same way as audio tracks except their inputs must be assigned to a hardware input or internal bus. (See Figure 3.32.) They don't route audio directly to or from the hard drive; rather audio is routed through them. Aux inputs are in there so you can process audio as it comes in from a hardware input, as it's routed from channel to channel, or channel to output. So if you really wanted to pass an incoming signal through a compressor before recording it, you could assign the hardware inputs to an aux input, insert a plug-in, route the output to an internal bus, and assign that bus as the input to an audio track to record the signal.

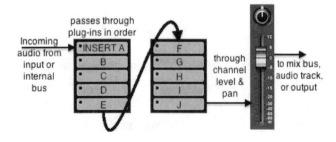

Figure 3.32 Signal flow chart for an aux input.

Instrument Tracks

Instrument tracks can be a little confusing to work with since they merge two different track types into one. (See Figure 3.33.) For audio and plug-ins they function just like aux inputs, but they also can record and playback MIDI data. The MIDI data can be received from any incoming MIDI source and routed to any software instrument or MIDI output. Even if there is an instrument plug-in active for that track, the MIDI data can be routed somewhere else. Once you get the hang of things, this dual function can streamline a session by keeping things a bit more organized. Until then, and especially if you are new to MIDI and software instruments, it can be a little confusing.

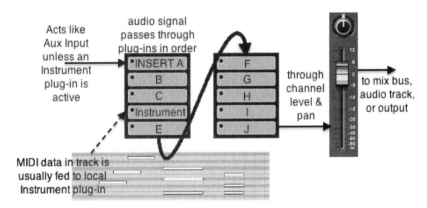

Figure 3.33 The signal flow chart for an instrument track is similar to an aux input with the extra MIDI data along for the ride.

Instrument plug-ins can be assigned anywhere any other plug-in can be assigned—instrument tracks, aux inputs, audio tracks, or even master faders. If you're unfamiliar with MIDI in general, it will probably be a lot easier to grasp what's going on if you use a MIDI track to hold the data and use an aux input to hold the instrument plug-in. That will help reinforce the idea that the data and the instrument are separate parts of the equation. Once you're comfortable working with the data and getting it to the instrument, the instrument track will make more sense.

The software instrument plug-ins themselves can be a little confusing as well since they generate their own sounds rather than simply processing sound as it passes through them. Most of them also require some kind of external control to tell them what to do. Simply activating a piano plug-in doesn't give you a great piano track until you tell it what notes to play.

Master Faders and the Post-Fader Plug-In

Master faders are a little different from the other track types covered so far. Audio signals are passed through them, but you don't get to choose an input source and output destination. Instead, you select an internal bus or hardware output and assign the master fader as the last control before that signal reaches its destination. Figure 3.34 shows several audio tracks assigned to internal busses, passed through an aux input, and routed to the hardware output.

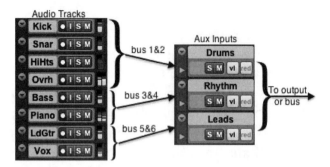

Figure 3.34 Audio tracks are assigned to internal busses, passed through an aux input, and routed to an output.

In this configuration, master faders could be added to each of the internal busses and to the hardware output as shown in Figure 3.35.

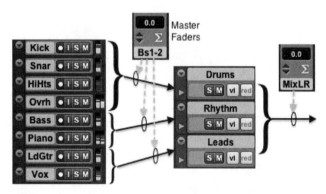

Figure 3.35 Master faders can be added in at any or all of these locations.

Once they are in place, master faders function in a very similar way to aux inputs, with two primary differences. First, only one master fader can be applied to any bus or hardware output. That's the whole point of a *master* fader. If two of them were set up to control your main stereo output, and you push the volume up on one and down on the other, which one would have the final say in whether the volume goes up or down? You can set up two aux inputs with the same source input and the same output destination if you would like to have competing volume controls to see which one would win. That is an easy way to set up a parallel compression process as described in Chapter 5. But master faders are set up to only allow one master per bus or output.

The other difference in using a master fader that relates specifically to plug-ins is that the insert points for plug-ins on a master fader are post fader. (See Figure 3.36.)

Having the plug-ins appear after the fader provides a few interesting advantages. The most obvious is that you can adjust the level going into the plug-ins with the standard volume control rather than having to add a Trim plug-in (Chapter 8) or automating the input-level control of

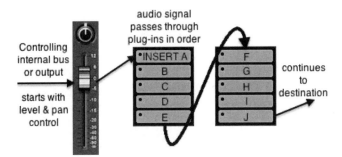

Figure 3.36 Signal flow chart for a master fader.

your first plug-in. Another advantage is that measurement plug-ins give an accurate reading of what kind of signals are leaving that bus or output. Pull down the volume control, and the meter will actually reflect that change. One more advantage is that dithering plug-ins are able to make smoother fades since the volume change happens at the higher sample rate before being truncated to the lower rate. But that's a far more complicated explanation than we will get into here.

Other Track Types

The four track types described above are the ones that accommodate plug-ins at their insert points. MIDI tracks, VCA master faders (Pro Tools HD only), and video tracks have no insert points available for audio plug-ins.

Native versus DSP: Who's on First?

There are two different kinds of real-time plug-in processors available in Pro Tools: native in the form of Real-Time Audio Suite (RTAS) and AAX Native plug-ins, and DSP-based in the form of Time Division Multiplexing (TDM) and AAX DSP plug-ins. Native plug-ins are available for every version of Pro Tools, but the TDM or AAX DSP plug-ins are available only with Pro Tools HD and HDX systems. That's because native plug-ins are processed by the host computer's CPU while DSP-based plug-ins are processed by the DSP engines housed on Pro Tools HD Core, Accel, or HDX processing cards. All systems will have a host computer, but only HD systems will have extra cards installed.

When it comes to managing your system resources, processing power is the big one to watch. With native Pro Tools systems, there isn't much of a choice because the native power of the host CPU is all you have. The more powerful your host computer is, the more complex and loaded with plug-ins your Pro Tools sessions can be. But if you're using Pro Tools HD or HDX, then choosing whether to use native of DSP-powered versions of plug-ins can really affect your system resources and performance. Getting into all of the specifics of when to use one or the other would make for a fairly long discussion. A simple guideline would be that if you have the available power to run a TDM or AAX-DSP plug-in, then start there. That's what those cards are meant to do and it will keep your system running strong. Reserve the native CPU power for when you're running low on DSP engines on your cards or when you need to run plug-ins like software instruments that are only available as RTAS or AAX-Native. There's nothing dramatically wrong with using both native and DSP-powered plug-ins on a single track, but it's important to know what's going on when you do that. It all comes down to voices.

Remember: regardless of the number of hardware inputs and outputs or the number of tracks you might create, every Pro Tools system has a limited number of available voices. A standard mono audio track in Pro Tools HD is routed from the hard drive, through the host system (including any native processing), and then into the TDM engines. That takes one voice. (See Figure 3.37.)

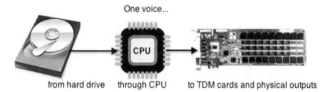

Figure 3.37 An audio signal is read from the hard drive, passes through the system, and is routed to the TDM processors.

If you plug in one or more RTAS or AAX-native processors, then that signal will leave the hard drive, be processed by the system CPU, and then pass to the TDM processor. If you add any number of TDM or AAX-DSP plug-ins after that, then they will be processed once the signal reaches the TDM processors. (See Figure 3.38.) It will still require only one voice.

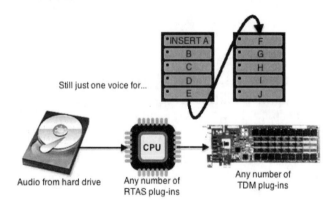

Figure 3.38 Add an RTAS plug-in, a TDM plug-in, or both, and it still takes only one voice.

The difficulty occurs when you add native RTAS plug-ins after DSP-powered, TDM ones. Not in terms of time, of course, but in the order of operations. Remember that Pro Tools will process the 10 insert points, A–J, in order from A through J. You can have any number of native plug-ins before any number of DSP-powered plug-ins and be just fine. As soon as you place an RTAS plug-in after a TDM plug-in (Figure 3.39), the system will rearrange the voicing structure to do what you've requested. That means it will assign an extra voice to carry the signal out of the TDM environment back to the host CPU, and yet another voice to get the signal back to the TDM environment. That's now three voices total.

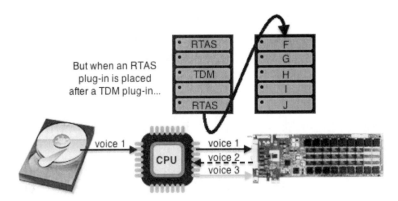

Figure 3.39 Place an RTAS plug-in after a TDM plug-in and additional voices are required to move things around.

If that mono track were a stereo track instead, then you would lose six voices to this plug-in chain. Try it with a 5.1 surround track and 18 voices are required. You can see how quickly things add up until all your voices are used up. Of course, if you're only working with a couple of tracks, then don't worry. The quality of the sound and processing won't change, but the number of available voices will be limited.

The total number of voices available in a Pro Tools HD or HDX system changes based on the number of cards installed, the sample rate, and the number of DSP chips you assign to the TDM mixer environment. To see how things are set up for your system, choose Setup > Playback Engine and see what is assigned in the Number of Voices pull-down menu.

Mono versus Mono/Stereo Plug-Ins

When activating a real-time plug-in for any mono track or bus, you'll notice that each of the plug-in names has a tag in parentheses after it that says either (mono) or (mono/stereo) (Figure 3.40). Some plug-ins even have both options available. In case that's not enough, multichannel systems will include options for mono/LCR, mono/5.1, and more.

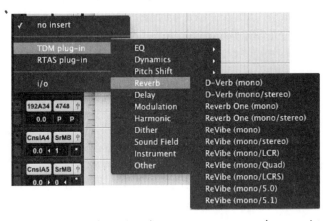

Figure 3.40 Choosing between mono and mono/stereo versions of plug-ins.

The mono/stereo distinction means that plug-in is designed to take a mono input and deliver a stereo output. A reverb processor is a good example. We generally use reverb to make things sound more spacious, but we determine the apparent size of a space by comparing the different sounds arriving at each ear. So if I send a mono signal into a reverb processor, it makes sense to get a stereo signal in return.

The catch to using the mono/stereo version of a plug-in is that you need to make sure your mono track is routed to a stereo (or larger) bus or hardware output in order to hear the stereo effect. You also need to make sure that subsequent plug-ins are set up as stereo, but the software will help you with that part. Once the mono/stereo plug-in is in place, all insert points after it will open the stereo versions of the plug-ins. If you already have mono plug-ins running and add a mono/stereo plug-in before them, Pro Tools will change the later plug-ins to stereo if it can. But be careful because it will close plug-ins that cannot be converted and your settings will go with them.

Multichannel versus Multi-Mono Plug-Ins

When activating real-time plug-ins for stereo or larger multi channel tracks, you will have a choice in the pull-down menu to activate a plug-in from either the multichannel or multi-mono menu. (Figure 3.41) Some plug-ins are only available in one format or the other; some plug-ins are available in both. So what's going on in there?

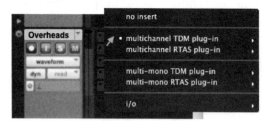

Figure 3.41 Selecting between multichannel and multi-mono plug-ins.

Simply put, this option is about control. A multichannel plug-in will have one set of controls, and the same process will be applied to all of the channels. A multi-mono processor has an extra set of controls at the top (Figure 3.42) that allow you to link or separate channels and then to select which channel you are adjusting.

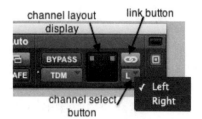

Figure 3.42 Multi-mono plug-ins can control settings for each channel independently.

The advantage here is that you can apply one plug-in to a stereo or multichannel track, but apply different kinds of processing to each channel. For example, if you recorded an acoustic guitar with two microphones, one for the body of the instrument and one near the neck, you might want to apply different EQ settings to the two channels. Keeping them separated as two mono tracks is an option, but it makes editing and keeping track of the separated tracks a little harder. Using a stereo track with a multi-mono plug-in keeps the session neat and organized but still allows some flexibility in processing.

Side-Chain Inputs

When working with most dynamics processors, whether compressors, limiters, or gates, you will see an option for a side-chain input. (Figure 3.43).

Figure 3.43   Side-chain input assignment.

This input allows you to control the processor with a different signal than the one being processed. That's a little easier to understand when you consider what a dynamics processor does. At the simplest level, all dynamics processors are automatic volume controls. They take an incoming signal and split it for two uses (Figure 3.44). One side of the split is used to measure the original level and adjust the automatic volume control. The other side is sent through the volume control and on to the output.

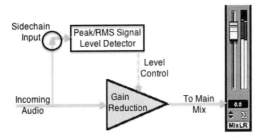

Figure 3.44   Signal flow chart for a dynamics processor.

A side-chain input allows you to send another audio signal into the measurement side of the processor and control what happens with the volume control. This function has many applications and uses, including a few that have become standard processors on their own, such de-essers and duckers. Those are described in much more detail in Chapter 5, "Dynamics Processors."

Moving and Copying Plug-Ins

Outside of the computer, in the "real" world of audio processors residing in little boxes interconnected by miles of wire, it's usually easy to rearrange your plug-ins so that an equalizer catches the signal before the reverb that's followed by the delay processor, and so on. In the virtual domain of Pro Tools, it's even easier. To reorganize plug-ins on a particular track, simply click on the insert button (Figure 3.45) and drag the plug-in to a different insert position.

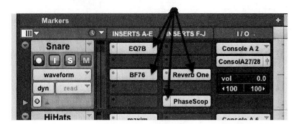

Figure 3.45 The insert buttons for four active plug-ins at insert points A, C, H, and J.

You can even drag a plug-in to an entirely different track, provided the input and output formats are the same. That just means a stereo plug-in needs to be dropped into a track that will feed it a stereo input. Mono plug-ins can move into stereo tracks and will be changed to their stereo versions, but going the other way won't work.

Copying plug-ins is almost as easy. Simply hold down the Alt button (Option for Mac) while clicking and dragging the plug-in's insert button to another track to create a new copy of that plug-in with all the same settings in place.

In either case, whether moving or copying plug-ins, be careful about dropping the plug-in onto occupied insert points. The plug-in that was there first will be closed and replaced with the new plug-in, and any settings will be lost.

Presets, Settings, and Keeping Things Organized

With all of the different processors available and all of the possibilities for settings, you need to organize things in a way that makes sense for you. Luckily, there are several ways to view and keep track of all of the plug-ins installed on your system, and to save, copy, and organize the settings used on individual plug-ins.

Organizing Your Plug-Ins and Playing Favorites

On its own, Pro Tools comes with a lot of plug-ins. If that's not enough, there are hundreds, perhaps thousands, of additional plug-ins available from Avid and other third-party software developers. Just finding the plug-in you're looking for can be quite a task. For that reason, the pulldown menu can be arranged in several different ways.

From the menu at the top of the screen, select Setup > Preferences and go to the Display tab of the Preferences window (Figure 3.46) to find the "Organize Plug-In Menus By:" pull-down menu.

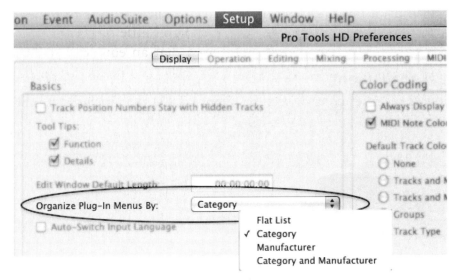

Figure 3.46 Go to Setup > Preferences to change how your plug-in menu is organized.

The flat list option may look impressive, but it can be hard to find what you're looking for, especially if you are looking for a particular kind of processor but aren't familiar with all of the names. "Compressor/Limiter Dyn 3" might be an obvious plug-in name, but "Boom" and "Smack!" are less obvious. For that reason, try using the Category option for organizing your plug-ins until you are familiar with all the names. Organizing by manufacturer isn't helpful when only using the basic plug-in included with your system, but it can help you discover what new goodies are included if you buy a plug-in bundle from a third-party developer.

As you become familiar with various plug-ins and find yourself reaching for the same handful of tools over and over again, you might find it helpful to pick a few plug-ins to designate as favorites. This can be done with the regular plug-in selector buttons in either the Edit or Mix windows. Simply hold down the Ctrl button (Command for Mac) while you click on any plug-in selector button and find your favorite plug-in on the menu. The plug-in won't be activated, but the next time you open the pull-down menu (Figure 3.47), your favorite plug-in will be at the top of the list before the plug-in categories and will be highlighted in bold in the category or manufacturer folders.

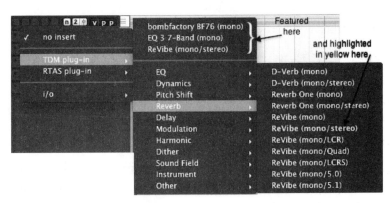

Figure 3.47 Favorite plug-ins appear at the top of the plug-in category list and in bold within the category folder.

If that particular tool eventually falls out of favor, simply repeat the Ctrl-click process to remove it from favorite plug-in status.

Copying Settings and Preset Management

At the top of every plug-in window is a Preset control section (Figure 3.48) that includes a pull-down menu along with a few other controls.

Figure 3.48   Plug-in preset control section.

The preset selector pull-down menu is the largest control and likely the one you will use first. It opens a menu of all of the factory and user presets that have been saved for that particular plug-in. The menu shown in Figure 3.49 is for the EQ 3 7-band equalizer.

Figure 3.49   Preset menu for the EQ 3 7-band equalizer.

Some plug-ins have lots of factory presets while others have only a few or none at all. Almost every plug-in has the ability to save user presets. When you find a great setting for a particular instrument, voice, or other sound, save it for future use or reference. Click the small arrow to the right of the Preset section heading (Figure 3.50) to open the Plug-In Settings Menu.

From that menu you can copy and paste settings from one instance of a plug-in to another, and you can save the current settings you have dialed in as your own preset. Selecting the Save Preset

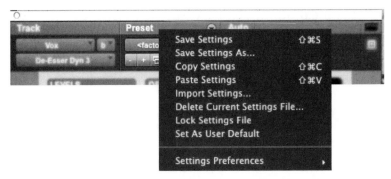

Figure 3.50 Open the plug-in settings menu to copy, paste, and save settings as presets.

As option opens a standard file dialog window (Figure 3.51) that will allow you to organize your presets into folders alongside the factory presets.

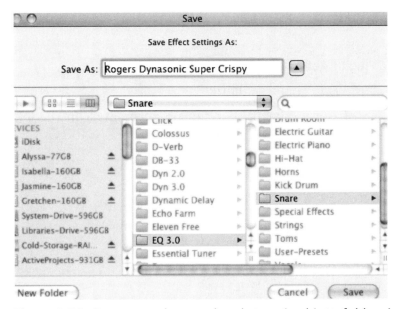

Figure 3.51 Presets can be saved and organized into folders just like any other file.

Below the preset selector pull-down menu are a pair of small Next (+) and Previous (-) selector buttons (Figure 3.52) that allow you to cycle through all of the presets available for the plug-in. This is helpful when trying to find the right kind of effect from a long list of possibilities, and it works for any kind of plug-in. Cycling through instrument sounds, reverb settings, or special effects is much easier this way.

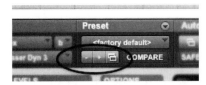

Figure 3.52 Use the – and + buttons to cycle through saved presets.

When you find a preset that's just about right, you can make some extra adjustments to fine-tune the sound and then use the compare button to switch back and forth between the current settings and the original preset.

Automating Plug-In Controls

With all of those controls, it would be a shame if you had to pick one setting and stick with it for an entire mix. Luckily, the options for automating plug-in controls are extensive. Simply put, if it's in there, you can automate it.

Under the Auto heading at the top of any real-time plug-in, click the Auto button (Figure 3.53) to open the plug-in automation dialog window.

Figure 3.53   Click the Auto button to open the Plug-In Automation window.

Once the window is open, you will see a list of every control that can be automated on the left side of the window. (See Figure 3.54.)

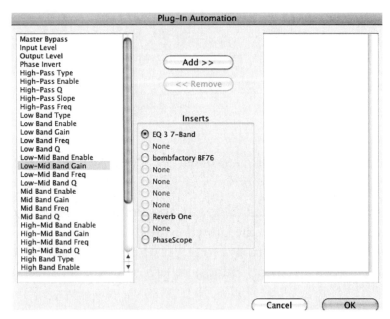

Figure 3.54   Every function that can be automated is listed on the left side of the window.

From this window, simply select the control you want to automate and click the Add button. That controller name now appears on the right side of the window and among the controller options for the track containing the plug-in. (See Figure 3.55.)

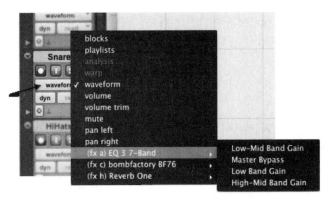

Figure 3.55 Once a controller is automated, the controls are accessible by selecting the Track View selector.

If that process is too complicated (it can be time-consuming), you can use a convenient keyboard shortcut. Although it's called the "3-finger salute," it doesn't have anything to do with your system crashing, so don't worry. Hold down the Ctrl, Start, and Alt keys (Control, Option, and Command for Mac) and click on the control in the plug-in window you want to automate. A dialog window pops open (Figure 3.56) asking if you would like to enable automation for that particular control or open the Plug-In Automation dialog window.

Figure 3.56 Hold down Control-Start-Alt while clicking a plug-in control to enable automation for that control.

Once you have activated automation for a plug-in, moving and copying that plug-in also moves the automation around, but changing to a different plug-in causes the software to remove that automation data. Also, if you make manual adjustments to a control that has been automated, those adjustments will be gone when the automation is played back unless you switch off the automation playback (Figure 3.57).

Figure 3.57 Set the automation mode from Read to Off to try manual adjustments to a plug-in.

When the automation playback is deactivated for a track, you can adjust settings manually and hear the results. Once it's reactivated, all automation for the track plays back and resets any manual adjustments to those controls.

Other Plug-In Controls

A few more plug-in controls standard to almost all of the real-time plug-ins are located in the upper right-hand corner of the plug-in window (Figure 3.58) and include the Bypass button, clip indicator, Target button, and Convert Plug-In button.

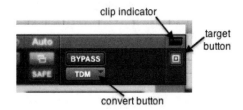

Figure 3.58   Other standard plug-in controls

The Bypass button allows you to temporarily deactivate a plug-in to hear the sound of your track with and without the effect. It's easy to turn a knob up slowly and not notice any change in the sound until the settings are pretty severe. So being able to switch the processor on and off is especially helpful for making sure the settings you've dialed in really do sound better and aren't too intense.

The clip indicator light appears on most real-time plug-ins and lets you know if the signal is clipping on its way through the plug-in. It lights the same whether the signal is peaking as it enters the plug-in or because of the processing being applied, and it functions like all other clip indicators in Pro Tools.

The Target button allows you to open multiple plug-in windows at the same time. If you click the button to turn off the little red indicator, the window stays open when other plug-ins are open. This is handy for having a complete signal path available while working on a track or for keeping specialized meter plug-ins open while you are working.

The Convert Plug-In button is available only in Pro Tools HD or HDX systems. It allows a plug-in to be switched between the RTAS or TDM version of the plug-in for older Pro Tools HD systems, and to switch between the AAX Native and DSP versions in new Pro Tools HDX systems. That option would, of course, depend on whether the plug-in is available in both formats. If so, it can be seamlessly switched between formats while the transport is stopped and you won't even lose your settings.

Delay Compensation

Delay compensation can be a tricky issue when dealing with plug-ins. In the past, automatic delay compensation was only available to Pro Tools HD users, but with the arrival of Pro

Tools 9, this feature has become standard equipment. The process itself is complicated and taxing on the system resources. Every other track will need to be held back in a delay buffer while waiting for the one slowpoke with all the intense plug-in processing on it.

Processing audio takes time. The more complicated the process, the longer it takes. The time we're talking about is measured in milliseconds, but it adds up quickly. When it crosses a certain threshold it can be audible, but even below that threshold it can affect the sound of your tracks by knocking them out of alignment with one another.

In Pro Tools 9, 10, and earlier Pro Tools HD systems, an automatic delay compensation process is available but needs to be activated. From the top menu, select Setup > Playback Engine (Figure 3.59) and an option in the dialog window allows you to activate the Delay Compensation Engine.

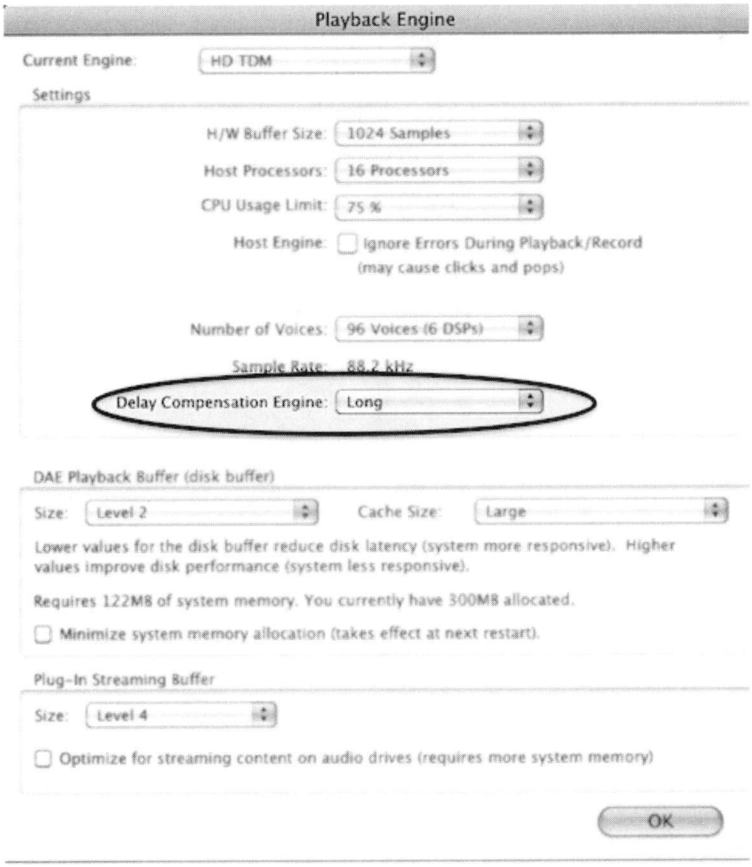

Figure 3.59 Automatic delay compensation is available in Pro Tools 9, 10, or earlier HD systems.

The option includes the ability to set the delay compensation to short, long, or none. Switching the engine on assigns DSP resources to the task of compensating for the delay. The short setting reserves less of your DSP resources than the long setting, so try to use less if it's possible. An indicator light in the Edit window's main clock display (Figure 3.60) changes from green to red if you have exceeded the capabilities of the short or even the long ADC buffer.

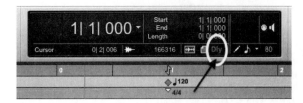

Figure 3.60 If this icon is red, then one of your tracks has too much delay for the current ADC setting.

Once ADC is activated, all of the tracks will be held back momentarily in a buffer so they will line up with the track that has the slowest processing time. This process should also compensate for the delay caused by analog-to-digital conversion at your I/O, as long as it's a device the Pro Tools software recognizes. To your ears, everything should sound perfectly normal, since all of the delay occurs between the moment you hit Play and the moment the first sounds start coming out of your speakers.

For earlier Pro Tools LE and M-Powered systems before Pro Tools 9, the process isn't so easy. For these systems, the track delay has to be identified by you on a track-by-track basis and corrected with the TimeAdjuster plug-in described in Chapter 7. Even though delay compensation is available as an automated feature in the newest versions of the software, read up on the process for a solid foundation in how it works and what to do if you exceed the limits of the automatic delay compensation.

4 Equalizers

In the beginning there was sound, and the plug-ins made them equal...

After basic gain controls, equalizers seem to be the most ubiquitous audio processors in recording gear, live-sound rigs, broadcast, right down to your car stereo. Yet for as much as we see them (and use them), many novice engineers aren't sure what to do with them.

Most equalizers are designed to either cut in very poorly defined and broad strokes, such as the "treble" and "bass" tone controls of your car stereo, or to dial in overly precise measurements like +1.2dB at 187 Hz with a plug-in on your vocal track. To make matters worse, we are often taught to reach for these tools to adjust the tone of a sound according to arbitrary descriptions.

You might be asked to make a sound "brighter" or "warmer" without agreement about what those terms mean. Does warmer sound mean more lows, more harmonic content, or something else entirely? Where does "brighter" stop and "shrill" begin? The controls on the devices won't help since they don't measure sound in such helpful adjectives. So unless you know what all those Hz, Q, kHz, and dB numbers are supposed to mean, it can be confusing.

So let's start with a refresher to better understand what frequency is all about.

Refresher

Since Equalizer plug-ins deal directly with narrow parts of the audio spectrum, make sure you understand terms like frequency, bands, harmonics, and spectrum. Even if you think you have a good handle on them, skim through this section and remind yourself of some of the various ranges and values.

As with other topics covered in this book, entire volumes have been written on the subjects of the physics of sound and how we perceive sounds in the world around us. I won't go into that kind of depth. However, since this is where the art and science of recording begins, it's important to have a strong foundation.

Fundamentals

When something happens once, it's an event. When it continues to happen again and again, it has a frequency. The simplest definition of frequency is how often something happens. The earth goes around the sun once a year; it spins around on its axis 365 times in a year (or once every day); and your heart beats about 70 times every minute. The audio frequencies we deal with when recording rocket along at much faster speeds but share a few basic concepts. Frequencies are always measured in some unit of time—with repetitions per second in the case of sound and audio. You will never see a frequency of zero since that would technically mean that no event ever happened. And, similarly, they can never be negative since that would mean that the event was "unhappening."

In the audio world, the events we are talking about are sound waves: changes in air pressure moving away from a source. Whether the sound is coming from a voice, an instrument, or a tree falling in the woods, it causes changes in the air pressure that ripple out into the space around the source. We capture those changes in air pressure with microphones, measure the intensity of the change, and represent it as a graph (Figure 4.1) of intensity (amplitude) over time.

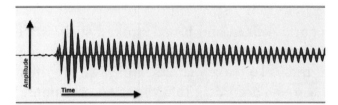

Figure 4.1 We represent a sound wave as a graph of amplitude (vertical) over time (horizontal).

Of course, we can't hear every sound that is made in the world (and it has nothing to do with how far away we are from the trees). Some sound waves repeat too slowly for us to hear them, while others repeat too quickly. There is a narrow "sweet spot" in the middle of the entire spectrum of frequencies that is the human range of hearing.

The Human Range of Hearing

The frequency of sound waves is measured in Hertz, a unit of measure named in honor of Heinrich Hertz, who was an early pioneer in electromagnetism. The name Hertz replaced the previous, less confusing, term of cycles-per-second. Similarly, kilohertz or kHz means thousands of cycles per second, and Megahertz (MHz) means millions of cycles per second.

It might seem like fun to have super-human hearing that can sense lower lows and higher highs than most people, but we're probably lucky our range of hearing stops where it does. The average range of human hearing extends from about 20 Hz at the low end up to about 20 kHz (20,000 Hz) at the high end. In Figure 4.2, the rough curve is the measured average, while the smoother curve is an approximation used in audio manufacturing and measurement called "A-Weighting."

This range is an average—especially at the upper limit. Children can generally hear higher frequencies, up to perhaps 22–23 kHz, but as people age, that high-frequency threshold drops off.

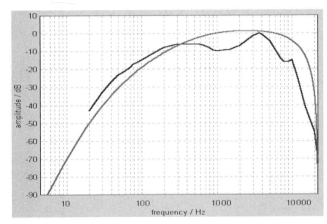

Figure 4.2 The average range of human hearing is usually about 20 to 20,000 Hz.

It usually happens gradually, although health and environment are contributing factors. So if you had lots of ear infections, worked around noisy equipment, or if you've been pumping 110dB worth of hard-rockin' tunes straight into your ears through little, white ear-buds four hours a day for the last decade, then you might not be hearing quite as much as you think you are. Still, it helps to have an average, and this range of 20–20,000 Hz has become a well-established target for equipment manufacturers and software designers.

As you record and alter your sounds with equalizer plug-ins, remember that just because we can't hear certain frequencies doesn't mean they aren't there. Sounds with frequencies lower than 20 Hz are called infrasound and are in the seismic range: think earthquakes. Sounds with frequencies higher than 20 kHz are called ultrasound and can actually be produced and heard by many other animal species: think dog whistles. It's unlikely you'll produce any earthquakes or be overrun by a pack of dogs, but those sounds can damage other parts of your audio system, especially speakers. There's more info on how to avoid turning up the stuff you can't hear in the "Overuse, Abuse, and Danger Zones" section later in this chapter.

Where Do the Instruments Fit?

Knowing the limits of the human range of hearing helps establish boundaries to work within, but that's still a big set of numbers that doesn't say much about where different kinds of instruments fit into the picture. Even describing the range as running from 20 Hz to 20 kHz doesn't say enough about how much sonic space that really is. Where, for example, do the seven-and-a-half octaves of piano keys fit into the picture?

Every engineer should remember some of the basic laws of physics related to sound, particularly the relationship of octaves. When talking about frequencies, an octave is a doubling (or halving) of the frequency. So from the standard tuning pitch of A=440 Hz, one octave higher would be A=880 Hz, while one octave lower is A=220 Hz. Do you notice, though, that the lower octave, from 220 to 440, seems like it is half as wide as the higher octave that runs from 440 to 880? It's not, since they are both one octave wide, but this isn't a linear scale.

Consider the very bottom and top of the human range of hearing. An octave higher than 20 Hz is 40 Hz. While an octave lower than 20,000 Hz is 10,000 Hz. That seems like a huge difference in numbers, but both of those ranges are just an octave wide. So maybe that human range of hearing isn't quite as wide as it first seems. Counting up in octaves (Figure 4.3), you can see that it only spans about 10 octaves, and the piano keyboard accounts for seven and a half of those just with its fundamental frequencies!

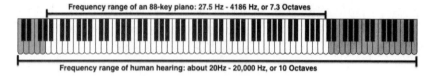

Figure 4.3 Measuring a different way, the human range of hearing is only 10 octaves wide.

That means everything you will ever hear fits within that seemingly narrow range of about 10 octaves. It also means that the numbers you will be dialing into the Pro Tools equalizer plug-ins might mean something a little different than you would expect. Look at the ranges covered by a few of the instruments you are likely to encounter in the recording studio (Figure 4.4) and consider how they fit into the overall picture of what we can hear.

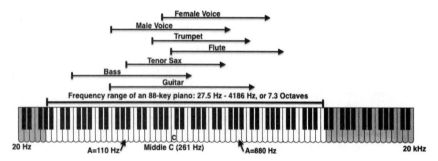

Figure 4.4 Here's how a few common instruments fit into the picture.

Those are just a handful of the instruments you might encounter in the studio or on the concert stage (and it doesn't factor in everyday sounds), but it's a good starting place. Notice two important things about this diagram: look at how most of the instrument ranges seem stacked on top of each other in the middle of our range of hearing; and notice that I've drawn each of the ranges with an arrow extending up into the higher harmonics.

> If you're trying to EQ an unusual sound, like the hum of a car engine, for a sound effect, try to relate it to the instrument that sounds closest to it—maybe an electric guitar or electric bass—and use that as a frame of reference. You could also hum a pitch in the range you're trying to adjust and then find that note on a piano or keyboard.

Remember that instrument sounds don't start and end at the fundamental frequency of the note it's playing. If that were the case, every instrument would sound the same when playing the same note. The difference in sound that we call timbre comes from the harmonics that sound at the same time, and these can extend far higher than the written range of the instruments. So every instrument you encounter can produce a much wider range of frequencies than even the performers may understand—but that's why they need you to engineer their album.

Why Does Your A-440 Sound Different From Mine?

If you have listened to a group of musicians tuning up their instruments, whether it was a garage band, a high school marching band, or a symphony orchestra, you heard a number of different instruments playing the same note. But while they were all playing that note, did you notice that each instrument still sounded unique? You can recreate the effect using a keyboard or instrument plug-in by playing the same note on different instruments. If they are all playing the same note, why do they sound different?

That difference in sound is called timbre (pronounced tam-burr), and it's created by the different way each instrument generates harmonics (overtones) above the note it's playing. Some instruments create their sounds with very few harmonics and produce very pure-sounding tones, like a flute or a vibraphone. Others create sounds with lots of harmonics and so produce very dense or rich sounding tones, like bowed strings.

Remember how the frequency relationship of octaves is a doubling of the frequency? So starting from, say, A=110 Hz, the next octave higher would be A=220 Hz, then A=440 Hz, then A=880 Hz, and so on. The series of harmonics produced by any instrument also follow a physical pattern, but it is a simple linear multiple—the starting frequency times one, then times two, then times three, four, five, and so on. Starting from A=110 Hz again, the "harmonic series" would be the frequencies 110 Hz, 220 Hz, 330 Hz, 440 Hz, 550 Hz, 660 Hz, and so on (Figure 4.5).

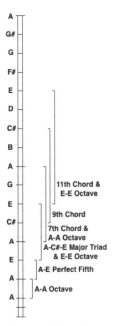

Figure 4.5 Octaves double the frequency, while harmonics are a linea

As an instrument produces a sound, a fundamental (starting) pitch, it sounds that frequency along some combination of the harmonics above it, all in different proportions. It's that difference in the proportions that makes instruments sound different, and they become almost a sonic fingerprint of the instrument. The average violin creates a sound that contains some typical proportion of various overtones, and we hear the sound and immediately recognize it to be a violin. But even within that characteristic sound, there are instruments like those by Stradivari, Guarneri, or Amati that may speak a little stronger, resonate a little longer, and favor certain harmonics in slightly different proportions. In some cases, such subtle differences in timbre means the difference between an instrument that is worth thousands of dollars and one that is worth millions.

So what does all of this talk of harmonics have to do with equalizer plug-ins? There are several things to consider. Remember that an equalizer is designed to boost or cut individual frequency bands rather than simply turning the volume up or down for an entire track. So changing one frequency range while leaving another means you may be changing the timbre of an instrument. It's highly unlikely you will accidentally turn a knob that makes someone's electric guitar suddenly sound like a set of bagpipes. But when a person's individual tone is their musical signature, knowing how to treat it gently might keep them coming back as a client.

The other important thing to remember about tone and timbre is that as sounds become more complex, as they sound richer, they add more and louder harmonic content. Some of that harmonic content will inevitably get in the way of other instruments. Take another look at the harmonic series starting from the A=110 Hz, which is the second-lowest string on an electric guitar (Figure 4.6).

Figure 4.6 The harmonic series as musical notes, starting from the lowest A on a guitar.

Take an electric guitar and add a lot of distortion to it, and the physical effect that makes the sound gritty, crunchy, and, well, distorted, is an increase in the number and volume of the harmonics that are sounding with each note. When the guitarist plays, even down at the lowest of the instrument, that guitar will also sound a big cluster of harmonics that land right on the soprano vocal range. Don't worry: I'm not saying anyone needs to turn down the distortion on the guitars. But it is something you are likely to encounter as an engineer, and knowing way around the equalizer plug-ins and the audio spectrum may help you carve out a midrange for your lead vocals to call home.

Is That a High-Pass or a Low-Cut?

To many engineers this seems like a silly question of semantics. But to plenty of folks just getting started, it can be confusing. Why is the same function, the same control, the same very basic feature, labeled differently everywhere? It happens on plug-ins, software, and hardware, even from the same manufacturers. We see the little icons on switches almost everywhere (Figure 4.7).

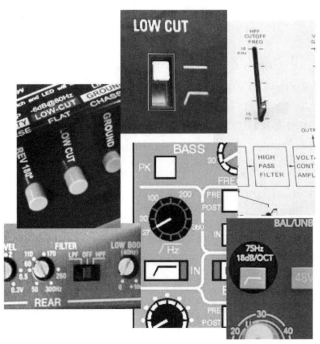

Figure 4.7 Low-Cut filters appear on every kind of audio gear.

The basic function of this audio filter is simple. Starting from a corner frequency, the volume level is turned down proportionally by a certain number of decibels per octave (the slope). The audio below the corner frequency is cut, while the audio above the corner frequency is allowed to pass through. So it really is *both* a Low-Cut filter *and* a High-Pass filter. And the same holds true at the other end of the spectrum, where you will see the counterpart high-frequency filter labeled as either High-Cut or Low-Pass.

Is there really any difference? For the most part it's a matter of opinion. I prefer to avoid confusion by using labels that describe what is being changed, not what stays the same. The very word "filter" means it's a device that takes something away. I never switch on a Low-Cut filter to let the highs pass through; I switch it on to cut the low frequencies. More accurately, I know they "roll-off" the lows or highs at a certain number of decibels per octave, but arguing for that label would be an even more ambitious fight. The important thing to remember is that the filter is only meant to affect the low frequencies—that's what it's changing. On the other end of the spectrum, a High-Cut filter is used to cut the high frequencies—and, again, that's what changes. Filters are easier to understand when the name describes what is being changed.

Throughout this chapter (and all others), I will refer to these filters according to their labels within the plug-in. If the programmers label the control as a "Low-Cut Filter," it will appear that way in the text. If the plug-in has the control labeled as a "High-Pass Filter," it will appear that way with an extra "(Low-Cut)" designation next to it. Someday there may be a consensus. Until then, I'll do my best to help you keep track of what these ubiquitous devices are trying to accomplish.

When to Reach for These Tools

You might occasionally find some of the pioneers of this industry talking about the good-old days when equalizers were referred to as "correctional devices," though that doesn't mean they were like prisons for your audio signal. It's a different way of thinking about equalizers than we do today: use them to correct a problem with the signal, not to create a particular tone or texture.

Of course, today we've learned creative ways to use all our tools. But it's still helpful to have this concept in mind as you choose *when* to activate an equalizer plug-in: are you looking for a corrective tool or a creative one?

Use Equalizers Creatively During Composition or Songwriting

When you're writing new material and creating new ideas, you won't have much use for corrective EQ options like filtering out low-frequency rumbles. That doesn't mean you can't explore some of the more extreme settings on your equalizer plug-ins as inspiration.

Just as hearing a little reverb might inspire you to sing (whether it's in the studio or the shower), using a telephone-effect EQ filter might inspire a particular sound or style while you are writing. A plug-in like the AIR Kill-EQ (Figure 4.8) is designed like a real-time DJ-style effect more than a clinically precise, corrective tool. Using it to change the tone of your voice, guitar, keyboard, or any other instrument could help you to tap into some new ideas.

Figure 4.8 AIR Kill-EQ is designed to be a creative tool.

If you are playing around with a guitar or other rhythm instrument and you're stuck for ideas, try running it through the AIR Kill-EQ plug-in to hear what some dramatic shifts in the tone can do. Sometimes dropping out all the highs or all the lows on a familiar instrument can make it sound different enough that it kick-starts your creativity. When it opens, the preset should drop the lows below 200 Hz, so clicking the low button will "kill" the lower half of your tone, leaving just the upper mids and highs. Play for a bit to see if the new sound takes you in a new direction.

Use Sparingly During Tracking and Overdubbing

Audio engineers debate how much processing should be done to incoming signals while recording. The two most common processors employed at this stage are Equalizers and Compressors (see Chapter 5), but the original reasons for using these processors had more to do with limitations of the equipment and recording medium. Using a Low-Cut filter to remove the rumbling air conditioner noise or compressing a signal to keep the quietest parts above the noise floor of a tape machine are probably the two most common situations. There are times to use equalizers as creative tools too. And that's where you need to make a decision.

I've found that keeping my options open while recording has been helpful and sometimes a life-saver (well, maybe more of a session-saver) for most recording projects. This is a commentary you can expect me to repeat often throughout later chapters. It's difficult to know how all of the sounds and textures of your project are going to fit together until you get all of them recorded. It might sound very cool to dramatically boost or cut frequency bands on some of your tracks, but it's often a safer bet to record the signals unprocessed and apply the effect afterward. This way you can make changes without having to correct for them later.

Remember that something as small as a –3dB dip in a frequency band means that you are only recording *half* the energy in that band. If you turn it down while tracking only to turn it up again while mixing, you'll also be raising the noise floor in that range as well. Not a big deal most of the time, but it adds up across multiple tracks. A much bigger problem would be if you applied something intense like a telephone effect to the lead vocals during tracking only to have your artist ask to turn it off during mixdown. Tell your diva you'll need to set everything up again and re-record that perfect take and see how she responds.

The only exception I make to this approach is when rolling off low frequencies from wind, HVAC, traffic, or other environmental problems. I want those problems corrected early in the signal chain, before they mess with the material I am trying to capture. But ultimately you are going to be the one to decide how and when to use your equalizer plug-ins—and how dramatically they are going to change the sounds you are recording.

Using Equalizers while Editing

Resource management is a recurring theme when using the Pro Tools plug-in suite, and it's while you are doing detailed editing work that you may find the Audio Suite versions of the EQ plug-ins most useful. When you encounter a smaller audio clip that needs treatment without changing the rest of the track, use the Audio Suite plug-ins rather than activating a real-time version.

You'll save on real-time processing power and won't have to automate the plug-in to switch on and off when it's needed.

A great example of this is when you're editing a vocal track and need to remove a "P" pop. The technique is described in more detail later in the section about the 7-Band EQ-III plug-in, but here's the basic idea. When you're going through vocal takes to build a composite of the best parts, you're likely to run into a strong plosive sound, a "P" pop. It's a place where a sudden burst of air causes a brief spike of low-frequency energy (Figure 4.9).

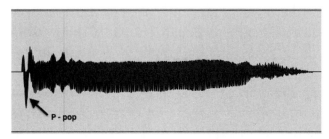

Figure 4.9   In a "P" pop, a sudden burst of air movement, causes a spike of low-frequency energy.

Selecting a small audio clip and applying a Low-Cut filter with the Audio Suite version of the EQ-III plug-in is an easy way to remove this kind of problem (Figure 4.10). The burst of lows won't cause a thump in your mix, but you'll still be able to hear the higher frequencies clearly so it will still sound like a "P" in the final mix.

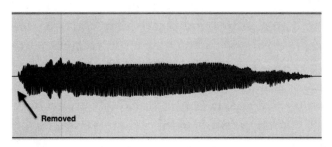

Figure 4.10   The plosive is edited out with an EQ plug-in.

The editing stage of the recording process is largely about fixing problems and correcting mistakes, so equalizer plug-ins as "correctional devices" have an obvious place in the process. You might use them briefly to remove individual bumps, thumps, and pops from a few notes, or you might run them over an entire track to reduce the amount of hi-hat sound in the snare drum mic, or to tune some buzzing sound out of a horn or electric guitar track. However you use them, remember these tools exist to help get your tracks cleaned up and ready to mix.

Equalizers Are a Mix's Best Friend

There's no hard-and-fast rule that says you have to use equalizers while you are mixing or anywhere else in the recording process. If you are recording a great-sounding instrument in a quiet room with a microphone that matches the sound, you might never need to switch on an EQ for that track.

Of course, there's nothing wrong with using equalizers when you need them...or want them. The three main uses for equalizer plug-ins during your mixing sessions are for correction, protection, and creativity.

Corrective uses fall into any range of the audio spectrum: a noisy room, a bright-sounding microphone, a muddy guitar, a nasally vocal sound. Many of the things we identify as problems with the tone of an instrument, voice, or sound, are issues that can be fixed with an equalizer. Reduce the lower midrange to thin out a muddy guitar, or reduce the upper midrange to tame a nasally vocal sound. The possibilities are endless, but a number of examples are covered later in this chapter.

Protection probably seems like an odd use for equalizers, especially if you are new to mixing, but it's an important use. This is the main role of the Low-Cut and High-Cut filters provided on the Pro Tools equalizer plug-ins and so many other audio devices. The recordings you create in the studio will be played back on real-world audio systems that have real-world limitations. At the low-end of the spectrum, for example, many speaker systems can't reproduce very low frequencies, but that doesn't mean they just go away peacefully. Low-frequency sounds are still boosted by the amplifier and sent to your speakers. If the speaker can't reproduce the sound though, all that energy is turned into heat—the kind that damages the speakers. I'll cover that in more detail in the "Overuse, Abuse, and Danger Zones" section at the end of the chapter.

It's fun to use equalizer plug-ins creatively while you're mixing. The work we do as engineers doesn't always have to be clinical, methodical, or technical. It might not seem like an obviously "fun" thing to carve a big hole in the middle of your rhythm guitar tone, but it can create a great effect in the right situation. It might be a functional way to help a vocal cut through, but it might also be a great way to make that introduction riff sound hollow and unnatural, so the listener expects this track to go in a different direction than all the others. Once you factor in the ability to automate all of the plug-in settings, there's no limit to how you might use sweeping peaks or notch filters to create sounds that tell stories...or cause nightmares.

Whether you use equalizers in your mixing and audio production heavily or very sparingly, the important thing is to be comfortable enough with the tools and techniques to use them any way you need to. There's a reason equalizers and "tone controls" are second only to volume controls in the mix of tools we are given to process audio. Most of the requests we receive from artists, producers, or directors can be solved by either turning the overall volume of a track up or down, or turning certain parts of the audio spectrum up or down. We equalize the tone, the blend, and the balance of each sound to create the perfect final texture. Isn't that the whole idea of mixing?

Equalizers Are the Cornerstone of Mastering
Whether you call them the cornerstone of mastering or the front-line weapon for mastering, equalizers are some of the most important tools for mastering engineers.

Whether you are dealing with mixes arriving from different engineers, or that were mixed at different studios, or just material you mixed on different days, the tonal balance of each mix is going to be a little different. That in itself isn't such a big deal, but it is part of the challenge of mastering a project—all those different mixes have to come together to sound like they belong on the same album. Matching the volume levels is one part of that, but a much more subtle (and difficult) task is matching the levels of different components within each mix.

Listening to a finished CD from track to track, you expect the vocals for each song to be at about the same level. You expect the low end to sound tight on every track. You expect each track to have a similar sparkle or glow, even as each piece of music may be constructed quite differently. Since remixing everything isn't an option, you need a solution to apply to the entire track—and equalizer plug-ins play a critical role here.

There are two key ways to utilize equalizer plug-ins when mastering. You can apply the plug-in to a track just as you would normally add a real-time EQ plug-in on an individual track in a mix. Subtle adjustments are made to narrower bands to bring out some sounds while settling back others: such as bringing out the airy highs of the percussion while settling back a slightly muddy bass guitar. The first technique is described in more detail in the "Advanced Techniques" section of this chapter. You can also use the equalizer to process the side-chain loop for a compressor. This technique creates a kind of automatic volume level for certain parts of the signal, and it's described more in Chapter 6.

Whether you are mastering music for CD release, sound effects for a theatre or film production, or the sound on video clips for the Web, the Pro Tools equalizer plug-ins are critically important for getting the job done.

What's in the Box?

Pro Tools includes two different equalizer plug-ins designed for substantially different purposes. The AIR Kill EQ equalizer plug-in is designed as a real-time performance effect more than a corrective tool, and it is only available as an RTAS real-time processor. While it has the ability to boost or cut separate frequency bands within an audio signal, its three "Kill" switches allow you to incorporate cool DJ-style effects into your productions. On the other end of the spectrum, there are several versions of EQ-III available. The EQ-III plug-ins cover the entire spectrum, both in terms of frequency range and being equally adept at clinically accurate corrective processing or dramatic, creative processing. You can choose a 1-Band, 4-Band, or 7-Band version of the processor to run in real-time as either RTAS or TDM, and the 1-Band and 7-Band versions also appear under the Audio Suite menu for offline rendering. (Versions of the plug-in that would run under the AAX Native or AAX DSP environments for Pro Tools 10 have not yet been introduced, but considering the update to Mod Delay III [Chapter 6], the update may include a push to an entirely new version.)

Although there are different versions listed, all of the EQ-III plug-ins are built over the same algorithms. The reason for having multiple versions with different numbers of available bands is, of course, to conserve system resources. Even if you haven't dialed a setting into a particular band of an EQ processor, the system needs to reserve a certain amount of processing power to run the entire plug-in, including that band, just in case you do decide to use it. As with other resource-intensive plug-ins, if you're working on a smaller project or a more powerful system, you may never have an issue and might safely use a 7-Band EQ-III on every channel. However, it's good practice to be efficient with every plug-in you activate for a track. If you only need a single filter, try using the 1-Band version. But don't feel you must limit yourself if you need the extra bands—that's why they are in there.

EQ-III (7-Band and 4-Band)

This plug-in should appear three times in your drop-down menus, as the "EQ 3 1-Band," the "EQ-3 4-Band," and the "EQ-3 7-Band." In the bottom right corner of the plug-in window, they're all labeled as "EQ-III" because they are really just different configurations of the same underlying processor. However, the look and behavior are different enough with the 1-Band version that it seemed a good idea to list it separately. But it's best to read both entries to get a sense of how each version can work for you.

Take a quick glance across the plug-in window of the EQ-III plug-in (Figure 4.11) and three main groups of controls should stand out; the very obvious graphic display in the upper right corner, the small set of controls in the upper left corner, and the colorful (at least in the computer) set of five controller groups across the bottom half of the window.

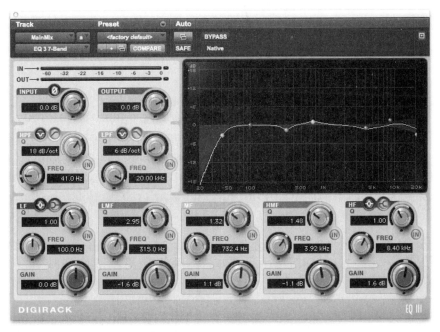

Figure 4.11 The EQ-III plug-in display is split into three main groups of controls.

Throughout the plug-in window, there are many ways to enter or change values for the various controls. You can click on and "turn" a virtual knob, or click on any of the small, green value displays to type in a specific value. You can also click and drag any of the colored dots in the graphic display window, but that will be covered later.

For the 7-Band version of EQ-III, all seven of the filter bands are available at any time. That's the five Peak/Notch filters at the bottom of the plug-in window along with the HPF and LPF filters just above them on the left. The 4-Band version can run any combination of the seven filters up to four total, but with one odd little quirk. The HPF and more filters are a little more processor intensive, so they take the signal processing power of two of the other bands. So you can run any four of the bottom five, or you can run one roll-off filter plus any two of the bottom five, or you can run just the two roll-off filters.

Starting with the control group in the upper-left corner, there are two groups of functions displayed, the I/O controls and the Roll-Off filters.

Input/Output Controls

This first set of controls for the EQ-III plug-in includes a pair of meters and three simple, yet useful, controls (Figure 4.12). The Input and Output control knobs are only set to their extreme settings for illustration though; that's probably not a good place to set them.

Figure 4.12 Notice that only one input and one output meter are provided.

The input and output meters are definitely helpful when working with any equalizer, although they are a little limited in multichannel situations since there is only one meter displayed for all inputs and one for all outputs. So when using the stereo version of the plug-in, the two channels are summed to mono for the purpose of metering. This has no effect on the sound but might change the readings on the meters—though either way you slice it, you're better off keeping things under control and your signal out of the red.

The Input and Output gain controls both provide a range of adjustment from –20dB up to +6dB on either the input or output side of the processor. It's a narrower range than some other plug-ins allow, but it's included here as a convenience feature and a safety net.

Working with any equalizer, it's easy to push your audio signal into distortion. You might not even see that displayed as a red line on the meters since it's easy to push one frequency band into distortion while the rest of the signal shows a lower average level. An easy solution is to grab the Input level control and turn down the overall signal before turning up any specific frequency band. Unfortunately, changing the Input and Output level controls will not change the graphic display at the right of the window for a visual representation of how all the levels will now be balanced.

The last control provided in this section is the Phase Invert switch, which is probably included as a convenience feature to avoid the need for adding another plug-in like Trim (Chapter 8), although it could also be used for a special effect. Experiment with a stereo track and a multi-mono version of the EQ-III plug-in. Dial a midrange bump into the left channel, along with a dip in the right channel, and then invert the Phase on one of them for a weird, wide-stereo effect.

HPF and LPF Roll-Off Filters

Next in line below the I/O controls are the Roll-Off filters, which are labeled as an "HPF," *High Pass Filter* and as an "LPF," *Low Pass Filter* (Figure 4.13). As already explained, I prefer to name equalizer bands (and any other audio tools) according to what they are changing rather than by what will remain the same. For that reason I will refer to their functions as a Low-Cut filter and a High-Pass filter.

Figure 4.13 EQ-III includes "High-Pass" (Low-Cut) and "Low-Pass" (High-Cut) filters.

The controls for these two filters are identical except for being set to control opposite ends of the spectrum. Each filter has a pair of filter-type switches at the top to select whether the filter will function as a Roll-Off or a Band-Reject filter. These are accompanied by two virtual knobs to control the frequency and the bandwidth of the filters. There is also an On/Off switch labeled In that glows blue when the filter is active. The one control that is conspicuously absent from these filters is the Gain control, but that is because these aren't designed to boost signals, only to cut them...cut them deep.

When you activate the plug-in, the default setting will set these filters as Roll-Off filters. This means the filter is intended to reduce all signals below or above a corner frequency by a consistent amount down into nothing. For example, you might choose to reduce all of the high frequencies above 1 kHz by 6dB/octave (Figure 4.14). That means the signal level will start dropping at 1 kHz until it is lower by –6dB at 2 kHz, and then it will lower by –12dB (total) at 4 kHz, then lower by –18dB at 8 kHz, and so on up the spectrum and down into nothingness.

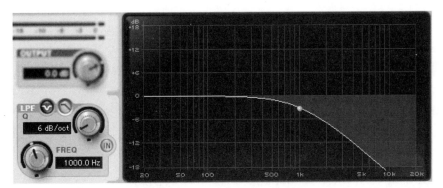

Figure 4.14 High frequencies above 1 kHz are reduced at a rate of –6dB per octave.

Selecting the Notch filter type changes either of these two filters into a Band-Reject filter. More than just reducing the midrange of your signal a little bit, this is like putting a black hole in the middle of it—nothing escapes. In this mode, the Frequency control will select the center of the Notch while the Bandwidth (Q) control adjusts the width. It's a fairly severe filter for most applications but can be a lifesaver when working with live audio or live recordings with feedback since the specific frequencies can be targeted and eliminated with precision.

Of course, the two largest controls for each filter are the virtual knobs that control the frequency and the Q. These are probably the first controls you will reach for when using this filter type, although their functions do change based on the filter type.

When running as a Roll-Off filter, use the Frequency knob to select the frequency where the filter starts to reduce the signal. It's a common mistake to think the filter will drop everything below or above the corner you set or even have much effect on the corner frequency itself. This is simply the point where the filter activates, so it should remain at normal volume while everything past that point is reduced gradually.

The speed at which the filter is dragged down into the darkness is controlled by the Q control that, in this case, is functioning as a Slope control. The display for this control is selectable as 6, 12, 18, or 24 "decibels per octave." Keep in mind the signal will drop off by this consistent amount for each octave below or above the corner frequency. So setting a Low-Cut (HPF) with a frequency of 50 Hz and a slope of only 6dB per octave does *not* remove 50 Hz. It doesn't even do much with the audible bass since it would only be –6dB down at 25 Hz and only about –9dB down by the time you wouldn't hear it anyway. That's significant, make no mistake, but it's not the same as starting at, say, 100 Hz and dropping at rate of –18dB per octave.

When you are applying Low- or High-Cut filters to treat specific problems such as environmental noise in a recording, consider where the troublesome frequency range is located and how intensely it needs to be cut. That will help you decide where to set the corner frequency and how steep to set the slope.

Midrange Peak/Notch Filters

At first glance, the five groups of controls that occupy the bottom half of the plug-in window look like five identical filters. All of them can function as Peak/Notch filters, although the lowest and highest ones, labeled LF and HF, can be switched into a shelving mode that will be described more in the next section. Apart from this difference, all five bands share similar controls and functions (Figure 4.15).

Figure 4.15   Each of the five Peak/Notch bands has three virtual knobs and an On/Off switch.

The In switch for each frequency band operates as a simple On/Off switch that glows blue when each filter is active in the signal path. This is a convenient way of testing how your settings are altering the signal since you can switch one band on and off to hear how it is affecting the sound. And like every other control, the In switches can also be automated to create quick tone changes as the track is rolling. For the 4-Band EQ-III, these switches are also essential for selecting which filters will be active.

The Q or bandwidth control adjusts how wide the peak or notch filter will be. The range for all of the controllers is from 0.10 at the widest to 10.0 at the narrowest. It looks at first glance like this might be a measure of a portion of an octave, but it's not. Instead the Q represents the "quality factor" of the filter shape.

The exact mathematics gets a little involved, but try to remember a few reference points. At the narrow setting of Q=10.0, the width would be about 0.144 octaves, or roughly one-seventh of an octave, or about a whole step. At Q=0.10, the width is about 6.67 octaves, which is about 80 notes out of the 88 on a piano. But you can easily remember it as going from about seven octaves to about one-seventh of an octave. To add one more number in the middle, a Q of 1.4 means a filter that is one octave wide. Knowing those reference points should get you through most normal usage.

The next control is the Frequency knob, which selects the center of the peak or notch filter. Here each band has a slightly different range from low to high so that you can dial in a more accurate number with its "sweet range" and so the processor can be tuned to act more like an analog filter circuit.

The last of the virtual knobs for each Peak/Notch band is the Gain control. This allows each filter to be set to boost the selected band as high as +18dB or cut it as low as –18dB. Remember though that a boost or cut of as little as 3dB represents a doubling or halving of the energy in a particular band, but we can't always hear a gradual change in volume level until it is at least 3dB. So it's good practice after setting an EQ filter to switch the individual filter or even the entire plug-in on and off so you can hear the abrupt change in level across all the various frequency bands.

It's sometimes easier to zero in on the exact frequency range you are trying to cut by boosting it instead—or vice versa. So the EQ-III plug-in has an interesting, somewhat-hidden feature to make this easier. With any of the five Peak/Notch filters, you can hold the Shift key and click on either the Gain knob or the colored dot on the graphic display to flip the gain amount from a boost to a cut, or from a cut to a boost.

Low Shelf and High Shelf

Two of the filter bands break from the rest of the pack to offer one more variation on filter shape. These are the lowest and highest of the five filters, labeled as the LF and HF bands, and they are differentiated with the extra filter Type switch that changes them from Peak/Notch filters into Shelving filters (Figure 4.16).

Figure 4.16 Two lowest and highest Peak/Notch filter bands can be switched into a Shelving filter mode.

A Shelving filter is like a hybrid between the Roll-Off and the Peak/Notch filter types. Like Roll-Off filters, the Shelving filter will extend past the end of the human range of hearing, either below 20 Hz, or above 20,000 Hz, and the Frequency controller will no longer select the center frequency of the filter, but rather the corner frequency of the shelf. However, rather than only dropping the signal level by an increasing number of decibels every octave, these filters can cut or boost the signal (like a Peak/Notch filter) by a consistent amount above or below the selected corner frequency.

That last part can be a little confusing to follow, so let's use an example instead. A High Shelf filter is so named because the frequency response chart should look like a shelf was drawn onto the graph. Set a High Shelf filter to increase +6.0dB at 2.5 kHz, and you will see that all frequencies above 2.5 kHz are raised by the same +6.0dB (Figure 4.17).

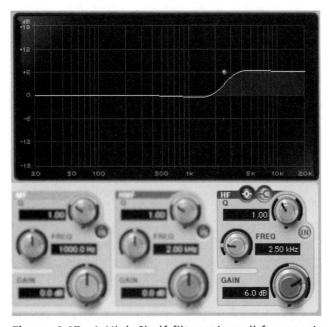

Figure 4.17 A High Shelf filter raises all frequencies above 2.5 kHz by +6.0dB.

Of course, the filter cannot raise the level immediately at the 2.5 kHz mark, so instead the display shows a little ramp in the graph representing the gradual increase in level up to the +6.0dB target. Maybe you're wondering how you can adjust that slope to make the rise happen faster... and funny you should ask. In addition to changing the shape of filter, and changing the Frequency controller from a center frequency to a corner frequency, switching to a Shelving filter also changes the Q control from a measure of width to a measure of slope (Figure 4.18).

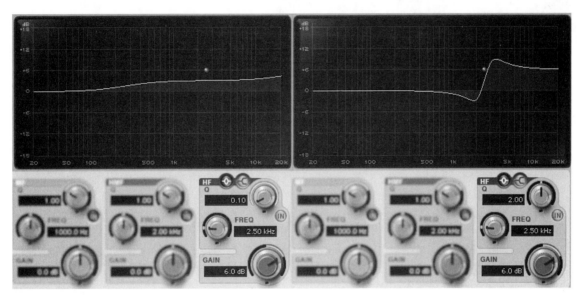

Figure 4.18 The same filter again with a very wide (left) and narrow (right) slope setting.

The very wide and shallow slope setting on the left begins shifting the level upward several octaves below the corner frequency and doesn't even achieve the full 6.0dB boost until the signal is past the limits of our hearing. Think of it as something like a high-frequency "tilt" filter instead, since it is so gradual. Meanwhile, the steep slope setting on the right is so intense that it causes the level increase to overshoot the mark by a couple of decibels before settling back into the consistent +6.0dB level. That's not just a function of the graphics programming. It is displaying the struggle the signal processor must go through to pull off such a steep slope, and that is actually consistent with the anomalies found in analog circuitry as well.

There's no escaping the physics involved in manipulating audio signals in such severe ways, but sometimes it's not such a bad thing. Consider a situation where there's a build-up of sub-bass frequencies that are weighing down a mix and making it seem muddy. Using a Low Shelf filter to reduce the signal by about –6dB could help thin the mix down below about 80 Hz. But if the male vocalist is singing notes as low as 100 Hz (a reasonable range for a baritone or bass), the filter needs to activate quickly (Figure 4.19). Setting a steeper slope might do just the trick.

With these settings, the lowest notes of the singer will actually get just a slight boost, the signal will be down just about –6.0dB at about 80 Hz, and will only level off to a consistent –5.0dB at a point that is already approaching the limits of human hearing.

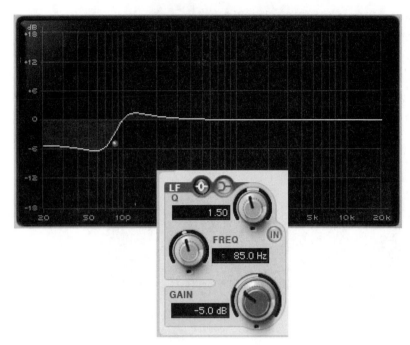

Figure 4.19 Setting the Low Shelf filter at 85 Hz, –5.0dB, and a 1.50 slope does the trick.

The most important thing about using Shelving filters to *increase* is that they will continue to increase the signal right on past the range of human hearing. That might not seem like a big deal, but remember that your amplifiers will still amplify the signals you can't hear, and your speakers will try to play the frequencies they cannot play. I've explained this subject in more detail in the "Overuse, Abuse, and Danger Zones" section at the end of this chapter, but it's worth reminding you here that energy your speakers cannot turn back into sound gets turned into heat instead—the kind of heat that can cook the voice coil of a speaker. Shelving filters are one of the easiest places to make that sort of trouble happen.

Graphic Controls and Other Fancy Tricks

Just in case all of these knobs, switches, and little numerical displays across seven bands of filters aren't enough layers of control for you, these equalizer plug-ins have a couple more tricks hiding...well, hiding wherever plug-ins traditionally hide such things. It's either right there in front of you like the graphic display controls, or hidden in a keyboard shortcut like quick-flip or Band-Pass listen features.

You may have noticed that in the graphic display window of the EQ-III plug-in, there are several colored dots representing the Frequency and Gain settings for each of the active bands (Figure 4.20). What you may not have realized is that each of these dots is also a control interface for the corresponding filter.

Not every option can be controlled from this point, but it does allow for simultaneous adjustment of the Frequency control and the Gain of the Peak/Notch and Shelf filters. The Q control,

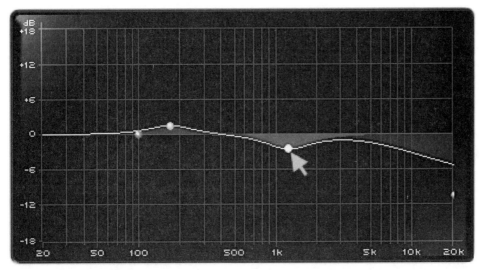

Figure 4.20 Grab any of the control dots on the graphic display to adjust the corresponding filter.

whether acting as a bandwidth or slope controller, cannot be adjusted from the graphic display. Mostly this feature can be a great time-saver when you're dialing in an initial EQ setting and need to slide the controls back and forth a little to find just the right spot. Although there is one very cool application for this control interface, and that's when you use it to write automation. Enable the automation for both the frequency and gain of one or more filter bands and set the track automation control to Auto Touch. While the track is playing, you can grab a dot on the display and swirl it around to write in awesome sweep effects. Set the automation control back to Auto Read, and the track will dutifully play back all of your movements. And the fun doesn't stop there.

It is sometimes easier to zero in on the exact frequency range you are trying to cut by boosting it instead—or vice versa. The EQ-III plug-in has an interesting, somewhat-hidden feature to make this easier. With any of the five Peak/Notch filters, you can hold the Shift key and click on either the Gain knob or the colored dot on the graphic display to flip the gain amount from a boost to a cut, or from a cut to a boost. So if you dial in a +6dB boost so you can sweep around and find the frequency that's poking your ear, you can Shift+Click and flip that to a −6dB cut. And since you can click the control dot as well, this means you can slide around the dot to focus on your target, then Shift+Click to knock it out or to bring it up.

If you still need a more dramatic way to zero in on the exact frequency target you are hearing, then consider using the Band-Pass Listen feature. This is purely a listening feature, meaning that the filter will not stay in this mode when you release the controls, although you can adjust the frequency, gain, or the Q settings for any band. Hold down the Shift+Start keys (Control+Shift for Mac) while clicking on any rotary controller or graphic display control dot to throw the selected filter into Band-Pass mode (Figure 4.21).

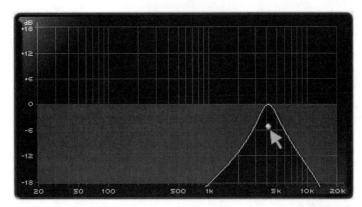

Figure 4.21 Hold down Shift+Start and click any knob or control dot to listen in Band-Pass mode.

A Band-Pass filter is kind of like taking a Low-Cut and High-Cut filter and setting them to the same corner frequency so only one tiny bit of the spectrum comes through while everything above and below is cut out. All of the rotary control knobs will function as you click and adjust them, although you won't hear a difference from the Gain controls since the Band-Pass filter doesn't boost or cut the selected frequency. Adjusting the frequency or the Q controls will, however, change the sound of the filter and allow you to sweep across the spectrum and find exactly the frequency you are looking for. Once you've found the spot, you can release the Shift and Start keys, the plug-in will jump back to normal operation, and you can adjust the Gain controls to your liking.

Real-Time Use (RTAS and TDM)

The EQ-III plug-ins are available for real-time processing in both RTAS and TDM formats for Pro Tools 9 HD and earlier Pro Tools HD systems. On Pro Tools 9 or earlier Pro Tools LE or M-Powered systems, only the RTAS version is available. For Pro Tools 10, only these RTAS and TDM versions are included since AAX Native and AAX DSP versions have not yet been released. Equalizer plug-ins can be a little resource intensive; that's why there are 7-Band, 4-Band, and 1-Band versions available.

Remember that the plug-in reserves processing power based on the total number of bands available, not the number you're actually using. So plan accordingly and try to use the 4-Band version if you are worried about processing power or only need a couple of filters. You can freely switch back and forth between the 4-Band and 7-Band version without losing any of your settings. You'll have to switch each band back on or off when you make the change though.

Usage Example I: Beefing Up a Weak, Acoustic Guitar Pickup

Face it, most acoustic guitar pickups really sound weak. Thin, quacky, brittle, and downright irritating are the standard sounds. But they are practical in many live-sound and live-recording settings, so there's a good chance you're going to have to deal with one eventually. Dialing in a good, corrective EQ setting to get a more balanced tone is definitely the first step to improving the sound.

First you'll have to activate a 7-Band EQ-III on the channel with the acoustic guitar recording. Then start with the stuff that needs to be cut (Figure 4.22). That should keep you from boosting to match the levels of stuff you don't want to keep.

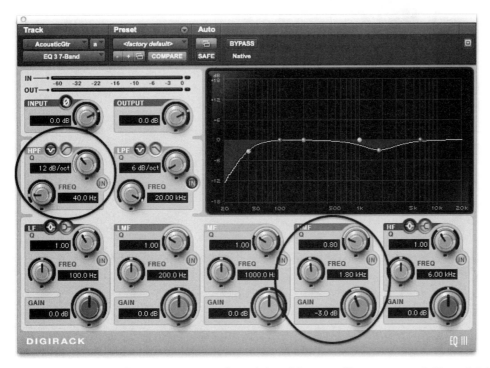

Figure 4.22 Start by cutting. Use the High-Midrange filter to cut –3dB at 1.8 kHz and set the HPF to 40 Hz and 12dB per octave.

Using the Low-Cut filter might seem contradictory when you're trying to fix a thin and weak-sounding DI acoustic guitar track. Trust me, it's an important safety net and will actually make your low end tighter when you get to boosting it.

The cut to the upper midrange is meant to take out some of the more brittle top end that's typical of many pickups. Your pickup's peak might hang a little higher or lower than this frequency. In that case, dial a deeper cut, maybe –6dB, and slowly sweep back and forth until the worst spot is pulled down and the tone seems more balanced. Then, while you're still listening, turn the gain back to 0dB, wait a moment, and then slowly cut until you have just the right amount taken away. Switch that filter band off and on a couple times to confirm it's the right spot.

Next, try boosting the Low-Midrange band by about +3dB centered on 150 Hz with a Q setting about 1.0 wide (Figure 4.23). This should give a strong push to the first two octaves of the guitar's fundamentals.

Depending on both the pickup you are using and the function of the guitar, you might push the frequency up or down a little. For lead acoustic parts, favor a slightly higher setting of about 180 Hz, and for rhythm tracks, aim a little lower at about 125 Hz. If 3dB isn't enough, you can push a little more—just make sure to listen. Switch the filter on and off to make sure you aren't going

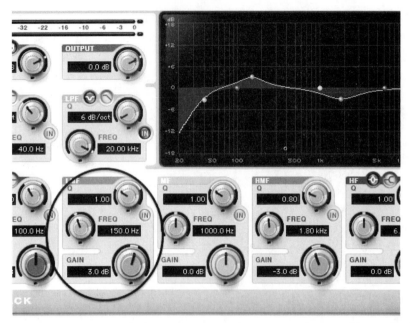

Figure 4.23 Next dial in a boost to the Low-Midrange filter of +3dB at 150 Hz with Q = 1.0.

too far. Also be sure to listen with the whole mix going so you know if you're overpowering the bass, keyboard, or vocals.

> If you're the one playing the guitar, ask someone else to listen to the balance against the rest of the mix. We always want our own instrument to be louder than the others…it's a musician's nature.

Your guitar track might still need fine-tuning, but this should be a good starting point for most DI acoustic tracks. Next, add a little light compression (Chapter 5) to thicken up the sound, and make sure to send a little of the signal to a nice-sounding reverb (Chapter 6) to make it sound less like the track was recorded from inside the guitar (even though it was!). And, of course, don't be afraid to revisit your EQ-III settings to take away any other bad stuff that may have floated to the surface along with the deeper, richer guitar tone you managed to find.

Audio Suite Use

You may have noticed that there are only two versions of the EQ-III plug-in listed in the Audio Suite pull-down menu: the 7-Band version and the 1-Band version. If you are using the 4-Band version in a real-time setup and want to copy your settings into the Audio Suite version to render some audio clips offline, don't worry. Simply copy and paste the settings into the 7-Band version. Since the Audio Suite plug-ins run offline, there's no need to limit the number of available bands to anything less than the full seven. Any filters you weren't using in the real-time version simply won't be switched on. The 1-Band EQ-III plug-in, however, has a unique enough layout and design that settings cannot be cut and pasted into other versions.

Usage Example III: Un-Popping Your Vocal Plosives

You have heard "P" pops from live sound systems, on radio broadcasts, on recordings, and in many other situations, so I probably don't need to explain what they sound like. You may not be aware that they can happen on consonant sounds besides the dreaded "P." It's common to hear them with a "B" or a "T" at the beginning of a word. I worked with a singer who managed to pop on a "W" sound and another who could pop on the ends of some words.

Whatever the specific phonetic sounds are that cause them, the problem is the same—a sudden rush of air causes a short, very low-frequency burst of sound. Think of what happens when you say a word like "Pow!". You close your lips and build up air pressure behind them. A quick opening allows the rush of air out to make the "P," followed by the more steady air flow you use to produce the tone "ow." That short rush of air is less of a sound and more a tiny, focused, burst of wind.

You can treat this kind of plosive sound like wind and add foam windscreens to your microphones, switch on the Low-Cut filters at your mics or preamps, or use a Low-Cut filter on your favorite EQ plug-in. Although the pop sound is very low, it might have some higher components that are in the same range as the vocals you are hoping to keep. In these situations, an offline EQ-III plug-in can handle the task.

Zoom in on your vocal track and find the section where the plosive sound occurred (Figure 4.24). Here's a great example from a jazz vocal recording.

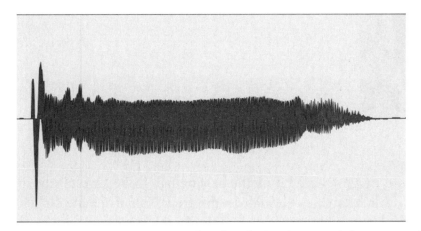

Figure 4.24   Here's an example of a plosive ("P" pop) from a vocal jazz recording.

At first glance you might think the offending pop is only that extra blob before the note and that you might be able to remove it with a simple cut and fade-in. But look more closely (Figure 4.25) when I overlay the curve of the low-frequency pop further into the note.

The most obvious part of the plosive sound is definitely the part just ahead of the note I want to keep, but the pop is still "ringing" in the air, and it's modulating the note. This one is clearly a job for an EQ filter. Just remember to select enough of the note to catch all of that extra ringing. If the note being sung is higher than your EQ filter, you can select the whole thing.

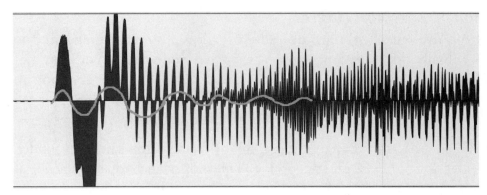

Figure 4.25 With the low-frequency curve drawn in, you can see how long the pop rings.

Depending on the pitch of the note the vocalist is singing, you might be able to use a simple Low-Cut filter alone to fix the problem. I usually start with an HPF (Low-Cut filter) set to 100 Hz and a Q of 12dB per octave (Figure 4.26). That's a nice target that will catch a lot of plosives right off the bat.

Figure 4.26 Apply a Low-Cut set at 100 Hz and a Q of 12dB per octave to start.

For a male vocalist, this might be into the range where he might be singing, so be careful not to cut the tone. A steeper Q and slightly lower frequency should do the trick. For a female singer, you might be able to push as high as 150 Hz, which should definitely do the trick.

In some cases, I find that stacking a Low-Shelf and a Low-Cut will do the best job on tougher plosive problems. Try a low-shelf set at –3dB below 180 Hz along with a low-cut set at 12dB per octave below 80 Hz (Figure 4.27). That should take care of any pop your singer springs on you.

When it's all done, you should still have all of the higher harmonics and attack characteristics that will tell your ear it's a "P" she is singing, but without the explosive that thumps your sub-woofers (Figure 4.28).

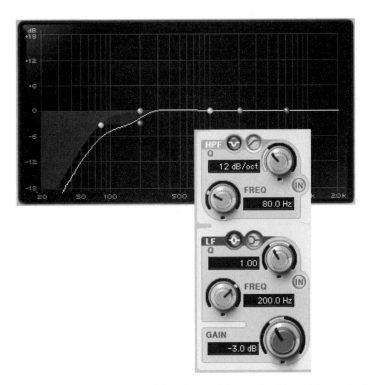

Figure 4.27 Try a combination of Low-Shelf and Low-Cut to take care of tougher pop sounds.

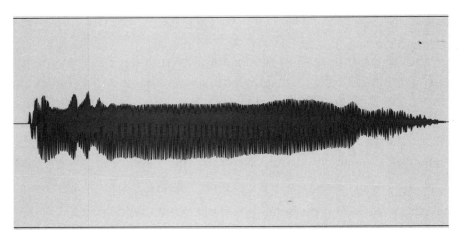

Figure 4.28 Here's the wave with the plosive filtered out.

Notice in particular that by reaching a little farther into the note, I removed the ringing low fre-quency so now the tone is more even and centered on the zero line of the track. That shows just how much that low-frequency energy was affecting more than just the attack. Once you get the hang of it, make this kind of process a normal part of your vocal compositing procedure. Save a couple of your favorite settings as presets, and you'll be ready to take on any vocal track that comes your way.

EQ-III 1-Band

The 1-Band version of the EQ 3 plug-in really is built over the same underlying algorithms as the larger 4-Band and 7-Band versions. That made it tough to decide whether to break this description out on its own or simply include it with the main one. The two big differences between the 1-Band version and its larger siblings are the design of the plug-in window and the ability of this lonely little band to transform into any filter shape centered on any frequency. (See Figure 4.29.) Taken together, those differences seemed enough to earn the EQ-III 1-Band plug-in its own entry. However, this plug-in is still part of the larger EQ-III plug-in, so if you're new to this plug-in or equalizers in general, read about the 4-Band and 7-Band versions too.

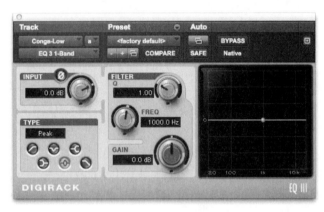

Figure 4.29 It may look a lot smaller, but this version is still an EQ-III plug-in.

Although the size of the interface window for this version is substantially smaller, there are many similarities to its bigger brothers. The frequency graph display still shows the intended behavior of the equalizer across the spectrum from 20 Hz to 20 kHz; the display is just scaled down to a smaller size. The virtual knobs of the filter control section function like any individual band of the larger versions. Controlling all of the functions also works in the same way. You can click and "turn" a virtual knob, type exact controller values directly into the display, or grab a dot on the graphic display.

This version is included, as you'll see with other plug-ins, so you can manage limited system resources. Activating plug-ins takes processing power from your system. As the processors get more complex, they need larger allocations of CPU or DSP-engine power to run. Using the smallest version of a plug-in possible (that still gets the job done) preserves limited system resources so you can run more tracks or more plug-ins.

Efficiency, however, is not the only benefit to having the 1-Band EQ-III plug-in available. It is a convenient analysis tool, like a little audio tape measure. If you are hunting for a particular band of frequencies where your track needs help, this simple filter can help you zero in on the trouble. Switch on the plug-in, for example, to zero in on the sibilant sounds so you can set a De-Esser (Chapter 5) to get them under control. Or find the frequency band where the vocals are centered so you can carve a notch into your synth pad and keep it from drowning out the lyrics. It's also very easy to automate when you want to create frequency sweep effects. Whether you find creative or technical uses for it, this is a helpful tool.

Input/Output Controls

In addition to limiting the plug-in to just one filter, the designers have also scaled back on the input and output controls (Figure 4.30). The input and output meters are gone, along with the Output Gain control.

Figure 4.30 Streamlining of the 1-Band version extends to the I/O controls as well.

What remains in this version is the Input Gain control with the same range from –20.0dB to +6.0dB, so you can boost an incoming signal slightly or reduce it a little so the filter settings don't drive the track into overload. The Phase Invert switch is also still included, if you need to correct absolute phase issues (Chapter 7) or to create special phase-related effects.

Filter Type Selector

Several bands in the larger 4-Band or 7-Band version of EQ-III have filter Type switches, so these should be familiar feature. This version, however, can be set to any of the six different shapes you might need (Figure 4.31). Only one filter Type can be selected at a time (since there's only one band available). Switching between some filter Types will change the behavior of the other controls.

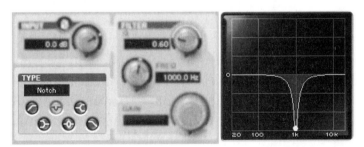

Figure 4.31 Choose one of the six available filter Types to change the behavior of the 1-Band EQ-III.

Choose a High-Pass (Low-Cut) filter to reduce or roll-off all the frequencies *below* a corner frequency by an increasing number of decibels per octave. On the opposite end of the spectrum, choose a Low-Pass (High-Cut) filter to reduce all of the frequencies *above* a corner frequency by an increasing number of decibels per octave. The frequency graph displays (Figure 4.32) for these filter types show how they behave.

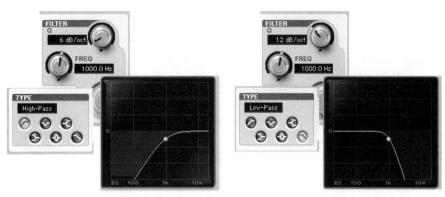

Figure 4.32 A High-Pass filter cuts low frequencies –6dB per octave (left), while a Low-Pass filter reduces the highs by –12dB per octave (right).

Selecting a Low-Shelf filter allows you to cut or boost all the material *below* a corner frequency by a consistent amount you can choose. Similarly, a High-Shelf filter allows you to cut or boost all the material *above* a corner frequency by the same amount. The frequency graph displays (Figure 4.33) for these filter types show how they behave differently from the previous types. Notice in particular that the amount of boost or cut will continue out past the human range of hearing.

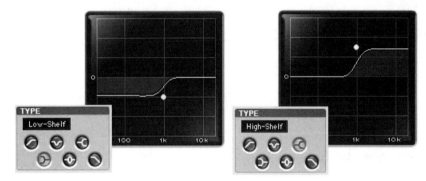

Figure 4.33 A Low-Shelf filter cuts low frequencies by –6dB (left), while a High-Shelf filter boosts the highs by +9dB (right).

Two more filter types cover the middle of the spectrum. Clicking the selection button in the middle of the top row switches the plug-in to a "band-reject" filter that is called a Notch filter in the plug-in display (Figure 4.34). This filter type functions similarly to Low-Cut or High-Cut filters in that it only reduces the signal, and it aims to completely remove all material at a particular band.

The Notch filter is actually successful at the second part since it will completely remove the centered frequency shown in the display window. To see how accurate this audio black hole really is, I ran a quick test that you might want to duplicate. Try using the Signal Generator plug-in set to play a 500 Hz tone followed by the EQ-III 1-Band set to notch out 500 Hz. It can all be set up on a single Aux Input track. Use the Bypass switch on the equalizer to test the effectiveness of the Notch filter. I found that it killed that frequency dead, but gradually started letting signal

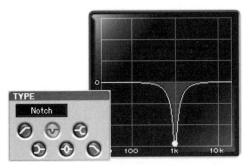

Figure 4.34 The Notch setting puts the filter into a band-reject mode that aims to completely remove all material at a particular band.

pass again as I dialed the generated frequency only 1 Hz up or down. Adjusting the Q setting will widen or narrow the band of frequencies cut by the filter.

Stepping away from the extreme band-reject function, you'll find the Peak filter setting in the middle of the bottom row of the Filter Type switches (Figure 4.35). This setting functions as you would expect a peak/notch filter to and as five of the seven bands of the 7-Band EQ-III plug-in are designed to operate. Select a center frequency and a bandwidth, and then adjust the gain to boost up to +18dB or cut down to –18dB in that band.

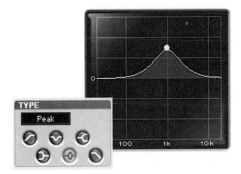

Figure 4.35 The Peak selection is a peak/notch filter that can boost or cut +/–18dB at a selectable center frequency.

Once you have selected the filter Type you want to use, it's time for a little fine-tuning.

Filter Controls

Three virtual-knob, rotary controls are clustered under the Filter heading that allow you to dial in the exact filter settings you need (Figure 4.36). These are the same controls, in the same layout, as the larger versions of EQ-III, and, for the most part, they function the same way.

At the top of the group is the Q control, which functions as a width control when the plug-in is running as either a Notch or Peak filter, and as a Slope control for Roll-Off or Shelf filter functions.

Figure 4.36 The filter controls allow you to fine-tune the EQ-III settings.

Although a Q or "quality factor" is technically different from the bandwidth of a filter, the specific details are beyond the scope of this text. Instead, observe that the control has a range from the very wide Q=0.1 (bandwidth of 6.67 octaves) to the very narrow Q=10.0 (bandwidth of about 0.144 octaves). That might be tough to remember, so instead remember the dividing line at Q=1.4. Q values smaller than 1.4 are wider than one octave, while values larger than 1.4 are narrower than an octave.

When you select either Roll-Off or Shelf filter types, the Q control will shift into different modes, controlling the slope instead. For the HPF or LPF filter types, the Q has a range of four values: 6, 12, 18, or 24 decibels per octave. That adjusts how rapidly the signal is cut at frequencies beyond the corner frequency. When the plug-in is acting as either a Low-Shelf or High-Shelf filter, the Q control will adjust how quickly the signal is boosted or cut to the shelf level.

In the middle of the filter control section is the Frequency control, which functions similarly to the same controls in the 4-Band or 7-Band EQ-III but with an interesting extra feature. As you would expect, the control selects the center frequency of a Notch or Peak filter but changes to select a corner frequency when the plug-in is operating as a Roll-Off or Shelving filter. The difference here is that, since there is only one filter available, it has to have a broader frequency range. So this Frequency control can be set anywhere from 20 to 20,000 Hz—the complete range of human hearing.

That subtle difference might not seem like a big deal since, taken together, the five Peak/Notch filters of the 7-Band EQ-III cover that entire range and even overlap from one filter to the next. However, that broad range only extends to the Roll-Off and Shelving filters in *this* version of the plug-in. With the 1-Band EQ-III plug-in, there is no limit to how high or low you can set the corner frequency of any filter.

This wider frequency range seems like a simple solution the plug-in designers chose to use. But don't overlook it, as it's useful if you are trying to create more specialized EQ effects, particularly for electronic music or sound effects. In the "full" version of EQ-III, the Low-Cut (High-Pass) filter can only be set as high as 8 kHz, and the Low-Shelf can only be pulled as high as 500 Hz. The ranges for the high-frequency counterparts are similarly narrow. But here in this "limited" version of EQ-III, any filter can be set to any corner or center frequency from 20 Hz up to 20 kHz. You might never *need* (or even want) to use such extreme settings, but it's nice to know you *can* if you choose.

At the bottom of the filter control section of the plug-in is the Gain control, which operates exactly as you'd expect. For Peak filters, the Gain control had a range of cut or boost from

–18dB to +18dB. This range shrinks to anywhere from –12dB to +12dB for Low-Shelf or High-Shelf filters. And for the High-Pass filter, the Low-Pass filter, or the Notch (Band-Reject) filter types, the control is unavailable since it is not relevant to those filter types.

The specialized control features of the larger versions of EQ-III are also available in the 1-Band version. This includes the Band-Pass listen feature (Figure 4.37) where you can hold down Shift +Start (Control+Shift on Mac) and click a control to throw the filter into Band-Pass mode to zero in on the exact frequency band you are trying to control.

Figure 4.37 The 1-Band EQ-III plug-in also includes the Band-Pass listen function.

You can also use the quick-flip function to change a boost to a cut, or vice-versa, by holding the Shift key while clicking either the Gain control knob or the control dot in the graphic display. That is still, however, a feature only available for the Peak filter type.

Real-Time Use (RTAS and TDM)

The 1-Band version of EQ-III, like its larger siblings, can be run under both RTAS and TDM environments, in both multichannel and multi-mono configurations. There are three main reasons to use the 1-Band version over the others. It is a simple and streamlined interface that delivers the most essential functions, especially if you only need one EQ filter to get the job done. It uses fewer system resources compared to the larger versions that reserve processing power even if you don't use all of the other bands. And it has a broader frequency range for some of the filters, so you can create more dramatic effects.

You'll probably use the 1-Band EQ-III most for little filtering tasks that need to continue running throughout a session. This might be a subtle bump or dip to compensate for the tonal relationship of microphone and instrument. It might be a High-Cut filter meant to remove squealing ultrasound from computer monitors. Or you might find yourself trying to notch an electrical hum out of a "vintage" guitar amplifier.

Usage Example I: Filtering out a 60-Cycle Hum

Before we start down this path, I have to say the best way to handle electrical hums is to avoid recording them in the first place—but a full explanation of how to do that is beyond the scope of this text. With research into proper grounding, ground plane differentials, induction, and transformers, you can start learning how to deal with this issue on the front end. However, you may not be able to kill every electrical issue at the source, and you might receive compromised tracks from some other engineer, so here's a way to tackle the problem.

There are two main problems when dealing with electrical hum issues. First, they don't reside exclusively at 60 Hz; there are usually other harmonics present. Second, those extra harmonic frequencies involved, 60 Hz, 120 Hz, 180 Hz, and so on, are also places where you are likely to have a lot of instrument sounds. Oh, and if you're working in other countries or with tracks from other countries, keep in mind that 60 Hz power is used mainly in North and South America, while most countries use 50 Hz power.

If you are definitely dealing with a low-frequency "hum" and not a higher-frequency "buzz," then using the 1-Band EQ-III to carve a narrow notch out of the signal at 60 Hz might help you. Using the Notch filter type instead of the Peak filter is a little extreme since it's designed to completely remove the selected frequency, but it is highly effective and allows for a deeper cut than the maximum –18dB available with a Peak filter. Setup is simple, with a real-time 1-Band EQ-III plug-in (Figure 4.38) activated and set to notch at a frequency of 60 Hz and a Q of 2.0 (the narrowest available).

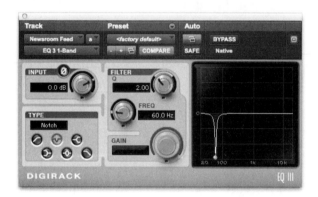

Figure 4.38 Set the 1-Band EQ-III plug-in to a Notch filter at 60 Hz with a Q of 2.0.

In most cases, this intense removal of the narrow band around 60 Hz (or 50 Hz) should be sufficient to knock out much of the electrical hum problem. The narrow band of the filter will, of course, also knock out some of the sound of your bass, guitars, piano, or other instruments, but here's where harmonics are both a friend and an enemy. Remember that when we hear the upper harmonics of a familiar instrument sound, our brains will fill in the missing fundamental. That works for both the hum you're trying to defeat as well as the instruments you're trying to keep. The instruments have a slight edge, however, since they generate more harmonic content than AC power, and 60 Hz happens to lie in between two standard musical notes.

You might still have some higher harmonic ring from the electrical hum, but you can deal with it in several ways. Any harmonics would occur at linear multiples of the power frequency, so 60, 120, 180, 240, 320, and so on could be cut in a similar way or with a less severe Peak filter. Try activating a second 1-Band EQ-III filter and setting a similar Notch filter at 120 Hz. Listen carefully and change the frequency to 180 Hz and then 240 Hz. If one of these settings has a significant effect on reducing the hum without poking a big hole in the signal you want to keep, then leave it set to that frequency. You can also try switching between a Notch and a Peak-type filter to see if a less severe cut does the job. Of course, if one filter does the job, then you're done.

This approach can be used to chase down other narrow-band sounds that might creep into your audio. A large university lecture hall where I occasionally record recently installed a new wireless Internet router that has an audible, high-frequency squeal, most likely from a switch-mode power supply. The room functions as a classroom, so taking it down isn't an option, and requesting a different device could literally require an act of congress (state congress). However inconvenient the sound may be, it is conveniently a very narrow, high-pitched sound that lands right around 9.8 kHz. So when I record in that space, it takes just a moment to set up a Notch filter, sweep around to find the exact frequency, and knock it out of the recording. All the other high-frequency content is preserved, so the room sounds spacious and reverberant. A quick and easy fix.

Audio Suite Use

With seven bands of the same EQ-III algorithm already available among the Audio Suite plug-ins, it might seem like overkill for the programmers to include the 1-Band EQ-III as well. There are, however, a couple of good reasons it's included.

First, it's helpful when you need to shift from a real-time version of the plug-in to the Audio Suite version to save processing resources. You cannot copy and paste settings from the 1-Band EQ-III into the 7-Band version, whether you're working with real-time or Audio Suite versions.

Second, because of the quirks of its design, the 1-Band version has a broader frequency range for some filter types. This is especially helpful with the High-Pass and Low-Pass filters.

Usage Example II: Band-Limiting the LFE in a 5.1 Mix

While mixing to 5.1 surround is easy in Pro Tools, the programming has one hidden flaw that can cause trouble for your mixes. The surround panner (Figure 4.39) for any of your tracks has a control to adjust the signal level that track is sending to the LFE (subwoofer) channel. The problem is the signal sent to the subwoofer is full-range, meaning it has more signal than most subwoofers can handle.

Most LFE subwoofer channels are delivered with only a narrow two-to-three-octaves worth of the lowest material from the audio track. You can limit the higher frequencies at any point you'd like, though the standard tends to be at 120 Hz. Some people may aim a little lower, around 100 Hz or even 80 Hz, and some will go a little high. I tend to roll-off a little higher at 150 Hz because I know that most home theater systems include a filter that can be set to 80 Hz, 100 Hz, or 120 Hz, and I want to leave a little extra room for the filter to respond more smoothly.

If you choose to limit your LFE channel at 120 Hz or higher, then the other EQ-III versions can manage the task. But if you choose to limit your LFE channel at 60 Hz, 80 Hz, or 100 Hz, you

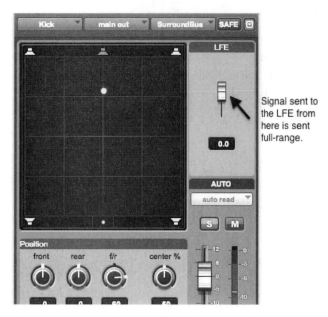

Figure 4.39 Routing audio from a track to the LFE channel is easy with the surround panner.

won't be able to use the 7-Band EQ-III plug-in because the Low-Pass filter (High-Cut) can't be set that low (Figure 4.40). This is where the unassuming little 1-Band EQ-III helps with its full 20-20,000 Hz frequency range. Simply select the whole LFE track from your final 5.1 mix session, open the Audio Suite version of the 1-Band EQ-III plug-in, set up a High-Pass (Low-Cut) filter, and dial in the frequency and slope wherever you choose. It's not a huge difference in the available range, but why should you have to work with any limitations?

Figure 4.40 A quirk in the design allows you to set more extreme values in the 1-Band EQ-III.

This arrangement can, of course, be set up with the real-time version of the 1-Band EQ-III plug-in as well. In a live 5.1 mixing environment, you can even use a multi-mono version of the plug-in, unlock the channel controls, and set different filters for each of your six speaker outputs to limit the highs sent to the subwoofers and the lows sent to the mains. Just remember that doing so will not create a crossover that sends the lows from the other five channels into the sub; it will just throw them away. But it can also deliver a tighter overall bass sound with less wear and tear on the low-end of your mains.

AIR Kill EQ

Moving away from the accuracy and fine layers of control afforded by the versions of the EQ-III plug-in, the AIR Kill EQ goes in a totally different direction. This ain't no subtle, corrective tool; it's built for special effects.

Of course, since it's designed to operate within the Pro Tools environment, it's not likely to end up nestled between a pair of turntables on the DJ stand at your local club. Instead, the AIR Kill EQ (Figure 4.41) brings some of the DJ's favorite tricks home to the studio for beat production, electronic music, or wherever your imagination takes you.

Figure 4.41 The AIR Kill EQ places fine adjustment controls in the middle with the "Kill" switches down the side.

The plug-in interface is simple and streamlined with only a few key controls and only three frequency bands to manage. The aim is to allow broad frequency bands to be boosted or cut slightly for tone shaping but then to abruptly drop out entire frequency bands by hitting one or more of the "Kill" switches. The controls are similar to the controls on a small club mixer or a guitar pedal. On the inside, however, the processing acts more like a crossover than an equalizer.

A standard crossover doesn't divide a signal so that some frequencies are sent in one direction while other frequencies are sent in another. Instead, the incoming audio signal is copied (split) into two, three, or more parts—in this case, three. Each of the copied signals is then processed by a Low-Cut filter, a High-Cut filter, or both to leave only a certain portion of the signal (Figure 4.42). The result in this case is three separate signals: the lows, mids, and highs of the original signal.

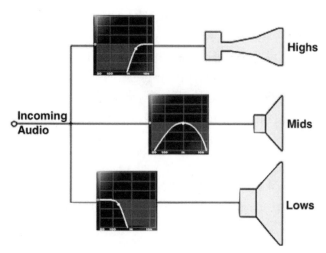

Figure 4.42 In a crossover, the incoming signal is split and filtered to produce three frequency bands.

Following the signal path through the plug-in, the incoming audio signal is split into three frequency bands based on the settings in the Frequency section. The levels of all three bands can then be adjusted in the Gain section or simply muted with the Kill switches. Then the three signals are mixed back together with the final level set by the Output control.

Frequency Section

Set in an equalizer plug-in and grouped with the Gain controls as they are, you might expect the Frequency controls (Figure 4.43) to select the corner frequencies for Low-Shelf and High-Shelf filters. That's what I expected the first time I glanced at this plug-in, but I quickly realized that's not the case.

Figure 4.43 The Frequency controls adjust the crossover points between the bands.

Rather than corner frequencies, these Low and High controls allow you to adjust two crossover points, where the low frequency band gives way to the midrange band, and the midrange band gives way to the high-frequency band. As you adjust either one of these controls up and down, you are changing the width of the midrange band as well as the Low or High band.

In the middle of these two crossover controls is the confusing Sweep control. The function of this control isn't obvious, and, of course, the programming is proprietary, so the details aren't public knowledge. Inside the processor two parameters are being adjusted against one another—much like how a pan control raises the volume of one side while lowering the volume of the other. But in this case, the adjustment is made to the slope of crossover filters.

Starting at the factory default settings, turning the Sweep control appears to have no function, although it is changing the behavior of the crossovers. At a setting of +100%, the slope of the low-frequency crossover is set so wide that it encompasses the entire audio spectrum, regardless of where the Low-Frequency control is set. At that point, any adjustments made to the mid and high bands are irrelevant, even the Kill switches don't matter as only the low band contains any signal.

At the other extreme, setting the Sweep value to –100% sets the slope of the High-Frequency filter so wide that it encompasses the entire audio spectrum, and only the High-Band controls will be active.

Of course, it also means the Sweep control defeats the purpose of the plug-in at its most extreme settings. Use it within a range from about –50% to +50% to create an effect without shutting down two of the frequency bands. Within that range, the Sweep control will adjust the two crossover points against one another, allowing you to create some fantastic swept filter effects. You'll have to adjust the level of one of the Gain controls or activate one of the Kill switches to hear what's going on. With a little practice and some clever automation, you can create some cool effects.

Gain Section

At the top of the center section are three knobs that act as tone controls for the incoming signal when the Kill switches for each band are not active (Figure 4.44).

Figure 4.44   These Gain controls act more like faders for a three-channel mixer.

These are a little different from the Gain controls of other equalizers because the range is set more like a channel fader, from –∞ at the lowest to +12.0dB at the highest level. The plug-in is designed more like a crossover than an equalizer. The incoming signal is split into three frequency bands that are then mixed back together into one signal. Each "channel" of the internal mixer has a mute (Kill) switch and a channel fader labeled as the Gain control.

The sonic result of boosting or cutting any of the three bands is similar to what you would hear if you boosted or cut the frequency band with an equalizer. Set the Low-Frequency control to 200 Hz and boost the Low Gain by +6dB, and the result should be fairly close to what you would hear from a Low-Shelf filter, except the transition into the midrange should overlap more smoothly and occur above the corner frequency.

Kill Switches

Grouped together on the left side of the plug-in window are the Kill switches (Figure 4.45). They look like normal On/Off switches, which is what they are, except they are also the whole point behind the design (and name) of the plug-in.

Figure 4.45 The Kill switches drop out the signal in each of three adjustable-frequency bands.

These three switches are simply mute switches going by a different name. Like other mute switches, turning them on and off seems contradictory. Activating a Kill switch turns off the signal for its frequency band, while deactivating restores the signal. Their function is that simple. The incoming signal is split into three frequency bands, and then each band passes through a level control and a mute switch before being mixed back together.

Final Output Level

For this plug-in, the Output control may be the only control with an obvious function. After the three frequency bands are mixed back together, the Output control adjusts the final signal level. This plug-in will likely see the most use processing complete stereo mixes, so be careful how high you push the output gain. The control has a range of –20.0dB to +20.0dB, but there aren't any meters on the plug-in so watch the track meters to avoid red-lining your signal.

The whole idea of the AIR Kill EQ is to help you recreate an effect that is popular with club DJs and in electronic music production. The Kill switches make it possible to drop whole frequency bands and create swept filter effects. It's not something you're likely to use in a live setting, but with a little creative automation, you can easily include some of these effects into your beat production, electronic music, or sound effects design.

Real-Time Use (RTAS)

The AIR Kill EQ plug-in is part of the Pro Tools Creative Collection™ along with all the other AIR plug-ins on your software. There's a familiar look and layout shared with the other AIR plug-ins as well as some of the quirks, and it's definitely designed for creative applications rather than utility.

As you'll see with all of the AIR family of plug-ins, the AIR Kill EQ is only available as a real-time processor. Keep that in mind while working, in case you run up against the limits of your system resources. If you need to conserve processing power, bounce processed tracks to disk, or print your processed channels to new tracks, and then disable the original tracks as described in Chapter 3.

The AIR Kill EQ can be activated as either a mono or stereo plug-in, but like the rest of the AIR family as of the time of this writing, none of them can be started as a mono-to-stereo plug-in (labeled as "Mono/Stereo" within Pro Tools). If you are activating any of them on an auxiliary track, this won't be an issue as you can simply create a stereo aux bus, insert the stereo version of the plug-in, and feed stereo or mono signals to it. Although with a processor like this, you're just as likely to activate it directly into the chain for a single track or mix bus, so keep this in mind.

Usage Example I: Outside the Club

It's a familiar sound to almost everyone. You are walking toward the club, the concert hall, the basketball court, or whatever the space might be. The sound from inside is mostly dull thuds, but as the door opens, all the rest of the spectrum sweeps back into place and you hear all the sounds properly.

This might seem like an effect that's only suited to film, video, and sound design work, but it's an interesting tool that can be used anywhere you are looking for the effect of "leaving the party behind." With the AIR Kill EQ and a little clever automation, you can open and close the doors over and over again on any noisy space you choose.

Since this is an effect that's more likely to be applied to an entire mix or a broadband track within something like a film mix, it makes sense to activate the Kill EQ plug-in on a Master Fader for a sub group. Once you have the processor in place, dial in a few starting settings (Figure 4.46). Leave all the Kill switches alone. Set the Gain controls to low=0.0dB, mid=–6.0dB, and high= –32dB. Then set the Frequency controls to low=250 Hz, sweep=–10%, and high=1.3 kHz.

Figure 4.46 Set the Gain controls to low=0.0dB, mid=–6.0dB, and high=–32dB. Then set the Frequency controls to low=250 Hz, sweep=–10%, and high=1.3 kHz.

Listen to your track through that setting, and you should have a pretty good "outside of the club" sound, but it may take a little tweaking to get it just right for the scene you are trying to create. For a thicker, heavier door, or to add more distance, lower the gain a little more on the Mid and High controls. For an interior door to a restroom, you might put a little more high-end back in to simulate the splashy sound of the tiled walls.

Once you have the right sound in place, slowly dial the Sweep control up to about +75% to enter the room. Dial it back down to about –10% to leave it again. Turn it up to +25% for the door to open halfway so your buddy can stick his head out and invite you in. The possibilities are almost endless.

Now activate the automation for the Sweep control, and you'll have a controller available to automate the approach to the club, the door opening, and the door closing as the bouncer decides he doesn't like the look of you. It doesn't matter though. There's a better club down the street, and all the cool people are hanging there waiting for you.

Usage Example II: Turn AIR Kill EQ into a Three-Way Crossover

In the unlikely event that you need a crossover, AIR Kill EQ can handle the task. That is, after all, exactly what's going on inside the plug-in, although it's going to take a little work to bring that function to the outside.

Say you're in a situation where you are using tracks output directly from Pro Tools in a live sound environment, and you would like to control all of the aspects of the audio processing from inside the software. You can use an equalizer plug-in to balance the tone of the speakers within the room. You can use a limiter to keep the overall levels within bounds. Why not also use a crossover so your output signals can go directly to the power amplifiers? You'll need more than one pair of available analog outputs, but the rest is in the box.

The AIR Kill EQ plug-in already is a three-way crossover on the inside, although it's unfortunately not designed to output its three frequency bands separately. But why should that stop you? Inside your session, locate your main stereo mix output and reroute the output to an internal bus pair. Then create three new Aux Input tracks, set their inputs to the bus pair from the stereo mix, and assign each track to its own hardware output (Figure 4.47). Don't forget to label the tracks Highs, Middle, and Lows so you know which is which.

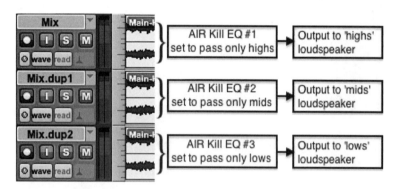

Figure 4.47 Route the stereo mix from your session to three Aux Input tracks.

Now activate an AIR Kill EQ plug-in on only one of the Aux tracks. Click on the Kill switches for the mid- and low-frequency bands so you are only monitoring the high band. Then play your audio and adjust the crossover point of the high band to a place that delivers only the material you want to send to the high-frequency drivers of your PA system.

Next you should kill the mid and high bands so you are only monitoring the low band. Play your audio again and adjust the crossover point for the low band until it is right for your system. This only leaves the mid band, which should already be set to a good spot for the system—but double-check it just to be sure.

Once the crossover points are set, you can duplicate the plug-in into the other Aux Input tracks. Then kill the mid and low bands on the "highs" output channel; kill the high and low bands on the "middle" output channel; and kill the mid and high bands on the "lows" output channel. Feed the analog outputs to your amplifiers, and you should have a software crossover setup within Pro Tools.

You can use other plug-ins to process the signal even further. Add a 7-Band EQ-III plug-in to the main stereo mix to balance the overall tone of the speakers within the room. Adding a limiter (Chapter 5) after each Kill EQ plug-in can help keep your system safe from damage caused by clipped signals. Or add a PhaseScope plug-in (chapter 8) after each Kill EQ to see how the phase alignment holds up within different bands and to provide higher resolution output meters.

Of course, live-sound situations are not the only place where crossover functions can be helpful. You could also use the Air Kill EQ to filter the LFE (subwoofer) track in a 5.1 surround mix. Or split a mono drum overhead into three bands so you can adjust the level, panning, and processing of the kick, snare, and cymbals separately.

I'll also describe how to take this concept one step further to create a multi-band compressor in the next chapter on Dynamics Processors.

Advanced Techniques and Good Practice

If you have spent some time around audio equipment, you've probably noticed equalizers and filters are everywhere. From the humble looking low-frequency roll-off switch on your microphone to the four or more bands of EQ built into every channel of your mixing console, equalizers are everywhere.

With so many equalizers out there, it seems there should be an example of how to apply EQ to every kind of instrument, voice, sound, or effect that exists. I could try to provide such examples, but then nothing else would fit in this book, and there are so many other cool plug-ins to tell you about.

Taking a closer look at a few examples and some good practice should give you a few good ideas to start with and the tools to develop your own sound and style.

Words Can't Describe It

I wasn't sure I should include this section and the accompanying chart of descriptive terms and frequency ranges. Many recording and mixing textbooks include a chart of frequency targets for getting certain sound characteristics out of various instruments—for example, "Turn up 800 Hz to add 'thwack' to your snare drum." Even before I learned much about recording, these kinds of target frequencies seemed unrealistic. How did the author know what kind of snare drum I was using? A 15″ × 6″ wood snare with calfskin heads sounds a lot different than a 13″ × 3″ steel piccolo snare—and that's before I decide whether to record it with a dynamic, condenser, or ribbon mic.

On the other hand, I see value in trying to connect common tone descriptions to specific frequencies. That's because recording clients, whether they are musicians, producers, film makers, theatre directors, or video game designers, don't speak to us in terms of numbers. They speak in ideas. Translating the ideas to numbers is your job.

The trouble is the numbers aren't always the same. The words don't always mean the same thing either. If I ask you to make an instrument sound "warmer," you might turn up the low midrange, maybe even some specific range about 100 Hz. But what if I ask you to make a flute sound warmer? It doesn't even play notes lower than middle C, so where is the "warm" range for that instrument? (By the way, if you thought of *turning down* the upper midrange, then you just earned an A for today's lesson.)

It's all about context. If we were sitting in the same room, listening to the same track, and then I asked you to make the flute track sound warmer, you would have more information about the sonic target. Dialing in the right kind of boost or cut would then be much easier. If your client asks you to make her guitar sound more "orange," then it's up to you to find a way to make it sound more orange. Is that any weirder than asking you to make it sound more "crisp," or "shiny," or "rich?" A theatre director once asked me to make it sound "hot" on stage during a street fight scene in *Romeo and Juliet*. I gave it some thought and listened to the sound effects I had playing (cicadas and other summer bugs). I applied a Low-Shelf EQ to drop the lows by about −4.5dB below 500 Hz. That made the sound thin and edgy, like you would hear on a hot, dry day with no wind. It seemed to do the job. Then again, I also asked the lighting technician if she could push up the whites and yellows for that scene, and I'm sure that helped too. It's all about context.

Having said all that, I *am* including a chart (Fig 4.48) that connects descriptive words and phrases to the audio bands most people relate to them. These are terms you're likely to hear, and there is some degree of standard interpretation. The trick is seeing the deeper picture.

Most novice engineers who look at this, see a familiar word like "warmth" and assume that adding warmth means boosting in the 120–280 Hz range. That's not the right idea.

Take another look at the chart and see what terms overlap in that range. Do you notice that "thickness" and "muddy" also cross into that range? All of these ideas of how to describe are interrelated and need to balance with each other.

When you receive a request to make a sound "warmer," you can't assume it means "turn up the warm knob." Sometimes it means "turn down the *bright* knob." That's because adding warmth is not the same as creating warmth or revealing warmth. It also all depends on the frequency range of the instrument. The warm part of a flute sound isn't the same as the warm part of a bass guitar sound.

Description	Approximate Frequency Range
Rumble	15 - 50 Hz
Depth	30 - 150 Hz
Fatness	50 - 250 Hz
Muddy	80 - 250 Hz
Warmth	120 - 280 Hz
Tone	150 - 800 Hz
Thickness	200 - 400 Hz
Honk	350 - 1200 Hz
Boxiness	600 - 1200 Hz
Tinny	800 Hz - 2 kHz
Edge	1 kHz - 8 kHz
Crunch	1.5 kHz - 3.5 kHz
Articulation	1.5 kHz - 6 kHz
Air	6 kHz - 14 kHz
Brilliance	8 kHz - 16 kHz
Space	10,000 - 25,000 Hz

Figure 4.48 Here are common terms and phrases used to describe audio frequency ranges.

All of equalizing, mixing, and recording in general is a balancing act. It's not a tug-of-war where one side has to win, but a game of subtle pushing and pulling so everything stays balanced. Adding more "warmth" may lead to "darkness" overall, and if you counter that by adding "brightness," then you're just chasing your tail.

It's a musician's nature to ask for more of what they think is missing rather than asking for less of what is standing out. It's your job as an engineer to figure out what is really going on, and then translate that target into numbers on the dial.

Subtractive versus Additive EQ

Grandma always said, "It's better to give than to receive." I never really believed her. But, sure enough, it's a lot safer to give the signal away in the places where it's too strong than it is to add more in the places where it's weak. In more common terms, it's usually better to cut than to boost.

But it's hard to think this way. Psychoacoustic tests that measure how we perceive sound have found that we perceive a 6dB boost to be about the same as a 9dB cut. What does that mean, exactly? We don't notice frequency bands being taken away as quickly (or accurately) as we notice them being boosted.

Your brain is actually wired to be happier faster when you hear *more* of something! And believe me, the audio salesmen have known this for years and very cleverly push the volume a little louder on the more expensive piece of gear, and then tell you how much better it sounds.

So why am I telling you to do something that's completely contrary to how your brain understands sound? Well, just like eating your veggies, it's good for you.

A couple of things happen when you start pushing up frequency bands. The first is level creep. As you turn up the low-midrange on something like a guitar that sounds too bright, you are also making that part of the guitar sound louder than the bass. So you turn up the bass a little to compensate and find the kick drum is too weak. Turn up the kick a little and it starts to make the snare seem out of balance. So you turn up the snare to a good spot and it starts to overshadow the vocals. Up the vocals a bit and the guitar seems too quiet in the low-midrange. And before you know it, you've basically turned up the entire mix, the whole thing is pushing into the red, and you're not sure how to dig yourself out. The answer, of course, is to not start down that path in the first place.

The other reason to be careful about boosting rather than cutting is it's hard to tell when you are pushing the signal into distortion. As of this writing, the one metering plug-in Pro Tools doesn't include that would be most helpful is a frequency analyzer, which is like a 30-Band crossover mixed with a bunch of individual meters (Figure 4.49). It's meant to show the volume level at each frequency band.

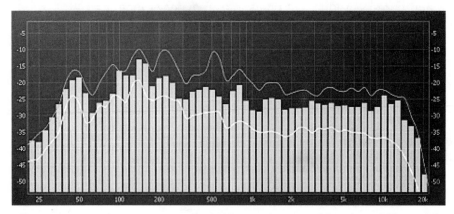

Figure 4.49 A frequency analyzer shows the signal level at different frequency bands.

The regular audio meters in Pro Tools, and even some of the fancier plug-ins specifically for metering (Chapter 8), only show the average signal level over the entire audio spectrum. It's possible to boost a signal in a narrow midrange band until it distorts without having that problem show up on the meters because it's balanced against the rest of the spectrum. This can be especially tricky in the upper midrange where lots of harmonics and presence peaks build up very quickly and create an edgy and shrill-sounding mix that might not register as being very "loud" in the overall scheme of things.

I'm not saying you should never use an EQ to boost a frequency band. I've already given you many usage examples that involve boosting different frequency bands. The point is to be aware of what direction you are going and why you're going that way.

One of my favorite descriptions of this balancing act is: "Cut to make things sound better; boost to make things sound different." More often than not, if you hear a sound and think something's wrong, you want to boost something. Instead, take a moment to think about cutting at the opposite end. If you want a warmer piano sound, is it because the low-midrange is too weak or because the upper-midrange is too strong. Cut to make things sound better. Boost when you want to make things sound different.

EQ for Drums—Filters Are Your Friends

Engineers seem to love overdoing the microphones when it comes to drums. No wonder the bass players hate hanging around through the sound check. One mic for the snare, another for the kick drum, one for each tom, a couple up above, maybe one for the high-hat. With all those stands and cables and then the levels to check and recheck, it seems like it will never end. Then you hand the bass player a cable attached to a DI box and say, "We're all set." And why do we all love to do it that way? Because you know it's fun.

The catch, of course, is that then you're left with 8, 10, maybe 12 tracks of drums that all need to come together and sound like one guy playing one drum set, with a bunch of other guys playing other instruments in front of him. Mixing all those tracks together can be a nightmare unless you know what you're doing with your favorite EQ plug-ins.

Start by taking a quick accounting of all the drum tracks you have recorded and what you expect to hear from each. One pair in particular, usually the overheads, should be your reference starting point. I won't get into the philosophy of overheads capturing the whole set versus just being "cymbal mics"—that can wait for a different book. But something should be a reference microphone that captures the sound of the whole kit.

To the main pair, you are going to add your other drum tracks to give each instrument a little extra push, presence, or "oomph" as needed. This is where Low-Cut and High-Cut filters will instantly become your friends.

Even though you pointed the microphone so very carefully at the floor tom, that didn't stop the drummer from playing his ride cymbal and getting lots of high-frequency cymbal wash into that track. If you add the track to the others without any treatment, it will just smear the sound of everything else it captured, especially if the drummer only played the drum two or three times during the song.

Start by adding an equalizer plug-in to each of the extra drum tracks and switch on the Low-Cut and High-Cut filters while you're at it (Figure 4.50). Set the slope on both filters to 12dB per octave and start dialing them inward to cut out everything that's not what each track was meant to record.

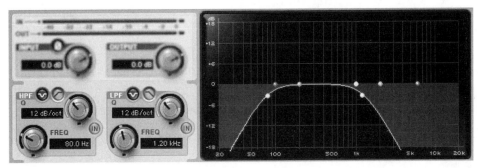

Figure 4.50 For a floor tom track, set the Low-Cut to about 80 Hz and the High-Cut to 1.2 kHz.

For something like the floor tom track, you might start with a setting of about 80 Hz on the Low-Cut filter and 1.2 kHz on the High-Cut filter. The goal is to keep the rich tone of the drum but to cut out the bass drum, high tom, snare, and cymbals if at all possible. Set the Low-Cut a little lower for bigger drums and a little higher for smaller ones. Don't bring the High-Cut filter down too far, or the drum will sound unnatural. You could use a shallower slope up there so the top end is taken down more naturally.

Here are a couple of filter settings for other drum tracks.

- For the high tom, start with a Low-Cut of about 120 Hz and a High-Cut at about 1.8 kHz.

- For the snare, set the Low-Cut at 100 Hz but steeper at 18dB per octave, and set the High-Cut at 2.0 kHz but with only a 6dB-per-octave slope.

- To keep the snare out of your hi-hat track, try a Low-Cut at about 250 Hz, and set the High-Cut way up at 10 kHz and only 6dB per octave.

- Focus the energy of your kick drum with a steep 18dB-per-octave Low-Cut at 40 Hz, and a 12dB-per-octave High-Cut at 1 kHz. (Add an extra +3dB bump at 85 Hz with a peak filter for a deeper thump too!)

The only filter you should put on your main pair should be a steep 18dB-per-octave Low-Cut at 40 Hz as a safety net for the low end of your overall mix. You might still visit these mics with a slight dip in the 4–8 kHz range so the upper midrange doesn't get too dense and shrill. A slight bump in the 16 kHz range can open up the top end for a more spacious and airy sound.

One of the trickiest parts of managing a big pile of drum tracks is that it's easy to forget that every one of those microphones is perfectly capable of capturing every frequency produced by the entire drum set. Just because the mic is pointed at one drum doesn't mean that's all it's going to hear. Filter out the most obviously unnecessary frequency bands from the secondary mics, and they will be able to support the main pair without all that pesky buildup that makes a muddy bottom end.

EQ for Mastering

The equalizer is one of the frontline weapons the mastering engineer uses when starting to work on a track. Since any processing done during mastering is typically done to completed mixes rather than to individual tracks, the engineer has a limited set of tools to start with. A simple task like turning up the snare drum is easy for the mixing engineer who has a separate track for the snare microphone. The mastering engineer must find the narrow space in the frequency spectrum where the snare drum resides and then bring that sound forward without bringing along everything else.

Clever use of automation with your equalizer plug-ins is one way to conquer these sorts of challenges. More intricate ways of combining equalizer and compressor functions are also very effective, but those will be covered more in the next chapter. First, look at how a sophisticated plug-in like the 7-Band EQ-III (Figure 4.51) can help you master your tracks, and learn about some of the key frequency ranges you'll need to address.

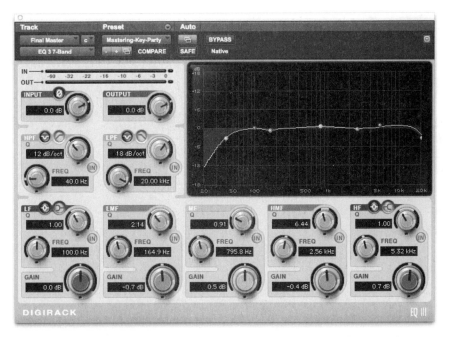

Figure 4.51 The sophisticated 7-Band EQ-III is a powerful tool for mastering your tracks.

The goal of mastering your tracks isn't to reshape them into something totally new. If you are mastering a single track, give it one last listen and do the slightest bit of extra processing to bring out the best features of the sound and give a smooth polish so it sounds more like a mix than a bunch of individual channels. If you are mastering multiple tracks, create a consistent tone across all the tracks so none stands out as more bass-heavy, or edgy, or brighter than the others.

From Bottom to Top

The first best place to start is at the top and bottom of the frequency range—or rather, the bottom and then the top. What's going on with the very low and very high material? On the low end in particular, it's easy to have a lot of build-up that leads to a muddy-sounding track. Or you might have a track that seems to need a punchier bass, and you're tempted to turn it up. Don't do it. Instead, grab the HPF (Low-Cut) filter of your EQ-III plug-in (Figure 4.52), set the slope to 12dB per octave, and slowly start sweeping the frequency up from 20 Hz to see how it changes your sound.

You might not even notice the filter is doing anything until you hit about 40 Hz. Remember: that's a whole octave above the bottom, and the next one is squeezed between 40 and 80 Hz. As you hear the filter starting to thin the sound a little, back it off a touch and use the On/Off switch to hear how it is changing the sound. A muddy track may still need more help higher up, but a weak bass track may already have more definition, since your system will be putting more effort into the bass than the sub-bass.

Next stop is the top end. You can repeat this process coming down from the top end, although it will probably work better to use a steeper slope. Try 18dB per octave to start. Once you hear the

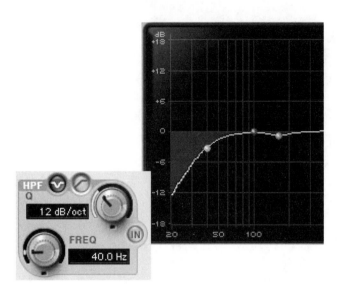

Figure 4.52 Start at the low end with a High-Pass (Low-Cut) filter set at a 12dB per octave slope.

top end start to sound different, back off a little and use the On/Off switch again. But before you adjust the frequency again, click the slope back down to 6dB per octave and listen again. You might even decide to go as shallow as 6dB per octave, but you'll need to start steeper than that to make sure you don't pull the frequency too low. Think of this filter as a safety net to ensure other changes you might make don't continue past the audible range.

Now for the tricky part: all that stuff in the middle. Every project you mix will sound a little different, but there are a few key ranges to consider as starting points.

Punchy Bass versus Muddy Bass

It's a fine line between getting the bass to sound punchy and tight without making it sound muddy. A slight push of maybe 1.5dB to the range from 60 to 100 Hz (Figure 4.53) can give extra depth and fullness to your low end, supporting the bass guitar and getting more tone out of the bass drum. This is shown with the low roll-off still in place.

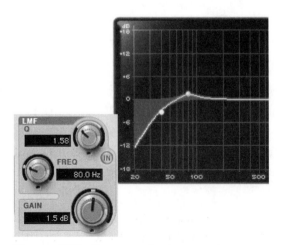

Figure 4.53 Support the bass and get more tone from the kick by boosting 60–100 Hz by 1.5dB.

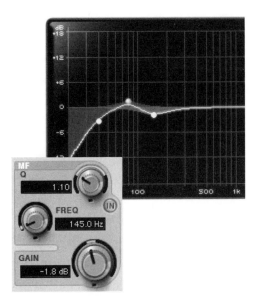

Figure 4.54 Thin out the mud and boominess with a 1.5–3.0dB dip from 110–180 Hz.

A slight dip of maybe 1.5dB–3dB just above that from about 110–180 Hz (Figure 4.54) can take care of muddiness and keep things from sounding boomy.

The range from 160 to 240 Hz is definitely the trickiest spot in the low end. In a vocal-heavy mix this would likely be a place to cut out some of the muddiness of the midrange instruments and voices (Figure 4.55). In a more energetic, instrument-driven mix, this is a place to bump if you want more impact from the sweet range of the bass and kick drum.

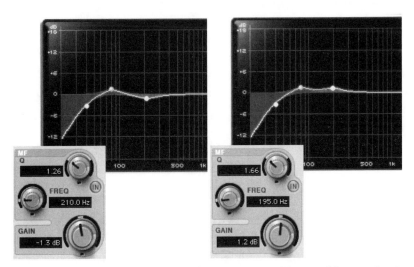

Figure 4.55 160–240 Hz is tricky. Cut it to thin muddy vocal mixes or boost it for punchier bass and kick.

Mastering Midrange Magic

Asking engineers for their EQ settings is like asking a chef for his recipes. Some will share, and some will take their secrets to the grave. Of course, the recipes you do get will all be a little

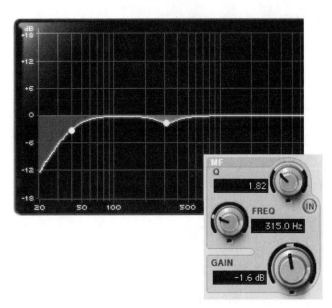

Figure 4.56   Try a slight dip in the secret sweet spot of 315 Hz.

different. There is, however, one secret spot in the midrange that many mastering and even some mixing engineers have mentioned that lands around 315 Hz (Figure 4.56).

It's pretty high up in the frequency spectrum by most measures, and not a spot you immediately think of as causing muddiness. But this little area around middle-C carries a lot of weight in your mixes. Try taking it down 2, 3, even 4dB and see if it helps a heavy, sluggish-feeling mix sound lighter, more open, and even a little stronger on the bottom end.

Part of the reason for the dense sound in this range is that it's in the middle of a range that represents the third octave above the fundamental frequencies of your lower rhythm-section tracks. That's where all the spaces between the harmonics start shrinking to very narrow intervals. It's a densely packed frequency band, especially if the levels of your low instrument tracks were pushed up in the mix. All of those harmonics are clogging up the works. Layers of guitars and vocals also are trying to fight their way through. Pull it back a little and hear how quickly the mix opens up for you.

Real Vocal Clarity

Another classic "secret target" frequency for mastering engineers centers around 2 kHz. Most of the energy of your vocal tracks, the fundamental frequencies for either a male or female vocalist, reside in a two-and-a-half octave range from 100 to 600 Hz. (Yes, there's more than that, if you are working with very low or very high voices.) That means you will be getting a lot of harmonic content and articulation starting another octave or two higher, from about 1.5 kHz to 2.5 kHz.

Many of the studio microphones you use for recording vocals already have a substantial bump in the upper-midrange that the manufacturers refer to as a "presence peak." (There's more on presence peaks later in this section.) The trouble is that most of these presence peaks start climbing after this range, at about the 3 kHz mark, which leaves your vocals wanting more attention in this crucial area.

It doesn't take much of a push in this range to get things to pop out since there's already a lot of sound energy crossing paths right there (Figure 4.57). Apply a very slight bump of between 1–2dB, centered on 2 kHz, with a Q of between 1.0-1.5 (remember: a Q of 1.4 is one octave wide).

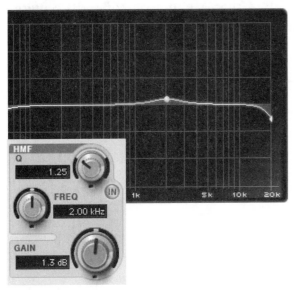

Figure 4.57 Pull vocals and lead instruments forward with a 1–2dB bump at 2 kHz.

This is a critical spot for vocal articulation as well as the clarity and attack of instruments like acoustic guitar. Of course, if that's all you have playing on a song, this range may be plenty strong already. But in most cases, a small bump here can fill in the hole in the middle of the fundamentals of your vocal tracks and the presence peak delivered by most microphones.

This very critical frequency band is already compromised (weakened) in many speaker systems, because the majority of speaker systems in studios, home stereos, and even on stage, use a two-way main speaker design. That kind of design uses a woofer to cover the lows, low-midrange, and midrange, leaving the high-midrange and highs to the tweeter. The center of the crossover point (where the sound tapers off in one driver and picks up in the other) is usually located between 1.5 and 2.5 kHz. You should never alter your mix or mastering sound for any one specific sound system, but realize that many systems will indeed be working against you in this critical range.

Air, Space, and Shimmer

I am a big fan of space—not just because I like sci-fi—because I record a lot of acoustic music and live performances. Hearing sounds in large spaces all the time, it's easy to get hooked on the sound of spaciousness. The trick is knowing the right places to give that little extra push in mastering to open up the top end and create a bigger sense of space.

Even if you aren't listening all the time, your ears constantly hear all of the sounds around you. High frequencies in particular are important to your brain, as it subconsciously analyzes the sounds coming in to determine what kind of space you're in. (More on that when we talk reverb in Chapter 6.) The key frequency range that has the biggest impact on our perception of air and space around the instruments runs from about 8 kHz up to 20 kHz.

Be careful, though, because this is also the domain of sibilance (hissing "S" sounds), and this range can make many sounds seem piercing or shrill. I find that a bump of 2dB–3dB centered on 16 kHz with a Q of about 1.2–1.4, and maybe even a little wider (Figure 4.58), is almost the perfect spot to give a sense of airiness to natural and artificial reverb and to add shimmer to instruments.

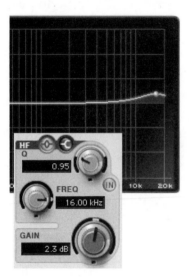

Figure 4.58 A small bump around 16 kHz can bring out the air and space around your instruments.

If you are working around a sibilant vocalist, aim on the high side and keep the Q set more narrowly. But in most other cases, adding this little push to the top end can open up a mix that feels too claustrophobic.

If you put a Low-Pass (High-Cut) filter on your track at the beginning of this process, switch it off and on a few times to make sure it's not interfering with any boost you put on the top end. If it is, dial the corner frequency up a little higher and test again. Keeping the High-Cut filter in place is important for protecting your system, especially while you are boosting audible high-frequency content. Don't burn up your tweeters.

There are many other directions you can go with equalizer settings for mastering—this is one small starting point. Remember that subtlety is the name of the game. Dial in just far enough that you can notice and then pull the level back a little and use the On/Off switch to hear how things are working. Also, if you're mastering several tracks from the same recording or mixing session, save your mastering EQ preset as a starting place for the next track. Be sure to switch the various bands off and back on one at a time to hear exactly what each filter does. Tweak here or there as you go, and you should be able to dial in a nice matching tone before you know it.

One-mic-itis

"So, what microphone do you use?" the high school student asks me.

"All of them," I reply.

Part of the fun (and trouble) of running a university recording studio is that I get a lot of tour groups. It might be one high school student with her parents touring the school of music, or it might be 25 ninth-graders on a field trip. When they get to our building, they are inevitably led to my door to see the big, fancy, million-dollar studio. It's not so great when I'm busy, but it can be a lot of fun to hear some of the questions.

That question I mentioned has stuck with me because it provides a unique insight into a problem home-recording studios face that you might never realize is a problem: What microphone do you use?

There aren't any good statistics on how many microphones the typical home recordist owns, but it's probably a fairly low number. The indie-rock, singer-songwriter types probably have three or four, including a small, bluish-gray dynamic mic popular for live sound; its fraternal twin vocal mic, a Chinese-made large-diaphragm condenser; and if he's staying trendy, maybe a ribbon mic. Meanwhile, the rap/hip-hop home studio will likely have just one, reasonably high-quality, large-diaphragm condenser.

Maybe you have the little bluish-gray dynamic mic with the frequency response chart that looks like Figure 4.59.

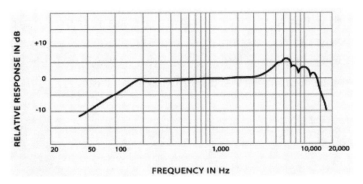

Figure 4.59 Frequency response chart of a popular dynamic microphone.

Maybe you have an inexpensive Chinese-built large diaphragm condenser with a response chart like Fig 4.60.

You might even have a large-diaphragm condenser from a renowned European maker with a chart like Figure 4.61.

The point is not the make and model of your microphone, but what's going on in the high frequencies on all three of those charts. Notice any similarities? Maybe you noticed that big bump in the upper midrange?

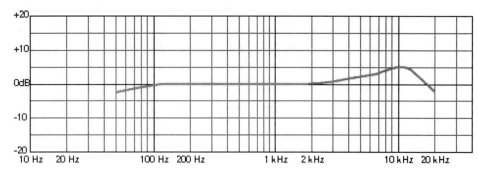

Figure 4.60 Frequency response chart of an inexpensive large-diaphragm condenser.

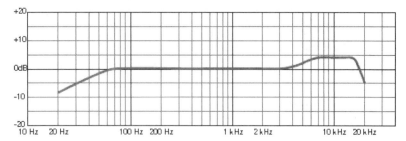

Figure 4.61 Frequency response chart of a high-end European condenser microphone.

There's a phrase used in the computer industry that fits here: "It's not a bug, it's a feature." Sure enough, the manufacturers will tell you that boost in the upper midrange is there to help you with vocal clarity and articulation. That's funny since Figure 4.62 shows the average frequency response of the human ear, and it looks like we can hear pretty well right in that range.

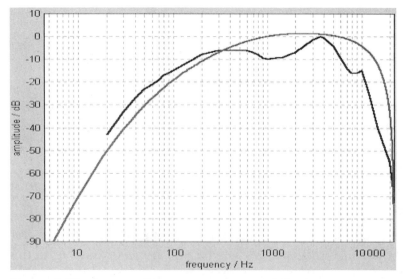

Figure 4.62 Average frequency response of the human ear along with the A-Weighting curve.

So, what's going on here? And why should any of this matter to you when you're learning about equalizer plug-ins? First of all, lots of microphones have these kinds of "presence peaks" in the high midrange. If you are recording at home, or even in a small studio, you might be using the same microphone over and over again as you overdub tracks. You might only own that one microphone. Don't worry though because there's nothing inherently wrong with that. It's a standard practice. Even with 60 or 70 mics in the locker, I still use my handful of favorites often, and so do plenty of experienced, professional engineers. If you use the same microphone over and over, you might end up with a build-up of energy in a particular frequency range.

Think about it for a moment: If your microphone has a 6dB bump between 2 and 6 kHz, or 6 and 10kHz, or wherever it may be, and you record three or four overdub tracks of your screaming electric guitar, there's going to be a lot of build-up in that range. On the other side of the spectrum (and the response curve), what if your microphone is particularly weak in the lower midrange? You might find your layers and layers of overdubs sounding weaker and thinner since the top end is building up while the bottom end stays underpowered. You can hear it happening from either direction.

Why Are Microphones Built This Way? This kind of microphone tuning first became popular in the early days of multi-track analog tape. As the tape plays back and forth over the record and playback heads, through take after take of overdubs and mixing, the signal slowly degrades. The first parts of the signal to fade away are the high frequencies. After 30, 50, even 100 passes over the tape heads, the signal might sound really dull—unless it was recorded with a big 6dB boost to start with!

Decades later, here you are recording to Pro Tools where the same tracks can be played back thousands of times without losing the high-frequency content in that way. Yet the microphones you are using are built to mirror these popular tools of the past. If your mixes are sounding a little brighter than you'd like, don't boost the low stuff until you check to see what's going on with the high stuff.

While the high-midrange presence peak is a common "feature" of many microphones, it's by no means the only quirk you're going to see on the frequency response chart. If you only have one microphone to work with, use it—but realize that its own peaks and dips are going to be compounded with each track you overdub. If you have more microphones, get to know them well; learn which are brighter, darker, smooth, or edgy. Then use them in ways that complement the sounds of the instruments you record. Use a bright microphone to help a bright-sounding guitar leap forward in the mix. While the darker mics can help keep the grumbling rhythm instruments at the back of the band. And, of course, use your equalizer plug-ins to smooth out any bumps and tease out the sweet spots to build a great-sounding mix.

Overuse, Abuse, and Danger Zones

Equalizers are powerful tools. They can save you lots of time finding the right tone for an instrument; they can fix environmental problems like HVAC noise; and they can help you create fabulous textures and effects. However, they can also get out of hand and cause trouble in your mix that might have you running around in circles trying to get things to sound right again.

Most of the "Advanced Techniques and Good Practice" recommendations in the previous pages deal with avoiding the danger zones, so it's worth making sure you're comfortable with all of the ideas from both that section and this one. It's especially important to watch what's going on out past the range of your hearing—specifically, the very high and very low frequencies. Be mindful of where your range of hearing ends, and be aware of the limits of your speaker systems.

Boosting What You Can't Hear

Earlier in this chapter, I mentioned the average range of human hearing runs from approximately 20 Hz to 20 kHz. But remember—that's the *average*. Children can hear a little higher than that, but as you age you lose some of that. Spend lots of time in front of a screaming guitar stack and it will go away even faster. But that's not the only limitation you might encounter. Beyond your own frequency response limit, have you looked closely at what your speakers can reproduce?

Here's a frequency response chart for a particular set of two-way speakers that have been wildly popular (for some bizarre reason) around studios for decades (Figure 4.63). Look at the overall frequency response but pay particular attention to the low-end response.

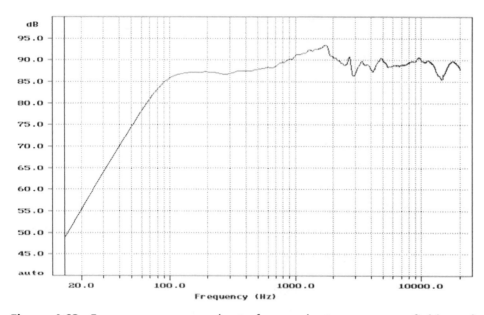

Figure 4.63 Frequency response chart of a popular two-way near-field speaker.

Apart from all the ups and downs at the top end and the 4dB peak right around 1.8 kHz that's followed by a –4dB dip at about 2.8 kHz, do you notice the precipitous drop in the low frequency starting just below 100 Hz? The frequency response plummets by a rate of about –15dB per octave below 80 Hz.

That last part isn't at all unusual for small, two-way, bookshelf speaker designs; it's hard to get much bass response out of a small, two-way loudspeaker. Take a look at the specifications for the monitors you are using and see where they drop off. Does that mean you should only be recording if your speakers can deliver 20 Hz? Of course not. Indeed, that's a hard task to manage for less than a couple thousand dollars, and you'll need to have some substantial acoustic treatment to keep all that energy under control.

What it does mean is that you need to be aware of what you are (and *aren't*) hearing before you try to turn up the low end. It's possible your bass is too loud already, but you can't hear it. What's worse is that some people, in particular your listeners, will hear more lows (or highs) than you do. These are the two places quickest to offend people, so watch what you're doing.

The simplest way to play it safe at the extremes is to follow three simple rules:

- Learn the frequency response limits of all the monitor speakers you commonly use. Write them on a piece of tape and stick it to the front of each speaker to remind you.

- Listen to many commercially released recordings on your monitors—from CDs, not from MP3s! Not indie releases recorded in home studios, and not low-res files with many of the lows and highs removed anyway.

- Choose the right kinds of filter types when you are boosting your signals close to the edges of your hearing or the edge of your monitoring.

There's nothing wrong with adding a little bump in the highest or lowest octaves, but *how* you choose to do it will make a difference. Most inexpensive analog mixers use shelving filters for the high and low bands of their equalizers (Figure 4.64). Remember: these filter types continue to boost well beyond the audible range.

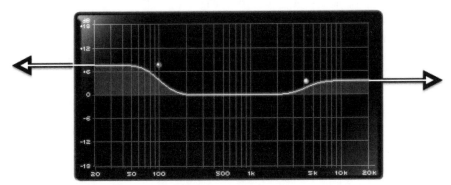

Figure 4.64 Low- and High-Shelf filters continue to boost the signal beyond the audible range.

Adding simple Low-Cut and High-Cut filters to the picture will help reign in some of the extra energy that might be up in that range (Figure 4.65).

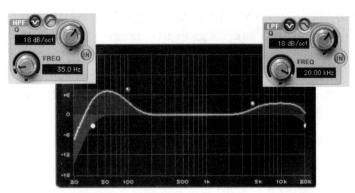

Figure 4.65 Reign in Low- and High-Shelf filters with Low-Cut and High-Cut filters.

You can also use narrower Peak filters in these ranges to get the boost you need with tighter boundaries above and below your target.

Knowledge is power when it comes to getting your audio to sound its best without coloring too far outside the lines. Know your ears, know your speakers, and know what your equalizers are doing in the extremes. And while you're at it, take a closer look at some of the instruments you are recording as well.

Is Your Instrument Producing the Frequency You're Turning up?

Just as you should be aware of what part of the audio spectrum you can or can't hear, you should be aware of the frequencies your instruments can and can't produce. At the beginning of this chapter I included a chart of the frequency ranges of some common studio instruments. It doesn't include everything you might encounter but looking at it again can help put this idea into perspective.

Most instruments have a well-defined range, at least for their fundamental frequencies. The 88 notes of a piano run from A=27.5 Hz to C=4,186 Hz, but an electric bass only runs from E=41 Hz to G=392 Hz. There are harmonics above those frequencies as well as other characteristic sounds, like the impact of the piano hammers or the attack of a pick or slap on the bass strings. Still, there is a point above and below where every instrument effectively stops producing sound, and that's the place you want to know about.

Many books, magazines, Web sites, and other resources can give you information about how to record, mix, and master your music. Many will include suggestions for frequency ranges that impart special qualities to your sound: "boost here for attack," "boost here for crunch," "boost here for woodiness," and so on. Of course, it's good advice, but you have to listen to know if the advice is pointing you in the right direction.

You might ask, "Why should it matter if I turn up the EQ when nothing is there? It can't really hurt anything, right?" Well, there are a couple of reasons. First, you're not fixing the problem you were hearing in the first place. And second, there might be system or room noise that you're turning up instead.

The simple solution is to solo the track you're working on, dial the settings into the EQ, and see how they sound. Make sure the frequency range you're aiming for actually exists in that sound and actually sounds better when you change it. Then—this is the most important part—turn the EQ gain back to 0dB, un-solo the track, and listen to the whole mix while you make adjustments to the EQ for that track. Use the Bypass switch to compare the sound before and after the change. It's a slow process, but the sound you create in the end will be worth the trouble.

The Limitations of Real-World Audio Systems (Don't burn up the listener's subwoofer)

Back in high school, or maybe college, or maybe in your favorite sci-fi movie, you heard someone explain the first law of thermodynamics. Whether you realized it or not, someone, at some point, explained it to you. You're likely to remember it as a statement along the lines of, "Energy cannot be created or destroyed; it can only change forms."

Before you turn off to the idea of more physics being thrown at you, take a moment to consider that statement. "Energy cannot be destroyed." "Energy changes forms." Why is that so important? Because the audio signals we manipulate in Pro Tools represent energy.

All those wavy lines on your computer screen represent several forms of energy, from the electrical energy that will be created when the digital signals are turned back into analog voltages, to the mechanical energy when the speakers start pushing air around to create the acoustical energy we call sound.

Holding that mouse, clicking that controller, changing that level, you are (if only figuratively) holding all of this power in the palm of your hand. Didn't some superhero teach you that, "With great power comes great responsibility?" If you're not careful, you have the power to damage speakers without even realizing it; and equalizer plug-ins in particular are the dangerous tools capable of such destruction.

How does it work? All the audio signals you send out of your system get amplified and sent to your speakers. The speakers will work their little hearts out trying to turn all your signal back into sound, but some of the very low and very high stuff just won't work. The speakers are just not able to hit some frequencies, but that doesn't mean the energy just goes away. It can't be destroyed, so instead it changes form. It turns into heat—the kind of heat that burns up the voice coils inside tweeters and subwoofers.

Consider an EQ setting like the one below (Figure 4.66), where a Low-Shelf filter is being used to raise everything below 120 Hz by 4.5dB, and a High-Shelf filter is being used to raise everything about 8 kHz by 6dB. This would be a common setting to dial into the high and low EQ bands of an analog mixing console.

Maybe the engineer is looking for a little more "warmth," "thickness," or "power" in the low end, and a little more "brilliance," or "space," or "air" at the top end. The trouble is what happens to the frequencies at the limits of the audio system. You know very easy to have an equalizer turn up a bunch of frequencies that you can't even hear. It's easier still to turn up frequencies

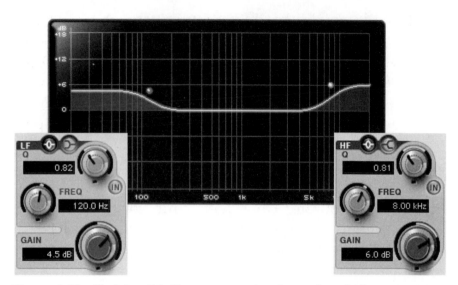

Figure 4.66 Shelving EQ filters are used to boost low frequencies by 4.5dB and highs by 6dB.

that your speakers can't reproduce. Even if the instruments can create it, and you can hear it, and the system can record it; that still doesn't mean your listeners can play it all back.

Now that I've got you all kinds of scared about it, let's back up a moment. The goal isn't to always mix as though your album is only going to be played over the telephone. Just be aware of what can happen, and think about all the changes you are making to different tracks in your mix. Here are some tips to keep things under control:

- If you are going to use a shelving EQ to boost the highs on a track, either reduce the overall level of the track to compensate, or add a High-Cut (Low-Pass) filter to bring things back down after about 18 kHz.

- If you want to add more sparkle to a finished mix, use a wider Q setting on a Peak filter instead of a High-Shelf.

- If you are using a Low-Shelf to increase the bass on a track then also switch on a Low-Cut filter at 30 Hz to keep the sub-bass and infrasonic stuff down.

- Remember that you'll usually get a tighter bass sound when there is less material in the 20–40 Hz range; try giving a little push in the 60–120 Hz range instead.

- Consider using a multiband compressor (Chapter 5) to bring up the average levels of your highs and lows without bringing up the peak levels.

- If you are mixing for a specific audio system (theatrical sound design, live mixing, tracks to play at your church), then find out the limitations of that system and work within that range.

- Be safe, but be subtle. It may only take a 6dB-per-octave roll-off to bring the extreme highs and lows down to a safe level.

- Try to mix on the most revealing monitors you can, but know their limits too. Most small monitors can't reach lower than about 40 Hz, but they should hit 20 kHz.

There's no crime in burning up the voice coils in your speakers, but it can be an expensive hobby if you do it often. The last time I did it was in the control room at work, and I wasn't even mixing, just demonstrating different waveforms with the Signal Generator plug-in. The voice coils burned up on both 1-inch titanium tweeters in my main speakers—first one, then the other, faster than I could tell it had happened. At about $150 per tweeter, I got off easier than the guy who burned up all four drivers in a pair of rented, dual-18-inch subwoofers when I worked at a pro-audio shop. One night of pushing the bass too hard on the dance floor cost him about $450 per driver. Your equalizer plug-ins are powerful tools. Whether you use them for good or for evil is entirely up to you.

5 Dynamics Processors

Hey, this track practically mixes itself...

When we first start mixing, there's an expectation, or maybe just a hope, that it's possible to set each channel fader at one level and simply leave it there. Then, as all the other tracks fall into place, the sounds will play back perfectly mixed from start to finish.

It's worth a try. After all, if all of the musicians are adjusting to each other, then all of the little ups and downs along the way should still fit together seamlessly. But as you've probably discovered, real sounds change, especially in volume level. Some parts of the track are louder while others are softer. Sometimes the level changes dramatically from one note to the next.

Automating every channel fader throughout the whole project is one option, but it can be a long and tedious process. There must be some other way of doing this since not everyone can automate mixes that way. You need some kind of automated fader: something that can adjust the levels up or down when you want it to—not something you have to set manually throughout the track, but something that changes automatically based on a few settings you choose. You need something to automatically adjust the dynamic range of your tracks.

A close second behind the equalizer, some of the most common effects processors you're likely to use for recording, mixing, mastering, or live sound, are dynamics processors. This family includes compressors, expanders, limiters, and gates—different types of tools that share one common family trait: they are all automatic volume controls.

Refresher

Dynamics processors deal directly with the overall volume levels of audio clips, regions, channels, busses, and mixes. They are automatic volume controls that alter the relationship between the softest and loudest parts of a track. A formula is set up to determine how each processor should behave, the signal levels are measured, and a gain control is adjusted. Lots of numbers will go whizzing by in this chapter, including peak levels, averages, thresholds, makeup gain, and more. So let's start with a quick reminder of what exactly all those numbers mean.

Fundamentals

What exactly is a decibel? For that matter, what is really going on with all these volume controls? Why is there one control that goes from –18dB to +18dB right next to another that goes from 0dB at the top to -∞dB at the bottom? As always, the goal is to learn to use this group of plug-ins to make your recordings sound their best, and understanding any dynamics processor starts with understanding the numbers.

The Decibel Scale

So what is a decibel? Why it's a tenth of a Bell, of course, named in honor of the inventor of the telephone. Wasn't that easy? Well, it was easy to write, but probably not particularly helpful. The trouble is that there really isn't a single definition of what a decibel is, partly because it identifies the difference between two power measurements. That might be the difference between the input level and the output level, or the difference between the signal level measured and no signal at all. Either way, you have to have two measurements to have a decibel relationship.

Once you know that is going on, it makes the decibel a little easier to understand. You can think of it as the measurement of change from one value to another. Now the only thing is to relate the decibel scale to more everyday values.

One scientific definition of the decibel explains that, "...two amounts of power differ by 1 decibel when they are in the ratio of $10^{0.1}$ and any two amounts of power differ by N decibels when they are in the ratio of $10^{N(0.1)}$." Doing a little quick math on the calculator shows that this means increasing a signal by 1dB is the same as multiplying it by 1.26, and increasing it by 3dB is the same as multiplying it by 1.99 (about double). That's the scale for decibels of sound power level (dB-SPL) used for acoustic power, the measurement of real air and sound energy moving around.

Inside audio electronics and software like Pro Tools, the scale is slightly different, but not by much. In there, two signals differ by 1 decibel when they are in a ratio of $10^{0.05}$. I know, that's probably still not helpful, but it's going to get easier.

Remember that the decibel is a ratio of one measurement to another, like the ratio of input level to output level. So let's say you're sending an audio signal into a Gain control and you dial the gain up to +1dB. You know the signal will increase, but it won't increase by having 1 more of anything added to it. The "ratio of $10^{0.05}$" means the signal will be multiplied by 1.12. That's the reason for this weird scale. It's not linear addition; the signal level is actually multiplied by that amount again and again for every decibel you add.

Figure 5.1 converts the decibel scale used inside Pro Tools and other audio electronics and software into the multiplication factor.

A few key values are highlighted for reference. Notice that a change of 6 decibels is roughly double the signal strength. Add another 6dB and the signal strength doubles again at 12, and then doubles again at 18dB. Of course, the ratio also works in the other direction—reducing a signal by –20dB, –40dB, or –60dB is equivalent to dividing it by 10, 100, or 1000.

Decibels	Multiplication Factor	
0	× 1.000	(Unity Gain / No Change)
1	× 1.122	
2	× 1.259	
3	× 1.413	(Roughly √2)
4	× 1.585	
5	× 1.778	
6	× 1.995	(Roughly double / half)
7	× 2.239	
8	× 2.512	
9	× 2.818	
10	× 3.162	
12	× 3.981	(Roughly 4×)
18	× 7.943	(Roughly 8×)
20	× 10.00	
40	× 100.00	
60	× 1000.00	

Figure 5.1 Decibel values and their equivalent multiplication factor.

Meanwhile, Back in the Real World…

So what if boosting a signal by 40dB means multiplying it by 100? What does that really mean? Remember that analog audio signals are really just waves of alternating current flowing through wires or electronics. A microphone converts the acoustic energy of air pressure changes into an electrical signal…and it's a tiny signal, on the order of maybe about 10 millivolts. But to safely travel around an audio system, it needs a signal strength closer to a volt. So you plug the microphone signal into a "preamplifier" that boosts the signal by about +40dB, multiplying the 10-millivolt signal by 100 so it measures 1,000mv, or about 1 volt.

Now is it starting to make more sense? These audio signals you are capturing from keyboards, guitars, and microphones are electrical currents zipping around through all those miles of cables behind your desk. When they are captured and converted to digital data, you deal with them as information for a time, but the information has to eventually turn back into an electrical signal sent to your amplifier and speakers.

Remember that the decibel is not necessarily a measurement of voltage; it's simply a measurement of change. The same decibel scale can be used to measure the intensity of electrical power, radio waves, radar, or even light. In the analog audio world, either the dBV or dBu units are used specifically to measure electrical voltage, while inside a digital system like Pro Tools, the dB-FS (Full Scale) unit is used. The difference between the scales is where they are calibrated (Figure 5.2).

This is partly why your audio signals read as different levels on the meters inside of Pro Tools compared to how they appear outside on your analog electronics. Outside of the box, the meters are measuring voltage, while the computer is measuring the difference from a "full-scale" level. Full-scale means that your loudest peaks are hitting the top or bottom of the digital scale; either all ones or all zeros.

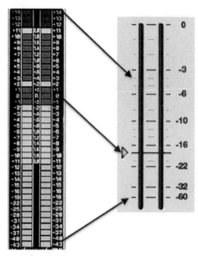

Figure 5.2 The 0dB value is calibrated to different measurements to create different scales.

When you think about it, all of the possible measurements of a 16-bit audio signal have to land somewhere between the binary numbers 0000-0000-0000-0000 and 1111-1111-1111-1111. That's the bottom (all zeros) and top (all ones) of the graphic display for every one of your audio tracks, and it's the loudest possible signal you can record. Going any louder isn't an option, because none of those ones will ever flip over to become a two.

Getting Technical   That absolute limit is the calibration point for the dBFS scale, but it's hard to calibrate to the outside world at the highest possible limit of the system. Instead, most Pro Tools systems are calibrated to the outside world where −18dBFS = 0dBVU = +4dBu = 0.775 volts. It might also be displayed as +22dBu = 0dBFS. Different calibration standards are required in many broadcasting systems and vary from country to country, so look up the standards for your location.

The technical details of everything that's going on in there can be overwhelming. The math isn't as complicated as it looks, but just keeping track of all the different values can be tough. The thing to remember as you are working with any audio software, and especially when you are working with dynamics processors, is what is really happening when you boost or cut a signal by 3dB, 6dB, 10dB, or more. That +6dB change means the signal you send out into the world will be going out with about twice the energy it had before. A small adjustment on a fader can mean a huge change in your signal level.

Peak versus Average Levels

I'm sure you've run into this problem: you have a track that's just too quiet in the mix, but you can't possibly turn it up anymore because it's already hitting the red clip indicators. Other tracks in your mix might still sound louder even though they aren't hitting anywhere close to clipping. So what's going on?

This situation is a perfect example of the difference between the peak and average levels of a track. Most of the time, the track is too quiet, but there are occasional bursts of energy that go right up to the limit. The average level is low, but the peak level is as high as it can go. You'd like to turn up the volume for the track, but you would have to watch for all of those little peaks and back the level off for a moment so they don't clip. Sounds like a job for an automatic volume control, doesn't it?

This is the essential role of the compressor, although it probably doesn't look like it at first. The compressor watches the level of the incoming audio signal and turns the volume down when it crosses a certain threshold. That in itself doesn't sound like the formula for making the average level of your track louder—until you remember the makeup gain control.

Figure 5.3 compares the volume level of the input signal versus the level of the output signal. This graph gives you an idea of what the processor is doing to the audio signal it's processing.

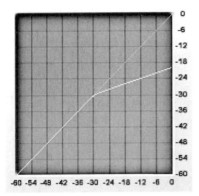

Figure 5.3 Graphing the input level (horizontal) against the output level (vertical).

Read the graph by finding the peak level of your incoming audio signal along the bottom. Then follow that value vertically up to the diagonal line and then across to the left to see what the output level would be. A processor that isn't changing the signal level would show an even 45° line, where the input value equals the output value (Figure 5.4).

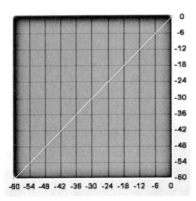

Figure 5.4 A processor that isn't changing the signal level shows a smooth 45° line.

In a compressor, a threshold volume level is selected to control when the processor becomes active. Above that level, the audio signal is turned down by a consistent ratio. Imagine a setup where every additional 2dB of input signal only changes the output signal by 1dB: a ratio of 2:1 (Figure 5.5). The graph would show a normal slope up to the threshold point that then turns to a shallower slope as less output level is delivered.

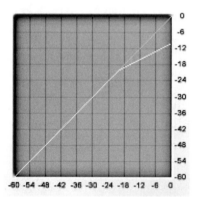

Figure 5.5 Graphing the response of a compressor with a 2:1 ratio above a threshold of –20dB.

Look closely and you'll see that a peak on the input side of the signal that would have hit 0dB should now only hit –10dB at the output. It probably doesn't seem like that's going to help your track that's already too quiet, but it will. This kind of gain reduction of the loudest peaks allows you to increase the overall level of your track by as much as +10dB (Figure 5.6). Once you do, the whole picture changes.

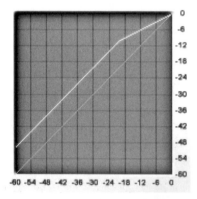

Figure 5.6 Increasing the signal level of the whole track brings the peak level back up to 0dB.

Now a peak on the input side that would have hit 0dB will still hit 0dB, but a peak that would have only hit as high as –20dB will be pushed up to –10dB. The quietest material on the track can be raised an entire +10dB louder without pushing the highest peaks into clipping. The whole dynamic range of the track is "compressed," meaning that the level difference from the softest material to the loudest is squeezed into a narrower range (Figure 5.7). Imagine taking the range from pianissimo to fortissimo and squeezing them a little closer together.

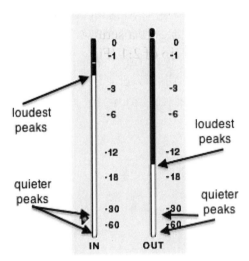

Figure 5.7 The whole dynamic range from softest to loudest is squeezed into a narrower range.

This particular example deals directly with overcoming the challenging difference between peak and average levels, but in itself, it's not a definition of those terms. Peak level is definitely the easier term to explain. This is the measure of how loud the signal level gets at any given moment. Remember though that when you're zoomed in close on a waveform, the highest peaks don't just happen on the positive side of the graph; they're just as likely to be on the negative side (Figure 5.8). Here's a close-up view of a bass drum note that has a stronger negative peak.

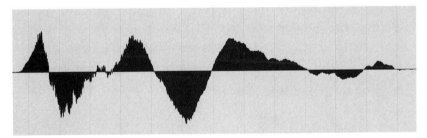

Figure 5.8 The loudest peaks are not always on the positive side of the graphic display.

The trouble is that most audio signals aren't running at their highest peak levels all the time. There might even be a huge difference between the audio level for most of the track and the level of a handful of the loudest peaks. The average level of an audio track is really a measure of how loud the signal is averaged over time. Compare it to driving 100 miles over about two hours. Your average speed may have been 50 mph, but if you spent most of the time in traffic doing about 30 mph and then shot up to 80 mph when it cleared, your average may well have been 50 mph, but the cop is still going to give you a ticket based on your peak level.

So how much time is averaged? That depends on the situation. If you select an audio clip that is two minutes long and analyze it with the Gain plug-in (Chapter 8), then it will tell you the average over the entire two minutes. But if you are watching an analog VU (volume units) meter in real-time, the average is over about 165 milliseconds. Real-time PPM (peak program) meters should run about a 10 ms average, while digital meters will run about a 5-ms average.

You can't win, right? Watching your meters within Pro Tools should give you a sense of where your tracks are averaging, even if there aren't any specific numbers displayed. If you need a more accurate measure, look at some of the other measurement plug-ins (including more advance meters) in Chapter 8.

Noise Floors Inside and Outside of the Studio
Shhhhh, listen.

What do you hear?

Sitting here in my living room late at night, I hear a slight whining whir (with a noticeable peak around 350 Hz) from the fan in the laptop under my fingers. I hear the clock on the wall to my left ticking. From the kitchen, I hear the compressor in the refrigerator. I hear occasional hints of cars outside, but not many since it's kind of late, and the cars aren't too close to my little back street.

That's my noise floor, at least right now as I'm typing this section. I might estimate it at about 30dB SPL, but it's so hard to judge that low. Maybe it's more like 35dB, but that's just one half of the story.

How loud would I turn up the music if I were going to play some right now? Going as loud as 60dB SPL would be a little louder than turning on the dishwasher and a little quieter than typical TV-watching level. The Environmental Protection Agency says that 70dB SPL is the maximum to protect against hearing loss, stress, or sleep disturbance. But I do this stuff for a living, so I'm not afraid of a little real-world level, so let's say I'd listen at 70dB SPL. How much dynamic range do I have between the loudest sound I'm comfortable hearing and the quietest sound that will get lost in the noise floor?

Probably about 35–40 decibels, but I mentioned earlier in the "Decibel Scale" refresher that the scales are different for acoustic and electrical measurements, so that 35dB range right now in my living room would represent about a 70dB dynamic range. I could listen to some seriously broad-ranged music... but that's not at all typical (Figure 5.9).

I wouldn't say my living room is abnormally quiet right now, but it's quieter than it is during the daytime. There's more air movement, more people movement, more traffic, and other disruptions and distractions during the daytime. That might move the noise floor up to about 45dB or even 50dB SPL. And I might not be willing to listen to music as loud if someone else is in the room who isn't as comfortable with stronger levels, so the maximum playback might drop to 65dB SPL. That leaves 15dB of acoustic range and about 30dB worth of electrical range to keep me entertained.

That's more like the real world, although it's still not as bad as it can get. Imagine that your listener is in the kitchen washing dishes with a little clock radio playing on the counter. Imagine he

Figure 5.9   Your audience won't hear your music in the studio; it will be in the real world.

is in a car on the highway with the windows halfway down. Imagine she is on an airplane with the rumble and rush of a couple of jet engines just outside the window.

In real-world situations, you are lucky to find listeners who will have 10dB or 15dB worth of acoustic dynamic range when the music is playing in the background. When they hear the loudest peaks of your mixes, listeners will adjust the volume control until those are at a level that's comfortable for them. This kind of adjustment might drop your average level down into the noise floor of the listener's kitchen, office, or car. If they turn it up, they'll hear the quieter sections, but the highest peaks will probably be too loud.

This isn't a recommendation to start crushing the life out of all your mixes until they only have a 5dB dynamic range left. It's not all about mixing for the lowest common denominator—the guy with the worst listening environment. It's about being aware of real-world situations and scaling your dynamic range to your target audience.

If you expect your music to be loaded onto an MP3 player and shuffled in with commercial tracks, you don't necessarily want your track to be the loudest one, but it probably shouldn't be quieter by a mile than all the other songs. The idea is to stay comfortably close to the other material. If your listeners will hear your work in quieter, more controlled settings, you can open up the range a little more.

I generally aim for most pop/rock/jazz tracks to land at an *average* level of somewhere between –24dBFS for the ballads and –15dBFS for the heavier songs. For classical I might let the average hang a little closer to –30dBFS, but even here I aim a little higher as long as it doesn't affect the tone of the recording. Peak levels will, of course, still land close to the 0dB mark for every track. The average levels determine where the listener sets the volume control. The loudest peaks shouldn't land so far above this average that they irritate the listener, and they shouldn't be so low that there's no drama left in the track. Aim for that sweet spot in the middle that sounds just right.

Building an Automatic Volume Control

At the center of every dynamics processor is an automatic volume control. It's the *dynamic* adjustment of the signal level that gives this family of processors its name. But how exactly can we create an automatic volume control (Figure 5.10)? It's easy to say that's what the processor is doing, but you need to understand what's going on under the hood if you want to make the most of these amazing tools.

Figure 5.10 Listen to a CD and ride the volume to turn up the quiet stuff and turn down the loud stuff; you are compressing the signal.

In the analog world, the device that is most often at the center of a dynamics processor is a voltage-controlled amplifier. That's an amplifier circuit that turns the gain up or down based on a separate voltage being sent to it. Send less voltage and the amplifier turns the signal down; send more voltage and the amplifier turns the signal up. The technique in the digital world of plug-in dynamics processors is essentially the same, except it's all done with software so the control voltage is simply a control value based on the audio signal being measured. In either case, there are two important things to keep in mind about how it all works:

- The control signal doesn't have to come from the audio signal that's being amplified.

- The control signal doesn't have anything to do with the actual amplification of the signal; it's just a controller.

For most dynamics processors, the control signal will be derived from the audio signal being controlled (although it doesn't have to come from there) (Figure 5.11). The incoming signal is split into two parts. One part is sent to a logic circuit that measures the signal level and creates a control voltage. The other part is sent through the amplifier circuit and back out into the world.

From this simple conceptual design, it's possible to build any kind of dynamics processor. Set the system up so that the amplifier is turned up when a signal is louder than a certain threshold and

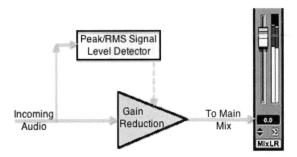

Figure 5.11 This block diagram shows the basic procedure going on inside any dynamics processor.

then turned down when it falls below that threshold, and you've built an expander/gate processor (Figure 5.12).

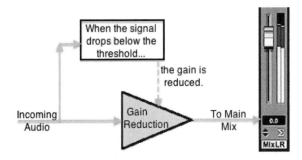

Figure 5.12 An expander/gate turns the amplifier *up* when the signal is *above* a certain threshold.

Set the system up so the amplifier is turned up when the signal level is low but then gets turned down as the signal crosses a certain threshold, and you've built a compressor/limiter processor (Figure 5.13).

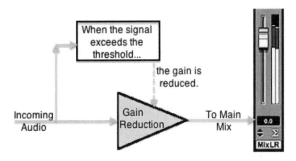

Figure 5.13 A compressor/limiter turns the amplifier *down* when the signal is *above* the threshold.

You can even do some clever things with the control signal side of the system. Running that signal through an equalizer before it is measured and turned into a control voltage creates what is called a spectral compressor (Figure 5.14). One specialized type of compressor called a "de-esser" boosts the high frequencies so the compressor turns the signal down only when the high frequencies get too loud.

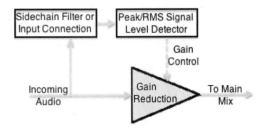

Figure 5.14 Adding an equalizer to the control signal creates a spectral compressor that turns things down only when certain frequency bands get too loud.

It's even possible to have a completely unrelated signal generate the control voltage through a technique called side-chaining. I've included examples of how to use side-chains to make a kick drum track open and close a gate on a signal generator and how to create a ducker that lets your vocal track automatically turn down the guitar track.

Many possibilities exist for interconnecting dynamics plug-ins to create powerful mixing tools. Once you understand how these processors work, you'll discover new ways to solve strange audio problems and to create amazing mixes.

When to Reach for These Tools

Even when you understand that dynamics processors are a very simple form of automation built around an automatic volume control, it's not always obvious how to use them in your projects. Flipping through books or searching online for tips on recording will probably make matters worse. Some suggest using compressors, limiters, or gates on almost every track and channel, while others complain that everything is over-compressed these days. So what's the real story?

There is no single "real" story. Dynamics plug-ins are just another set of tools that can make or break your project. You could use them on every single track and create the most amazing mix ever, or you could completely overdo it and crush all the life out of your sounds. There isn't even any magical place in the middle that's "just right" either. Everything will depend on what kind of project you are working on and what kind of sound you are trying to create. As with all plug-ins available within Pro Tools, before you use one, identify which part of the recording process you are working on and whether you are trying to fix a problem or create something new.

Not Likely to Help with Composition and Songwriting

There is no question that dynamics processors can be used creatively to help you breathe life into your sounds, keep your tracks from fighting each other, or pull your final mix together. But that part comes later. It's not the kind of creative edge that's useful when you're writing new material.

There are exceptions, but activating a gate, limiter, or compressor probably won't have the same inspirational effect you're likely to get from other processors because the change of volume is usually more noticeable than any change in tone.

Expanders and gates reduce the level on a track when the original volume drops below a certain threshold. Compressors and limiters reduce the level when the original climbs above the threshold. At their core, these are really just volume controls, and if turning the volume up or down was likely to inspire your work it could just as easily come from changing the channel fader.

However, sometimes it's the exception that proves the rule—and I would never encourage you to stop experimenting. Guitar and bass players know that compressor/sustainer effects seem to stretch their notes, since the volume level of the quiet decay is turned up a little louder. Gate thresholds can be set so close to the loudest peaks that your notes are cut off abruptly to create a tight, staccato effect. If that kind of sustain or separation inspires a smooth groove or a funky riff, then go for it. But if you need something more remarkable to get your ideas flowing, then dynamics might not be the first place to look.

Compressors but Not Gates when Recording

Considering that the function of a gate is to turn off the incoming signal, it's obviously not a great processor to use when recording. If the threshold is set too high, the signal could drop out and never even make it into the recording. But setting the threshold too low defeats the purpose of running the gate since hardly anything will be dropped out. The risk of completely losing part of the signal before it's even recorded far outweighs the benefit of dropping a little unwanted noise that could easily be removed at almost any other time during post production. Don't risk losing a great performance without a very good reason.

At the other end of the volume control, using a compressor or limiter while recording is common for safety as well as tone, although how you do it depends on your own recording technique. The only compressor I consistently use during tracking sessions is on the upright bass track so the musicians can hear it more clearly in the headphone mix. The track is still recorded raw with the compressor on the output side just for monitoring. However, I rarely use any processors to alter tracks before they are recorded, but I'm aware of the long-standing tradition of compressing incoming audio signals before they are recorded, even if many engineers don't know why they do.

The main reason for this practice goes back to the days of analog tape machines. While you hear endless love stories about the wondrous sounds of tape, you have to dig a little deeper to find out that the medium itself had one particular flaw that drove engineers of the '60s and '70s up the wall: a high noise floor. Tape is a noisy medium (Figure 5.15). High-quality machines running at 15ips (inches per second) certainly perform better than smaller consumer decks or the ghastly cassette tape, but they still had a lot of self-noise. Rooms, microphones, preamplifiers, and mixing consoles all started out with noise too, but they were easier to fix, leaving the noble tape machine as the noisiest part of the signal chain.

The key to recording to a noisy medium is to keep your signal levels as far above the noise as possible. Simply turning up the volume at the microphone preamp would be enough if you didn't also have to worry about clipping the electronics at the top end when the signal gets too loud. And how do you turn up the quietest signals while keeping the loudest ones from clipping? You need some kind of automatic volume control.

Figure 5.15 The venerable open-reel tape machine was unfortunately a rather noisy medium.

And so compressors found a favored place at the front end of many recording systems. The standard signal chain became microphone, into preamp, into compressor, into tape machine. Even as the quality of tape machines improved and the noise floors dropped, the compressors stayed in place.

In a modern digital studio with Pro Tools as the recording medium, the noise floor of the recording medium is so low, especially with a 24-bit signal path, that the recording medium might just be the quietest part of the signal chain. The noisiest part of your recording chain is probably your room, unless you happen to be recording in a purpose-built, well-designed recording facility. Turning up the levels while you're tracking won't make your signal any louder without also turning up the noise.

On the other hand, there's nothing wrong with a bit of light compression or limiting on the way in. Even in a digital environment with a low noise floor, it's still best to get strong levels into the recorder as long as you don't overdo it. Boosting the signal level of your digital tracks still brings up the noise floor. Yes, you could boost the recorded signal as much as 12dB and still keep the noise floor lower than many high-end tape machines, but if you don't have to raise the level, then the noise stays even lower. But noise is definitely not the only issue.

The big killer for digital tracks is hitting the 0dBFS peak on the way in. Remember: this level is the end of the line for digital signals—the spot where the highest peaks in your waveform are all ones (or all zeros), and none of them will ever cross over to become a two. Setting your preamp gain so the loudest incoming peaks land between –12dB and –6dB is a reasonable target, but if you are concerned about the performer having a very wide dynamic range, then use a compressor or limiter while you are recording. Keep the settings light and don't let latency spoil your timing.

Avoid Using Dynamics Plug-ins While Editing
Turn off all the compressors, limiters, gates, and other dynamics processors running on any tracks you are editing. In some cases, you might also switch off dynamics processors on other tracks to get the best sense of how all your tracks relate to each other.

Editing is one of those steps during production where you really need to focus on all of the details within your track. Especially when compositing vocal tracks—hearing each nuance and inflection accurately enables you to decide what to keep and what to cut. Even a light compressor setting alters the sound of your tracks, taming higher peaks and bringing quieter sounds forward. Running a de-esser plug-in while you're editing vocals also masks some problems that you might want to handle with more specific editing. You need to hear the details and differences to know if each take sounds good before adding any extra help.

It should be obvious why you wouldn't want to run an expander/gate plug-in while editing. Those devices act as automatic editors, but they'll drop out the signals you need to hear while you're editing. If you're focused on cutting parts out of a track, then switching the gate on and off while editing can be helpful. If you're trimming something like the tom tracks for a drum-set part and trying to make sure only the actual tom hits are coming through, then you are doing the same function the gate is trying to do automatically. You just happen to be a better judge of whether that loud spot is really from the high-tom and not just a loud snare hit.

Definitely Use Your Dynamics Plug-Ins for Mixing

That's exactly what these things were built to do. The point of an automatic volume control is to provide a basic level of automation to your tracks. Your project won't mix itself, but it will behave better, and the dynamics plug-in will handle some of the more tedious chores for you. Could you say dynamics processors help free your mind from the mundane details so you're free to explore the heights of creativity? Well, maybe that's too ambitious, but it's aiming in the right direction.

- Use your **expander plug-ins** to keep a noisy guitar-amp sound pulled down except for when it's playing the sounds you want to hear.

- Use your **compressor plug-ins** to thicken up a bass track and keep the foundation of your mix solid and stable.

- Use your **gate plug-ins** to drop out drum tracks for toms or other less-used instruments so they only open up when there's a sound you want to hear in the mix.

- Use your **limiter plug-ins** to push your vocal track up to the front without clipping.

Once you get the hang of these tools, you'll find uses for them on every track. You'll quickly realize why many digital consoles and high-end analog consoles include compressors along with the equalizers for every channel on the board. They are an essential part of creating a controlled, full, focused, and cohesive mix.

Using a dynamics plug-in on every track doesn't mean you're overdoing it—unless you are. But that's more a question of how intense the settings are, not how often you use it. I equate using compressors while mixing to using the sustain pedal on a piano. That's a strong statement, especially to classical musicians, who are probably familiar with the words of the great pianist Anton Rubenstein: "The more I play, the more I am convinced the pedal is the soul of the pianoforte!"

Do I think the compressor is the "soul" of the recording process? Well, I wouldn't be embarrassed to say so.

But don't overdo it by pouring on the compression until all the life is choked out of your sound. I don't think Rubinstein was thinking of a dripping bucket of new-age muddiness where the sustain pedal is never lifted. It's all about technique, subtlety, and putting just the right amount of that soul into each sound, each track, each mix that you create. Dynamics processors might be little more than automatic volume controls on the inside, but in bringing up the quieter parts of your tracks, they also bring up the hidden nuance. Warmth, space, depth, and color are subtleties that can be lost behind louder sounds. Bring these forward while keeping the loudest parts under control, and you'll hear the soul emerge from your mixes.

Dynamics Plug-Ins for Mastering

Much has been written and said about the magic, mystery, and artistry of the mastering engineer's trade in recent years. This could be a legitimate observation of the talents of these master technicians or a fortunate bit of good publicity that keeps them in business during the home-recording revolution. In any case, what's going on behind the curtain, in the shadowy spaces where the mastering engineer works? What tools are in use there, making things sound so wonderful? More important: can you get your hands on that kind of magic too?

If you've never visited a commercial mastering studio, look online to find photos of the control rooms at various mastering houses. One thing that should stand out about most of them, apart from the enormous speakers, is the conspicuous absence of a mixing console. And what's sitting in the key position where most recording studios would have their mixing console? An equalizer and a compressor.

Probably you'll see a couple of different equalizers and compressors and maybe a small mastering console that selects between various sources and listening destinations. The point is dynamics processors, particularly compressors and limiters, are as critically important to the mastering process as the mixing console is for the recording and mixing engineers.

A mastering engineer is tasked with both putting the final bit of sparkle and polish on each track and with balancing the tone and level from one track to the next on an album. The tracks that are brought together to make a finished album might all have different instrument sounds, they will have been mixed at different times, maybe even by different engineers, and possibly at different studios. With only finished stereo mixes to work from, the mastering engineer doesn't have the option to turn up the snare track here and turn down the vocal track there; it all has to be done with tonal balance and level control—with equalizers and dynamics processors.

Be sure not to limit yourself at limiters. There are so many other possibilities for putting the final touches on your projects. The basics of using dynamics processors for mastering involve a lot of ideas you already know. Expanders can open up the dynamic range on tracks that have been squashed too tight, while compressors close up the dynamic range on tracks that peak very high but are too weak on average. Gates drop out low-level noise in between tracks, and limiters can make sure the loudest peaks don't exceed the maximum level your delivery format can handle.

It doesn't stop there. From those basic building blocks, you're able to incorporate equalizers and other processors on the control side of the dynamics processors so you can compress certain frequency bands more than others. That kind of detail work can actually move certain instrument sounds and tracks forward or back in the mix without remixing. It will take some practice along with the guidance and examples offered here. Mastering is all about subtlety, and dynamics processors form another cornerstone of the mastering engineer's art.

What's in the Box?

Pro Tools software includes several different dynamics processors as standard equipment to cover most of your needs for mixing and mastering. Three of the processors are part of the Dynamics III package that is the third revision of the basic Pro Tools plug-in suite, similar to the EQ-III (Chapter 4) and the Delay-II (Chapter 7) plug-ins. Included in the Dynamics-III package are the Compressor/Limiter, De-Esser, and Expander/Gate plug-ins. These three processors are joined by the Bomb Factory BF76 Peak Limiter and the Maxim look-ahead limiter.

Several similar controls are shared across several dynamics plug-ins, such as Threshold, Makeup Gain, and Ratio controls. If the description for a control isn't particularly clear when you're reading about one plug-in, flip back a few pages and check out another one. The controls may be identical, but each description is a little different, so there should be something that makes sense. Of course, each unique plug-in will have some unique controls as well, and those descriptions are a little more detailed.

Common Features of Dynamics III Plug-Ins

The three plug-ins of the Dynamics III package share a few common controls and displays worth looking at separately before reading about each individual processor. Differences in how these features are implemented is covered with each plug-in.

The first and most obvious of the common features across this group of plug-ins is the set of Input, Output, and Gain Reduction meters provided on the left side of the plug-in window (Figure 5.16). These are bracketed together under the Levels heading.

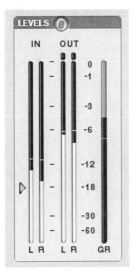

Figure 5.16 Input, Output, and Gain Reduction meters are provided for each Dynamics III plug-in.

The Input meter shows the peak levels of the highest 60dB of the incoming audio signal while the Output meter shows the peak levels for the same range for the outgoing, compressed signal. The standard display will show one, two, or three of each meter for mono, stereo, or LCR tracks, respectively. Any larger track configurations, from LCRS up to 7.1 will show either the Input or Output meters and will include a switch for you to select which meters you need. The small, orange triangle to the left of the Input meter shows and controls the current Threshold level. Click and drag the triangle to set the threshold point near the average level of your track.

The last meter on the right displays the amount of gain reduction being applied. This inverted meter starts at the 0dB mark at the top and extends downward to show how deeply the signal level is being cut. An orange display means the reduction is within the knee range of the processor while a darker orange indicates gain reduction at the full ratio.

A Phase Reversal switch is also included at the top of the Levels section as a convenience feature so you won't need to activate an additional plug-in to correct for out-of-phase signals.

Another somewhat curious feature of the Dynamics III plug-ins is the Options section (Figure 5.17). It could have just as easily been labeled the "Extras" section since the controls placed there aren't as optional as you might expect.

Figure 5.17   Each of the Dynamics III plug-ins has a few extra switches in the Options section.

The Expander/Gate plug-in has the option to activate or deactivate the Look-Ahead feature. The De-Esser has the option to process the high frequencies only and to listen to the processed control signal. And the Compressor/Limiter only has an LFE Enable option when running in a 5.1, 6.1, or 7.1 surround configuration.

The last common feature of the Dynamics III family is the graphic display window (Figure 5.18). This window shows a graph of the input-to-output level relationship for the Compressor/Limiter and the Expander/Gate plug-ins.

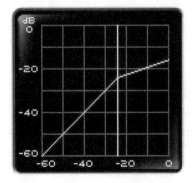

Figure 5.18   The graphic display window illustrates how the plug-in will alter the signal.

The De-Esser display is a little different, showing the signal level and gain reduction against frequency. When audio is running through any of the plug-ins, either a moving cursor or line shows how the processor is performing.

Compressor/Limiter Dyn 3

Take a quick look at the control window for the Compressor/Limiter plug-in and you'll see the window divided into five groups of controls and displays (Figure 5.19). The standard graphic display, Levels section, and Options section are joined by the specialized Comp/Limit controls and Side-Chain.

Figure 5.19   The Compressor/Limiter control window.

While the standard components are, well, standard, there are some subtle differences in how they behave within this plug-in. Look at how the standard controls function here or even flip back a page or two to see how they function for other Dynamics III plug-ins, and then continue to the specific Compressor/Limiter controls to get an idea of how to use and understand this tool.

Levels Section

Although this section is a standard feature on all of the Dynamic III plug-ins, there are some subtle differences among the different processors. The Phase invert switch is provided as a convenience feature and operates as any similar switch, allowing you to invert the signal for that channel for corrective or creative effects.

The GR (gain reduction) meter will only appear as a single inverted meter showing the amount of attenuation being applied to the loudest peaks of the signal. It may seem strange that only one meter appears for any channel configuration from mono to 7.1, but remember that the Compressor/Limiter plug-in can only be activated as a multichannel plug-in, and not multi-mono. That means all of the channels are linked so that when the signal in any one channel crosses the threshold, the level for all of the channels is reduced. There's more about this idea in the "Advanced Techniques and Good Practice" section at the end of this chapter.

The Compressor/Limiter plug-in can operate in any channel configuration including mono, stereo, and multi-channel up to 7.1 surround. That's a lot of input and output meters to display at once, so the display will only show input and output meters together for mono, stereo, and LCR configurations. At four channels or more, a selector switch appears in this section of the window (Figure 5.20) that allows you to switch between input and output meters.

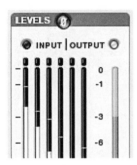

Figure 5.20 With four-channel or larger configurations, choose to display either input or output levels.

The input meters always include the small orange triangle that shows the current Threshold level, but that goes away when switching to view the output meters. Don't forget that you can click and drag that display to quickly adjust the Threshold level graphically. That's handy for getting it set right at the edge of your average peak level.

Options or Standard Equipment?

In most typical music production situations, you might wonder why there is an Options control section set aside on the plug-in window when there are no options available for you to choose. That's because the control that appears in this section only appears when you are working with multi-channel configurations that include a ".1" or LFE (low-frequency effects) channel—those are the 5.1, 6.1, or 7.1 surround modes. When you are working in any of those modes, an LFE Enable toggle switch appears in the Options section (Figure 5.21) of the plug-in.

Figure 5.21 In 5.1, 6.1, and 7.1 surround modes, an LFE Enable option appears.

The default position for this option is "on," meaning that the LFE channel will be linked and compressed along with all the other channels. When you think about it though, it's ironic that this option is even included. There isn't an option for a multi-mono version of the plug-in since it's best to have all your compressor channels firing together, but then this option allows the LFE to run through without processing. This could create a scenario on a 5.1 film mix, for example, where loud dialog in the center channel triggers the compressor to turn down the L, C, R, Ls, and Rs channels, but not the LFE subwoofer that might still be thumping away with the bottom end of the score and sound effects. If the voices and all the other channels are pulled down but the LFE signal remains unchecked, the actors' words could be overshadowed by the LFE.

That's just one example of splitting control between the full-range and LFE channels. There will be times when separate control of the LFE will make sense. But then, there is a reason why the LFE Enable option defaults to the active position, and in most circumstances you'll want to leave it there.

Graphic Display

As with the other Dynamics III plug-ins, the graphic display window shows the relationship between the incoming signal and the processed signal being sent back out into the world (Figure 5.22). It's a small graph, and the scale is rather large, from –60dB to 0dB (digital "full scale"), but a close look shows it's still easy to see what the processor is trying to do.

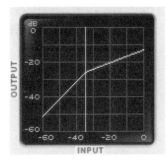

Figure 5.22 The graphic display shows input signal level (horizontal) versus output level (vertical).

A vertical orange line shows where the Threshold level is set, and adjusting the makeup gain level or knee control changes the graphic display so you always have a quick reference to what the plug-in is doing to the audio. Unlike the EQ-III plug-ins, you cannot click and adjust settings from the graphic display, but all those controls are right below in the next section of the display.

When audio is actively running through the plug-in, a small cursor appears in the graphic display to illustrate where the current input level falls along the graph and how it is being affected by the plug-in (Figure 5.23). It's not a control cursor, just another type of visual display that shows the amount of compression being applied to the signal.

The cursor is trying to show you all of what is going on with your audio signal, including marking the real-time point on the graph where your current input and output levels converge. It

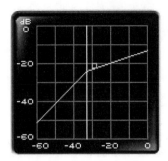

Figure 5.23 When audio is actively running, a cursor displays the gain reduction.

appears as a white box when the signal level is below the threshold, a red box when the signal is being compressed, or as an orange box when the signal is within the knee range and not yet at full compression. It mirrors (to some extent) the Gain Reduction meter in the Levels section. If you see the little cursor blinking out periodically, that shows when transient signals are making it through faster than the attack time of the compressor. It means the signal should be compressed based on the threshold and ratio settings, but is being missed because of a long attack time.

Comp/Limiter Section—The Big Three Controls

Six virtual control knobs with accompanying value displays allow you to adjust all of the basic functions and features of the Compressor/Limiter plug-in (Figure 5.24). They are not arranged in the most intuitive order, so I'll approach them in a way that makes sense for the order of operations, starting with the big three: threshold, ratio, and gain.

Figure 5.24 Six controls adjust how the Compressor/Limiter does its job.

The function of any compressor or limiter begins at the Threshold control since this sets the volume level where the device activates and begins to affect your track. Threshold is the orange knob in the lower right corner that corresponds to the orange line in the graphic display and the orange triangle alongside the input level meters. For this plug-in the available range for the control is from –60dB up to 0dB on the digital, full-scale range.

- A very high setting, close to the maximum level of 0dBFS, means the processor is only activated for the loudest peaks and has only a narrow range in which to work. This would be a more common setting for a Limiter than a Compressor.

■ At the other end of the scale, a very low setting that is lower than the average signal level ensures that the processor is active nearly all the time. This is good for adding a very subtle, almost undetectable, amount of compression to bring the average level of a track up without any risk that a listener would notice the effect.

■ A common and comfortable middle-ground threshold would land right around where the track's average signal strength is landing. Watch the meters for this or use the Gain plug-in (Chapter 8) to measure the average level. The compressor will then gently take effect as the signal exceeds the average.

To relate the Threshold control to the rest of what's going on inside the compressor, think of it as determining the range that will be affected by the processor. The maximum level you can hit inside Pro Tools is the 0dBFS, full-scale level. The threshold point will be somewhere below that. And the operational range of the plug-in will be between those two points. Set it at –10dB and the plug-in has a 10dB range to do its job. Set it at –40dB and the plug-in has a 40dB range. Set the range too narrow and you won't have much room for the processor to do its job, and the other settings will have to be more intense. Set the range wider and you'll get a smoother and subtler effect.

On to the Ratio control. You've already set the threshold point where the compressor activates, now the ratio will determine what the compressor is doing. This adjusts the relationship of the input level to the output level in a ratio of X:1, meaning that for every X number of decibels coming in, the output level is increased by 1 more decibel. The range for this control is from 1:1, which is effectively off, to 100:1, which is effectively an absolute limit on the output level.

The Ratio control of a compressor can be a little difficult to understand at first, but it is the most important part of the processor. It *is* the compressor. A compressor simply measures the level of the incoming audio signal and reduces it when it exceeds the Threshold level. The Ratio that determines how much more output you get once you cross that line.

Let's say you're working on a track that's averaging a level around –24dBFS with a few loud peaks that are hitting pretty close to 0dBFS, but you need the track to seem louder. Set the Threshold level down at –24dB and you'll have 24dB of range for the compressor to work. Setting a ratio of 1.5:1 means a peak that traveled the whole 24dB range up to 0dBFS would now only reach –8dB. Controlling those loudest peaks allows you to easily turn the track up by +6dB. Doing that would place your average level around –18dBFS with the loudest peaks staying safely out of the red.

The red-colored makeup Gain control adjusts the output level of the plug-in after all the other processing has happened. It might seem odd to describe this control now, before covering some of the others, but it's a key component to how compressors are used.

By itself, a compressor simply reduces the overall dynamic range of an audio signal (Figure 5.25). A track with a very broad range from its softest sounds to its loudest can have that range squeezed down to a more manageable difference.

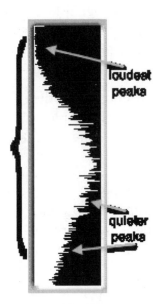

Figure 5.25 Compressors reduce a broad dynamic range to something more manageable.

Simply changing the overall range only gets you part of the way. The next step is to slide that range up or down so it can relate to other tracks in the mix, other songs on the album, or other albums out there in the world (Figure 5.26). Increasing the gain brings the average level up while ensuring the quietest sounds aren't lost in a noisy environment (your listeners won't always be in a quiet room) and that the loudest sounds aren't clipped or distorted.

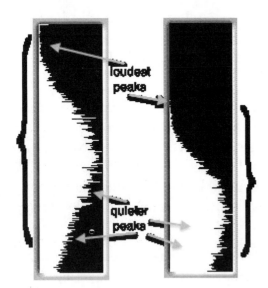

Figure 5.26 Move this narrower range up or down to change the perceived level.

The Gain control has a huge range from +0dB to +40dB, allowing you to amplify your track as much as 100 times its original volume. That's a lot of power, but remember you'll also bring up any noise that might be lingering down there at the lowest levels. Environmental noise like

HVAC and wind, system noise from microphones and preamplifiers, and digital noise from within the software and the plug-in itself can all be brought along for the ride, so listen carefully as you push up toward the more extreme levels. There's a more detailed explanation of the relationship between threshold, ratio, and makeup gain in the "Advanced Techniques and Good Practice" section at the end of this chapter.

Comp/Limiter Section—Refining the Automatic Level Control

Three more controls in this group help to refine the performance of the compressor, allowing you to dial in an effect that is intense and obvious, subtle and controlled, or anywhere in between. The Knee control is adjustable from 0dB to 30dB and adjusts how quickly the compressor reaches its full ratio once the signal level reaches the threshold point. It spreads the transition from no compression to full compression across a wider range so the effect activates more gradually—and less noticeably.

If you set a 4:1 compressor to activate at, say, –20dB and then set the Knee control to 0dB, the incoming signal will start being compressed at 4:1 as soon as it exceeds –20dB. But if you set the knee to, say, 20dB, then compression will start at a more subtle ratio of about 1.1:1 at a lower-volume level of –30dB, growing more intense until it reaches the full 4:1 compression at about –10dB. This difference is referred to as hard-knee versus soft-knee compression (Figure 5.27). It's easier to follow when you see it on the graphic display.

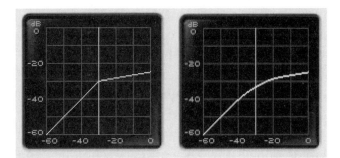

Figure 5.27 A hard knee (left) activates quickly while a soft knee (right) smoothes the transition.

Although it's common to describe a hard-knee compressor as activating "quickly" and a soft knee as activating "slowly," it's important to remember that the Knee control has nothing to do with time. Instead, it creates an automated threshold and ratio control that delivers lighter compression at lower volume levels and stronger compression at higher volume levels. Timing is controlled by the Attack and Release controls.

The Attack control adjusts how quickly the compressor activates once the signal level crosses the threshold point. The attack time can be set anywhere from 10 µs (microseconds) at the fastest to 300 ms at the slowest.

It might seem odd to even have a control for adjusting how quickly the automatic controller activates; wouldn't it make sense to have it happen instantly? For some sounds, it does make sense to move as quickly as possible. Percussive sounds (drums) that reach their maximum volume levels right at the beginning of each note usually need very fast Attack settings.

Vocals or strings, on the other hand, can take a little longer to build up to their loudest levels. The attack time could still be set to activate very quickly, but it might make the effect more noticeable if, for example, heavier compression settings are used on a very dynamic vocal track. Setting the attack time a little slower can help with vocal intelligibility by letting important transient sounds like hard consonants through at full volume, and then springing into action to control the pitched vowel sounds. For most acoustic instrument sounds, try starting with a setting of about 4 ms, and then adjust up or down from there to dial in just the right balance of attack and sustain levels.

At the other end of each note, it's important to listen carefully to the release times of your compressors. The Release control has a range from 5 ms to a full 4 seconds. Release times should generally be set long enough to cover the full decay time of the notes. Setting the time too short on something like a piano note delivers a quiet piano attack that gets louder as the note decays—an effect that can't happen naturally. On the other hand, setting the Release time too long could cause a brief, loud sound to trigger a compressor that continues to reduce the signal level and lose the quiet sounds that follow. For most acoustic instrument sounds, you could safely start with a release of about 200–250 ms, and then adjust up or down from there to catch just the right spot.

Side-Chain Section

The Compressor/Limiter Dyn 3 plug-in includes a side-chain section that can be activated in two distinctly different ways: with an external key input or with its own two-band equalizer. A side-chain signal is usually just a split copy of the incoming audio signal. The intensity of this signal is measured and used to control the gain reduction of the compressor (Figure 5.28). Altering the signal with an equalizer or using a separate audio signal to control the processor can deliver some useful effects. More information about what a side-chain is and how to use it are found in the "Refresher" section at the beginning of this chapter and in the "Advanced Techniques and Good Practice" section at the end of the chapter.

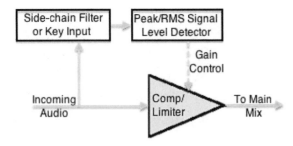

Figure 5.28 The side-chain signal is the part that gets measured to control the compressor.

The general idea of a side-chain is to alter the signal that is being measured, the control signal of the compressor, so the plug-in behaves differently. The most common way of altering the signal is to process it with an equalizer filter (more about those in Chapter 4), and that's why the Side-Chain section of the Compressor/Limiter Dyn 3 includes two filters (Figure 5.29). Two filters, labeled as HF and LF (high frequency and low frequency), are provided although they both can cover the complete frequency spectrum from 20 to 20,000 Hz.

Figure 5.29 Two broad bandwidth filters are provided in the Side-Chain section.

Each filter has a pair of switches that can be set to deliver either a Band-Pass-type filter, or a Roll-Off filter. The Band-Pass filter drops off the audio signal above *and* below the center frequency at a rate of 12dB per octave, leaving only a narrow band of midrange frequencies to trigger the compressor. The HF filter can run as a high-frequency roll-off filter that drops out everything above the corner frequency at a slope of 12dB per octave. The LF filter covers the other end of the spectrum, dropping anything below the corner frequency at a slope of 12dB per octave. Neither of the filters can boost the side-chain signal in any way.

The idea is to reduce the level of certain frequency bands so the compressor is triggered by certain frequency ranges but not by others. It can be confusing at first, but with some practice it makes more sense. If you are having trouble with a sub-mixed drum track that has a bass drum turned up a little too loud, you can use the side-chain to drop all of the high frequencies above 150 Hz. Then dial in a light compressor setting that drops the sub-mix level by about −3dB. Whenever the bass drum is played, the overall level of the drum sub-mix will dip down for a moment so the bass drum isn't so intense, but the compressor won't be triggered by the snare drum or the cymbals.

Each of the two Side-Chain filters can be switched on and off independently and even automated in case the frequency range needs to be adjusted for different parts of the song. To zero in on exactly the right spot to catch the target sounds with the compressor, you can activate the Side-Chain Listen button (Figure 5.30). It's the little button at the top with the icon that looks like a schematic symbol for a speaker.

Figure 5.30 Click the Side-Chain Listen button to hear exactly what the control signal is targeting.

There is also a button with a small key logo on it. Activating this switch bypasses the internal Side-Chain filters and allows another signal to control the processor. You'll need to select a Key Input connection from the pull-down menu at the upper left corner of the plug-in window (Figure 5.31). This is typically an internal bus, although it could also be a hardware audio input.

Figure 5.31 Select a key input connection, usually a bus or input, to control the processor.

There are lots of ways you can use this connection point to control the compression of the audio signal being processed by the plug-in. You can create a specialized compressor arrangement called a ducker that drops the signal level of one track (the one being processed by the plug-in) every time there is a sound present on the key input connection. You might, for example, set up a compressor on a hi-hat track that is keyed by the snare drum track so the hi-hat is turned down slightly every time the snare drum is played (Figure 5.32). There's a more detailed description of how to create a ducker in the "Advanced Techniques and Good Practices" section of this chapter.

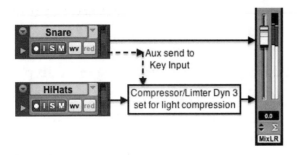

Figure 5.32 Try "ducking" the level of a hi-hat track so the snare track is heard more clearly.

As a very nice bonus, the two on-board equalizer filters are still available to process external key inputs as well. So you can roll the highs off of that snare drum on the side-chain to make sure any bleed from the hi-hats isn't inadvertently turning down the hi-hats track.

Another very common use of the side-chain connection involves using an equalizer to adjust the timbre of the audio signal being processed so that certain sounds trigger the compressor more easily than others. That is the reason for the EQ filters already built into the Compressor/Limiter Dyn 3, but using a more comprehensive equalizer like the 7-Band EQ-III plug-in (Chapter 4) allows for much more precise targeting (Figure 5.33).

Boosting a frequency band with the equalizer makes those sounds appear louder at the control input of the compressor. That means the compressor will be triggered more easily by that frequency band, causing the processed signal to be turned down. It seems contradictory at first, but

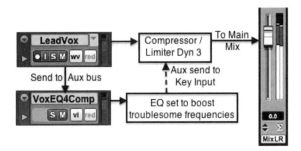

Figure 5.33 Route your track to a bus with an EQ plug-in, and then use that signal to control the compressor.

that's the idea. Turning something up on the control signal causes it to be compressed more easily on the processed signal. Similarly, turning a frequency band down on the control signal causes it to pass through the compressor without being turned down.

At first glance, this seems like a very complicated equalizer circuit jumping through a lot of extra hoops just to turn down the highs or the lows. In a way, that is what's happening, but it's more clever than that. A normal equalizer would simply turn a frequency band up or down throughout the mix (unless you automate it). A side-chained compressor can create a type of automatic equalizer that turns down the entire track only when a particular frequency band gets truly too loud for you. The track (and that frequency band) is left alone when the signal level is in a range you like.

Real-Time Use (RTAS and TDM)

The Compressor/Limiter Dyn 3 plug-in can run in real-time within both the RTAS and TDM environments. (Pro Tools 10 includes these older versions since a newer AAX version has not yet been released.) It can run as mono plug-in or in multichannel mode for anywhere from stereo to 7.1 surround. It does not, however, run as a multi-mono processor for real-time applications, although an option for independent mono operation appears in the Audio Suite version.

Usage Example I—Controlling a Rowdy Bass Player

All right, there are no guarantees this plug-in will help your bass player stay out of bar fights, keep away from the cops, or show up to rehearsals on time. It will, however, help you keep his tracks under control. Electric basses deliver a broad dynamic range with all the slapping, popping, and plucking effects pushing the peaks up pretty loud while some notes don't speak very loudly. With the bass forming the foundation of your mix, it's essential to keep that foundation solid.

Try activating a Compressor/Limiter Dyn 3 plug-in on the bass track and dialing in a fairly aggressive setting to start things off. Set the threshold to –24, the ratio to 3:1, and the gain to +12dB (Figure 5.34). This starting point means that a peak that would have hit 0dB should only hit –6dB, although the track should be 12dB louder on average.

Figure 5.34   Start with a threshold of –24dB, ratio of 3:1, and gain of +12dB.

You'll need to listen to set the exact attack and release times, but you can probably start at about 2 ms for the attack and 250 ms for the release. If the track is clipping on slaps and other fast transients, set the attack time lower to 1 ms or even less. If sustained notes seem to be wavering in volume, then set the release time longer so the compressor stays active through most of the longer notes.

Remember, the idea is to keep the bass under control and pull the total dynamic range in so it can be a more solid and consistent foundation through the song. If the dynamic range is still too wide, and you feel like you're losing the bass under other instruments, try pulling the threshold down a little further, maybe to –30dB or –35dB. You may have to ease up on the Ratio as well, but you can also use the makeup gain control to place the reduced range right where it needs to be within the mix. Try not to push the peaks up to 0dB since you'll still need room for other tracks to be mixed in and for other effects that you might add to the whole mix.

De-Esser Dyn 3

Before describing the specifics of the De-Esser Dyn 3 plug-in, it's worth explaining what a de-esser is. If you've never used one of these processors before, the first question you might have is, "What the heck is a de-esser anyway?" Why, it's a plug-in that can remove an "S" for you, what else what it be? And just think of the possibilities....

Why, with the click of a mouse, you could turn a fast man into a fat man. You could go all super villain and turn the land of Spain into the land of Pain—muah-ha-ha! Or maybe it's the magical plug-in that can finally make a "hit" out of a song that had previously sounded like...oh well, let's just say "crap." You could even leave this poor little guy in need of a new logo for the front of his Halloween costume (Figure 5.35).

All right, so that's not the kind of "S" this plug-in is meant to remove. Its purpose is to reduce sibilant sounds, the hissing "S" sounds we hear in quiet voices, lisping singers, and large groups of people reciting something together. Words with an "S," a "C," or a "Z" are the common culprits. Although it's the sound more than the letter, so you might also hear the same effect from a "T," an "F," or a "Ch" sound.

The trouble with sibilant sounds is how we make them. The tip of your tongue moves up against the roof of your mouth to restrict airflow, causing a more focused stream of high-pressure air.

Figure 5.35 Don't worry Superman, that's not the "S" we'll be removing.

That's probably a little technical, but think of other places where high-pressure air is released in a similar way, like when you open a can of soda, a bottle of beer, or use an aerosol spray. The resulting sound is a short burst of high-frequency, broad-band noise, with most of the energy landing between about 6 kHz to 12 kHz.

You're probably thinking that sounds like a job for an equalizer, right? You're right since an equalizer is required, but there's more to it than that. Turning down the highs with an EQ would take them down throughout the entire track and would make a vocal track sound dull or confined. Automating the equalizer is one possibility, but you would have so many sounds to chase down, it would be quite a chore. You need something more like an automatic volume control that only turns down the high stuff.

A de-esser is just a specialized compressor designed to listen for high-frequency noise and turn the volume down quickly when it appears. The setup involves sending the internal side-chain signal through an equalizer that boosts the high frequencies. When a sibilant sound shows up, it activates the compressor and the output level is turned down.

The De-Esser Dyn 3 plug-in shares some similar displays with the rest of the Dynamics III family and also has a few extra features to make it more specific to the task of de-essing (Figure 5.36). You should recognize the Levels and Options sections along with the graphic display, and these are joined by the De-Esser controls section.

Standard Equipment—Level Meters and Graphic Display

The De-Esser Dyn 3 plug-in shares the same Levels section with the other Dynamics III plug-ins, although it is slightly different than the other processors. The Phase switch is still available as a convenience feature to invert the signal polarity should you need to do so for corrective or creative reasons. The Input and Output meters are arranged similarly and function as they do for the other plug-ins. However, since the De-Esser only runs in mono or stereo configurations, there is

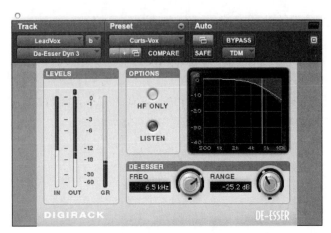

Figure 5.36 The De-Esser Dyn 3 is a specialized compressor with a streamlined set of controls.

no need for the switchable Input or Output display used in the multichannel modes. There is also no orange threshold triangle since there is no adjustable threshold setting for the De-Esser plug-in. The GR (gain reduction) meter functions similarly to the other plug-ins, as an inverted meter that displays how much the audio signal is being attenuated by the de-esser.

The graphic display is also a little different from the other Dynamics III plug-ins since it displays the output signal level (vertical axis) over the frequency range from 500 Hz up to 20 kHz (Figure 5.37). This graphic display provides a more accurate picture of how the plug-in is altering the audio signal than the Output and Gain Reduction meters provide.

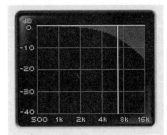

Figure 5.37 The graphic display shows the output signal as gain reduction over frequency.

While the De-Esser Dyn 3 does not have multichannel options available, it is the only Dynamics III plug-in with the ability to run in multi-mono mode. You can activate the plug-in on a stereo track and set different control values for the left and right channels. This isn't usually a good idea to do with most compressors since it can cause the stereo image to "wobble" from side to side if one channel is compressed while the other isn't. On the other hand, this effect can be minimized with the HF Only option activated. Use this feature for independent de-essing of a stereo backing-vocals track to have the plug-in tame hissing "S" sounds that might arrive from each side at different times and intensities.

Specialized Control—Frequency, Range, and the Option Switches

While the De-Esser Dyn 3 is indeed a compressor on the inside, it has a much more streamlined control interface than its Compressor/Limiter Dyn 3 sibling. There is no Threshold control since this is incorporated into the Range control. There is no gain control since this plug-in will only attenuate the audio signal. And there are no Attack and Release Time controls since these settings are fixed at fairly short times so the plug-in can catch offending sounds quickly.

The two knobs that adjust most of the behavior of the plug-in are the Frequency and Range controls (Figure 5.38).

Figure 5.38 The Frequency and Range knobs adjust most of the behavior of the plug-in.

Use the Range control to adjust how much the audio signal is attenuated by the de-esser. It has a very broad range from 0dB to –40dB of attenuation. Although it's rare to need such severe gain reduction when compressing the entire audio signal, this large range makes more sense when targeting just the high frequencies in HF Only mode.

The Frequency control serves a double purpose in the plug-in. Under normal operation, this adjusts the corner frequency where the processor will be listening for high-frequency content. The available range tops out at 16 kHz since detecting anything above that for attenuation would be irrelevant as the human range of hearing ends at around 20 kHz. But the frequency range does extend all the way down to 500 Hz, which is well below where most sibilant sounds occur. This broad range allows you to seek out exactly the range of the sounds that are causing trouble, so they can be contained.

The second function of the Frequency control relates to what portion of the audio signal is attenuated by the De-Esser when it is operating in the HF Only mode. It seems at first glance that using the HF Only mode would make the processor act more like an automated High-Cut filter, adjusting the slope of the filter steeper to attenuate more of the signal. But by pulling the controls to their extremes, it's clear this isn't the case (Figure 5.39). Instead, the Frequency control seems to adjust the corner frequency of a shelving filter with a fairly shallow Q-factor.

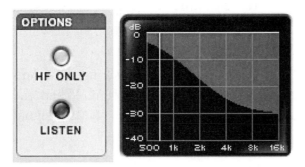

Figure 5.39 Setting the Frequency very low in the HF Only mode shows the filter shape being used.

Knowing that the filter shape being applied is closer to a shelving EQ than a high-frequency roll-off means that you can feel safer using lower Frequency settings. As long as your range value isn't set too severely, you can target a wider frequency band, down to where it starts to be very obvious, without worrying about losing more of your high-frequency components to a High-Cut filter. This is particularly helpful if you are trying to knock sibilant sounds out of lower male voices or if you are trying to tame the highs on certain instrument sounds like the "chiff" of a flute or the clash of a half-open hi-hat.

To zero in on exactly the part of the sound you're trying to control, listen to the control signal rather than the processed audio signal. This is why the Listen control is included. Click the button to activate the Listen control and you'll be hearing just the high frequencies the plug-in is sending through the side-chain to control the compressor.

While you're listening, adjust the Frequency control up and down until you hear all of the sound you're trying to control and as little as possible of the sound you want to preserve. You might want to loop a small portion of the track where you hear the worst sibilance so you know you're on target. Then deactivate the Listen control and adjust the range until those pesky "S" sounds are under control.

You might be confused when you first learn about what's going on under the hood of the De-Esser, but once you understand it, the whole thing is pretty easy.

Expander/Gate Dyn 3

Wouldn't it be nice if your audio tracks could automatically turn down the volume, or even mute themselves, when the sounds you *want* to hear from them stop? Any extra noise they pick up from other stuff in the room could be dropped out, leaving only what those microphones were *meant* to hear. It seems like an ambitious dream, but it's the basic idea behind a processor typically called a "noise gate" or a "downward expander" that you'll find labeled as the Expander/Gate Dyn 3 inside Pro Tools.

If the level is just turned down a little, we refer to that as an expander. If it's cut out completely, then it's considered a gate. It's a lot like how a limiter is really just a compressor at a more extreme setting, and that's why this plug-in is labeled as both Expander and Gate.

This third sibling in the Dynamics III family looks almost identical to the Compressor/Limiter, although you don't want to get them confused since it works in quite the opposite direction. A compressor attenuates the signal when it's above the threshold, and an expander attenuates it when it's below. Since a compressor is meant to compress the dynamic range of your track, it shouldn't surprise you that an expander is meant to expand the dynamic range, keeping the loud parts loud while the quiet parts get quieter.

The tough part is that it's not always clear which direction the gate is trying to swing. It's common to hear noise gates described according to the way most engineers use them: When the incoming audio signal crosses the volume threshold, the gate opens up and lets the signal through. This would be a gate that's normally closed and then opens to let sound through. But that's not quite how it works. Instead, the volume level is being turned *down* when the signal falls *below* the threshold. So the gate is normally open.

The most typical task for a noise gate or downward expander is to reduce noise like tape hiss, HVAC, or wind whenever the instruments aren't playing, or the speakers aren't talking. On a recorded audio track, the setup might look something like the drawing (Figure 5.40). The gate is normally open for louder sounds and closes for the quiet ones.

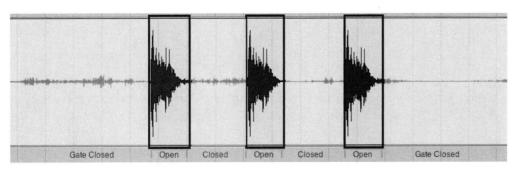

Figure 5.40   The gate is open when a loud signal is present but closes to reduce low-level noise.

The Expander/Gate Dyn 3 works this way, although some of the controls, particularly the Attack and Release time controls, are arranged differently. Those are labeled as though the gate is normally closed for quiet sounds, and opens to let louder sounds through. It's a subtle distinction that will be explained in more detail after the basic controls are covered.

The Basics—Input, Output, and Gain Reduction Meters

The Expander/Gate Dyn 3 plug-in shares the same Levels section as the Compressor/Limiter plug-in. There is a Phase switch (Figure 5.41) available as a convenience feature to invert the signal polarity for corrective or creative reasons.

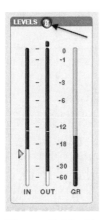

Figure 5.41   The Levels section includes a Phase switch along with input, output, and gain reduction meters.

Expander/Gate Dyn 3 can operate in any channel configuration including mono, stereo, and multi-channel up to 7.1 surround, but that's too many input and output meters to display at once. Instead of crowding the screen, a configuration with four channels or more will add a selector switch in this section of the window (Figure 5.42) that allows you to switch between input and output meters.

Figure 5.42 With four-channel or larger configurations, choose to display either input or output levels.

The input meters will always include the small, orange, click-and-drag triangle that shows the current Threshold level, although it only appears with the Input meters. Sliding the little triangle up and down provides a visual reference as you place the threshold or your gate down near the noise floor.

The GR (gain reduction) meter functions similarly to the other plug-ins, as an inverted meter that displays how much the audio signal is being attenuated by the expander or gate.

Graphic Display

The graphic display window shows the relationship between the incoming signal and the processed signal being sent back out into the world (Figure 5.43). It's a small graph with a –60dB to 0dB range but still gives you a rough idea of how the processor is performing.

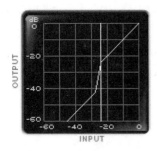

Figure 5.43 The graphic display shows input signal level (horizontal) versus output level (vertical).

A vertical orange line shows where the Threshold level is set, and adjusting the Range or Ratio control changes the graphic display so you always have a quick reference to how the plug-in is changing the levels. You can't click and adjust settings from the graphic display like some other plug-ins, but there are plenty of other controls for that.

When audio is actively running through the plug-in, a small cursor appears in the graphic display to illustrate where the current input level falls along the graph and how it is being controlled (Figure 5.44). It's not a control cursor, just a specialized meter that shows where the current peak level falls along the graph.

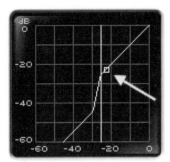

Figure 5.44 When audio is actively running, a cursor displays the current peak level.

The cursor is designed to mark the intersection point on the graph where your current input level and output level converge. It will appear as a white box when the signal level is above the threshold or as an orange box when the signal is being attenuated. If you don't see the cursor, or if it seems to drop off the bottom of the graph, that's perfectly normal when your Range and Ratio settings are strong enough to drop the output signal below –60dBFS.

Essential Controls—Threshold, Range, and Ratio

The function of any dynamics processor begins at the Threshold control since this sets the volume level where the device activates and begins to affect your track. For this plug-in, the threshold can be set anywhere from –60dB up to 0dB on the digital, full-scale range. It's adjusted by the orange knob in the lower right corner or the orange triangle alongside the input level meters, and it is represented visually as the vertical orange line in the graphic display.

Just as in a compressor, the Threshold control determines the range that will be affected by the processor. Here's where that confusion about whether the gate is "active" when closed or when open comes into play. The threshold point will be somewhere below the 0dBFS maximum level, and the processor will be active when the signal level is below that point. Think of it this way:

- A *very high setting*, close to the maximum level of 0dBFS, means the processor is always active and working to reduce the signal level. This is great for *expanding* your dynamic range, but not useful in gating.

- At the other end of the scale, *a very low setting* that's a lot lower than the average signal level will leave the processor off most the time. That's good for true *noise gating* if you want to pull the level down only when the low-level noise is exposed.

- A comfortable, middle-ground threshold would land just below the track's average signal strength. Watch the meters to set this, and the expander will take effect as the signal drops below the average.

Set the threshold at –10dB and the loudest 10dB will remain unaffected while anything quieter than that is turned down or "expanded." Set it at –40dB and the loudest 40dB of your track will remain unchanged while the rest is attenuated. Once you have decided whether you're trying to expand or gate your track and have the threshold level set, adjust the Range and Ratio controls to create an effect that's exaggerated and abrupt, or smooth and subtle.

Adjusting the Range control next seems alarming at first, since it seems like your audio signal is falling off a cliff. It even looks that way on the graphic display (Figure 5.45), since something like a –10dB range below a threshold of –20dB looks like you're flushing a lot of your audio away.

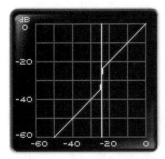

Figure 5.45   Even a –10dB range looks like a severe drop on the graphic display.

The Range control can be set as high as 0dB, which effectively turns off the processor, or as low as –80dB for more extreme noise-gating. The Range control allows you to select both the decibel range over which the processor will be active and the maximum amount of gain reduction that will be applied. So, the –10dB range you just saw is a relatively mild expander setting and can be made less severe by changing the slope of the drop with the Ratio control.

Once you've set the threshold point and range of the Expander/Gate, adjust the ratio, which determines how noticeably the level will drop as the signal strength falls below the threshold. The ratio is still expressed as a value of X:1 decibels as it is for a compressor, but in this case the relationship is reversed. For every 1 decibel lower the signal falls, the plug-in will reduce the output by X decibels, *until* the range is met. That last bit is really quite important though, so consider how that works out. If you set the previous example to a 2:1 ratio (Figure 5.46), you'll see that the sudden drop doesn't seem as severe.

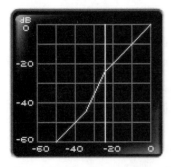

Figure 5.46   Set a ratio of 2:1 and the sudden drop won't seem so severe.

The default settings of the Expander/Gate Dyn 3 plug-in land well over on the gating side rather than the expanding side. But an expander can be set to be very subtle, opening up the dynamic range of tracks that might have been over-compressed or that just need more breathing room. The Ratio control can be set anywhere from 1.0:1, which is effectively off, to 100:1, which should drop your level like a brick. Use the higher setting of both the ratio and range to gate drums or to drop out low-level noise from wind, traffic, or HVAC. But remember: it's the lower settings, 1.2:1, 1.5:1, or 2:1, where you can use the plug-in to restore some dynamic contrast to your tracks.

Attack, Hold, and Release—Don't Let the Gate Hit You...

Placing either an Attack, Hold, or Release control within an expander/gate processor presents an interesting problem. Whether you think the gate opens to let loud sounds through or closes to keep quiet sounds out is like arguing over whether the glass is half full or half empty. Both ideas are similar, but you need to consider what the programmers were thinking so you know whether the attack time controls the speed of the gate opening or closing.

The programmers for this plug-in seem to have tried to cover both points of view. The Expander/Gate Dyn 3 functions as any gate should, by turning the signal level down (or off) as it drops below the threshold. But they have reversed the labeling of the Attack and Release controls so they describe the speed of the gate opening (attack) and closing (release). It seems like the obvious way to do it, especially if you're familiar with MIDI and the ADSR envelope. But believe me—it's not so obvious for the plug-in. Even the plug-in manual has it listed wrong, explaining that both controls adjust how quickly the processor turns down signals as they drop below the threshold.

So, to make sure you're following me, here's a diagram to show how these controls are working (Figure 5.47). The Attack control changes how quickly the processor opens up (deactivates) to let sound through. The Release control changes how quickly the processor closes (reactivates) to turn the signal down.

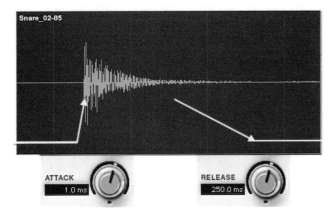

Figure 5.47 Attack adjusts how quickly the gate opens, and release adjusts how quickly it closes.

The attack time can be set anywhere from 10 μs (microseconds) at the fastest to 300 ms at the slowest. It seems to make more sense to have the gate open instantly—and it does for some sounds. Percussive sounds (drums) that reach their maximum volume levels right at the beginning of each note usually need very fast attack settings, if you want to preserve that initial attack sound … but maybe you don't.

Setting the attack time a little slower helps smooth hard consonants on vocals and take the edge off percussion attacks. But it can also wreak havoc on vocal intelligibility, so be careful how far you go with that kind of effect. If you want to try it but aren't sure if you've gone too far, have someone who isn't familiar with the lyrics listen to see if they can still understand all the words.

The Hold control adjusts how long the Expander/Gate is held open, regardless of whether the signal level drops back below the threshold. It's adjustable from 5 ms to 4 seconds, so you can choose whether the gate will stay open across a series of short sounds or attempt to close briefly in between each of them. For a vocal track, try setting the Hold control between 250 and 500 ms to make sure the Expander/Gate doesn't drop out quieter sounds in the middle of words. Set it a little longer if the person is speaking slowly, pauses a lot, or is generally soft-spoken.

At the other end of each note, the Release control also has a range from 5 ms to a full 4 seconds. Release times should generally be set long enough to cover the full decay time of the note, unless you want to (or need to) cut them short. A quick release time can ensure that any system or environmental noise is dropped out quickly as the note decays, but it can also be used for creative effects.

Try setting a fast release time with a high threshold on an electric bass or rhythm guitar track. It can deliver a very cool, on/off, staccato effect, as if the track is pumping sound in and out. It's an effect you can't get any other way unless your bassist is really good at palm muting. For most acoustic instrument sounds, you could safely start with a release of about 200–250 ms, and then adjust up or down from there to catch just the right spot.

Looking Ahead

One problem when using an expander or gate on your audio track is the risk the gate won't open fast enough for your sound to get through. It's an ironic opposite to the problem of a compressor not moving fast enough to control quick, transient sounds. In this case, however, it's a problem of missing the fast transients that you *do* want to hear, which is especially common if you are running gates on percussion tracks, since percussive attacks happen fast. If only the gate could see a moment into the future to make sure it's able to open in time. And as it happens….

Under the Options section, there's a button that switches on or off the Look Ahead feature (Figure 5.48). As the name implies, this feature allows the plug-in to glance into the future to watch the signal level for anything that might pop up above the threshold.

Figure 5.48 Use the Look Ahead feature to avoid losing fast transients.

When using Look Ahead, start opening the gate 2.0 ms before a sound crosses the threshold level so you are certain to protect those fast transient attacks. You've probably seen plenty of movies and know a trip into the future always comes at a price, and in this case the price is delay. Even if you aren't using the Look Ahead feature, the plug-in reserves the CPU or DSP processing time and the delay time in case you decide to activate it. So the Expander/Gate has a longer internal delay time than the other Dynamics III plug-ins, longer by about 88 samples at 44.1 kHz, which happens to be about 2 ms worth.

So as long as you're paying for the delay time on your system, why would you want to turn the Look Ahead off? Well, sometimes you might *want* to lose some transients.

If you're working with an instrument or voice that has a harsh-sounding attack, you might like to soften it by turning off the Look Ahead function and stretching the Attack time just a little longer. That can deliver the effect of a tiny fade-in at the front end of each note. I'll describe this idea in more detail in the usage examples.

Side-Chain Section

The Expander/Gate Dyn 3 plug-in includes the same side-chain section that you'll see in the Compressor/Limiter. It can be activated in two different ways, with an external Key Input or with its own two-band equalizer.

A side-chain signal is the split copy of the incoming audio signal that is measured and used to activate a dynamics processor (Figure 5.49). You can create some interesting effects if you alter the signal with an equalizer or use a separate audio signal to open and close the gate.

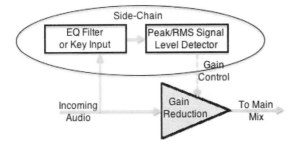

Figure 5.49 The side-chain signal is measured and used to control a dynamics processor.

Altering the side-chain signal or using an external input as the control signal of the compressor causes the plug-in to behave differently when it's processing the audio signal. One way of altering the signal is to process it with an equalizer (Chapter 4), which is why the onboard Side-Chain section of the Expander/Gate Dyn 3 includes two filters (Figure 5.50). Two filters are provided and are labeled as HF and LF (high frequency and low frequency), although they both can cover the complete frequency spectrum from 20 to 20,000 Hz.

Each of the two Side-Chain filters can be switched on and off independently, and each can be set to either a Band-Pass or a Roll-Off filter. The Band-Pass filter drops off the audio signal above

Figure 5.50 Two broad-bandwidth filters are provided in the Side-Chain section.

and below the center frequency at a rate of 12dB per octave, leaving only a narrow band of mid-range frequencies to trigger the processor. The HF filter can run as a high-frequency roll-off filter that drops out everything above the corner frequency at a slope of 12dB per octave. The LF filter covers the other end of the spectrum, dropping anything below the corner frequency at a slope of 12dB per octave. Neither of the two filters can boost the side-chain signal in any way.

The idea here is to reduce the level of certain frequency bands so the gate opens for sounds in certain frequency ranges but not for others. It can be a little confusing at first, but with some practice it makes a little more sense. If you are trying to use an expander on a snare drum track but find that the hi-hat sounds that were also captured on the channel keep opening the gate, you could try using the side-chain to drop all of the high frequencies above about 1 kHz. Then dial in an expander with a ratio of 2:1 that drops the snare drum track by about –12dB when the signal level falls below about –24dB (Figure 5.51). As always, you'll need to listen and make some fine adjustments to make sure you're dropping out the sounds you don't want, but keeping all the stuff that you do.

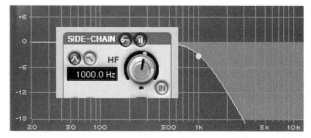

Figure 5.51 Use a High-Cut filter at about 1 kHz so the hi-hat doesn't open the snare drum gate.

To zero in on exactly the right spot to catch the target sounds, use the Side-Chain Listen button (Figure 5.52). That's the little button at the top with the drawing of a speaker.

Figure 5.52 Use the Side-Chain Listen button to hear exactly what sounds are opening the gate.

Activating the button with the key logo on it bypasses the internal Side-Chain filters and allows another signal to open or close the gate. Select a key input connection from the menu at the upper left corner of the plug-in window (Figure 5.53). This is normally fed from an internal bus, although it can be any input that shows up on your list.

Figure 5.53   Select a bus or other input to act as an external key for the processor.

There are many ways you can use this connection point. Imagine a situation where you would like one sound to be triggered every time another sound is present. The effect doesn't even have to be instant—remember that you can adjust the attack and decay time of the gate. Try creating an ethereal, other-worldly voice effect by routing your normal lead vocal track into the mix while sending a copy to another Aux Input channel. Put on a special effect like D-Verb (Chapter 6), and dial in something that sounds kind of cool. Then put an Expander/Gate plug-in after that processor and set up the Side-Chain input so it is triggered by the vocal track (Figure 5.54). The setup sounds a little more complicated than it really is.

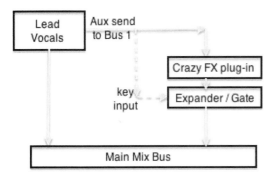

Figure 5.54   Feed a vocal track through a special effect, but use the dry signal to open a gate.

You can then set the threshold very low so the effect comes through a lot, or set it higher up so only the loudest parts get the effect, which can be especially effective with a very dynamic vocalist. And don't forget that just like the Side-Chain section of the Compressor/Limiter, you can still use the two onboard filters to process an external control signal. That means you can roll off some of the highs so your singer's hissing "S" sounds don't trigger the reverb, or roll off the lows to make sure the "P" pops don't open the gate on a pitch-shift effect

Real-Time Use (RTAS and TDM)

You can run the Expander/Gate Dyn 3 plug-in under RTAS or TDM formats for real-time use and in configurations from mono to 7.1 surround. Just remember that the look-ahead feature adds a bit more delay time to this plug-in than you'll see on the other Dynamics III plug-ins. Switching off the feature doesn't change the delay either since the time is already reserved in case you turn it back on. For newer Pro Tools 10 systems, the older plug-in versions are included since a new AAX format replacement has not yet been released. Although the automatic delay compensation that is now standard across all levels of Pro Tools 10 helps to take care of that look-ahead delay issue.

Non-Usage Example I—Gating Drums

One of the most popular (and least effective) places to use noise gates is on drums. It's a great idea considering that something like a floor tom track might only contain two or three hits over the course of a song, However, the open mic will still hear all of the other drum sounds. Using a noise gate that stays closed through most of the noise and only opens for the notes you want seems obvious, but it doesn't always work as planned (Figure 5.55).

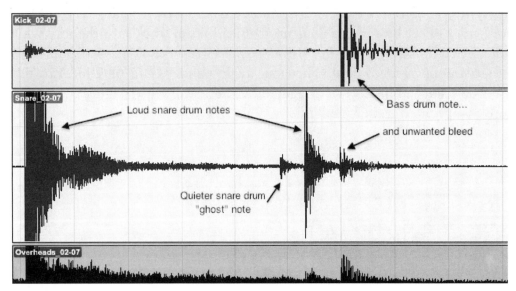

Figure 5.55 It's common for drum notes you want to be quieter than the noise you don't want.

If your drummer plays with any kind of dynamic contrast (honest, there are some of us who do), it's possible to have notes that you want to keep that are actually quieter than the sounds that "bleed" into the mic from other drums. Since the gate is only opened when the volume level crosses a particular threshold, the louder, unwanted sound will pass through while the softer, wanted sound is lost.

I personally prefer to scan through tom and other drum tracks to "manually" gate the tracks by cutting the unwanted parts out and adding fades around each note I want to keep. But that doesn't involve any plug-ins at all, and this is a book about plug-ins. Another option is to use the Expander/Gate but to automate the Threshold control. That sounds like quite a chore, but you can probably scan through, or even play through, your whole track in about five minutes and pull the threshold down to make sure all your tom notes are heard. Then push it up to make sure the gate stays closed for any other sounds that try to sneak in. It's like adding a musical "doggie door" to your track.

Usage Example II—Make Your Bass Drum Sing

One place I love using the Expander/Gate plug-in for drums isn't actually used to gate the sound of the drum. Instead, I use the bass drum track to feed the side-chain key input on a gate that is controlling a Signal Generator plug-in. The Signal Generator is set up to produce a low-frequency sine wave, and the Expander/Gate is set up to be a true gate that's closed up tight. Every time the bass drum is played, the gate pops open to let the sine wave tone through. It may seem like a strange idea, but it can be very effective for putting some life and tone back into a dull and thuddy-sounding kick.

The whole thing starts with switching on a pre-fader aux send from your bass drum since you'll need that for the side-chain key input. Then set up an aux track below your kick drum track and activate a Signal Generator plug-in there. The default sound should be a sine wave at 1 kHz that you'll want to pull down to between 70 and 80 Hz. If I'm feeling ambitious I might tune the tone to the key of the song, but usually I just go with what sounds best. Start at 75 Hz and you can adjust it later. Activate an Expander/Gate after the Signal Generator and select the aux feed from the kick as the key input. The signal path should look something like this (Figure 5.56):

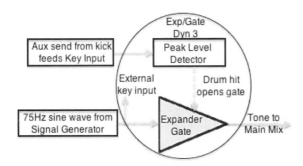

Figure 5.56 The kick track serves as the side-chain key for the gated tone generator.

Set the Expander/Gate to key off the side-chain input. Then dial in a severe gate with a range of –80dB and a ratio of 100:1. The threshold level will need to be set just below the quietest bass drum notes, but –24dB is probably a good starting point. Then set the Attack to 3 ms, the Hold to 40 ms, and the Release to 40 ms (Figure 5.57). Then it's time to listen and make some fine adjustments.

Solo the kick and the tone tracks so you can focus on just the effect you are creating. The tone should sound whenever the bass drum is played, but you'll need to adjust the hold and release times to get it just right. A shorter time will add some depth and tone without sounding artificial. Longer times can deliver that classic "808" drum machine sound. For more tone, turn up the output level of the Signal Generator plug-in.

Figure 5.57 Start with an extreme gate and set the Attack to 3 ms, Hold to 40 ms, and Release to 40 ms.

If you are getting some snare drum bleed in the bass drum track, use the Side-Chain filters on the Expander/Gate plug-in to filter the high frequencies out of the control signal. That will ensure only the bass drum gets the tone.

For hardcore industrial sounds, you can use the same technique to add a burst of pink noise onto your snare drum tracks. For electronica or dance mixes, you can use this technique with a shallower expander setting to control synth pads or bass tracks for a rhythmic pumping effect. Once you learn the basics, experiment and make it your own.

BF76 Peak Limiter—Recreating a Classic

There are good things and bad things about trying to recreate anything that's considered a "classic." It doesn't matter whether you're trying to remake a car, a film, a hairstyle, or a compressor; similar difficulties will arise. What made the original thing become a classic is a combination of the design, the parts, the time-period and marketplace, who used the originals, how they were used, and how they aged over time. To be fair, the BF76 Peak Limiter plug-in (Figure 5.58) can't even be called a recreation at all since it's actually a digital simulation of the original. But it's the thought, creativity, and effort that make this an effective recreation by any measure.

The BF76 is modeled after the famous (and classic) 1176 Peak Limiter, an analog audio processor, originally designed in 1967 by engineer Bill Putnam, Sr., that was manufactured and sold by his company called United Recording Electronics Industries or UREI for short. The 1176 limiter (Figure 5.59) was based on a new (at the time) technology called a field-effect transistor that Putnam used as the basis for a voltage-controlled, variable resistor that became the gain control element of the compressor circuit.

Basing an audio device on transistors (solid-state) versus tube circuitry generally made for a quieter, more linear performance with greater reliability. Along its production timeline, the 1176 saw several design revisions to improve its sound, noise performance, and other features. All of

Figure 5.58 The BF76 Peak Limiter plug-in is a digital simulation of the original UREI 1176.

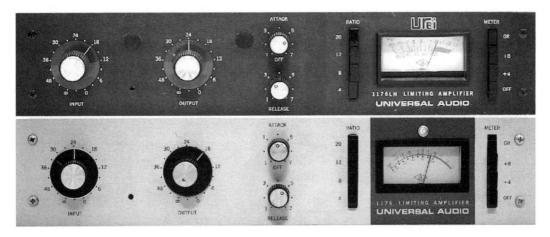

Figure 5.59 Later revisions of the 1176 wore different faceplates over similar internal designs.

the various versions were known for having a slightly bright sound as well. More of a gentle tilt than a high-end lift, this "feature" probably helped increase their popularity in the age of analog tape.

Many factors contributed to the success of the original 1176 Peak Limiter, which continues to be one of the most popular analog compressors in recording studios today. You might encounter the new reissues or even come across a highly prized vintage original—but you already have the BF-76 recreation included with your Pro Tools software. Best of all, you're not limited to the number of physical units filling your equipment racks since you can easily activate one of these famous compressors on any track, aux bus, or master fader in your session. These digital versions can also operate in stereo or with a side-chain input, both of which were a challenge on the original model. And like all the Pro Tools plug-ins, you can automate all of the controls—something none of the originals could ever do.

Where Are All the Controls?

One quick look at this plug-in and it looks like it should be a piece of cake to operate. There's one big Input knob followed by another Output knob with then just a couple of little extras that look almost like afterthoughts (Figure 5.60). But if this is a limiter, and a limiter is really just an extreme version of a compressor, where are all the other controls?

Figure 5.60   Two large knobs for Input and Output control more than just levels.

The numbers around the outside of both the Input and Output controls range from $-\infty$ to 0, which would normally suggest that they represent decibels on a digital, full-scale range. Unfortunately, though, these are the same markings as appear on the original analog units. Yes, they represent decibels, but only as a ratio relationship within the processor, not relative to the 0dB point within Pro Tools.

The Input control does, naturally, turn up the level of the signal being fed into the processor, but it also controls the threshold level of the compression circuit. That explains the absence of a Threshold control and why adjusting the input level also changes the intensity of the overall compression.

The Output control is only controlling the output level and can be thought of as the makeup gain control for this plug-in. When you have set the Ratio and Input controls to the best levels for the sound you're trying to achieve, then adjust the Output control to the output level you need. This will make up for any overall level lost to gain reduction.

Fast, Faster, Fastest, and Backward?

Staying true to the design of the original analog processor, the Attack and Release controls are labeled with values from 1 to 7 rather than with actual time values. There are good and bad things about this kind of approach. It can help your creative side not obsess about the numbers or precision and simply let your ears be your guide. On the other hand, a good engineer really should know what's going on inside and whether the numbers being dialed in can actually do the job. Is the processor actually firing fast enough to catch all of those transients and keep them under control?

It's also helpful to know if the designers are thinking the same way you are. Knowing that the controls are *backward* from what you might normally expect is kind of helpful. The values from

1 to 7 represent increasing speed on the original processor, not increasing time. That means turning the Attack knob all the way to the left delivers the slowest attack time of 5.7 ms, while turning it to the right delivers the fastest time of 0.4 ms. Either way you go, it's a pretty fast attack time. It's good to know, though, if you're going to catch that initial snare drum attack or not. Also, the fastest attack times on the original units introduced some distortion noise, and that effect is still present on this digital recreation.

The same holds true for the Release control that is at its slowest setting of 1.1 seconds when it's all the way to the left, and at a very short 60 ms when it's all the way to the right. Try to always set the release times fast enough that there are no unnatural instrument decays, but not so fast that you create a pumping sound as the limiter disengages and reengages between several loud sounds...unless that's the sound you're looking for.

A quick search online about how people like to use the 1176 Peak Limiter should turn up a few references to the "Dr. Pepper" setting. This refers to an old advertising campaign that the soft drink manufacturer used during the 1940s and '50s (Figure 5.61). The idea was based on research that showed workers' energy levels would drop around 10 a.m., 2:30 p.m., and 4:30 p.m., and so the beverage maker encouraged people to drink a Dr. Pepper at 10, 2, and 4.

Figure 5.61 The "Dr. Pepper" settings of 10, 2, and 4 became a popular starting point.

As it happens, this popular starting point is already built into the factory default settings for the BF-76 Peak Limiter. The idea is to set the attack time at 10:00 (3 on the plug-in), set the release time to 2:00 (5 on the plug-in), and set the ratio to 4:1 compression. Give it a try to see if it's the right setting to perk up a sluggish vocal track.

Ratio Switches: 4, 8, 12, 20, and British?

Four Ratio switches are provided along the left side of the VU Meter to control the compression characteristics of the plug-in (Figure 5.62). Although there are four switches, there are actually five settings available.

Figure 5.62   Four Ratio switches control the intensity of the compression.

It's certainly not as flexible as the continuous control of the Compressor/Limiter Dyn 3, but these four switches are an accurate representation of the original processor and should cover most of your needs. As with any Ratio control, these switches select the relationship of the input level to the output level, or the intensity of the gain reduction that will be applied. For a ratio setting of 4:1, for example, the incoming signal is left alone until it crosses the threshold point. Then the signal is attenuated so that for each additional 4dB of input signal, there will be only a 1dB increase of the output signal. Higher ratio settings mean more intense compression. The following options are available:

- **20** — Selects a 20:1 ratio (hard limiting)
- **12** — Selects a 12:1 ratio (mild limiting)
- **8** — Selects an 8:1 ratio (severe compression)
- **4** — Selects a 4:1 ratio (moderate compression)
- **All Buttons In** — Selects a modified 20:1 ratio

The All Buttons In mode can be selected from the presets pull-down menu or by holding the Shift key while clicking any of the four Ratio switches. This sets the compressor in an extreme setting that is often called "British Mode," because it was popular among many British engineers of the late 1960s and early '70s. The setting exploited some odd characteristics of the original analog processor and is recreated here in the plug-in.

Part of the characteristic sound of this extreme setting comes from the stacked Ratio switches that change the compressor's behavior. The ratio does not go to any higher setting, rather it lands somewhere between the 12:1 and 20:1 settings. But it causes the processor to act more like an optical compressor. Since the FET transistor in the 1176 acts as a variable resistor, there is a point where it reaches maximum resistance. At this point, the compressor can't continue to reduce the incoming signal, and the ratio returns to a 1:1 relationship, although it is attenuated by the maximum amount available. This mode also affects bias points around the circuit, constantly alters the Attack and Release times, and increases distortion. Taken together, all of these change the tone and noise characteristics of the processor, making it as much a tone-shaping effect as a dynamics processor.

The details of what goes on inside the original analog processor are a little more involved, but also dive a little deeper into circuit design and electrical engineering. When it comes to the BF-76 Peak Limiter's recreation of this effect, the designers replicated the sound of the effect rather than the method. This also happens to be one of those effects that's best to hear and then decide whether or not it can help your sound. Try it on an electric bass to get some bite and growl out of the sound, or on hard rock vocals to really put them up in your face. This kind of "British" sound isn't about tea and crumpets.

Is That a VU Meter?

The original, analog 1176 Peak Limiter had a VU meter, so why shouldn't the plug-in version have one as well? The first reason it shouldn't have one that leaps to my mind is that you're not working with analog audio signals. The calibration range is different and that makes the meter considerably less useful than if it had been designed to *look* like the original but *act* like a digital meter.

Four switches appear to the right of the meter and they serve to change the behavior of the meter to suit various situations (Figure 5.63). Ironically, the –18dB and –24dB settings are not original values, they were chosen for the plug-in version, but the designers might have done better by sticking to the original.

Figure 5.63 Four selector switches change the behavior of the VU meter.

The default setting of the VU meter is in the GR position, which inverts the meter to show how much gain reduction is being applied by the processor. This is a very helpful feature to show how dramatically the processor is changing your audio signal. Unfortunately, the integration time is still set to a rather long time span, which means the meter responds too slowly to show how peaks are being controlled and simply shows an average of the gain reduction over time.

The two switches in the middle of the column are labeled –18 and –24 and are designed to recalibrate the meter so 0dBVU is equal to either –18dBFS or –24dBFS respectively. Unless you are working with very quiet passages, they might as well be labeled "almost pegged" and "pegged." Don't get me wrong: I generally advocate recording levels that are a little quieter so you don't risk clipping on the way in, and if you have a track that is averaging a level of between –24dB and –18dB, then the meter will show you most of that average range. But even if your average level is that low, it's not likely your peaks will all stay that low.

The catch here is that there's only 3dB of headroom above the 0dBVU point before you run out of meter. This means that peaks that are any higher than –15dBFS are going to peg the meter when you're in –18 mode. It also means that if you're at a louder part of a song and have a sound (or even a mix) averaging a level of about –15dBFS, then you're going to peg the meter. Using the –24 mode only makes matters worse.

The original analog units had selections of +8 and +4 for the meter recalibrations, which would both have set the meter calibration above the ranges available on the BF-76 plug-in. This would be equivalent to –10dBFS and –14dBFS ranges respectively, and either would do better at displaying how close your signal is to clipping at digital full-scale.

The last selector button turns the meter Off, which is nice for when you find yourself getting obsessed with the numbers and need to get back to trusting your ears instead.

Extra Features—Linked Stereo, Side-Chain, and Audio Suite

One of the most important extra features available in the BF-76 plug-in (that you probably never even considered as a bonus) is its ability to operate in stereo. That may seem like an obvious feature for most any plug-in, but remember that the original 1176 compressor was (and still is) a single-channel unit. Two units could be linked together for stereo operation, but this required the studio to own two units, and to wire them together with an extra interface module, *and* to calibrate the link so the two units would fire together. That last part is key: Stereo compressors need to fire together; otherwise the image will appear to drift to one side or the other as the signal levels are changed.

You can activate the BF-76 Peak Limiter as either a mono, multichannel stereo, or multi-mono stereo plug-in. You can operate a single channel when you're working with just a mono track like bass, snare drum, or vocals. You can take care of two tracks with a single control if you want to compress or limit your drum overheads, piano, or stereo mixes. Or you can run split control of a stereo pair so each side is compressed independently if you are working on a stereo sub mix of something like auxiliary percussion, rhythm guitars, or sound effects.

A feature that is noticeably absent from the original analog 1176 limiters and even many of their current reissues is a side-chain connection. That's not a particularly unreasonable oversight since the unit was designed to be a limiter and not a compressor. That means the amount of gain reduction applied is likely to be more severe unless you keep the settings at fairly low levels. Nevertheless, this is a feature some engineers modified into their original units, and it's included with the BF-76 plug-in (Figure 5.64).

Simply selecting a key input connection from the Side-Chain pull-down menu is all that it takes to use a secondary input to control your BF-76 plug-in. You might choose to use a different signal than the one being processed by the BF-76 to create a ducker effect, or you might use a copy

Figure 5.64 Selecting a side-chain key input from the pull-down menu is all it takes.

of the signal that's sent through an equalizer to create a de-esser effect. How you choose to use the side-chain is entirely up to you. The good news is that you don't have to open up the box and solder in your own connectors to make it happen.

You'll also find that the side-chain key input for the BF-76 Peak Limiter is available for the Audio Suite version of the plug-in as well. An older version of the plug-in documentation might tell you that you have to select a side-chain input or the Audio Suite version won't render your audio clip at all, but that's not the case. It will default to key from the audio you've selected, but you can also choose to have the plug-in keyed from any other audio track. It can't key from a bus in Audio Suite mode since that would require all of the other real-time effects to be running, which also means that you can't run through a real-time EQ filter. So de-essing isn't an option, but you can trigger the plug-in from a secondary audio track.

Real-Time Use (RTAS and TDM)

The BF-76 Peak Limiter is available as a real-time plug-in under both RTAS native and TDM formats. Pro Tools 10 systems currently include only the RTAS and/or TDM versions since a newer AAX format has not yet been released. In any format, the BF-76 can be activated in either mono, stereo multichannel, or multi-mono configurations. Mono instantiations should run exactly as you would expect, but it's always worth taking a moment to consider how you would like the processor to run for your stereo tracks.

A multichannel stereo configuration will allow the gain reduction processing to be triggered by either the left or right audio signal and will affect both channels equally. That will alter the average dynamic range of the track without changing the stereo balance.

A multi-mono approach will allow each channel to operate independently. This means one channel may have a loud enough peak to activate the gain reduction, but only that channel would be attenuated. The stereo balance will shift slightly to the opposite side for a moment while the uncompressed track is louder than the compressed one. To avoid that kind of wobble, stick to multichannel stereo or keep your multi-mono configurations linked together.

Usage Example I—Vocals, Vocals, Vocals

For many decades now, some of the greatest engineers in the business have sworn by their UREI 1176 Peak Limiters for mixing vocal tracks that sell platinum records and win Grammy awards. With that in mind, along with the knowledge that the BF-76 Peak Limiter is a pretty faithful recreation of that original, give it a try on some of your vocal tracks.

One trick I am partial to when it comes to vocals is layering multiple equalizers and compressors at very light settings to slowly dial the sound up to the level I need. This requires fairly light compression settings and very careful listening to make sure you're not layering on too much of the same colorations. The BF-76 is designed to have some of the same slightly bright top-end as the original 1176, so too much can make an overly bright lead vocal.

Start by listening to your lead vocal to see if you need any initial EQ adjustments. If you have some heavy plosive ("P" pop) sounds, muddiness, or hissing "S" sounds, you may want to tame those a bit with an equalizer in the first plug-in insert point. Then activate a BF-76 in the second plug in position and dial in these settings to start (Figure 5.65): Leave the Attack, Release, and Ratio settings at the "Dr. Pepper" settings of 10:00, 2:00, and 4:1.

Figure 5.65 Set the input to –4dB of gain reduction (about 35) and the output to 15.

Play the track and adjust the Input control until you are getting about –4dB of gain reduction and push the Output control up to 15 for a little bit of makeup gain. Listen carefully to make sure you're not coloring the track too much. If the tone has shifted a little, add another equalizer plug-in to the third insert point and shave a little bit off any frequency bands that seem to be pushing a little too hard.

Once things are rebalanced, add a second BF-76 to the fourth insert point. This time set the attack faster at about 3:00 to catch the fast transients, and set the release time to about 12:00. Leave the ratio at 4:1 but push a little harder on the Input control until you get about –8dB of gain reduction. Then push the Output level up until your channel meters are showing peaks just shy of the orange segments; that should be about –3dB.

Your average level will still be lower, so don't worry that you've overdone it. The track might even still be a bit soft for your needs, if it was originally recorded at a lower level or you have a very dynamic singer. If that's the case, just push the Input control up a bit more until it's pulling down by about –12dB and adjust the Output control to keep the channel meter hitting around –3dB.

The idea is to put a substantial amount of compression onto your lead vocal track so it can be pulled up to a powerful position at the front of your mix, but without adding a lot of the obvious sounds of severe compression. Compressing in two stages with an equalizer rebalancing the tone of the track in between can pull a lot of power, sustain, and articulation out of your vocals without letting any frequency band get out of control.

For very dynamic vocalists, you might try compressing a little more with the first BF-76, perhaps 8dB or even 10dB of gain reduction and makeup gain. Double-check the tonal balance and adjust the equalizer as needed. Then use the second BF-76 as more of a limiter with an 8:1 ratio and only about 4dB to 6dB of gain reduction, along with enough output gain to push the peaks up to about –2dB. You might get a little more of the characteristic grittiness, but you'll also get a vocal track that's ready to be front and center in your mix—right where it should be.

Audio Suite Use

The BF-76 Peak Limiter is also available as an Audio Suite plug-in to render your tracks offline. All of the same controls and features are available and you can, as always, copy and paste settings from a real-time version to the Audio Suite version and back again. This is great for running a quick finalizing limiter on a rough mix to send home with the band as a daily disc. Also use it for rendering your tracks offline to save system resources.

The Audio Suite version also contains a couple of optional controls so you can change how the plug-in deals with your audio clips (Figure 5.66). These are two extra drop-down menus in the upper left of the plug-in window.

Figure 5.66 Two pull-down menus in the Audio Suite version select operation mode and side-chain.

If you are processing a stereo audio track, you can choose to run the plug-in as either a linked stereo effect in stereo mode, or you can run it as independent mono channels in the mono/left mode. You can also select any other audio track to act as a side-chain key input if you are running a side-chain process like a ducker. Since the Audio Suite rendering will run offline, you cannot select an aux track or mix bus, and the key input will not be run through other real-time processors.

Usage Example II—The Magical Mastery Tool

It may not be dying to take you away, but this is a setup that can really help a daily rough mix, a drum sub mix, or maybe even your whole final mix. The 1176 Peak Limiter has been an incredibly popular audio processor for decades, and lots of engineers have found many ways to use it. The characteristic sound can make for a great bus compressor. This same technique could work as a real-time effect, but let's say you're grabbing the audio clip of your rough mix and making a quick export file to burn onto a CD to send home with the band overnight.

Open up the Audio Suite BF-76 Peak Limiter and dial in these settings as a starting point. Set the input to 30 and the output to 18. For up-tempo rock, set both the attack and release times fast at about 6 (3:00 on the dial). For slower/softer tracks you might lengthen the release time a bit. Then set the ratio to 8:1 and watch the gain reduction on the meters. The setup should look like this (Figure 5.67):

Figure 5.67 Set the BF-76 input to 30, output to 18, attack and release to 6, and ratio to 8:1.

Hit the Preview button and watch the GR meter. Dial the Input control up or down until you're getting 4dB or 5dB of gain reduction. (Hint: Turn the input up for more reduction and turn down for less.) Then watch the bar-graph meters at the bottom of the Audio Suite plug-in window and turn the Output control up as a makeup gain until the highest peaks land where you need them—probably just below 0dB for a rough or final mix.

While the BF-76 Peak Limiter is a digital simulation of the original analog processor, it has a pretty authentic sound. The light amount of compression, the subtly bright-sounding, top-end push, and that little bit of harmonic coloration can really pull a mix together and give it a sense of urgency and excitement.

For a little more edginess, pull the output down a bit, dial the Input control up until there's 10dB–12dB of gain reduction, and then bring the Output level back up to just below 0dB.

If you're using this on a final mix that's headed for a CD, back the Output level down to about –2dB and follow the BF-76 up with a Maxim limiter. Use the BF-76 for the vintage tone and classic color, and then use Maxim to lock your output firmly at –0.5dB and to dither the final audio file down to 16 bits for the CD. That's a one-two punch that just might roll up to take your mixes away.

Maxim

One of the toughest parts of creating finished, polished, and professional-sounding tracks is getting the overall levels to land in the right place. Compressors and limiters are designed to control the dynamic range and place the highest peaks where you want them, but it's hard to get it right when you're looking at the peaks from the bottom-up. Wouldn't it be easier if you could change them from the top-down instead?

Imagine setting a maximum level for your mix and then adjusting the input level and threshold points together until you get a stronger, more controlled sound, without going over your limit. Maxim (Figure 5.68) takes this idea, delivers it in an effective yet simple interface, and goes a step further. It uses a look-ahead feature to make sure it sees bigger peaks coming and adapts to them before they become a problem.

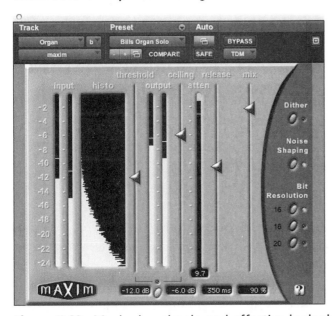

Figure 5.68 Maxim is a simple and effective look-ahead limiter.

The controls may appear simple, but there's a lot of power packed in there. Maxim also provides a lot of information to let you know what's going on with your sound, including a histogram that doesn't appear on any other plug-ins. The best place to start is with the information Maxim offers up to you.

Better Sound through Metering

Four meters are included to show the ins, outs, and in-betweens of what Maxim is doing with your audio. First in line on the left side of the window are the Input meters (Figure 5.69) that

Figure 5.69 Input meters display the top 24dB of incoming signal level.

display the level of the top 24dB of the incoming audio signal. Two meters will appear for a stereo version while one meter will appear in the mono and any other channel configuration from LCR to 7.1.

Next to the Input meters is the unique histogram display (Figure 5.70). This strange-looking window displays the relative number of peaks that reach a particular volume level. The graph is calculated as audio clips that are played through the plug-in and can be reset at any time by clicking inside the window.

Figure 5.70 The histogram display shows how many peaks reach a particular dB level.

A particularly wide horizontal line in the histogram display means you are getting a lot of peaks at that volume level. This can help you to decide where you place your threshold and Ceiling controls to adjust how much limiting is applied.

To the right of the histogram is the Output meter, which doesn't have dB level markings but is referenced to the same values for the other meters, so it also shows the top 24dB of the processed signal being sent out of the plug-in. One meter will appear in mono and multi-mono configurations, while two meters will appear in the multichannel stereo version of the plug-in. Watch this meter to make sure your output signal is not clipping and to gauge how your average level is changing compared to the Input level.

The last meter provided in Maxim is the Attenuation meter, an inverted meter that shows the amount of gain reduction being applied to the processed signal (Figure 5.71). The scale is the

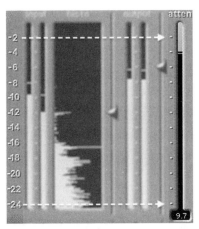

Figure 5.71 The Attenuation meter shows how much gain reduction is being applied.

same –24db to 0dB as the other meters, but an orange line will extend from the top downward to show how much the gain is being reduced above the threshold point.

Three Parameters Make for an Easy Limiter

Although a limiter is simply a compressor set to a more extreme setting, there are only three basic controls to adjust for Maxim to deliver your perfect sound, compared to the six controls of the Compressor/Limiter Dyn 3 plug-in. Three controls are all you need to get the job done with Maxim.

The best place to start is actually in the middle of the plug-in window with the Ceiling slider (Figure 5.72). This control allows you to select the maximum level you would like your track to output, between –24dBFS and 0dBFS.

Figure 5.72 Adjust the Ceiling slider to select the maximum output level of the plug-in.

If you are using Maxim on an individual track, channel, or subgroup, then this control should be set somewhat lower. This will control the dynamic range of the track but still leave you some room for other tracks to be added in the final mix. If you are using Maxim to limit a mix or output bus, then adjust the Ceiling closer to the maximum level.

I love using Maxim as the last stop for my mixes as they leave Pro Tools, and I generally set the Ceiling at −0.5dB rather than 0.0dB. I do this because when recreating the electrical signals that will be sent to the amplifiers, digital-to-analog converters use oversampling to calculate smooth waveforms. Some of these smooth waveforms will extend higher than the peak levels recorded in Pro Tools if the sample point happens to lie just a little before or after the actual peak of the wave. Extending the range too far can cause peaks that actually exceed the 0dBFS level once they are back in the analog domain, and that might cause clipping or distortion. So as a safety net, I set the ceiling just the tiniest bit below the full 0dB level.

After you've set the output ceiling where you want it, press play to get some audio running through your track and watch the histogram report of where the peaks are falling. Then slowly pull down the Threshold control to contain your loudest peaks and, of course, listen to the change in your audio signal since it should be getting louder.

The Ratio control that would normally be on a compressor or limiter is automatically shifting to accommodate the difference between the Threshold and Ceiling levels. That's why your audio track will get louder and louder as you pull the Threshold control lower: the overall amount of compression is changing, and the makeup gain is automatically being applied to bring the highest peaks back up to your ceiling point.

To make it easier and quicker to apply absolute limiting with no change in the average volume level, you can use the link feature (Figure 5.73) that is activated by the button in between the threshold and ceiling numerical displays at the bottom of the plug-in window.

Figure 5.73 Click the Link button to lock the threshold and ceiling levels together.

Linking these two controls will make them move together as you click and drag either one of the sliding controls. This means you can set an absolute, ∞:1 limiter right at your maximum output level for the track.

It's All About the Timing

The last control slider that changes the limiting function of Maxim adjusts the release time. But this begs the question, "What about the attack time?"

I've already mentioned that Maxim is a "look-ahead" limiter, which means that Maxim places audio in a buffer so it can be analyzed ahead of the current playback location. This is bad because it makes a huge delay time on the plug-in, which makes it basically impossible to use live or on a monitor track being fed to your musicians. Use the automatic delay compensation or a Time Adjuster plug-in (Chapter 7) to adjust for the delay. Luckily, it's all worth it since Maxim is fantastic for its functionality as a limiter.

As a look-ahead limiter, Maxim doesn't react to incoming audio peaks as they happen. It sees them coming and starts adjusting the level before they arrive. This preserves the original sound, clarity, and much of the dynamic contrast of fast attacks, from percussion and other sounds, while still keeping the levels under control.

So you won't see an attack control since it's effectively a perfect attack time of zero, but there is a Release control to adjust how quickly the limiter lets go of the gain reduction. Because Maxim has no attack time, the Release control has a very noticeable effect on the character of the limiter. If you are using more extreme settings for heavy limiting, you should probably use proportionally longer release times to avoid the pumping effect you may get when the processor is forced to activate and deactivate in response to changing signal levels. Lengthening the release time can smooth out these changes. Use short release times on material when your audio has fewer peaks that aren't as close to each other. You can set the release time to any value from 1 millisecond to 2 seconds.

Extra Controls for Flexibility and Convenience

There's a fourth sliding controller provided, the Mix control, that allows you to adjust the blend between your processed and unprocessed signal. That's kind of an unusual control for a dynamics processor, but one that you'll see more often with special effects plug-ins in later chapters.

So what's the Mix control doing here? It allows for an extra layer of flexibility in using Maxim at other points throughout your mix—not just as a final bus limiter. Mix literally controls the balance between unprocessed signal and processed signal, or limited and unlimited audio. It probably doesn't seem to make much sense that you might limit your audio signal to stay within a certain dynamic range, just to mix in a little of the original signal that isn't being limited, but it's a common technique normally referred to as "parallel compression."

The Mix control in Maxim can be set to blend anywhere from 0% processed (wet) and 100% unprocessed (dry) to the default setting of a 100% wet mix. Any setting in between would provide a blend of the two, allowing for some of the immediacy of the original attacks to be blended with the longer sustain of the compressed signal. It's an effect you could certainly use on an entire mix, but it's probably more at home on a sub mix, drum overheads, or sound effects. Any sound that can benefit from having some of the presence and immediacy of fast transient attacks combined back in with the processed signal is a good candidate. And don't worry about those unprocessed attacks clipping your output. They won't be amplified at all, so if they aren't clipping on the way in, they're not going to clip when mixed together since anything less than 100% dry will turn down the level of the dry signal against the wet one.

Dithering Down the Bits

Just to the right of the Mix are three more buttons that offer an extra convenience feature to Maxim called dithering (Figure 5.74). These buttons activate the dither feature, select whether noise-shaping will be employed, and select the bit resolution of the final output signal. Dithering is explained in much more detail in Chapter 8 where two other dither plug-ins are described.

Figure 5.74 Maxim also provides a convenient dither function for your final mixes.

Activating the dither feature should only be done when you are using Maxim as a finalizing limiter on your final mix. Dithering involves adding a layer of controlled, low-level noise designed to mask other noise and digital artifacts that may be lingering down at the lowest volume levels of your track. If you use the dither on other tracks within your mix, these layers of noise will build upon each other and may become more noticeable. Click the Dither switch to activate this feature and then select the next two options.

Selecting the Noise-Shaping option applies a layer of low-level noise that is filtered with an equalizer so it avoids the most sensitive ranges of human hearing. The idea is to ensure the noise layer does the job it needs to do while staying as inaudible as possible. Select the Noise-Shaping option when you are working with extremely quiet and delicate material where the listener's attention will be focused on the quiet subtlety and detail. Leave the option off for louder material that can benefit from more effective noise control without critical attention.

The third option is the bit resolution of the final output. Since the point of the Maxim limiter as a finalizing processor is to push your mix up to a stronger overall output level, you will be reducing the total dynamic range of your output signal or file. A digital signal can, in theory, deliver a dynamic range of about 6dB per bit of resolution. That means a 16-bit sample should yield a 96dB dynamic range; a 20-bit sample should deliver 120dB of dynamic range; and a 24-bit sample should get you 144dB of range.

It doesn't really work out that way, but that's the theoretical yield. In reality you can easily get more than 100dB of dynamic range between the loudest 0dBFS signal and the inherent noise of your system. That's much more dynamic range than the average listener will be able to hear on anything but the most extravagant home hi-fi systems. That's the whole point of compressing and limiting your projects in the first place. But what do you do with the excess range? The bit resolution control answers this question by throwing it away...in the best way possible.

If you are working with 24-bit original sessions (and you really should be), then all of the processing you do from a simple level change to the most complex special effects will shrink your dynamic range by building up low-level noise. The dither process adds to this in an attempt to mask it by layering controlled noise over the rest—like putting a rug down to hide the condition of old, worn-out, wood floors. That might be a bad analogy, since it would mean that changing the bit resolution throws out the rug and the floor beneath it, but that's kind of the point.

Lowering the output bit resolution preserves your broad dynamic range by eliminating the "least significant bits." Those are the bits that represent the quietest signals, and you already know there's nothing down there but lots of noise. By cutting those bits, you can drop them out before your signal is sent to its final destination. Since your final destination is likely to be a CD track that can only deliver a 16-bit signal, why would it matter if bits 17–24 are changed from noise to nothing? Better still, the final, 16-bit file can be written without a sample-rate conversion, which means it will simply take the last 16 bits it needs. That will deliver a file with the full 96dB of dynamic range. If the low-level noise were still there, it would be incorporated into the bottom of the 16-bit file, which would make it louder and further reduce your dynamic range.

This might seem too technical when you're just trying to learn about a mastering limiter, but it's a useful bonus feature Maxim makes available to you. So if you are using the plug-in on your final mix, try adding the Dither function. Set it to 20-bit resolution if you are outputting to a file that will be uploaded to another project or program. Set it to 18-bit if you're feeding the signal to older digital systems that might be running at an 18-bit depth (not likely anymore). Or set it to 16-bit if you are outputting the mix to a CD or to software that's expecting a 16-bit file.

Real-Time Use (RTAS and TDM)

When I was mixing across a console to an outboard CD recorder, I ignored Maxim because I thought of it as purely a finalizing limiter, and I already had one of those as an outboard processor. A few years ago I shifted things around in the studio, and while I still mix across a console, I now route the mix back into Pro Tools for mastering. I started using Maxim as the last step in my recording chain, and it quickly became one of my favorite, must-have plug-ins.

It's obviously useful as a finalizing limiter, but don't overlook its potential in other places throughout your work. It can be run in real-time as an RTAS or TDM plug-in, although there's no AAX version yet, but those environments both still work for Pro Tools 10. Maxim will also run in mono, linked stereo, and multi-mono formats from two channels all the way up to 7.1 surround.

The only problem with using Maxim all over your mix is that the delay time is *huge*! Remember: this is a look-ahead limiter exclusively, and in order to peer into the future to see what's coming, the plug-in is receiving the incoming audio signal and holding on to it long enough to know what's coming next. The lowest delay time is 1,024 samples and it goes up based on the sample rate you're running. Delay compensation is a must. It can't be running while you're tracking or overdubbing, so the real-time applications are limited with this limiter.

Usage Example I—A Finalizing Limiter with Parallel Function

Did I mention that I love using this as a final limiter on my mixes? Here's my starter setup: I bring the mix in from the console through an audio track that will record the mix and an aux track to run the mastering processors. I might drop in an equalizer or other processors on the aux track, but Maxim is the last in line before that track is routed to another audio track to record the mastered track. The signal path looks like this (Figure 5.75):

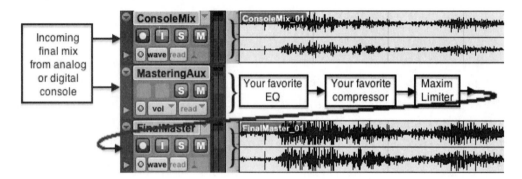

Figure 5.75 The console mix is run to an audio track and an aux track with Maxim.

Recording both the mix and the mastered audio adds flexibility. If I need to tweak some of the settings later, I can reroute the unprocessed stereo mix through the mastering channel and reprint the mastered track. Once you have Maxim set up, dial the ceiling down to –0.5dB, set the release to 500 ms, and pull the threshold down to –4dB (Figure 5.76). That should be a good starting point for a little safety net on the end of an already-strong mix.

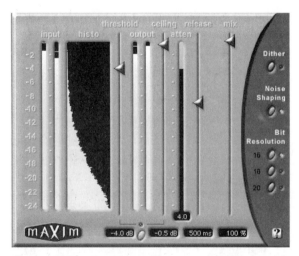

Figure 5.76 Set the ceiling at –0.5dB, the release at 500 ms, and the threshold at –4dB.

If your mix is a little quiet still and needs an extra push, pull the Threshold level down a little further. Just move slowly because the track will get a lot louder as you pull the controller down. If your track is moving a little quicker, you might also want to shorten the release time—but, again, be careful not to go too far. Too short of a release time can result in a pumping sound as the limiter engages and disengages between loud sounds.

If you have to bring the level of your mix up a lot, then don't forget about the Mix control on the right side of the plug-in. Squeezing too hard on a whole mix can really wreck the fast transient attacks in your mix, even with a look-ahead limiter as effective as Maxim. If you need to pull the Threshold control much lower than about –8dB, you should consider a parallel limiter (Figure 5.77). In this case, drop the threshold a little further still to maybe –10dB or –12dB. Bring the ceiling down as well to about –3dB and adjust the Mix control to 75%.

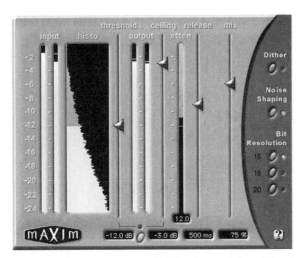

Figure 5.77 Try a parallel limiter with a threshold of –12, ceiling of –3, and mix of 75%.

This kind of parallel processing allows the original track to come through on the dry side of the mix to maintain the presence, feel, and clarity of the attacks and articulations. The processed side of the mix will provide power with the increased average level. The technique is often called "New York Compression," and there's more info about it in the "Advanced Techniques and Good Practice" section at the end of this chapter.

Audio Suite Use

A surprisingly plain-looking version of Maxim is available as an offline, Audio Suite plug-in as well. Without the meters and the dithering option, there are just four control sliders. Maxim also does not include the side-chain input or multi-mono features the other standard Pro Tools dynamics plug-ins include in their Audio Suite versions. Don't let the simple looks and streamlined controls fool you—it's every bit the same processor. And with so much delay on the real-time version, having an offline version means you can use Maxim on more tracks by printing the rendered audio before your final mix.

Usage Example II—Mixing with Maxim Offline

You can dodge Maxim's long delay time by using the real-time version of the plug-in to find the right sound and then using the Audio Suite version to print the rendered audio clip. This gives you additional access to a powerful and great-sounding plug-in for use on more tracks within your mix.

Try the technique on a pair of drum overheads or room mics where parallel compression really shines. Activate a real-time version of Maxim in the first insert position so any other plug-ins will fall in the same position—after Maxim. Set the threshold to –18dB, the ceiling to –6dB, the release to 300 ms, and the mix to 75% (Figure 5.78). The setup should look like this:

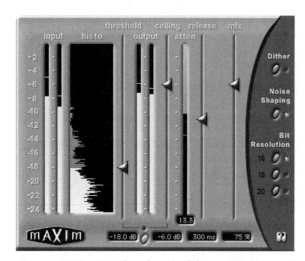

Figure 5.78   Set the threshold to –18, the ceiling to –6, release to 300 ms, and mix to 75%.

Solo the drum track, listen to the sound, and adjust the controls as necessary. Set the threshold higher (closer to 0) if the limited signal is too intense, or lower if you need more. Pay particular attention to the Mix control as well. Slide the setting up and down to hear how the wet and dry signals blend together.

If your system is up to the delay-compensation challenge, listen with the rest of the mix as well to see how things will blend. Make sure not to push the level too far with Maxim since you'll still be mixing this track with everything else and maybe even adding some other processing.

Once you have the sound where you need it, copy the settings from the real-time version into the Audio Suite plug-in and render all the clips in the drum track. Then switch off the real-time plug-in and get back to mixing. You'll have a drum track with a stronger average level that still has the punch and presence of all the original attacks—and you won't have to deal with all that delay compensation.

Advanced Techniques and Good Practice

I've mentioned a few times throughout the chapter that dynamics processors are among the most common audio tools, probably second only to equalizers. With so many engineers using so many dynamics processors on so many tracks, you can imagine how many great ideas and techniques there are to talk about. I'll bet if you searched hard enough, you'll find every possible combination of control settings recommended by someone for some instrument. That really wouldn't be very helpful.

So what I'll do instead is cover a few clever setups and some good, solid theory. This way, you know how to approach dynamics processors, what they can and can't do for you, and how to create your own perfect settings to make your music sound its best.

Doing the Math: Threshold, Ratio, and Makeup Gain

It can be a little confusing when you first try to figure out exactly how intense the settings of your dynamics processor should be. It might even seem unnecessary. Experienced engineers often reach out and turn the knobs until something sounds different, or until the numbers match a suggestion—or they reach for the settings that worked last time. "Doing the math" may seem unnerving, but it's pretty basic stuff once you know what's happening. It can also help you get the most out of your dynamics plug-ins.

With a plug-in like the Expander/Gate Dyn 3, it's actually done by setting the controls. The Range control selects how much gain control will occur, and the Ratio control selects how steeply the change will happen: not as a measure of time, but in terms of level in versus level out.

For the Compressor/Expander Dyn 3 and plenty of other compressors in the software and hardware worlds, you'll have to some quick math so you know what's going on. The Threshold control is the place to start since this setting will determine the range over which the compressor is working, and it's easy to figure out. Working in the digital world, the decibel scale you'll see starts at 0dB at the top and drops down to –infinity at the bottom. The top of the compressor range will always be 0dB, so the range is whatever you set at the threshold. Turn it to –6dB, and the compressor has a 6dB range to do its job. At –20dB, it has a 20dB range to get things under control. It's simple as that.

The Ratio control can be a little more confusing. Think of it is as the number of decibels coming in versus the number of decibels going out, though that's not really how it works since "decibels" is a measure of change. The "decibels in" is really a measure of how much louder the incoming signal is than your threshold. If your threshold is at –30 and the incoming signal peaks at –10, then there's a 20dB change in the level. If the ratio is set at 2dB-input to 1dB-output (2:1), then that 20dB of change above the threshold becomes only 10dB. It might be easier to understand with a few examples:

■ A limiting ratio of 50:1 means for every 50dB of signal level above your threshold, the output will only go up by 1dB more. To move the output to 2dB would take a 100dB change in level. (That's the difference between the quietest whisper you can hear and the loudest rock concert you might ever attend.)

- A limiting ratio of 20:1 means that for every increase of 20dB coming in, only 1dB will be added to the output. A 60dB range that represents a 1000x increase in signal strength would only amount to a 3dB or 1.41x increase.

- Ratios below 10:1 are considered compressing rather than limiting. A 60dB range would still only amount to a 6dB or 1.99x increase in signal strength.

- A ratio of 3:1 means for every additional 3dB at the input, the output will increase 1dB. This will still preserve some dynamic range. A 24dB change would be reduced to an 8dB change.

- Ratio settings of 2:1 and below are far more subtle and will retain a more natural dynamic contrast. A peak at 0dB above a –30dB threshold is a 30dB change that would be reduced to only a 15dB change.

Since so much of my work is with acoustic instruments playing classical and jazz styles, I tend to run compressors at the most subtle and undetectable levels. I'll still likely have to shrink the dynamic range by 10dB, 20dB, even 30dB to keep a track within a range that most listeners can manage, but it has to be undetectable. This means very low thresholds, soft knee settings, and ratios that are less than 2:1. Doing the math on a ratio of 1.5:1 can be obnoxious since you have to divide the range by 1.5. Think of them as whole numbers instead, and a 1.5:1 ratio becomes a 3:2 ratio, a 1.2:1 ratio becomes 5:4, and so on. From a –40dB threshold, a 5:4 (1.2:1) ratio will take a 0dB peak (40dB change) down to a –8dB peak. It might not be easier, but it helps. If you have to open a calculator on your computer, nobody will think any less of you. They'll probably think you're really smart.

Where Are the Multi-Mono Dynamics Plug-Ins?

First of all, you get extra credit for even noticing there's only one compressor option listed among the multi-mono plug-ins, and that's the Bomb Factory BF76 limiter. You will also notice the De-Esser Dyn 3 and Maxim plug-ins, but the Compressor/Limiter Dyn 3 and Expander/Gate Dyn 3 are conspicuously absent (Figure 5.79). Here's why.

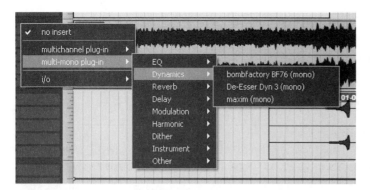

Figure 5.79 The Dynamics III Comp/Limiter and Expander/Gate don't run in multi-mono mode.

Consider what happens when you compress an audio signal—the volume levels, specifically the relationships between the softest and loudest levels, are changed. With stereo tracks, that level change can have some unintended effects. If you change the levels of both tracks together, then the track level simply shifts up and down a little. But if one channel changes without the other, then it can shift your image from side to side. Remember that a pan control shifts a mono track to the left or right by turning the signal level down on one side and up on the other. An unlinked stereo compressor will do the same thing.

Perhaps this is the kind of effect you are looking for, and, in that case, there are options for using your favorite plug-ins this way. To stick with real-time plug-ins, you can split the stereo track into two mono tracks and compress them independently. You can also activate the Audio Suite version for any of these dynamics plug-ins. There you will see a pull-down menu (Figure 5.80) that allows you to select Multi-input mode (linked) or Mono mode (unlinked).

Figure 5.80 Use the Audio Suite version to select an unlinked mono mode.

Sum and Difference Matrixing

Audio engineers have struggled with how to create effective linked-stereo compressors for decades. While the Pro Tools plug-ins largely cover this problem, there's another popular and powerful technique for final mixes and mastering. This is a little tougher to set up since Pro Tools doesn't include a sum and difference matrix plug-in. See if you can spare all the extra busses and aux tracks required. Here's the basic idea (Figure 5.81). Start with your stereo pair, matrix them to create a sum and difference channel, compress those two channels, and then matrix them again to recover the left and right channels.

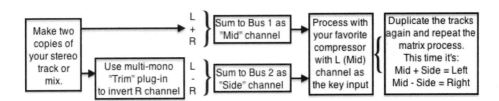

Figure 5.81 Using a sum and difference matrix for compression can create a very transparent effect.

It seems like a pretty complicated setup, but once you work it out, it's easy to operate and provides additional options. (The sum and difference part of the process is explained in more detail in Chapter 8 with the Air Stereo Width plug-in.) Any unevenness in the two channels doesn't result in a shift of the image from left to right. The processing is happening to tracks that both represent both sides of the stereo image. So when they are decoded to stereo, variations result in a stereo image that seems to get slightly wider or narrower, something that's much harder to detect.

The best part of this approach is that you can intentionally unlink the processor and change the apparent width of your stereo image. A stronger sum channel will result in a narrower, more centered, almost mono sound. A stronger difference channel will result in a wider, more diffused, stereo sound. It doesn't even matter if you are using a compressor or limiter to shrink the dynamic range, or using an expander to open it up. The process is the same, and the added ability to change the width makes all the complicated setup worth the effort. Try it on drums, piano, sound effects, a stereo subgroup, when mastering, or even on a commercial CD track for a little practice.

New York Compression

If you've ever ridden a New York City subway, crammed into an elevator in a New York City skyscraper, or pushed your way through a crowd at Times Square, or felt that rock-in-your-gut feeling after a New York street vendor hotdog.... Okay, so that's not the kind of compression we're talking about.

I'm talking about a very popular technique that goes by a lot of different names. You might see it referred to as "side-chain compression," although that term can be confused with true side-chain key input techniques. You might also see it called "subgroup compression," "upward compression," or, what I think is the most accurate term (coined by Bob Katz), "parallel compression."

The idea is fairly simple. If you just compress an audio track, subgroup, or mix, you enter into a constant struggle to push the level of the softest material up without ruining the immediacy and articulation of the fast transient peaks. Indeed, the whole point of a compressor is to attenuate those peaks so the overall level can be brought up.

What if, instead of just compressing your track, you split the track (copy it) so you can feed one side through a very aggressive compressor and leave the other side uncompressed. Then you could mix the two back together, preserving the clarity and impact of the highest peaks from the original track while pushing the level of the quietest material up from the compressed track. The only dynamics plug-in that provides its own mix control to blend compressed and uncompressed signals is Maxim, but you can still use other plug-ins with some creative setup. There are a few ways to route this around in Pro Tools (Figure 5.82) with aux sends, split outputs, or by duplicating the track.

Deciding which setup to use depends on what you're compressing. For an individual track, I like to just duplicate the track. You could also use a pre-fader aux send to route the uncompressed signal to the same output as the compressed main channel. For a subgroup or main mix, you can create two aux tracks that each receive the same bus output and apply compression to just

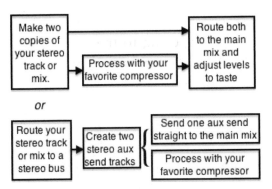

Figure 5.82 You can arrange a parallel compression setup in several ways.

one side. You can even use the Audio Suite version of any compressor plug-in to render a duplicate audio clip and then mix those together.

However you choose to set up your session, the idea is the same: heavy compression on one side is blended with very light or no compression on the other side. You still need to be careful with the attack and release times of your compressed signal to make sure you don't let very loud peaks crash through from that side and clip your outputs. With a little practice, you'll find just the right balance of increased intensity from the compressed track with the immediacy and presence of the original track. And you didn't even have to hail a cab and fight midtown traffic to get that classic sound.

What's This Side-Chain Thing All About?

Side-chain inputs can be confusing at first, but understanding how they work and why they're included with dynamics processors can open a lot of new possibilities for how you build your mixes. Remember that part of the job of a dynamics processor is to measure the incoming audio signal and use the measurements to change the output level of another signal. The side-chain is the signal that's sent to be measured (Figure 5.83), but the side-chain key input allows a secondary audio signal to be used for control.

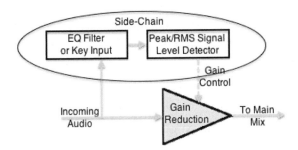

Figure 5.83 The side-chain input allows a secondary signal to control the dynamics processor.

The power of this connection point is that almost anything can be used to control the behavior of the processor. For analog processors, the side-chain provides one way to link two or more units for stereo or multichannel operation—something that's not so hard to do in Pro Tools.

Some analog processors provide a send-and-return loop for the side-chain, similar to a mixing console insert point. That allows the measured signal to be looped through another processor, like an equalizer, before it returns to control the dynamics processor. Several plug-ins have built-in equalizer filters that serve the same purpose.

It's even possible to use completely unrelated signals to control the processor. A noise gate on a synthesizer track can be opened and closed by a drum track. A compressor can reduce the level of an acoustic guitar track every time there's sound on the vocal track. You could even control a dynamics plug-in with an external microphone if you wanted the track to be processed every time you snap your fingers or clap your hands. There are lots of possibilities, but here are two common applications.

Spectral Compressing—A De-Esser for Any Frequency

If you haven't already read about the De-Esser Dyn 3 plug-in, then start there so you are familiar with how a purpose-built de-esser works. The idea in any de-esser is to reduce the gain of a track whenever high-frequency, sibiliant noise is present. The method uses an equalizer on the side-chain path to boost the high frequencies above a selectable frequency. The boosted highs on the side-chain cross the threshold level more often. That makes the compressor more likely to acti-vate and reduce the level of the processed signal whenever those high frequencies are present.

Take the same idea and consider other frequency bands. By boosting the low frequencies, you can set up a compressor so your mix bus is attenuated slightly when the bass drum hits. By boosting a narrow band in the midrange, you can raise the level of each snare drum hit so it causes the compressor to activate. You can even go the opposite direction and lower the level of any frequency band. In this case, use a low-shelf EQ to drop the low-end a little bit, which means that strong bass notes won't activate the compressor unless accompanied by loud midrange or high frequencies. This is called "spectral compression" because the compression levels vary across, and are used to reshape, the frequency spectrum.

The next logical step is to apply dynamics processors only on certain frequency bands, although there is no equalizer plug-in with side-chain control available for the level control of each filter. Instead, a more complicated arrangement must be made where the signal is split into high, mid-dle, and low frequencies. This concept is called multi-band compression (although any dynamics processor can be used), and it's an involved process explained further under the "1 Compressor, 2 Compressor…" heading.

Creating a "Ducker" or Priority Mixer

This is another specialty dynamics processor that isn't included with the Pro Tools plug-in suite because it's not commonly used in recording studios; it's more of a live sound tool.

Imagine a news conference where a large audience is listening to five people on stage who each have their own microphone. Any person can speak and their voice will be carried to the PA sys-tem, but you want the moderator or host microphone to have priority over the others. When he speaks, everyone else should quiet down to listen.

If you set up compressors on all of the guest microphones, you can feed copies of the moderator microphone to the side-chain key input. Set up each compressor with a –30dB threshold and a 1.5:1 ratio along with a 5 ms attack and a 1,000 ms release time. If an argument breaks out or a rambling speaker starts to dominate the discussion, the moderator can speak and the sound from his microphone will attenuate the other microphones. One input channel has priority over all the other channels.

You can make similar arrangements within Pro Tools to help almost any kind of project. Set up a compressor so the drum-set reverb channel is dropped –6dB every time the snare drum plays. This way the drums can sound like they are in a large space, while the snare drum sounds slightly drier and more present when it's played. Or set up a compressor so that every time your vocalist sings, her voice drops the level of the acoustic guitar track just a few decibels (Figure 5.84). Any track you choose can have priority on one, some, or all of the other tracks.

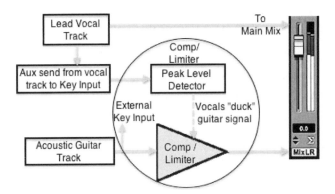

Figure 5.84 Send one track to the compressor's side-chain input for another track to make a ducker.

You can also go the other direction to create a reversed ducker that causes another sound to get louder by using an Expander/Gate plug-in instead of a compressor. If you feed a snare drum track into the key-input of an expander on your reverb bus, you can create a gated reverb effect. Set the controls so the gate stays closed most of the time but opens for each snare drum note. Leave the release time at about 500 ms so the reverb decay can ring out. Or set it below 100 ms for a very fast, dense burst of reverb sound.

Explore the possibilities for side-chain techniques. There are many ways to link, interconnect, process, and control your dynamics plug-ins, and some of them will take a little practice before feeling natural to you. Once you get the feel of these tools, you'll discover even more ways to use them.

1 Compressor, 2 Compressor, 3 Compressor, 4...

Just because the bass drum hits doesn't mean your vocal level should drop. Just because the vocalist screams doesn't mean the cymbals should get quieter. One of the difficulties in compressing or limiting an audio track is that the plug-in is designed to respond to, and change, the entire frequency spectrum.

You could use an equalizer plug-in to push the levels of the low end down while pushing the midrange up, but then you're back to the problem of using a simple channel fader to change the output level of your track. Some sounds will be louder while others are softer. Automating the equalizer is one option, but it's tedious and slow and won't catch all the subtle changes unless you put a lot of effort into the process. You know you need a dynamics processor, but how can you make it behave differently for different parts of the audio spectrum?

The solution is to use a multi-band compressor (or limiter or expander). This kind of processor splits the incoming signal into several frequency bands, feeds each split through a separate dynamics processor, and then mixes them together again.

Sounds fantastic, doesn't it? The only trouble is that Pro Tools doesn't include one. But with some help from the AIR Kill EQ plug-in (Chapter 4), you can build your own. It will even be better than a typical software or hardware multi-band compressor, because yours can be a compressor, limiter, expander, gate, or any combination of them all.

This effect is usually used on a final mix or during mastering, so we'll work from that idea—although you can use it anywhere it seems useful. If you're working from a single audio track, duplicate it twice so you have three tracks total. You can also route the output to an internal bus, create three aux input tracks that all receive that bus as an input, and route those back to your mix (Figure 5.85). Either way, you then add an AIR Kill EQ to each of the three splits.

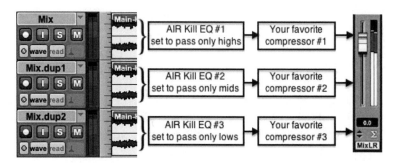

Figure 5.85 Duplicate your tracks or busses to create three copies with an AIR Kill EQ for each.

Follow the directions from Chapter 4 to set up the three copies of AIR Kill EQ as a three-way crossover. Once that's in place you can add a dynamics processor after each of the three equalizers and adjust them however you choose. The most common technique is to use three compressors set to roughly the same settings but with slightly different threshold and makeup-gain settings. Try using three copies of the Compressor/Limiter Dyn 3 with a 2 ms Attack, 350 ms Release, and a 1.5:1 Ratio (Figure 5.86). Then you can dial in different settings for the threshold and ratio for each frequency band.

Figure 5.86 Set three compressors to a 2 ms Attack, 350 ms Release, and a 1.5:1 Ratio

Then start pushing the levels around a little. Try setting –18dB threshold and +6dB gain on the lows and the highs, with –12dB threshold and +4dB gain on the midrange band. That should push the low end up for a solid foundation in the bass, pull up the highs for some sparkle and shimmer, and keep the vocals and melody under control in the midrange. Best of all, they will all fire independently, so a heavy bass drum hit won't pull the rug out from under a softer guitar or keyboard solo.

Fine-tune the settings to suit your track to get an idea of what's possible and then find a very heavily compressed commercial release and try using a multi-band expander to open it up. You can open the bottom end up a little so the foundation is still strong, open the midrange up a little more for a more dynamic melody, and open the top end up even more so there's room to add a nice reverb plug-in (Chapter 6) for a more spacious sound.

It may take a bit of work to set up a multi-band dynamics processor, but the new range of flexibility, control, and creative potential will definitely make your efforts worthwhile.

Overuse, Abuse, and Danger Zones

It's just a fancy volume control, what could possibly go wrong?

If you use them all carefully and listen even more carefully, then you shouldn't have any trouble. Then again, if the band rehearsed the song well enough, there would never be a need for a second take. Mistakes happen. They might come from simply dialing in a setting that isn't quite right, by not understanding how a particular control works, or by just plain going too far.

Cranking up the volume has the unique ability to make your track start spitting out noise from both ends. The highest peaks can start distorting as they are clipped or just crushed by the processing. On the other end, the quietest low-level system noise will tag along for the ride until it's quite audible in the mix.

Even turning down the levels with expanders and gates can cause problems. Important sounds may be cut off too quickly as gates slam closed, and clear, strong mixes can be thinned out to something delicate or just plain weak.

None of these are reasons to abandon dynamics processors in your production. As I said earlier, I've always considered the compressor the equivalent of the sustain pedal on a piano—it truly can bring out the soul in your sound. But you have to learn when to push and when to hold back. If it's all about loudness, power, and in-your-face sound, then you'll miss out on the subtlety, space, and detail. Do it, but don't overdo it.

But I'm Afraid of "Over-Compression"

Haven't you heard? It's all over the place, screaming from television, magazines, and Web sites from around the world: stuff is getting TOO LOUD!

You've certainly heard the phrase and maybe even used it without really understanding what is meant when something is called "over-compressed." That description is usually joined with a reference to the "loudness wars." I'm not saying the rumors aren't true, but I might say they're... overblown.

It's true that commercial recordings and radio airplay are getting louder. There's also a lot more history than most sources recognize (or that is appropriate here). Did it start in the 1990s, the '80s, the '70s, the '60s, or back when Edison's phonograph cylinder and Berliner's gramophone disc were rival technologies? Was it radio station DJs, broadcast engineers, station managers, record producers, mastering engineers, or musicians who demanded the louder levels? Truthfully, all that history doesn't matter nearly as much as what you choose to do about your own levels today, which are probably being set based on digital delivery via CD, DVD, or data files online.

When the compact disc (CD) first arrived on the scene in the early 1980s, mastering engineers weren't sure how to deal with the new technology, so it was largely handled with scientific precision. The specifications said that 0dB on an analog VU meter should correspond to –18dB on a digital, full-scale meter. So the equipment was calibrated that way; music was transferred from master tapes to digital data; and additional headroom went unused. Inevitably, some discs sounded louder than others, meaning they played louder on home stereo systems and on radio station broadcasts. If someone else's disc sounds louder and is getting more listener attention, it's logical you might want to crank up the volume on yours.

Before you decide to do that, here are some things you should know about your project:

- Know what kind of material you're working on. Will the Honduran marimba band need the same treatment as the heavy metal band?

- Know your target audience. Will people hear this work online, on TV, in a movie, in a dedicated listening room, or playing on the radio in their cubicle at work?

- Know your delivery system. Are you delivering uncompressed files for a larger project, download files for a band's Web site, or an old-fashioned CD to your fans?

- Know the consequences of making things louder. Will a louder track carry the same message, sound more exciting, fit in the soundtrack, or will it just be louder?

In the refresher section at the beginning of this chapter I wrote about noise floors inside and outside the recording studio to remind you the dynamic range of real-world listening environments is hard to predict. The loudest sounds will be set at whatever level the listener is comfortable hearing, and the quietest sounds should generally stay above the ambient noise floor. The space between those two points is your available dynamic range, and you'll probably never know how wide it really is.

How do you overcome this? Well, you could guess and hope. Or you can listen and measure. I describe many measurement plug-ins in Chapter 8 that can be used to analyze what's going on in your tracks as well as tracks you pull in from other sources. I like to use the Phase Scope or TL Master Meter real-time plug-ins along with the Gain offline plug-in, and the histogram display in Maxim to see what other engineers are doing on commercial releases, Web downloads, sound effects libraries, and files they send me for mixing or mastering. These tools provide a good view of where the peak levels are landing and how the average level changes throughout the track.

Once you have a basis for comparison, you can decide whether your own project should have a dynamic range that's wider, narrower, or about the same. I find that most of the finished mixes I produce land at an average level somewhere between –30dBFS and –15dBFS, with most of them landing within the narrower –18dB to –24dB range. The loudest peaks are almost always set to hit just below the 0dBFS mark. When I'm exporting tracks for another project or for someone else to master, I aim toward a lower average of maybe –24dB to –30dB and keep the loudest peaks down around the –6dB mark to make sure the next engineer has room to work.

The important thing to remember is that you shouldn't be mixing purely by the numbers; you have to listen to the sound as well. Remember that different parts of the song may well hit different average levels. Averages are just that, averages. The quiet acoustic guitar solo in the middle of the song might be a lot softer than the skull-splitting last chorus. If you push too hard across the whole track, you're going to lose the impact of that difference. Also, don't try to push the average level up to –12dB just because someone else did it, and don't drop it down to –30dB to avoid being too loud. Listen to your track and put it at the level that sounds best to you.

Every Time the Cymbal Crashes, the Level Drops

A cymbal crash is supposed to be loud, isn't it? So is an explosion in a film soundtrack or the primal scream when your singer comes back in after the ripping guitar solo. This kind of problem is common when using compressors on drum overhead tracks or whole mixes. There are several causes and several ways to fix them.

One problem can be bad compressor or limiter settings. When a cymbal crash or other loud peak appears, the compressor will spring into action to turn it down. If your incoming signal is running at an average level that's far below the peak level of the cymbal crash and also below the threshold setting of the dynamics plug-in, you're likely to run into trouble. Couple this with a higher ratio setting and maybe a slow attack time, and the problem gets worse. Try any one, or more, or all of these solutions:

- Use a lower threshold setting. This will make the compressor active through more of the track so the gain reduction is less obvious.

- Use a gentler ratio setting. Even a ratio of 3:1 can cause a dramatic change in level when the compressor activates.

- Use the knee control if it's available. If the plug-in has a soft-knee setting, use it to make the transition into gain reduction more gradual.

- Use a quicker attack time. If the initial attack of the crash comes through and then is compressed, the unnatural decay will be more obvious.

- Use a longer release time. If the compressor stays active longer, the level won't drop in between loud peaks.

As you get more comfortable with the different dynamics plug-ins and how to incorporate them into your mix, you'll reach for the most effective of these cures first.

Another problem you may run into is a compressor or limiter that's responding to an uneven tonal balance. A loud sound in one particular frequency range activates the compressor that then drops the level for the entire track. This is especially common on drum tracks, sound effects tracks, and whole mixes as well since any of these is likely to have louder-than-average peaks in different frequency ranges.

All of the previous bullet-point solutions are possible fixes for this kind of issue, but there are also other methods for dealing specifically with the tonal balance problem. One method is to run the control signal for the compressor (usually the track being compressed) through an equalizer and into the side-chain key input. By doing this you can reduce the high frequencies of the control signal so they don't activate the compressor as easily, and it doesn't change the sound of the cymbal crashes in the mix. Another possibility is to split the compression task across the frequency spectrum by creating a multi-band compressor. Here the lows, midrange, and highs are split into three tracks, each part is compressed separately, and the three are mixed back together. Both of these techniques are described in more detail earlier in this chapter in the "Advanced Techniques" section.

Just like the equalizer plug-ins of the previous chapter, your dynamics plug-ins are powerful tools for recording, editing, mixing, and mastering your projects. You'll find many ways to use them and maybe even some new ways to abuse them. Just make sure you're making great recordings either way.

6 Reverberation

This place sounds a lot bigger on the inside...

One of the most difficult terms to define in audio engineering is "realism," because the very act of recording sound is, to some degree, unreal. We choose the type of instrument and adjust the way it sounds while it is being played. We choose the room (if we can) and make minor changes to adjust how it sounds. The simple act of placing an instrument in a space means making a choice about how it will interact with the room. Acoustic energy doesn't blast out of a source like a laser beam. Instead, it spreads outward in every direction, wrapping around objects in its way. When the sound encounters an obstacle, whether it's a wall, floor, furniture, or person, some of the energy is absorbed, and some bounces back to spread across the space from a new direction.

We listen (don't forget that part) and pick out a microphone to complement the sound. It may be the only microphone you own, but you still chose that one at some point. Then it's time to figure out where to put it. We have to pick one point in space where our microphone will measure the sound energy flowing past it from all directions. Place it close to the instrument and the sound of the room isn't as noticeable. Move a little further away and the sound being recorded changes. It's easy to see how every choice we make narrows our sonic image. But which position gets us closest to what is really happening? The sound is no less real if you're recording from 5 inches away, 5 feet, or 5 miles. Each location may sound significantly different, but they're all equally "realistic."

The difference is that when we get up close and personal, we capture lots more of the direct sound of the instrument. That's fine, but it's not how we normally experience the world. Not many people are interested in sticking their heads inside the bass drum to hear their favorite band. In real life we experience real sound in real spaces, so we want our music to sound like it "really would" in a natural space. Trouble is, we can't always record where it would sound the best. So instead, we fake it.

Refresher

Reverberation processors create (or recreate) a sense of space around an instrument, voice, or other sound. It helps to understand what happens to sound in those real (and artificial) spaces. The sounds you record are going to interact with the places where you record them. Even if you try to remove all of that natural interaction, the sounds will simply seem, well, unnatural. They might not sound wrong, just unnatural. Let's review how our ears work, what's going on in natural acoustic spaces, and how reverb compares to other effects.

Fundamentals

It might be tough to capture the reality of the sounds we are recording, but for most audio production work we still want the end result to seem realistic. That probably sounds like a clever bit of double-talk but think of it this way: we might not want to hear *the room* where the sound was recorded, but we want it to sound like it was recorded in *a room*. It starts with our ears and our brains.

Hearing Our Place in the World

Our ears are constantly working to deliver information to our brains about the world around us. It's nearly impossible to be in a place that is absolutely silent, so there's almost always some kind of sound for our ears to hear. And no matter what the source of the sound may be, it still behaves like any sound we hear. It moves across the space, is absorbed by some material, and reflected by others. With so much raw data coming in all the time, our brains have developed some clever ways of putting the information to use.

As sound bounces around the space around us, the same sound is likely to pass us several times from several different directions, but at different times. Our ears hear all of those sounds, even if they are copies of the same sound again and again. Then our brains try to make sense of everything. The sounds that have a longer distance to travel, even just a few feet more, arrive a little later. The clever bit we have learned is to pay attention to the first arrival of a sound while ignoring similar sounds arriving within the first 30–50 ms. This is called the precedence effect, or the law of first wave fronts, and is described in more detail in Chapter 7 "Delay." The drawings in Figures 6.1 to 6.3 give a rough idea of the difference.

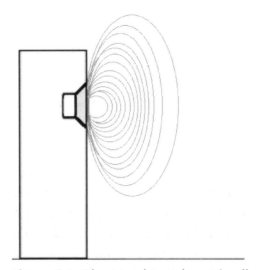

Figure 6.1 The sound travels out in all directions.

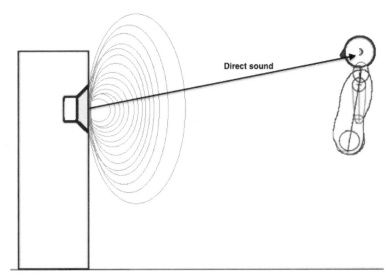

Figure 6.2 The sound traveling directly across arrives first.

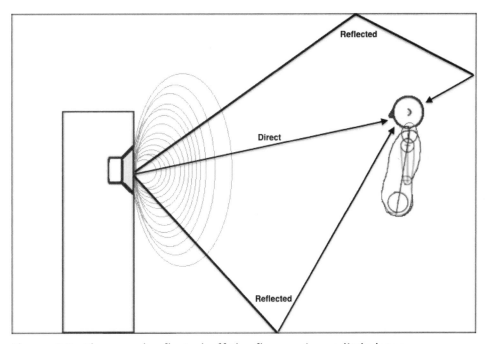

Figure 6.3 The sound reflected off the floor arrives a little later.

Sound travels 1 foot in less than 1 millisecond, about 0.9 ms. (Actually, it's about 8.865 ms per foot at 72°F, but that's harder to figure in your head.) So sound bouncing off a wall 15 feet away takes a little less than 15 ms to travel there and back. Once the sound travels far enough that it takes more than about 50 ms for the reflection to return, we hear a second, distinct sound that we call an echo. But all those extra reflections that arrive earlier aren't missed or thrown away. Our brain uses that information to tell us about our surroundings. Most of the time we don't even realize it is happening. We simply feel like we have a pretty good sense of where we are in the room around us and figure it's probably our eyes or our memory of where we placed ourselves in the room. Try this quick demonstration. Cup your hands and place them behind your ears like you see in Figure 6.4 below.

Figure 6.4 Blocking sound arriving from behind you tells your brain your back is against the wall.

When the sound arriving from behind is blocked it confuses your brain. So your brain starts telling the rest of your body that you have your back against the wall. That sense of location is actually real-time data from your ears making sure you know how far away all your boundaries are. It's part of our "fight or flight" mechanism in case we have to run away from a threat. And it's also part of why sounds without some small amount of space around them sound kind of strange. When something sounds out of place, including us, we notice it pretty quickly.

Natural and Artificial Flavors

So if the world around us is naturally reverberant, why do we need to use reverb plug-ins to create artificial reverb in the computer? If you're working with synthesized instruments or sound effects, this question may never have crossed your mind, but it's fairly common among most musicians. After all, why simulate the sound of a church when it's possible to simply record in a church? Here are many reasons why it's tough to record in real spaces:

- Real spaces have noise, whether it's electrical, ventilation, traffic, or creaky floors.
- Real spaces have schedules. You can only record when they are available.
- Real spaces require travel. You have to get the people and the equipment there.
- Real spaces can sometimes cost money to rent.
- Real spaces sound the way they sound, and that doesn't change easily.

Certainly some of these factors could apply to your main recording location as well. Whether it's a bedroom or a commercial studio, it's a real space, and real spaces have some noise. The two biggest factors that usually get in the way of using other acoustic spaces are schedule and flexibility of sound. Distance can be a factor if you're looking for something specific, like the Grand Canyon or Carnegie Hall. But even if there is a local church, theatre, or other venue that sounds fantastic and stays pretty quiet, it may be hard to schedule a time, and harder still to change the sound afterward.

Figure 6.5 Recording in a space like this might be nice but may also be impractical.

The reverb plug-ins available in Pro Tools are a modern answer to this problem that is more than a century old. Whether you're producing music, sound design, or something else entirely, we as humans expect sounds to occur in spaces. But it's hard to record in the spaces where the sounds need to occur.

For music this is usually a creative concern along the lines of wanting that one floor-tom strike to sound like it's in a canyon. But for sound design and video postproduction, it can be especially tricky. Imagine the image on the screen shows the hero running down a narrow alley in the rain. He hits some wet gravel, slides into a steel dumpster, and the crash echoes down the alley, causing the pigeons to take flight. Of course artificial reverb is going to make mixing those sounds easier, but how was it done before digital plug-ins?

The easiest way to create artificial reverb is to start with natural reverb but use it in an artificial way. Imagine recording music in the studio and then playing it back on speakers in a concert hall and recording the result. It seems like a roundabout process, but it can and did work in the early days of recording. Scheduling was easier since one engineer could work alone at any time of the day, but noisy rooms were still an issue. So studios built small, reverberant rooms in remote parts of their buildings. Those rooms could have a speaker and microphone set up and wired to the control room so audio could be sent down and returned in real-time while tracking or mixing. Some "reverb chambers" even became signature sounds for the studios, and artists would seek them out.

Specially built reverb chambers solved some of the problems of creating artificial reverb but still had some drawbacks. They were hardly portable; still took up space in a building; and in large studios with multiple control rooms, the reverb chamber schedule could get booked quickly. Plate and spring reverb units (Figure 6.6) were developed to overcome some of these issues.

Figure 6.6 Before digital, the magic boxes that made reverb looked a little different.

A plate reverb uses a thin sheet of metal as a two-dimensional model of a three-dimensional space. It acts like the still surface of a swimming pool. Drop something in the water, and the waves ripple across the surface, expanding in rings away from the impact. When the waves reach the side of the pool they are reflected back toward the middle, where they collide with the other ripples. Eventually all the reflections intersect to create a chaos of peaks and dips until they all settle down and the water is still again. Plate reverbs operate in much the same way. An audio signal triggers vibrations at one end of the plate, and little pickups capture the chaos of vibrations and reflections at the other end. A big plate simulates the sound of a big room. Spring reverbs work in much the same way but use a spring instead of a plate. These are all still artificial reverb units; the process just happens to be analog rather than digital.

Recreating Something Artificial?

Digital reverb processors, whether they are hardware boxes or the plug-ins included with Pro Tools, create reverb by processing digital audio data through a carefully designed algorithm. An algorithm is just a series of math functions applied to a digital audio signal. Think of them like recipes for different types of bread. They all use flour, water, salt, and yeast, but mix those in different proportions, bake a little longer, add an extra ingredient, and you could produce basic white bread, pizza dough, hard pretzels, or doughnuts.

The exact process will vary for different plug-ins, but it usually starts with measuring and analyzing the audio signal. Since reverberation is made up of lots of little echoes bouncing around a room, the signal is copied a few times, changed a little, and added back to the original. Then that is repeated and overlapped, again and again. This is an oversimplified view of the programming that goes into creating a good digital reverb, but it illustrates the general idea. A lot of time, effort, energy, and talent go into creating convincing algorithms.

A quick look at the Pro Tools reverb plug-ins and their preset lists shows that you have many options for different kinds of spaces. Recreating a natural acoustic space like a church or concert hall for music production, or perhaps a stairwell or car interior for video production, seem like obvious applications. But why spend the time developing algorithms to recreate sounds that were artificial in the first place (Figure 6.7)? Why fake something that was a fake already?

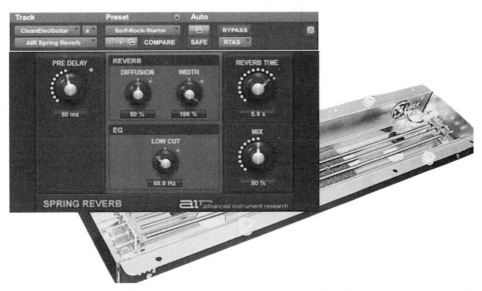

Figure 6.7 Plug-ins like the AIR Spring Reverb are simulations of analog artificial reverb.

The answer comes down to style. Although they are technically artificial reverb processors to begin with, chambers, plates, springs, and other effects have been used in audio production for a long time. Their sounds aren't quite the same as other acoustic spaces, but each still has a unique character. Over time those characteristic sounds have become familiar. The sound of a classic, 1960s, dripping-with-reverb, surf-rock guitar doesn't come from adding lots of concert hall or cathedral reverb; it comes from the metallic twang of the spring reverb built into the guitar amplifiers.

The sounds are now a part of our musical language. So naturally they have become standard-issue equipment in the audio production toolbox. But don't think they should only be used when you're aiming for something that sounds artificial. Listen to the options and get familiar with the colors and flavors they can add to your sound. Then choose what works best for each project.

Compression versus Reverb: Moving Sounds Forward and Back

Moving a sound from left to right or panning across the stereo sound field is a straightforward and familiar process. For a mono sound, simply send it to a stereo destination and turn the pan control to the left or right. There are other tricks like delaying the signal sent to one side or the other, but that's a discussion for a different chapter. Most of the time, you're likely to use a volume-based pan control. But moving sounds forward and back in the mix presents us with a few more options.

When we hear two sounds and try to figure out which is closer, our brains compare the sounds and check for a few key differences. First is volume: closer sounds are usually louder than distant ones. Volume alone isn't always enough; we also compare high-frequency content. Highs get weaker faster than lows as they travel because more of their energy is absorbed into the air. And, of course, usually there is also more reverberation as a sound moves away from us. In a closed space we hear reflections from walls, ceilings, and other objects that tell us the sound source is further away. Knowing about these natural effects can help when you're trying to place sounds in a mix (Figure 6.8).

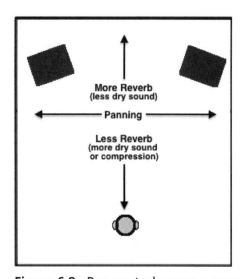

Figure 6.8 Pan controls move a sound left or right, and reverb can push a sound back in the mix.

So higher volumes, compression, and less reverb are all cues that tell us a sound is closer. Lower volume, less high-frequency content, and more reverb tell us a sound is further away. Keep that in mind while you are mixing—both as something to try if you want more depth in your mix, and as something to watch closely so your sounds don't sink too far away. With a little practice you should find it's easy to add a sense of depth to your recordings. You'll also notice some common goofs, like compressing the heck out of a bass drum while adding tons of reverb to the lead vocals. Who is going to sound like the front man in that band?

When to Reach for These Tools

Now you know more what reverberation is and some of the ways it can be generated, but that doesn't answer the questions of when and how to use it. Do you use it on every song or audio production? Should you apply it to every instrument, or just to certain sounds? Should you even add it at all?

With almost any other effect or plug-in, I would answer those questions with "maybe," but with reverb it's a resounding "yes!" Remember that in the real world every sound we hear occurs in a real space. And remember that our ears and brains work together to process reverb data in real-time to understand where we are in the world around us. Sounds that don't have at least a little spatial information in them sound artificial.

Use Reverb for Composition and Songwriting

Inspiration is one of the most important parts of any creative process. And what could be more inspiring than that splashy echo that gets us singing in the shower (Figure 6.9)? So try adding a splash of reverb when you're trying to find a creative direction for a project.

Figure 6.9 A little reverb can inspire some shameless performances.

Whether the sound you choose reminds you of a small room, a great hall, or an indoor swimming pool doesn't matter as long as it gets you going. As with other effects, don't get too attached to a particular sound in case it doesn't fit well in the final mix. Since reverberation is a time-based effect, it's important to gauge how much it is affecting the tempo or timing. If the particular setting you are using has a distinctive slap echo or delay, it may end up dictating the tempo of the project. There's more about that in Chapter 7. There's nothing wrong with that, as long as you know it is happening and plan accordingly. As you shift through writing, recording, and mixing, the tempo may want to shift up or down along the way.

If you're not sure how independent the material is from the effect, switch it off for a while. Sure, it might not sound as pretty, but how is the tempo? Try playing a little faster and then a little slower. Turn the reverb back on and adjust the Decay time (Reverb Time on some plug-ins) up and down a little. You'll quickly see how closely tied the material is to the effect. If they need to happen together, bus the processed signal to an extra audio track so you can record the reverb effect—in case any settings get changed down the line.

Use Reverb Cautiously When Tracking and Overdubbing

Regardless of how inspiring the reverb is, using a reverb plug-in during recording can be a little tricky. The latency of your particular system will likely be the biggest issue. And in case that's not enough, this is a time-based effect, which means a certain amount of delay and smearing of the time is built in.

If the system runs too slowly, the audible delay could cause confusion and become more harmful then helpful. On the other hand, even if your system runs fast enough to support feeding real-time reverb to the artist's monitor, you still need to be aware of how the performance might be changed because of the reverb. An experienced performer will adjust their timing based on how long the room rings, even if the "room" is a virtual one. Make sure your performers don't cut the notes too short, expecting the reverb to pick up the slack.

Sometimes that sound is very important to getting the right feel, tempo, or mood. But with latency or other factors getting in your way, using a plug-in may not be an option. You may have to look to a hardware option—perhaps an outboard, effects processor patched into the auxiliary send on your mixer, or maybe the spring reverb built into a guitar amp. In any case, recording the unprocessed signal and the processed signal onto separate tracks will give you the most flexibility later.

Once it's there, reverb doesn't go away—at least, not without putting up one heck of a fight. Look down your list of available plug-ins or processors in Pro Tools, or anywhere else, and count how many "Reverb Remover," "de-Reverb," or "Space Eliminator" plug-ins you find. It doesn't work that way. Remember that reverberation is made of many little echoes layered on top of the original sound. So until you are experienced enough to gauge how your raw sounds will come together in final mixes, aim for dry tracks.

Don't Use Reverb While Editing

Editing with the reverb on is like painting with sunglasses on. It might be more pleasant and easy on the ears (or eyes), but you won't get an accurate picture of what is going on. This is one part of the process where reverb probably hurts more than helps. Editing requires you pay careful attention to all the details around the beginnings and endings of each note or sound. If there's a reverb plug-in stretching out each sound, even just a little bit, that can get confusing.

It seems easy enough to switch off the reverb, edit the tracks that need editing, and then switch it back on for mixing, but sometimes it's not that easy. Let's say you're creating a composite track for a self-conscious singer or solo instrumentalist. When that lead track is soloed and played back with no effects, the artist might feel exposed and uncomfortable. Every hard articulation is clear and obvious, while all the releases seem short and abrupt. The artist may feel like none of the takes are good enough. In this case, have the reverb running but muted or at least turned way down in the mix while editing. Pop it back into the mix every so often to reassure the artist that things are still sounding pretty, and then pull it out again.

But don't let a bad edit hide behind the smear and shimmer of the reverb. It can be tempting. But there's no guarantee the reverb setting you are listening to while editing will stay the same through mixing. One little change could reveal all the things you hoped nobody would notice. So keep the sunglasses off and hear the naked truth of the recording—at least until you get to mixing.

Definitely Use Reverb for Mixing

Mixing is where all of the sounds you have brought together need to actually blend and start to sound like they are all meant to work together. Depending on the project, that may or may not mean they should all sound like they exist in the same space. A typical band recording will sound more natural to the listener if it sounds like the instruments were played in the same room. And that's not always an easy task if you recorded all the parts in different rooms. A sound design project for film, video, or theatre may need sounds to seem like they are coming from different places to be convincing. In either case, your reverb plug-ins will be powerful allies.

Like so much of mixing technique in general, learning the subtleties of applying reverb takes some time. There are many tips and cautions in this chapter to help get you started. Perhaps the most important tip is that even though it may help to add a little reverb to everything, don't add too much. It's not a magic pill that makes everything sound glossy and intentional. Yes, it may soften the edges a little to help hide some edits, or give a subtle blur to the timing. But it won't make wrong notes right. So use it, but don't overuse it.

Taking a moment to consider where you will actually plug in the plug-in will avoid overdoing it from the start. Adding just the right amount of reverb to all of your tracks doesn't necessarily mean you should add a reverb plug-in to every track (Figure 6.10). That takes lots of effort to set up and adjust and uses lots of CPU power.

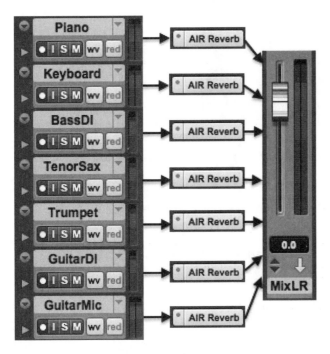

Figure 6.10 Adding a reverb processor to every track is difficult to manage.

That weighs heavily on the system resources, it's hard to manage, and usually makes every track sound like it's coming from a different space. And, unfortunately, adding one reverb plug-in to your master fader (Figure 6.11) usually isn't a good alternative.

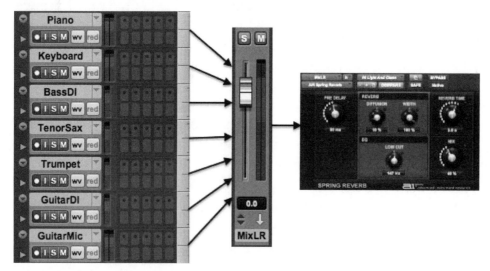

Figure 6.11 Dropping one reverb plug-in on the master bus loses individual control.

Instruments that already have a lot of sustain may not need as much extra help. The best approach is to activate a reverb plug-in on an auxiliary bus (Figure 6.12), so different amounts of each sound can be sent to the reverb plug-in.

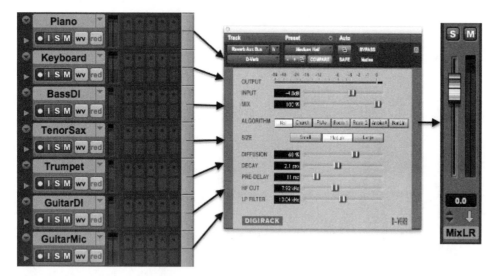

Figure 6.12 By using an aux bus for the reverb plug-in, each track has an individual control.

In this way, different amounts of each instrument sound can be sent to the processor, and the overall reverb level can be brought up or down in the final mix. This process is described in more detail later in the "Overuse, Abuse, and Danger Zones" section.

Yes, Reverb Can Be Used for Mastering Too

There are so many all-in-one hardware boxes that claim to be "one-box" solutions or, even worse, "one-button" instant mastering tools—but the only tools they provide are an equalizer and a compressor. It's enough to make a novice engineer think that's all there is to mastering. Just wait—there's more.

Reverb may not be the first tool that springs to mind when you think of mastering tools, but it certainly doesn't have to be the last. It's a tool, and tools exist to help us accomplish things. If you think mastering is something you do as soon as you complete a single mix, then, no, it's probably not a tool that will make sense. If the overall sense of space isn't quite right, jump back to mixing. Maybe you are compiling various mixes into an album, or adding a stereo mix into a sound design project, or you simply can't remix the original multi-track session. Relax and remember you have a few reverb plug-ins hiding in your toolbox.

Does this sound contradictory? Adding a reverb plug-in on your main-mix bus is usually a bad idea. That was just covered in the last section, and now the plug-in is back on the stereo bus. How did that happen? The trick to using reverb in mastering is remembering that it's all about subtlety.

During mixing it is best to have individual control over how each track interacts with the reverb plug-in. Once that task is done, you'll be listening to the final mix alongside others that will be on the same album, and one or more may sound out of place. If some of the mixes sound spacious while others feel closed in, dry, or even claustrophobic, you might need to balance things. You can't take away reverb from the spacious tracks, so the only option is to add a bit more to the drier tracks so they blend in with the crowd.

There are a few ways to add reverb to a finished stereo mix. You could drop a reverb plug-in inline on the stereo track and start playing with the controls (Figure 6.13). Place it somewhere in the plug-in chain that makes sense and works well with other effects you have running.

Pay careful attention to the wet/dry balance of the mix, since that will determine how much of the original mix is blended with the added reverb. The 80% shown would give you a dripping-wet final master for most reverb settings. Start with a setting down in the 25% range.

Another option is to arrange a parallel reverb plug-in for the mix (Figure 6.14).

In this arrangement, the reverb plug-in can be left at a 100% wet mix, and you can use the auxiliary send control to adjust how much signal is sent into the reverb processor. This will also allow you to add an equalizer or other processor to the reverb channel to change the sound of the processed signal.

However you choose to add reverb to a stereo mix, remember the original mix probably has reverb on it already, whether natural or artificial. Be careful not to make things sound muddy. Start with an algorithm that has very few early reflections. Set the pre-delay low but just enough

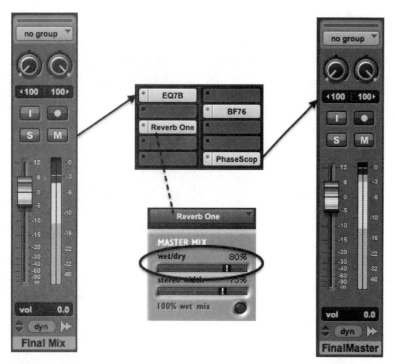

Figure 6.13 Drop a reverb plug-in inline on a finished mix and then adjust the wet/dry balance.

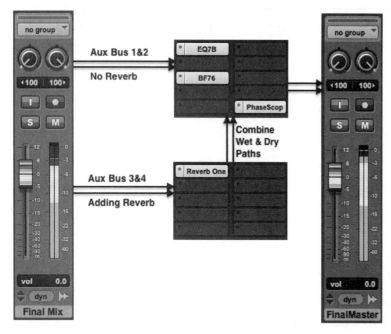

Figure 6.14 Setting up a parallel reverb plug-in makes finding a balance easier.

to stay out of the way of the articulation of the notes, maybe 15–30 ms. From there, find a nice decay time and overall wet/dry balance, then compare the results to other tracks or switch the reverb on and off. A few more subtle adjustments, and you can sneak the band into a bigger room without even having to hire a roadie.

What's in the Box?

Digital reverb processors can be designed to simulate many types of acoustic and analog reverberation, but those reverb types can't always be lumped together into a single program. An algorithm (sequence of math functions) designed to simulate a particular type of sound will require some specialized controls. Pro Tools software includes several reverb plug-ins, each designed to deliver a different sound, character, or special effect.

As with other processor types, reverb plug-ins share many similar controls. Pre Delay, Decay Time, and Wet/Dry Mix are in every reverb plug-in. If the description isn't clear to you when you're reading about one plug-in, flip back a few pages and check out another one. The controls may be identical, but none of the descriptions are copied and pasted, so there should be something that makes sense. Of course, each unique sound or feature has some unique controls as well. In those cases the descriptions will be a little more detailed.

D-Verb

D-Verb is the basic reverb processor included with every version of Pro Tools since 6.0; it runs in RTAS, TDM, and Audio Suite; and it's a great place to start when you're thinking reverb but aren't sure what kind will be right. It hasn't yet been updated to the new AAX Native or AAX DSP environments for Pro Tools 10, but don't worry because the RTAS and TDM versions work fine in the new software. The graphics aren't flashy, and the controls aren't as comprehensive as newer plug-ins, but they get the job done. Best of all, once you understand the layout (Figure 6.15) and what's going on under the hood, it's easy to use.

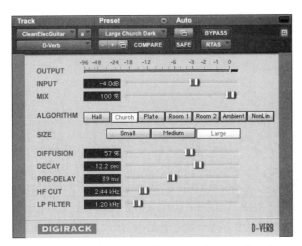

Figure 6.15 The D-Verb controls are simple and straightforward.

Level Controls

The organization of the first three items at the top of the plug-in window may seem strange. The Output meter is first, followed by the Input level control. The Input level also defaults to a value of –4dB when the plug-in is started. It may seem odd, but remember that adding reverb means adding processed copies of a sound to the original. Add a bunch of extra sound, and things get louder, possibly to the point of clipping. Also, if you're trying to make a sound seem away, it shouldn't get louder. So keep an eye on that Output meter and adjust the Input level to keep things balanced.

The wet-versus-dry Mix control operates as it does on other processors, balancing the processed (wet) signal output against the unprocessed (dry) signal. At 0% you will hear only the original signal and at 100% you will hear only the processed signal. If you have activated the plug-in on an audio track to process a single instrument or sound, then you need to adjust the control to get a good balance of dry and reverberant sound. If you are using the plug-in on an auxiliary bus to process multiple sounds, leave the mix set to 100% wet since the processed signal will be mixed with the original signals later.

The Input and Mix controls can be set where you need them and will not change if you click through the Algorithm and Size settings. However, the same is not true when cycling through the 20 factory-preset settings. The programmers figured you would be using the plug-in on an auxiliary bus so every preset defaults to –4dB input level and a 100% wet mix.

Algorithm and Size Controls

The 10 buttons across the middle of the plug-in control window visually separate the I/O level controls at the top from the reverb process controls at the bottom (Figure 6.16). Clicking on one of the seven Algorithm buttons causes the controls below to jump around, but don't mistake these seven buttons for simple presets. They fundamentally change the program and the kind of reverb sound you get from the plug-in.

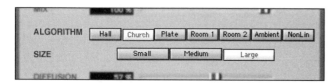

Figure 6.16 The Algorithm buttons select the type of reverb being simulated.

A plate reverb processor may serve the same function as a reverb chamber or a concert hall, but they all sound and function a little differently. It should seem reasonable that one algorithm can't reproduce all of them either. The seven algorithms change the plug-in into different reverb processors. Even though the same controls are used, the settings or even the range of control values may change. The algorithm choices aim to cover the most common reverb types.

- **Hall** aims to sound like a concert hall or auditorium
- **Church** has the diffuse, darker sound of a large, stone church or cathedral
- **Plate** has the dense and bright sound characteristic of metal-plate reverb
- **Room 1** has a more neutral, medium-sized room sound

- **Room 2** is a smaller, slightly brighter-sounding room, like a chamber reverb
- **Ambient** sounds spacious without many early reflections so there aren't clear walls
- **Non-Linear** has a natural build and unnatural cutoff to simulate gated reverb

The algorithm choices define the character and type of reverb, but they are just the starting point for the overall sound. The other controls will help to further refine the reverb process to suit your needs. Be careful about jumping to a different algorithm after you've made some changes. That will reset some of the other controls. So if you're searching for the right sound, start by finding an Algorithm you like, then adjust the Size, and then adjust the other parameters. If you need to go back and forth, use the preset save and copy controls like any other plug-in.

The Size buttons modify the algorithms and also adjust the ranges of the Decay control to allow for small, medium, and large variations of each. That means the already-large Church setting sounds biggest when set to Large, and the already small-sounding Room 2 setting sounds tiny when set to Small. While changing the size changes the range of values for the Decay control, you won't see the control sliders move, so it is safe to switch between different sizes while you're dialing in your sound.

The last five controls at the bottom of the window (Figure 6.17) are the fine-tuning controls for the D-Verb plug-in. Once you have selected an algorithm with the right character and have a rough idea of the size, you can make fine adjustments to make the sound as subtle or dramatic as you need.

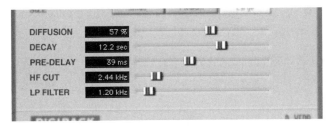

Figure 6.17 The last five controls in D-Verb allow you to fine-tune the reverb sound.

The Diffusion control always shows an available range from 0% to 100% and changes the density of early reflections in the processed signal. More early reflections (higher values) create a denser texture, as if the walls near the listener are hard and close. Be careful, though, because vocal clarity and instrument articulation can suffer if the early reflections are too dense.

The Decay time control adjusts how long the reverb will ring after a sound has triggered it. It's most noticeable with an abrupt percussive sound or when you stop playback and the sound is still ringing. The control range shifts for all of the algorithm and size combinations. At the extremes you can set decay times from a fraction of a second to infinite decay (not often a practical setting). The last setting before "Inf" is more instructive about the range of possibilities. The Decay control range for the small church algorithm runs from 200 ms to 33.5 seconds, which is hardly a small range. Some of the great cathedrals of Europe brag about reverb decays of 12 seconds. As with other reverbs, you'll have plenty more range than you'll need.

The Pre-Delay control is a confusing-sounding name. Is it there to delay something before you delay it, the same way an appetizer is what you eat before you eat to make you more hungry? Well, yeah...kind of. As with all reverb processors, the Pre-delay control adjusts the time between the original audio signal arriving at the processor and the start of the processed sound. Think of it as allowing the reverb to follow the original sound rather than riding on top of it. The control can be set from 0 to 300 ms. Adding pre-delay helps retain intelligibility and gives a sense that the sound source is centered in a larger room. Just remember that once the pre-delay exceeds 30–50 ms, you may perceive the start of the reverb as a distinct second sound.

The last two controls in the D-Verb plug-in look like they are doing exactly the same thing. After all, in the equalizer world (Chapter 4), a "High-Cut" filter and a "Low-Pass" filter are just two names for the same thing. But these two controls are slightly different. The HF Cut control sets the frequency where the processor starts changing the high-frequency decay. The high-frequency sounds won't ring as long as the low-frequency sounds. The LP Filter control operates as a standard equalizer filter, attenuating the high frequencies by 6dB per octave above the frequency you select. Both controls act only on the processed audio signal, not the original dry sound, and together they give a sense of harder or softer walls in the artificial space created by the reverb.

Real-Time Use (RTAS and TDM)

D-Verb is available for real-time processing as either an RTAS or TDM plug-in for Pro Tools HD systems. On Pro Tools LE or M-Powered systems, only the RTAS version will be available. There's no AAX version yet, but the RTAS or TDM versions work fine in the newest Pro Tools 10 or Pro Tools 10 HDX systems. Reverb processors are resource intensive, and D-Verb is no exception. So plan your mixing and processing accordingly. Adding a reverb plug-in to every track won't work unless your system is up to the task.

Audio Suite Use

Of the four basic reverb processors included with Pro Tools LE or M-Powered systems, D-Verb is the only one that is available as an Audio Suite plug-in. So for many users, it will be the only reverb processor available under Audio Suite. For that reason alone, don't ignore D-Verb for the flashier new stuff. It's a great processor with much potential, and you're bound to need it somewhere along the way.

Usage Example: One Big Boom

Mixing a project is about more than just setting a bunch of levels and sitting back while everything runs its course. There's something special that makes each piece sound unique. Finding the little moments and giving them extra attention makes all the difference.

Find a place in a song or soundtrack where adding a slightly longer or stronger reverb delivers a much bigger impact. Don't just find some random bit somewhere and overemphasize it: this is about adding something tasteful and creative. It may even be a corrective measure if, for example, the last guitar chord of the song was cut too short. Maybe you can give an extra push to the last drum hit before the rhythm section drops out at the bridge. Or make a door slam ring unusually long when the villain leaves. When you find a place where this seems like the right kind of treatment, here's a nice way to do it.

I'll use a strong, staccato, piano chord at the start of the chorus. Since this effect would only apply to one or two places in a project, it doesn't make sense to add an extra aux bus and reverb plug-in for that one note—especially if you're running short on system resources. And with other instruments still ringing, automating the reverb time would change the sound for everything. Using the Audio Suite version of D-Verb, you can select only the sound you want to emphasize, accentuate it with a bigger reverb setting, and not lose any real-time processing power to more tracks or plug-ins.

Hearing the sound before rendering the track is important, and there are two ways to do that. One is to set up a new track, activate the D-Verb plug-in for that track, pull the audio clips in, and dial up the right kind of sound (Figure 6.18). This way you can hear the sound within the context of the whole mix.

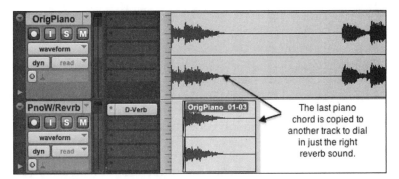

Figure 6.18 Find the right sound with the real-time D-Verb and then print it with the Audio Suite version.

Once the right reverb sound is dialed in, copy the settings to the Audio Suite version of D-Verb, print it for only the clips that need the rendering, move the clips back, and remove the extra plug-in and track. The other option is to select the clip you want to render and use the Preview function within the Audio Suite plug-in. It's considerably less work, but you can't hear it in context with the rest of the mix.

In either case, the most important thing about rendering any Audio Suite reverb plug-in is that you need to grab some extra time. If you select only the short note or sound you want to render and add a couple extra seconds of reverb, the software will only write a file as long as the audio region or clip you have selected (Figure 6.19). The reverb will be cut off too short, and you'll hear it drop off.

That defeats the purpose of adding the reverb. Selecting more time than you need looks strange onscreen since you may actually select empty space after a clip—but you are defining how long the new clip will be. If the plan is to add two seconds of reverb to a sound, make sure you select an extra two seconds after the sound you want to render (Figure 6.20).

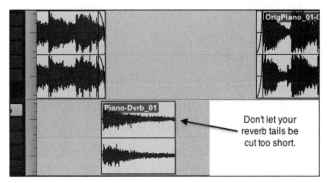

Figure 6.19 Selecting only a short clip means the rendered reverb signal will be cut short.

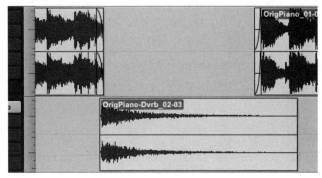

Figure 6.20 You're defining the length of the new clip, so select enough time for the reverb to ring.

You may want to extend a note that's too short, or you may want to make the sound of your hero's fist punching the bad guy sound like a thunderclap. Whether the effect you're going for is subtle and natural or over the top and obviously unreal, the method is the same. Once you render all the clips and audio regions where you want extra reverb, close the Audio Suite D-Verb plug-in and get back to mixing.

Pro Tools Creative Collection

The next three reverb plug-ins are similar in style and design, though quite different in their sounds. They are part of the Pro Tools Creative Collection™ labeled as the AIR plug-ins within your software. Instead of using the same set of controls to manage substantially different algorithms, each plug-in is streamlined to its specific task. There is a general-purpose reverb processor primarily designed to simulate natural acoustic spaces. The spring reverb processor is designed to simulate the sound of the little reverb tanks built into instrument amplifiers. And the non-linear reverb processor is designed to deliver unnatural reverb sounds for special effects.

Real-Time Use Only (RTAS and TDM)

As with all of the AIR family of plug-ins, the AIR Reverb, AIR Spring Reverb, and AIR Non-Linear Reverb are only available as real-time plug-ins running under the RTAS environment.

There's no AAX Native or DSP version yet for Pro Tools 10 users, but the RTAS version runs fine on the new software. This real-time-only limitation can be a problem if you encounter limits on your system resources. If you need to conserve processing power, do so by bouncing rendered tracks to disk or by printing your processed channels to new tracks and then disabling the original tracks as described in Chapter 3.

Mono versus Stereo

All three of the AIR reverb plug-ins can be activated as either mono or stereo plug-ins, but as of this writing none of them could be started as a mono-to-stereo plug-in (labeled as "Mono/Stereo" within Pro Tools). If you are activating any of them on an auxiliary track, this won't be an issue as you can simply create a stereo aux bus, insert the stereo version of the plug-in, and feed stereo or mono signals to it. If, however, you are activating directly into the plug-in chain for a track or mix bus, keep this in mind. You could, for example, add mono reverb to a mono track, but some of the features, like the width controls, will not function properly. If this is an issue, simply route the track to an unused stereo bus, create a new stereo aux track to catch the signal, route it back to the mix, and activate the reverb plug-in there.

AIR Reverb

The workhorse reverb plug-in of the AIR family is the AIR Reverb (Figure 6.21). It shares many of the same kinds of controls as the older D-Verb plug-in, with some streamlining, a few extra tools, and a more stylish look.

Figure 6.21 AIR Reverb divides its controls into seven sections.

As with most of the AIR plug-ins, the controls you will likely reach for the most are placed on the left- and right-side columns, with the fine-adjustment controls stacked in five sections down the middle. Also like the rest of the AIR plug-ins, the AIR Reverb interface has no meters and no input or output level controls. Keep that in mind when you set up your session and activate the plug-in. Simply follow the signal through the processor from top-left to bottom-right, starting with the Pre-Delay control (Figure 6.22).

Figure 6.22   The Pre-Delay control adjusts how soon reverberation starts.

The name can be confusing at first, but the idea is fairly simple. How soon should the reverb start? The Pre-Delay control determines how quickly the processed signal follows the original dry signal. Imagine your instrument or voice in a room. This is like a virtual distance control between the sound source and the closest wall that will bounce back the first echo. More time sounds like a bigger room; but remember, once you hit somewhere between 30 and 50 ms you start hearing that first echo as a separate attack.

Early Reflections

In natural acoustic environments, the early reflections are the first set of echoes we hear from the floor, walls, and ceiling. They help us determine where a sound is placed within a room, how big the room is, and whether the surfaces are hard or soft. Here those reflections are simulated with multiple delay taps (more on those in Chapter 7) spread across the stereo field. There are two controls in the Early Reflections section of the plug-in. The Type control is a pull-down menu (Figure 6.23) that allows you to choose the kind of space you are trying to simulate, while the Spread control adjusts the space between the delay taps.

Figure 6.23   Choose from 15 Early Reflection types, or choose none at all.

The different Type settings activate different room models that are similar to the Algorithm switches used in the D-Verb plug-in. Here, though, changing between them does not change any other control ranges or settings. But what exactly is the difference between early reflections of a church, a concert hall, or an opera house?

There isn't a good way to describe these kinds of models. The concert hall the programmer was thinking of might not sound like any concert hall you have ever visited. Short descriptions are available in the software documentation, but what is the difference between "medium and bright," "medium and live," or "medium and clear?" Experiment for yourself to hear which sounds are smaller or larger, brighter or darker, livelier or clearer. Then fine-tune the sound by adjusting how densely packed in time the early reflections are using the Spread control.

Reverb

There are three controls, Input Width, Output Width, and Delay, grouped together under the Reverb heading (Figure 6.24), with a fourth control, Reverb Time placed to the right of the group.

Figure 6.24 The Reverb section includes Width, Delay, and Reverb Time controls.

The Input Width and Output Width controls, while handy, are out of place graphically compared to their place in the signal path. Both are sum and difference matrix width controls similar to the AIR Stereo Width control described in Chapter 8. The Input control adjusts the apparent width of the incoming signal before any other processing begins; while the Output control works the same way but is the last stop before the wet-versus-dry Mix control described later.

The Delay control functions in a similar way to the Pre-Delay control described earlier, except that it adjusts the time between the start of the early reflections and the start of the long reverb tail. That is, when a sound arrives at the plug-in, the Pre-Delay adjusts the time before the early reflections start, and the Delay control adjusts how long *after that* the long reverb tail begins. Even if the early reflections are switched off, these two delays will stack. That allows for a total of anywhere from 0 to 500 ms of delay before the long reverb starts.

If it were not pulled out to the right side column, the Reverb Time control would be part of this grouping. Early reflections alone only tell part of the story of the space you are creating. Adding a longer reverb tail gives the impression of a larger or more resonant space. While the Delay control determines when that reverb tail starts, it's the Reverb Time control that adjusts how long it lasts. The setting can be anywhere from a short few ms to nearly 100 seconds or even infinite. Although a setting somewhere between 1 and 5 seconds will probably cover most situations.

Room

The Room section controls (Figure 6.25) allow for further refinement of the long reverb sound. They include the Room Size control on the left-side column as well as the Ambience and Density controls under the Room heading.

Figure 6.25 The Room section controls help refine the sound of your long reverb tails.

In a certain sense, all of these controls are meant to change the apparent size of the room, although they only affect the long reverb tail and not the early reflections. Adjust the Room Size along with the overall reverb time to adjust the overall balance of timing and sense of space in the room you are creating. Then fine-tune the size with the other two controls.

Ambience controls how quickly the long reverb develops. Think of it like a fade-in control for the long reverb. Lower settings mean a quicker build, like you would find in a smaller space; it doesn't take long for the more distant echoes to arrive. Density controls how the long reverb reflections build over time. A low setting has a more fluttery sound, as only a few long tails are returning. A higher setting sounds more smooth and rich, with lots of reflections adding to each other.

Balance

It doesn't have a heading of its own, but this is a good time to look at the Balance control (Figure 6.26) since this is where it fits into the general scheme of things. It adjusts the balance between the early reflections and the long reverb tails.

Figure 6.26 Use the Balance control to get the right blend of early reflections and long reverb.

When you first activate the AIR Reverb plug-in, the Balance will be set to 50%, meaning half early reflections and half long reverb. That's a good place to start while you are dialing in the right sound for your project. Once there, the balance control can help adjust the sense of space like so many of the other controls, but it can also give a sense of proximity. In a real acoustic setting, like a concert hall, we hear more long reverb and fewer early reflections if we are further away from the stage. Move up a few rows and the balance shifts even though the reverb time or density remains the same.

High Frequencies and Low Frequencies

At first glance these controls look something like an equalizer, but their function is quite different. The High- and Low-Frequency controls operate more like a three-way crossover (Figure 6.27) with variable timing controls for how long the high- and low-frequency reflections are allowed to ring.

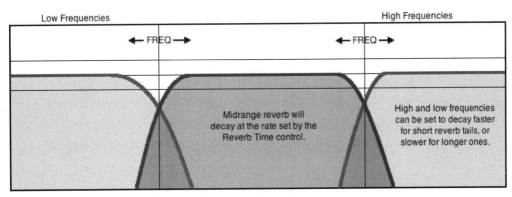

Figure 6.27   The High- and Low-Frequency controls split the signal into three frequency bands.

Use the Freq control in either the high or low section to set the crossover points that determine which parts of the signal are your low, middle, and high ranges. Then the Time control will adjust whether reflections in those ranges decay faster or slower than the overall setting. For example, if you find the overall reverb sounds good, but your low end is getting too muddy, you could adjust the crossover frequency high enough to cover the bottom of your mix, and set the LF Time to −50% lower to speed up the decay.

The Cut control in the High Frequencies section is more of a standard equalizer-type High-Cut filter. Set the corner frequency lower to roll-off the volume level of the reflections above that frequency. This will only change the processed signal, not the original dry signal, but it can be helpful if your reverb seems to ring a little too brightly.

Mix

The last control on the way out of the processor, as usual, is the wet-versus-dry Mix control. At 0% you are listening to only the original dry signal, and at 100% you are hearing only the processed reverb signal. If you have set up the AIR Reverb on an auxiliary bus so the output is fed into the main mix with the other dry signals, leave it set at 100% processed signal. If you have activated the plug-in on one individual track or mix bus, then you'll need to find a balance between the wet and dry signals. Changing settings on the Pre-Delay will only be noticeable in comparison to the original dry signal. So if you're turning that up but not hearing a result, this is probably why. Once you hear some dry sound with the wet sound, the Pre-Delay timing should be more obvious.

Usage Example: Fading Out versus Fading Away

The simple studio fade is a surprisingly controversial effect. Not controversial in the sense that politicians want to ban them for our musical safety, but controversial in the sense that some people love them and some hate them. They are no more a cliché in recording than in symphonic orchestra composition, where fading the end of a slow movement down to nothing has been a common technique for centuries. Perhaps the dislike of studio fades comes from the fact that simply turning down the volume is not enough to create the conceptual effect of the music fading off into the distance. If all you do is turn down the volume, then it sounds like all you did was turn down the volume.

If we hear a sound fading away in the distance, we not only hear the volume level decreasing, but we also hear a different balance in the reverberation. The balance of early reflections to long reverb tail changes as the ERs fade away in favor of the long tail. AIR Reverb has a unique control among the reverb plug-ins included with Pro Tools: a balance control for early reflections versus long reverb tail. Applying the plug-in and automating that control creates a far more convincing fade away.

You can use this technique on almost any kind of sound. To experiment, find a stereo track of an acoustic instrument like a guitar or piano. If necessary, import a suitable track from a favorite CD. If the track you're using already has a nice ending, use the trimmer tool to cut it off so the track ends more abruptly. (Save a copy of your work before you do anything too destructive.) Then add a linear fade of about 20–30 seconds to the end of the track so it looks something like the example below (Figure 6.28).

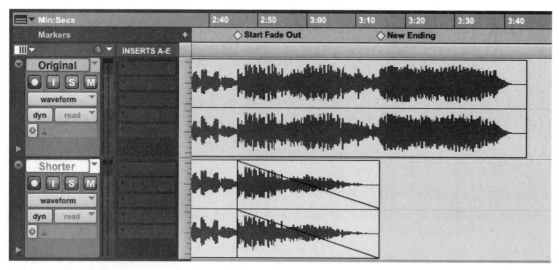

Figure 6.28 Top is the original acoustic guitar track I imported. Bottom is the same track cropped and faded out.

Now activate the AIR Reverb plug-in for the track and pull up preset "05 Medium Hall." It's an average-sounding reverb to get things started. Then adjust a few of the key settings. Since the plug-in is active directly on the track, set the Mix level to 50% dry. Then set the High Frequency Time control to –25% so the highs decay a little faster, and set the Balance control to 30% so we have more room to transition. The controls should look something like this (Figure 6.29):

Figure 6.29 Starting from preset "05 Medium Hall," make these adjustments.

Activate the automation for the Balance control by clicking the plug-in automation window button at the top of the interface window and selecting Balance from the list of controls. Then change your track view (Figure 6.30) to show the new automation control.

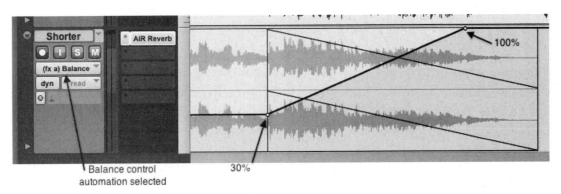

Figure 6.30 Change the track view to the Balance automation control and add breakpoints as shown.

Use the grabber tool to place one breakpoint on the 30% line at roughly the start of the fade-out, and another breakpoint at 100% about 3/4 of the way through the fade. Then listen to the result. Listen with the automation on and then with automation off to get a better sense of how it's changing the sound.

Some material will need a bit of fine-tuning to get the sound right, but the technique should be similar. If you're ambitious and want an even more realistic fade away try this. High frequencies decay faster over distance, so automate the High-Cut control too, and lower the corner frequency over the course of the fade. Or automate the Output Width control to shift higher so the space seems to expand while the sound fades. Experiment and be creative. You can use the same effect backward at the beginning of a song to create a more convincing fade-in as well.

AIR Spring Reverb

Remember that part about digitally recreating an analog artificial processor? Here's a plug-in designed to do exactly that. Analog spring reverb processors aren't realistic replacements for real acoustic spaces. Even the best sounds a little metallic with a recognizable splash of twang. However, they have been included on instrument amplifiers for so long that many people think that's what an electric guitar is supposed to sound like. The AIR Spring Reverb plug-in recreates that sound (Figure 6.31).

Figure 6.31 AIR Spring Reverb recreates the sound of an analog spring reverb.

But sometimes unnatural is the right way to go. The aim is to recreate the sound of the spring reverb from an instrument amplifier, but you can use it for many other applications. Spring reverbs naturally sound bright, metallic, and somewhat unrealistic. If you're working on a sound design or mixing project for a sci-fi film, for example, that kind of sound can give the spaces a recognizable but surrealistic sound.

What's the Same?

Several controls on the AIR Spring Reverb are similar to those found on the AIR Reverb, so a quick look at how they operate for that processor will help you make sense of them. The

Pre-Delay control is adjustable from 0 to 250 ms and serves the same function, adjusting the time between the arrival of the original signal and the start of the reverberation.

The wet-versus-dry Mix output is adjustable from 0% (all dry) to 100% (surf-rock heaven) and operates the same as on the AIR Reverb. With this reverb, however, it is more likely to be applied to only a single instrument track or bus. Guitars might sound naturally at home with a splash of springy goodness, but other sounds might not be as welcome. In that case, use the Mix control to dial in the right balance of original, dry signal and processed, wet signal.

Last is the Reverb Time control that functions much the same as it does on AIR Reverb, although the range is narrower. You can only adjust the time between 1 and 10 seconds. That seems limiting, but remember this is a model of an analog device, so certain limits are appropriate. Heck, most amplifiers don't have any control over the length of the reverb, just a single knob to control how much signal is sent through it.

What's Unique?

The center section of the AIR Spring Reverb interface (Figure 6.32) has three controls that are a little different from those in the AIR Reverb.

Figure 6.32 A trio of controls helps fine-tune the reverb sound.

The Diffusion control operates similarly to the Density control on the AIR Reverb. Use this to adjust how the reverb reflections build up over time. A higher setting means more reflections building upon each other, and a smoother sounding reverb tail.

The Width control functions similarly to the Output Width control of the AIR Reverb. It operates only on the processed reverb signal shifting from a mono reverb sound at 0% to a wider, stereo reverb at 100%. One nice feature here is that the original dry signal is left either mono or stereo as it passes through. Width only changes the apparent width of the processed signal so you can play around with stereo reverb from mono sources or vice-versa.

Also included is a Low-Cut control that, conveniently enough, operates exactly the way a Low-Cut filter should. Set the corner frequency and the volume of lower frequency sounds is reduced. Use this if the buildup of reverb reflections starts to make the low end a little muddy or just as good practice for keeping a tight low-end on your mixes.

Usage Example: Springing Life into DI Guitar

Guitar is one of the most common instruments to record in a home or project studio, and too often it's recorded through a direct box rather than through an amplifier. There is nothing wrong with recording through a DI; in fact, there are many benefits. Even when there's an amplifier in the studio, I also record the direct signal for the flexibility it adds down the line. Amplifiers form an important part of the tone and character we expect to hear from an electric guitar—and when that sound is missing, we notice its absence.

Many tools are available for recreating the sound of an amplifier, from amp-modeling plug-in software to reverse-DI boxes that allow the sound to be sent back out to a hardware amplifier. Whether you intend to use these approaches or not, you can add the flavor and flare of a great spring-reverb sound with the AIR Spring Reverb. It seems redundant since amp-modeling software has spring-reverb models built-in, and hardware amps may well have the real thing. The advantage to using this plug-in is that the controls are fantastically more flexible—and they can be automated.

Most amplifiers, and therefore most amp-modelers, have only one control for their reverb: volume. Using AIR Spring Reverb alone, or in conjunction with an amp or amp modeler, allows you to create a more customized spring reverb sound. Following are a couple example settings to try out: one for acoustic guitar and one for electric guitar with a surf-rock sound.

Since the DI input from your guitar is almost certainly a mono signal, you'll have to decide how to add the reverb since AIR plug-ins do not have a mono-to-stereo option. I suggest routing your DI signal to an unused stereo bus, creating a stereo aux input channel routed back to the mix, and activating the plug-in on the aux channel. Then dial in these settings (Figure 6.33) for an acoustic guitar. Pre-Delay to 10 ms, Diffusion to 75%, Width to 50%, Low Cut to 60 Hz, Reverb Time to 2.5 seconds, and Mix to 50%.

Figure 6.33 Try these settings as a starting point for acoustic guitar.

The DI pickups for most acoustic guitars tend to sound very bright and thin, so consider adding an equalizer plug-in before the reverb to tone down the highs and add extra weight to low midrange. With a balanced guitar sound, this reverb setting should give the right amount of springy splash without making the guitar sound synthetic. It should work well for acoustic guitar recorded with a microphone too.

For a surf-rock sound on electric guitar, the reverb should be dripping off the sound. Starting from the factory defaults, dial in these settings (Figure 6.34) to put some late-'50s twang on your sound. Pre-Delay to 50 ms, Diffusion to 50%, Width to 100%, Low Cut to 60 Hz, Reverb Time to 5.0 seconds, and Mix to 50%.

Figure 6.34 A stereo surf-rock starting point.

Adjust the Reverb Time and Mix levels to your own tastes, and with a bit of distortion from a plug-in like AIR Distortion, you might not need to run through an amp modeler. Truthfully, though, an authentic late-'50s or early-'60s surf-guitar sound wouldn't be coming out of the amp in stereo. Even most modern guitar amps still run in mono with only a mono spring reverb. You can choose whether to aim for that level of historical authenticity or not. I find this setting is a good starting point for adding this style and vibe to a modern recording where I want a sense of space as well as character.

AIR Non-Linear Reverb

Non-linear reverb is a refreshing change from all of this simulation, modeling, and recreation of natural spaces. It is blatantly unnatural—and that's the point. This isn't the reverb you are going to reach for to create a convincing concert hall sound for that solo violin recording. It's for special effects and creating strange sounds and textures.

The AIR Non-Linear Reverb plug-in adds delayed and processed copies of the original signal to simulate the sound reflecting off surrounding surfaces, but the volume level of those reflections doesn't follow the natural physics of sound. They build and decay more abruptly, creating a sound that seems more synthetic and artificial. Use it to accentuate certain elements in a song, like a classic, gated reverb for the snare drum. Or create an unearthly echo of the footsteps for the demon in your next horror-movie soundtrack. This is a creative tool meant for the engineer-as-artist more than the engineer-as-technician/documentarian.

Familiar Controls

The algorithm and the sound may be different, but many of the controls for the AIR Non-Linear Reverb (Figure 6.35) should seem familiar. The ranges may be slightly different, but the functions are similar to those found on the other reverb plug-ins.

Figure 6.35   Most of the controls on the AIR Non-Linear Reverb should seem familiar.

At the start and end of the process, the Pre-Delay and wet-versus-dry Mix controls operate the same as they do for the other AIR plug-ins. Pre-Delay controls the time between the arrival of sound at the plug-in and the start of the reverberation. Mix controls the balance between the original dry signal and the processed wet signal. If you activate the plug-in on an auxiliary bus track, it works best at 100% processed signal. If you activate the plug-in directly inline on a single audio track or mix bus, then the Mix control is important for balancing how much effect is added to the original signal.

The fine-tuning of the process is done with three controls that make up the reverb section of the processor: the Reverb Time, Diffusion, and Width controls (Figure 6.36). The Reverb Time control for this plug-in has a significantly shorter range than other reverb processors. It adjusts the length of time the reverberation rings to between 1 and 1,000 ms.

Figure 6.36   Fine-tune the sound with the Diffusion, Width, and Reverb Time controls.

The Diffusion and Width controls are similar to the same controls on the AIR Spring Reverb. Diffusion adjusts the number of reflections that build over time. Higher values mean more reflections and a more evenly sustained sound, while lower values mean fewer reflections. Since the volume levels of those reflections tend to be consistently louder, lower diffusion settings may seem like a distinctive stutter, especially with percussive sounds. The Width control adjusts the apparent stereo width of the effect by spreading the reflections out across the stereo field. As with the other AIR plug-ins, this will not be apparent on the mono version and will not affect the apparent width of the dry signal in the stereo version.

Two basic filters are also included in the EQ section of the plug-in interface (Figure 6.37). The Low-Cut control is similar to the same control provided on the AIR Spring Reverb. It reduces the low frequencies below the corner frequency of the processed signal only. The High Cut does the same on the opposite end, reducing high frequencies above the corner frequency you set.

Figure 6.37 The EQ section provides Low- and High-Cut filters to shape the sound.

Both are helpful tools for keeping your overall mix cleaner. Use the Low Cut to reduce muddiness and keep the low end of your sound tighter, and use the High Cut to reduce bright and edgy overtones. Don't forget, though, that these can be creative tools as well. Use them to pull the reverb sounds you create into a tighter midrange band for a different kind of synthetic sound.

Unusual Controls

While most of the controls provided for the AIR Non-Linear Reverb are similar in name and function to other reverb processors, two controls stand out as being somewhat unusual. The Reverse switch and the Dry-Delay control (Figure 6.38) are unique to this reverb plug-in.

Figure 6.38 The Reverse and Dry-Delay controls take unnatural sounds one step further.

Hitting the Reverse switch literally flips the reverb decay backward. Ironically, it might have a more dramatic effect if the reverb decay behaved naturally to begin with, but it can still be an effective tool for creating some interesting effects. Try it on a percussive sound like a snare drum, and you can hear the sound start soft and get louder, while the original drum sound does the opposite. Then dial up the Dry-Delay control, and you'll find it's the perfect companion for this effect.

As the name implies, the Dry-Delay control delays the dry signal while the processed signal does its thing. This means you can set up the plug-in so you hear the reverb before you hear the original dry sound. It can add a little rumble before each drum hit or lend an otherworldly sound to a vocal track.

Keep a few things in mind as you experiment with the Dry-Delay control. First, make sure the plug-in is set up on the track you are delaying. If the dry signal is sent to the mix somewhere else, that part will not be delayed. Second, make sure the wet-versus-dry Mix control isn't set to 100% processed signal. You have to hear the dry sound being delayed before it comes out of the plug-in. Third, turn down the Pre-Delay control. It only delays the processed signal and will fight against the effect you're trying to create. And fourth, all this delaying might throw off the timing of your track. That's going to make your drummer look bad, and you don't want him throwing sticks at your head while you're trying to mix.

Usage Example: Fake Reversed Reverb

Much of this example builds off of the "Unusual Controls" section immediately before this section. So if you've jumped to this page without reading that section, take a quick look at it to familiarize yourself with the Reverse and Dry-Delay controls that are unique to the AIR Non-Linear Reverb plug-in.

Why am I calling it fake reversed reverb? Well, the original reversed reverb trick is a little more complicated and comes from the venerable old analog tape machines. Tape is spooled up on one reel, gets unwound from that reel, dragged across the tape heads, and spooled up on another reel. That means the tape that's on the outside of the supply reel ends up on the inside of the take-up reel. Normally that means rewinding the tape (winding it from the take-up reel back to the supply) before playing it again. But if you simply lift the take-up reel and swap it with the supply reel, you can play the material backward.

That's not a fascinating development in itself, but it has led to some interesting experimentation and creativity. Back-masking, the trick of putting hidden messages into songs that can only be heard if you spin the record backward, is one such trick. Reverse reverb is a similar idea, where you play the tape in reverse, apply reverb to one or more tracks, and record that reverb onto an extra track. When the tape is played in the right direction again, there is an eerie pre-echo of sounds before they happen. The following trick is not the same—but it's a pretty good fake.

Decide which tracks will get the reverse treatment. If you're trying this out for the first time, use something regular and percussive, like a snare drum track. (If you are working on a real project, try duplicating the track with all of its audio clips and then making it inactive so it's available as a safety net or for lining things up afterward.) Then activate the AIR Non-Linear Reverb plug-in for that track and solo the track while you're experimenting so you can hear the process clearly.

The factory-default settings should come up; they're a good place to start as far as the reverb sound. Then change three key settings. Click the Reverse button to reverse the processed signal. Dial the Dry-Delay control up to 250 ms so the original signal is played after the reverb. And set the Mix control to 50% since you need to hear some of the dry signal to know the effect is happening. The controls should look something like Figure 6.39.

Figure 6.39   A basic reverse-reverb setting.

Put it all together and it should sound pretty convincing. Tweak the sound to your own tastes. Adjust the Diffusion and Width controls as usual to adjust the character of the reverb. Use the EQ filters to balance the highs and lows. You can also adjust the Mix control to change the balance of the effect versus dry signal. Adjusting the Reverb Time, however, is a little different. The reverb is now building up to the dry signal. It can be set to any value up to 1,000 ms, but you need to change the Dry-Delay signal to almost the same value to retain the overall effect.

Remember to keep your hands off the Pre-Delay control. Raising that delays the onset of the reverb, which defeats the purpose of a reverse reverb.

So what makes it "fake?" If you're working with a track in a larger mix, switch off the solo to hear what's wrong. A true reverse-reverb process leaves the original signal right where it belongs in time. This process is shifting your whole track out of alignment by whatever amount you have dialed in to the Dry-Delay setting. That means your track is playing late by maybe a quarter of a second or more. (Way to go, makin' the drummer look bad again.) Luckily, it's easy to fix this newly created problem.

Grab all the audio clips that are being processed by the reverse reverb and drag them backward in time by whatever amount you have set for the Dry Delay. Alternatively, you could delay all the other tracks by the same amount. It may seem like a lot of work, but all you have to do is activate and set one delay and then copy it to other tracks. I like this method because it leaves all my audio clips in their original time-stamped locations. Either way, since you know what caused the problem and the exact amount of delay, it's an easy fix. Plus you have a cool reverse reverb effect and a happy drummer.

What About the Big Guns?

The four plug-ins already described should be included and available with all current versions of Pro Tools LE, M-Powered, HD, and HDX. If you are using a Pro Tools HD or HDX system, you should find one or two other reverb plug-ins included with the basic software installation. Pro Tools HD and Venue systems include an additional TDM plug-in called Reverb One. It requires at least one HD Core card be installed in the host system. And Pro Tools HD Accel systems should include the ReVibe plug-in. It requires that at least one HD Accel card be installed. Both are powerful, professional, and sophisticated reverb processors designed for high-end studios and production houses.

These two processors are not covered in as much detail here for a couple reasons. First, they are not included with all of the Pro Tools systems, only the high-end, professional, Pro Tools HD, HD Accel, and Venue systems. They are also sophisticated pieces of software with many flexible control options. To give each of them the kind of detailed descriptions and usage examples they deserve would easily double the length of this chapter.

Most important, though, these tools are geared toward expert-level users. That's not to say novice or intermediate-level engineers couldn't or shouldn't use them, or that this text is only intended for beginners. But if you don't recognize most of the controls on those reverb processors without looking here, back up and learn the basics on something less complicated. Think of it like learning how to drive. You woulnd't want to start with something as complicated as an 18-wheeler—it's overwhelming. Instead, you start out on the nice, easy, four-cylinder automatic. That doesn't mean we're demoting you to the audio equivalent of a tricycle. That AIR Reverb is at least as challenging as learning to drive that expensive sports car your cool uncle drives to all the family reunions.

So, only a small amount of the unique features of Reverb One and ReVibe will be covered here. Any of their controls that aren't explained are similar enough to the ones on D-Verb or AIR Reverb that you can look them up there if you need a refresher.

Reverb One

The Reverb One's control interface (Figure 6.40) is divided into halves. The left side is packed with control sliders with familiar groupings and labels. The right side sports three graphic displays: two that look like equalizer graphs and one that's a little different.

Starting on the left side (to keep you waiting eagerly for the cool new stuff), you'll see basic reverb controls. The Master Mix section includes a wet-versus-dry mix control, a stereo width control, and a convenient switch that pops the plug-in to 100% wet mix to quickly hear only the processed signal while dialing in a nice balance. The Reverb section contains all the controls you would expect to dial in a nice, long reverb tail; decay time, diffusion, pre-delay.

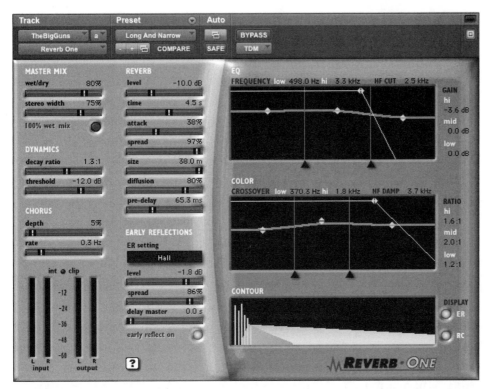

Figure 6.40 Familiar controls on the left are countered by three large graphic displays on the right.

The Early Reflections section starts with a pull-down menu with 16 space simulations, from rooms and studios to plate and non-linear settings. That menu is followed with level, spread, and delay controls along with another convenient on/off switch just for the early reflections. The balance between early reflections and long reverb is controlled via separate output level controls for each. That is a nice feature in some ways, but it's tougher to automate a shifting balance between the two than the single Balance control included on the AIR Reverb plug-in. The pre-delay for both reverb and early reflections is also independent, so don't let the label of "Delay Master" in the ER section fool you: it only moves the distinct delay taps as a group.

In the left-side control cluster, the most obvious departure from other reverb plug-ins is the addition of two sections labeled Dynamics and Chorus (Figure 6.41). Each of these options adds another level of creative possibility.

Dynamics

It's not quite a typical dynamics controller like a compressor, limiter, or gate, but the control mechanism of the Reverb One Dynamics section follows a similar idea. The volume level of the incoming signal is measured, you set a level threshold, and when the signal exceeds that threshold the processing is changed. In this case, however, it's not the volume level of the processed signal that changes; it's the decay time of the long reverb. The plug-in can be set so reverb rings longer on loud parts and shorter on quiet parts, or the other way around.

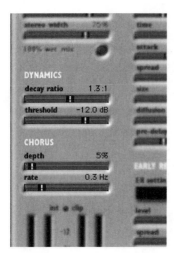

Figure 6.41 The Dynamics and Chorus sections add even more creative possibility.

To use the Dynamics section, watch the input-level meter to get a sense of where to set your threshold. If the level isn't clear enough, use a plug-in like Phase Scope or TL Master Meter (Chapter 8) to get a closer look. Slide the Threshold level to the left and set it low enough to catch all of the louder peaks you want to treat differently. It has a range from 0 down to –48dBFS. Then adjust the Ratio control to the left or right. Lower values (less than 1:1) deliver longer reverb times for the quieter material below the threshold, while higher values (greater than 1:1) mean longer reverb for the louder peaks. The ratio is a multiplier of the decay time set in the Reverb section. A value of 2:1 means the reverb for the louder peaks will ring twice as long. A setting of 0.5:1 means the reverb for the quieter material will ring twice as long.

Chorus

Since reverb processors add multiple copies of a sound back onto the original, it isn't a stretch to add a slight detuning feature to some of those delayed echoes to create a chorus effect. The Chorus section provides two simple controls to add a light chorusing effect to the processed sound. Adjusting the Depth control changes the amplitude of the sine wave driving the LFO that shifts the pitch up and down. Higher settings produce a more intense modulation and more noticeable effect. Adjust the Rate control to change the frequency of the LFO from a slow warble, to a distinct vibrato, all the way up to an audible range that will produce frequency modulation (FM) effects. It's adjustable from 0.1 Hz (that's one cycle every 10 seconds) up to 30 Hz.

Graphic Displays and Controls

The true standout feature of the Reverb One interface is the group of three graphic displays on the right side of the window (Figure 6.42). Two of them, however, are more than displays. They are the graphic controls for the tone-shaping controls.

The bottom of the three displays is labeled Contour, and it is purely a graphic display. It generates three stacked images representing the early reflections and the long reverb tail that can be viewed separately or together. The vertical axis of the graph represents signal, while the

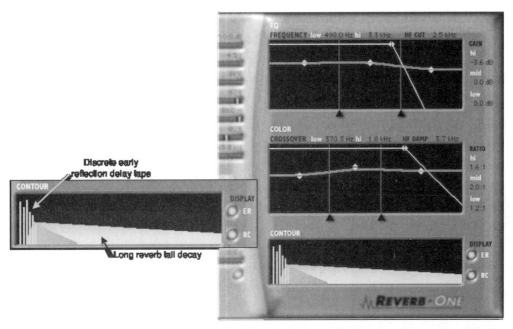

Figure 6.42   Three displays give a graphic depiction of what is going on inside the plug-in.

horizontal axis represents time, starting with an offset from the left side to illustrate the pre-delay. The representation of the long reverb tail shows the time from initial attack to full signal level, and then the gradual decay over time. The representation of the early reflections is overlaid in front of the long reverb. It illustrates the attack and decay envelope of this portion of the reverb sound. The early-reflections display also includes vertical yellow lines that represent distinctive individual delay taps.

The other two displays are different in that they are controls as well as displays. Click a breakpoint marker and drag it up, down, or side to side to adjust the control values displayed above and to the right of the display. The topmost graph, labeled EQ (Figure 6.43), is indeed a flexible equalizer for the processed signal. It provides four filters to shape the tone of the reverb.

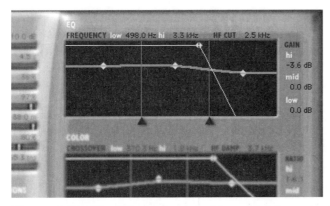

Figure 6.43   The EQ display provides graphic control over a three-band equalizer, plus a High-Cut filter.

Three bands of boost/cut equalizer are provided, including a low shelf, high shelf, and peak/notch midrange. Corner frequencies can be set for the low- and high-shelving filters, but the frequency center of the peak/notch filter is fixed. And just in case that isn't enough tone-shaping capacity, there is a 6dB/octave High-Cut filter with an adjustable corner frequency that can be adjusted to help tame an overly bright reverb tail.

At first glance, the middle display, labeled Color (Figure 6.44), looks like another equalizer, but it's designed to control the reverb-decay time.

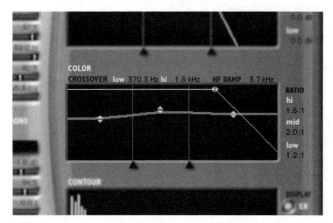

Figure 6.44   The Color graphic controller adjusts decay time instead of signal level.

As with the equalizer, you can simply click a breakpoint marker and move the control values around. High- and low-crossover point controls allow you to separate the processed signal into three bands. The relative decay time for each band can then be set to ratios higher than 1:1 for longer decay times or lower than 1:1 for shorter decay times. The corner frequency setting doesn't provide an instant shift to the new level. So, for example, set the breakpoint higher by an octave or two than the low frequencies you want to affect to make sure you catch them.

The last controller in the Color section that looks like a High-Cut filter is actually a high-frequency dampening control. Since high frequencies lose more energy to the air and absorptive materials in a room, it is natural they should ring a little shorter than lower frequencies. So this is different from the high-shelf style controller. Instead of adjusting the ratio up or down by a fixed amount above the corner frequency, this controller sets a corner and then cuts the decay time above it progressively shorter.

Online Help
The designers of the Reverb One plug-in realized you might need explanations close at hand. So, included in the plug-in interface is an online help function—not the kind that opens a Web browser or dials a $3-per-minute call to tech support. Simply click the name of any controller in the window, and a text box opens with a short reminder of what that controller does.

ReVibe

Looking at the progression of reverb processors from D-Verb to AIR Reverb to Reverb One, you see a steady increase in sophistication, complexity, and control options. Continuing this progression leads to ReVibe, which can be described as "more." More, more, more, more. It can process more channels, from mono to 5.1 surround. It has nine algorithms, along with over 200 early-reflection room types, and lots more control.

With all of that power under the hood, ReVibe is a truly comprehensive piece of software. But it's not a great place for beginners to start. The complexity can be intimidating, leading novice engineers (and pros alike) to select sounds only from the many factory-preset options and never learn all the plug-in has to offer.

Look across ReVibe's interface window (Figure 6.45), and you see much similarity to the Reverb One display. The controls are designed in a similar way, and they share many of the same labels and group headings.

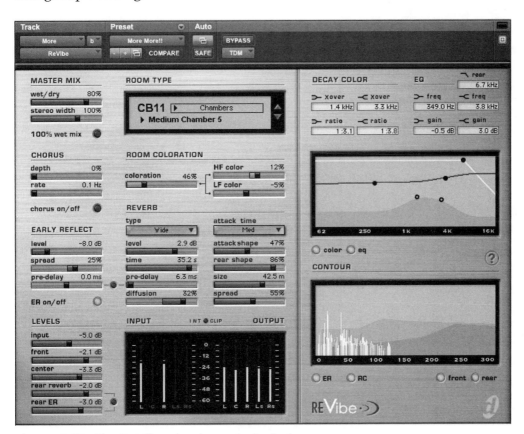

Figure 6.45 The ReVibe plug-in control window.

There is one place where there is less: the Dynamics section included with Reverb One is not present in ReVibe. But the Master Mix section and Chorus sections look and operate the same, and the other control sections are similar with a few extra features. There are only two graphic display/controls on the right side of the window, but not because anything was taken away. The

Decay Color and EQ graphic controls have been overlaid into a single display window. The big additions here are the early-reflections options and the multichannel controls.

More Early-Reflection Options   With over 200 choices for early-reflection characteristics, a simple pull-down menu is not enough. At the top-center of the plug-in window is a new display that, unfortunately, is easy to confuse with a preset-selection window. It's not. Presets are still managed above in the standard plug-in preset menu. This new display window is the Room Type menu (Figure 6.46), where all those early-reflection types are cataloged into 14 different categories.

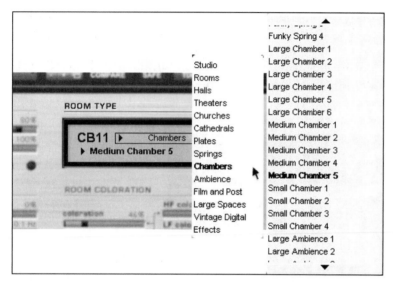

Figure 6.46   That's no preset window; use the Room Type window to select your ER model.

Having so many options can be overwhelming, even for the most experienced engineer. It's nice to be able to stick your sound into a small dark room, a large natural cathedral, or a metal garbage can (no, really, that's one of the models). But for practical purposes, it's much easier to group things into familiar categories like rooms, studios, churches, plates, springs, and even a nice selection of film and post models.

Once you've found exactly the right kind of model out of all those options, you can, of course, tweak it almost endlessly. The Early Reflections section (Figure 6.47) has familiar labels, including Level, Spread, and Pre-Delay.

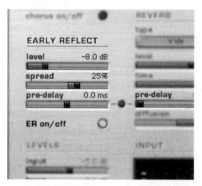

Figure 6.47   Primary controls for adjusting Early Reflections.

There are, however, two key differences in this Pre-Delay control. First, there is the control range that's adjustable from –300 to +300 ms. Negative pre-delay implies that the reverb starts before the sound arrives—but that's not what's happening. There are some room models that include built-in pre-delay, such as some of the slap-back settings. In those cases, dialing in a negative setting would counteract that effect. Indeed, you could also pull the pre-delay time back on any setting, and any delay taps that are pulled back before the arrival of the source simply won't sound.

Next to the Pre-Delay control is a Link button that links the two pre-delay controls for the early reflections and the long reverb tail. When this is active, the total of the two controls becomes the pre-delay setting, and negative values allow the early reflections to start before the long reverb.

The sound of the early reflections can also be modified using the Room Coloration section (Figure 6.48) that's located directly below the Room Type menu.

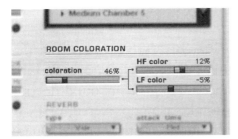

Figure 6.48 The Room Coloration section adjusts the tonal balance of the early reflections.

These controls affect only the early reflections by adjusting the amount of equalization applied within each of the room models. This has no relation to the EQ display section to the right; that section is only for the long reverb. Each room model has a built-in equalization curve to help shape the character of the sound. The Coloration control allows you to increase or decrease the overall amount of equalization applied to the early reflections, while the HF Color and LF Color controls allow you to target just the high- and low-frequency components. It's perfect for situations when the room setting is almost there, but you want to soften the walls a little by dropping the HF Color on those early reflections.

More Reverb Algorithms (Save Room for Dessert)   With over 200 early-reflection algorithms at your fingertips, you might feel you have too many options. What kind of plug-in designer would offer so many options and then leave you with only one long reverb tail algorithm? Not anyone working on ReVibe. At the top of the otherwise-familiar Reverb control heading, you should find two pull-down menus (Figure 6.49), one that allows you to select from 10 long reverb-envelope options, and another that allows you select a slow, medium, or long attack for each envelope.

Each reverb tail envelope can then, of course, be fine-tuned with the collection of controls below each menu, including Decay time, separate Attack Shape controls for front and rear channels,

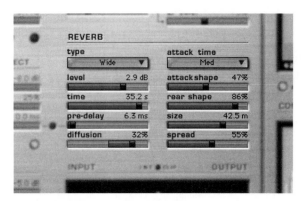

Figure 6.49 Ten algorithms and eight control parameters allow you to sculpt the perfect reverb tail as well.

Size, Spread, Diffusion, and more. With careful listening and adjustment, you can create almost any kind of space your heart (or client) might desire.

More Channels Sure, ReVibe creates fantastic-sounding mono or stereo reverb textures. But the '60s are over, man. Today there are a lot more channel configurations to explore, and ReVibe can also deliver LCR, LCRS, Quad, 5.0, or 5.1 surround. And since mixing in surround doesn't necessarily mean everything was recorded in surround, ReVibe can take a mono, stereo, or LCR input and output to any of the larger channel layouts. The only limitations are that LCRS, Quad, 5.0, or 5.1 only feed through to the same layout. So if you feed Quad in, you get Quad out. But, hey, if you feed 5.1 in, you get 5.1 out as well, so you won't be missing anything.

With more channels come more controls, but most of their functions should be clear to an experienced engineer. Under the Levels section are level-control sliders for the Center, the Rear Reverb, and Rear ER so that each component of the overall-reverb output can be balanced to suit your needs. An obvious oversight here is the lack of a separate control for the LFE channel. So if you are trying to keep a tight and tidy low end, consider using the 5.0 layout for general reverb and using 5.1 for score, Foley, or special effects.

Other controls for the rear channels are included around the plug-in window. Under the Reverb section, the Rear Shape slider controls the attack time to adjust how long the reverb tail takes to bloom across the rear channels relative to the front. Higher settings result in a longer development of the rear reverb to give the sense of a deeper room behind the listener. An additional graphic representation is also included in the Contour display window so you can see how the rear channels relate to other components.

The Same Amount of Online Help

Although there is no little question mark box on the display to let you know it's programmed in there, ReVibe includes the same kind of online help as Reverb One. Click on the name of any controller, and a small text box opens with a brief description of how the control works. The explanations aren't particularly in-depth but should provide enough of a reminder to keep you moving during a session...and the client won't even see you reaching for a manual.

Overall, ReVibe is a powerful reverb processor that can cover almost any situation. But that power comes at a price: it takes a lot of DSP power, and it can only be run on the Pro Tools HD Accel or the new Pro Tools HDX signal processing cards. Keep these limitations in mind as you lay out your mixing session.

Advanced Techniques and Good Practice

In case I haven't made it clear: reverb is a big topic to cover. We are surrounded by sound reverberations every moment of our lives, and yet we hardly notice them until we hear their absence in our recordings. We hear a sound, our brain makes some quick comparisons to localize it, and we turn our head to see where it originated. We don't even notice all the extra cues reminding us how far away we are from each wall in the room. Listing comprehensive examples of when and how to apply reverb to one kind of sound versus another could easily fill an entire book. Some examples have already been included with the individual plug-ins. Here, I'll give you extra examples that illustrate good practice; and I'll provide a starting point you can apply to many sounds and situations.

Blend Natural Room Sound with Artificial Reverb for a More "Realistic" Sound

I've already torn down some ideas about "realism" in a recording, and now I'm talking about a more "realistic" sound. You may be wondering, "Is this guy serious?" I am, and I promise it will make sense.

When we talk about capturing what happened in an actual room, we are talking about something that is extremely subjective. But when we talk about creating an artificial room that sounds realistic, that simply means making a believable-sounding space. It only needs to sound like it *could* be a real space; it doesn't have to sound recognizable as a specific location—unless you were hired to create a virtual reality tour of famous concert halls (if so, you're very brave).

Modern recording-studio designers know this method creates a more convincing sense of space, and they create spaces that are far more live than the old, dull, padded walls of studios from the '70s and '80s. Even if you don't work in such a specially designed room, you can use available spaces to create something new. Start by taking a quick inventory of the spaces around you. If you're working at home, are you in a bedroom? How does it sound? What about the hallway, the bathroom, the kitchen, or garage? Have a friend strum a guitar and walk around with you while you listen to your spaces.

Now, go back to the computer, record a close-up take of that same guitar strumming and switch on AIR Reverb. From the factory-default settings, dial the Mix back to 50%, the Balance back to 0% (all early reflections), set the ER Spread control to 50%, and start listening through the ER Type selections (Figure 6.50).

If the Small Studio setting sounds like your living room, for example, then you know you have a physical space that can replace the virtual space inside the plug-in. Once you find a good match,

Figure 6.50 Dial in these settings and then compare the sound of the ER Types to your own spaces.

dial the Balance back up to 50% and adjust the settings for the long reverb until you get a nice, overall-reverb sound you would be happy to hear on a finished recording.

Now for the fun part. Take your mics and guitar-playing friend back to the room you found as a match and record some guitar in there—but not so close! Back up a little further than you might usually record so you are sure to catch some of the room reflections as well. The direct sound will get quieter as you move away, so you might need to adjust the gain at the mic preamp a bit. Get a nice balance of guitar and room and head back to the reverb.

Set up the new recording with the same reverb setting you just had, except set the early reflection Type to Off. How does it sound? If it's not quite the same kind of balance, then adjust things until it gets closer to what you had before. Compare it to the close-up recording with only the artificial reverb added. You might find that you still want a little of the early reflection sound mixed in—although maybe not as much.

I can't guarantee you will like this approach better. The point is to understand the technique and know it's an option. In my early days as a recording engineer running a small location-recording business, I made many mixes for performers who could not believe we recorded in their living room.

Mono versus Stereo: Capturing versus Creating Space

It might seem contradictory to explain how to capture space through recording techniques when this chapter is all about reverb plug-ins. But using reverb well usually means creating a convincing sense of space, and our ability to perceive space relies on stereo listening.

If you are overdubbing sounds for a multi-track recording-and-mixing project, you probably record a lot of those sounds in mono. When those mono sounds are sent to the reverb processor, they will often be sent as mono signals dropped into the middle of the virtual room being created by the reverb plug-in. It may not seem like a huge difference for a single instrument, but over an entire mix, your reverb may be fighting its own purpose. By pulling the pan positions toward the center, the mix will sound more mono, while the point of the reverb is to create a larger sense of space. To fix, make sure your reverb sends for each channel follow the panning of the main mix (Figure 6.51).

Figure 6.51 Click the FMP button and the aux send will follow the main pan control.

By clicking the FMP button on a channel's aux send, you will link that pan control to the main-channel panner. It's a subtle difference, and the placement in the stereo field is still being created artificially, but it helps maintain the spaciousness of your mix. A more convincing approach is to record more of your sources in stereo.

Entire books have been written on the subject of stereo recording—and for good reason. We hear the world in stereo, so recording it in stereo makes sense. You don't have to capture every sound at once with a stereo pair, but try to capture more sounds in stereo when you can.

Capturing in stereo means you will have more information, in good ways and bad ways. Yes, it means you'll be using up tracks, system resources, and hard-drive space faster. It also means you'll have bigger sounds and more information about everything you record. Are there more highs coming from the left or the right? Is the instrument closer to one side or the other? Is the player moving while she strums the guitar? Do different sounds leave the instrument in different ways? A stereo recording generally captures a more detailed image of the event. Feeding that extra detail to your mix and reverb plug-ins creates a more convincing sense of space.

If you have the means to record in stereo (if you own or can borrow two matching microphones), then look up information on basic stereo techniques and record some of your tracks in stereo. Specifically, try setting up a stereo pair and recording different parts in different positions around the pair (Figure 6.52). Remember: you don't have to place the instrument directly in the center of the pair.

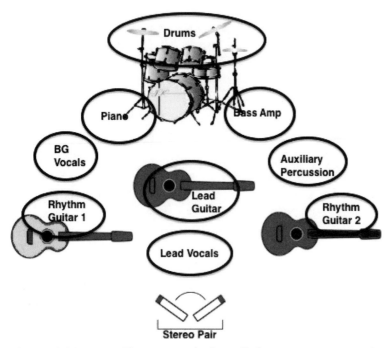

Figure 6.52 Even if you are playing all the parts, you can place the instruments at realistic locations.

Also keep in mind that even if you record several instruments in stereo, you don't have to dial the pan controls for the stereo track to hard left and right. You can still pull the pan controls into a tighter spread so perhaps the acoustic guitar is placed between 10:00 and 1:00, while the keyboard is spread from 12:00 to 3:00. Experiment and find your own blend of natural and artificial, your own balance between capturing and creating space.

Add a Sugar Coating to Keyboards or Drums

Nothing screams out "unfinished!" like layers of dry keyboard sounds, a dull drum mix that sounds like Mom's basement, or, worse, virtual instrument sounds with bits of built-in effects that all sound different. The sounds cry out for something to pull them together, to give them a common blend, a shared place to call home, a space to call their own. Wait a minute, isn't that exactly what reverb processors are designed to do?

While I usually suggest using the same (or at least similar) reverb settings for all the tracks in your mix, that may not be the sound or style you're looking for. Sometimes you just want that instant, sugary goodness for one particular instrument, group, or section. Start by re-routing the channels in question to an available stereo bus and then set up a stereo aux track to catch that bus and route it back to your mix (Figure 6.53). You know the routine.

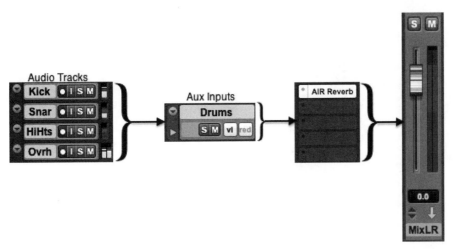

Figure 6.53 Send all the drum channels to an aux bus instead of sending them directly to the mix.

Once that's set up add a reverb plug-in to the stereo aux bus. I'm using AIR Reverb for this example, and activating it on insert C. That leaves available insert points before and after the reverb to add an equalizer, compressor, or other effect on either side of the reverb later on (it's good to keep your options open). Starting from the factory-default settings, there are a few adjustments to make. First, the Mix needs to be turned down since this reverb is in-line on the bus, so pull that down to 30%. Then set the Pre-Delay to 5 ms, the Room Size to 50%, and the early-reflection Type to Large Studio with a 50% Spread so the controls look like Figure 6.54.

It's not fair to say "instant sugar" without knowing what kind of source material you're starting with, but this is a very flexible beginning. If the highs are a little splashy and smearing a tight high-hat sound, reduce the room Density to 75% or even 50%. To keep the low end tight, bring the low-frequency Time control down a little, maybe to –25% to start, and the lows will decay a little faster. Adjust the Balance control to give the sense that you as the listener are closer or further from the instruments without changing the overall room size. More early reflections make the sound seem closer. Then make small increases to the Reverb Time to make the room seem more spacious or dramatic.

Figure 6.54 Starting from the factory default, dial in these settings.

As always, this is simply a starting point, but it's a solid starting point. Make the sound your own with subtle adjustments to one controller at a time until you find just the right balance. Then save the setup as your own preset recipe for the perfect candy coating.

Overuse, Abuse, and Danger Zones

Just as there are good ways to use reverb, there are bad ways as well. Maybe they aren't bad as much as they are common mistakes that leave you feeling frustrated or confused. Everybody in the studio has heard the term reverb, but few (especially the band members) know what it's all about. So here are a few common requests and common pitfalls to watch out for, along with some ideas for fixing them.

Just Dump a Bunch of Reverb on It...

This is a common request in the recording studio when an artist starts to get frustrated with getting a good take or editing a good composite. Maybe you've also heard this suggestion from an inexperienced audio engineer. Unfortunately, it's not usually the magic potion they are hoping for. Adding a little of the right kind of reverb helps in some situations. The trick is knowing what will work and what won't.

Reverb Can

- Create a sense of space

- Make a sound seem more distant

- Make short notes seem longer

- Hide small editing inconsistencies

- Add color and richness to a sound

- Help encourage a good performance

Reverb Cannot

- Be removed

- Hide tuning problems

- Make wrong notes sound right

- Correct badly cut edits

- Make a band play in-time

- Make a bad performance sound inspired

It's true that adding reverb can help breathe life into a dull recording. The depth and size of the presentation can lend a sense of drama and importance. The ringing of the artificial room can stretch notes that should have been held but weren't. It can even cover up little inconsistencies of timing as the delay taps of the early reflections smear the first few milliseconds of every beat.

On the other hand, throwing reverb at an out-of-tune singer makes it sound like he was singing out of tune in a bigger room. Dumping tons of soupy reverb on the rhythm guitar doesn't make the chords right, it just gives the dissonances more time to be offensive. And if the lyrics of a love song were delivered like an anti-smoking message from the guy in an iron lung, adding reverb isn't going to turn it back into the wedding song of the decade.

"I Think It Needs More Reverb"

Whether your client asks for more reverb or less, it probably means the same thing—they don't like the sound, and they think more (or less) reverb is a reasonable fix. It might even sound like a reasonable fix...until you try to decide which control to reach for.

What does it mean to add "more reverb?" Does it mean more of the processed sound versus the dry sound by turning up the level of the reverb return? Does it mean dialing in a longer decay time on the processor? Does it mean a denser reverb sound? Or maybe a brighter, more metallic sound? Or is one instrument simply sticking too far out in front of the others? Any of these are valid interpretations of "more reverb," although the client still may not be happy and may not be looking for a change in the reverb at all.

When this kind of request comes up, be diplomatic and try to deliver the right solution. The client is counting on you to have an expert understanding of the technology without making her feel completely clueless in her requests. The artist knows she doesn't like something, so in that sense, the customer is always right—even if she doesn't know what she is asking for. Start by asking if she wants "longer reverb time," "a denser reverb," or "more wet-versus-dry sound." If the artist is familiar with recording and mixing, she can be more specific. If the artist is not sure which it is, then ask what she is looking for in other terms that make sense to her.

That's why it's important to know how all those controls work. If the client wants the room to sound bigger, or the walls to sound softer, or a particular sound to seem more distant, you need to know to reach for the decay time, the high-frequency cut, or the wet/dry mix. If you're in doubt, jump back a few pages and double-check the description of the controls for the reverb plug-in you are using.

The Vocals Keep Sinking Further Away

Those who are new to mixing get mixed messages about what to do. "Always use this technique here," but "never use that technique there." "Lead vocals get reverb to make them sparkle." "Compress the life out of your kick drum, snare drum, and bass guitar!" "Whatever you do, don't over-compress your mix!" The messages say to add lots of this, but not too much of that, especially where the two counteracting forces of reverb and compression are concerned.

Do you remember how compression makes things sound closer while reverb makes things sound like they're further away? (If not, it's in the "Refresher" section of this chapter.) One issue that comes up often when mixing songs is losing tracks into the mix—especially your lead vocals.

It's frustrating, but take a step back and consider what effects have been placed on all of the sounds in the mix. Taken individually, what does each effect do? Reverb can certainly add color and sparkle to a voice, but its primary job is to make the voice sound further away or at least in a larger space. Compression has the opposite effect and tends to make things sound closer. Adding a chorus effect to your lead vocals gives them less focus and immediacy, which makes them fall back into the mix.

Equalizer settings will have some effect on the perceived distance. Remember that in natural spaces, high-frequency energy is absorbed into the air faster than lower frequencies. So taking out too many highs will make an instrument sound more distant. Boosting the lows or low-midrange makes an instrument sound closer.

Even the instrument sounds themselves can compete for presence and push vocals into the background. Electric guitars with lots of distortion have extra harmonic content in the upper-midrange that tends to dominate the top end of the mix, covering the key articulation and intelligibility range of the voice.

The solution to this problem may not lie in your reverb settings alone—although reverb is a common culprit, and adding too much won't help the problem. I can't give one or two specific reverb settings that would be helpful in all situations. Instead, here are some tricks for controlling how your reverb settings affect your vocals:

- Use less reverb on the vocals. "Less" in this sense usually means send less signal to the reverb plug-in, or adjust the wet/dry mix if the plug-in is on the vocal track.

- Use more reverb elsewhere. Don't overdo it, but sending a little bit of everything to the reverb plug-in helps make it seem like everyone is in the same room.

- Rebalance the reverb. Distant sounds have fewer early reflections, so boost the ERs and reduce the long reverb. The room can still sound big while the voice seems closer.

- Remove the early reflections. That's contrary to the last idea, but if dense ERs are smearing the articulation, cut them and see if that pulls the vocals closer.

- Try a more sparse sound. A dense plate reverb may add lots of color, but it will cloud the focus and intelligibility. Try a larger but less dense reverb sound.

- Increase the pre-delay. Even just 10–20 ms may be enough. This will let more of the dry signal through first, which should help the voice sound closer.

- Spread the long reverb wider. A wider stereo spread of the reverb tail can leave more space in the middle for the lead vocals to take center stage.

- Push the high-cut frequency higher on the vocal reverb. In nature, less high frequency means more distance. Don't cut as much, and the voice should sound closer.

- Turn the reverb off and listen. If the vocals are lost without any reverb running, then your problem may be somewhere else.

Lead vocals are often the most crucial element in a mix. Listeners generally want to know what the singer is saying to them. That's why lots of the examples and suggestions in this book deal with vocals. If none of these reverb solutions cure your disappearing vocals, you may need to look elsewhere. Look for similar examples related to equalizers (Chapter 4), compressors (Chapter 5), and chorus effects.

It Sounds Like Everyone's in Different Rooms

So the singer sounds like he's in a cathedral? The bass sounds like the amp is sitting on your chest? The electric guitars are rockin' all of downtown Surf City, and the drums sound like they're in the basement where they were recorded...except for the snare drum, which sounds like it's in the Grand Canyon. It might be time to rethink your whole reverb strategy.

Understanding how to apply reverb processors to the various channels, tracks, and mix busses when working in a DAW system is a common problem. Looking at the layout of the Pro Tools edit and mix windows, it seems logical to activate a reverb plug-in on every track that needs the effect, just as you would add an equalizer or compressor. Aside from being very taxing on the system resources, this approach usually leads to a mix that sounds like everyone is in a different room.

As with so many techniques, there is nothing inherently wrong with dropping a reverb plug-in onto every track. If you have the processing power or aren't running many tracks, that won't be an issue. The trouble arises when all of the reverb settings are different. If your mix sounds like everyone is in a different room, it's probably because they are being treated with reverbs that make it sound like they are in different rooms.

Imagine a real, physical, acoustic space. If all the instruments and sounds you created were playing in the same room, they would all reverberate within that room. Sure, the room might respond a little differently to high or low frequencies, absorbing some more than others, but every sound would reverberate together. Of course, that doesn't mean the solution is to drop a reverb plug-in on the whole mix, crank up the wet/dry mix, and call it good. There's a solution in between all or nothing that's usually just right.

In an analog-mixing environment with only one or two good reverb processors, the standard approach is to place the reverb processor on an auxiliary bus and feed the output back into the main mix. The diagram in Figure 6.55 illustrates the idea, using the Pro Tools mix window.

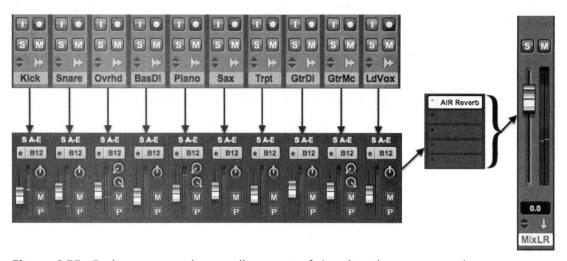

Figure 6.55 Each source sends a small amount of signal to the same reverb processor.

This arrangement is standard practice in the analog world and is easy to set up in Pro Tools; it's the same as setting up any other auxiliary bus send and return.

- Pick one of the 10 auxiliary sends, A–J.
- Route that send to an unused stereo bus on each track that needs reverb.
- Create a new stereo Aux Input track.

■ Set that Aux track to receive a signal from the bus and send it to the main mix.

■ Pick your favorite reverb plug-in and engage it on the Aux track.

Once you have that set up, you can adjust how much signal is sent from each track into the reverb processor. If you want the vocals to ring a little more while the bass rings a little less, dial it into the auxiliary send for that channel. You can even automate the send so the guitar gets more reverb during the solo, or so the bass gets less on the shorter notes. In this kind of setup the reverb output is usually set to a 100% wet mix, so the fader for that channel will control how much wet signal is added to the dry mix overall—and even that can be automated!

This is usually the quickest and most effective way to get all of the instruments and sounds back into the same room. Literally, they are all ringing the same virtual room. You can still bend the rules of physics a bit by having different instruments ring a little more or less. You can even add extra reverb to certain sounds. Guitar amps have spring reverbs built-in, and the sound they make echoes around the room. If all your actors are arguing in the same room, but you want the door slam to sound like it shook the world, dial in a different reverb for that.

This approach to reverb is a solid starting point to building a stronger mix. You can set up multiple reverbs in parallel on two or more auxiliary sends. Listen carefully (as always) to make sure things don't start sounding out of place again. Then dial some sounds into one, some into the other, and some into both. Whatever suits your project. Once you're comfortable with this and the other reverb techniques mentioned, it's time to start experimenting and exploring to develop your own sound and style.

7 Delay

Wait.... It's all about...timing.

Any good comedian will tell you that timing is everything. For that matter, so will most bakers, stock brokers, political analysts, and that cop who just decided it's your turn to be reminded not to drive so fast. Now I'll remind you that timing plays a huge role in audio production as well.

We measure the repetitive tones we call musical notes by their frequency, or how many times the vibration repeats in one second—a time-based measurement. We build and follow music in segments of time: notes and rests, bars and beats. The entire structure of Pro Tools as a recording and editing system is based on a timeline where audio events can be moved around each other in time. We enjoy hearing bands that play tightly in-time with each other, and make fun of movies when the sound and picture don't match up.

With so much emphasis placed on timing, you might expect there to be all kinds of plug-ins available to adjust the timing, or at least a few that move things backward or forward in time. But as it turns out, creating a plug-in to play sounds before they arrive isn't really possible without ripping holes in the fabric of the space-time continuum and potentially destroying the universe. So our plug-ins can only move events one direction in time: later. That might seem like a limitation, but there are many ways to use delay plug-ins both technically and creatively.

Refresher

The primary function of a delay plug-in is to make an audio signal arrive later. Keep in mind, though, that this doesn't mean the signal is played back slower. That would be time compression (speeding up) or expansion (slowing down). Delay doesn't change the length of the audio signal any more than waiting at a stoplight changes the length of your car. It simply holds back the audio signal for a moment before letting it go as normal.

Somewhere out there a guitarist is saying, "Hey, wait a minute! When I use a delay pedal, it plays back three or four little echoes for every note I play." That is an effect that can very easily be created with a delay. It only takes splitting the signal and allowing one part to play through in time while the other is delayed, just like any other dry versus wet, unprocessed versus processed balance. It's harder to think of it as a "wet" signal when it sounds the same as the original, but it truly is the same process. Split the signal, say, five times, and then delay four of them and you get

271

a multi-tap delay. Add lots of delayed echoes stacked on top of each other, and you get the basis of reverberation (Chapter 6). Plenty of creative effects can be created with delayed signals, but they all start with the basic idea of making an audio signal wait a moment…and then move on.

Fundamentals

Simply delaying an audio signal as a whole might not seem to have any obvious benefit, until you remember that sound takes time to travel. It may seem to move fast, but even the smallest amount of timing difference can have a surprisingly big impact on the sound. Our brains, for example, analyze the timing differences between sounds arriving at each ear to determine the location of the sound, and the distance between your ears is less than 1 foot. Understanding a little about the speed of sound and the way our brain interprets timing can help make sense of why some of those delay plug-ins are in there at all, and what else might be happening to the sound as you adjust the controls.

The Speed of Sound

To the average person, sound seems to move pretty quickly. Whether the source of the sound is near or far, it usually arrives without making us the least bit aware of the length of time needed to travel the distance. Considering that sound moves at roughly 1120 feet per second (768 mph), that seems only natural. It is, after all, travelling faster than any vehicle you're likely to travel in unless you happen to be a military pilot or an astronaut. That is, of course, until we compare it to what we see.

If you see something at a distance that you know should be making a distinct sound, like someone in a schoolyard across the street bouncing a basketball, you'll start to notice just how slow sound really is moving. Even at a distance of only 150 feet, the difference between how quickly light and sound reach us is staggering. It takes about 0.0000001525 seconds for the light to reach our eyes, while the sound wave plods along and takes about 0.1339 seconds to arrive. That's almost a million times slower. The light waves could have travelled all the way around world (about 24,860 miles) in the time it took the sound to cross the street!

All right, so sound moves slower than we might think; what's the big deal when the numbers still seem so tiny? The numbers are small, but they are significant. At a musical tempo of 120 beats per minute, each beat lasts .5 seconds, so that .1339 second delay is a little more than a 16th note off. Now in most cases you're not likely to record multiple instruments that are 150 feet apart. But even a short distance of, say, 15 feet from one side of a small studio to the other translates to a delay of about 13 milliseconds (0.013 sec.), and you don't even need that much delay to start running into phase cancellation.

Phase Cancellation

Phase cancellation is easily misunderstood and often poorly explained in many texts and online forums, and in this context I will only scratch the surface. The human range of hearing runs from about 20 Hz to 20 kHz, or 20 to 20,000 vibrations per second. It's described in more detail in Chapter 4 but is important to consider here when looking at real-world acoustic delay and delay plug-ins. Why? Well, because frequency is a measure of how many vibrations occur in each second, and the speed of sound describes how much distance is covered in each second.

Take the tuning frequency of 440 Hz. At 440 cycles per second, one single wave cycle happens about every 2.273 ms, and half a wave cycle takes only 1.136 ms. That probably seems insignificant, but sound doesn't move extremely fast and only covers about 16 inches in that much time. Now reverse that idea in your head and consider an instrument playing an A-440 that is being recorded with two microphones about 16 inches apart (Figure 7.1).

Figure 7.1 Two microphones capture sound from the same instrument at different times.

In this kind of situation, the sustained sound is moving along and the two microphones are catching the sound at slightly different times and different points in the wave cycle. While one microphone captures the positive peak of the wave, the other is capturing the negative peak. When the two sounds are combined during mix down some amount of cancellation can occur (Figure 7.2).

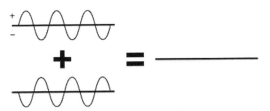

Figure 7.2 A very simplified view of phase cancellation—a positive peak cancels a negative one.

It might seem like an obvious and simple solution to invert the audio signal on one of the tracks and move along. The trouble with that is it only addresses a symptom—this is one particular frequency that's arriving at two microphones out of phase. Remember that the instrument is likely producing lots of additional overtones and will likely play more than just that one note. An octave higher at 880 Hz, for example, and the distance would be about one whole wavelength and the two signals would be back in phase. Now inverting one track would throw it out of phase with the other. Continuing up the spectrum, the signal would be out of phase again at 1320 Hz, in phase again at 1760 Hz, and so on. Clearly inverting one of the tracks isn't the answer.

There are many possible solutions to this kind of issue before the sound is recorded, but that's not always an option. Luckily, though, this is a problem caused by a timing difference, so why not change the timing to fix it?

You already know you can't make the "later" microphone sound any earlier, but we can make the "early" microphone sound a little later. Adding a delay to the close microphone makes the sound wait just a brief moment so the more distant microphone can catch up. Everything begins moving up and down, positive and negative, together again. There's a more specific explanation on using this technique for drum microphones later on in the "Advanced Techniques" section of this chapter.

The Precedence Effect

Also called the "law of first wave fronts" or the "law of first arrival" this is another way in which the relatively slow speed of sound affects how we use our ears to make sense of the space around us.

Don't believe me? Try this experiment: Start a new session at 44.1 kHz sample rate and import a finished mix from a favorite CD onto a stereo audio track. Route the signal to an output that gets to your monitors or headphones. Then activate a Time Adjuster Medium plug-in for the track. The factory default delay setting of 4 samples should come up for each channel. Hit Play and listen to the track, then click the Delay readout for only the left channel, dial in 48 samples and hit Enter (Figure 7.3). The delay is counted in samples, not milliseconds, so 48 samples minus the 4 on the right side is 44 samples difference, or about 1 millisecond at the 44.1 kHz sample rate.

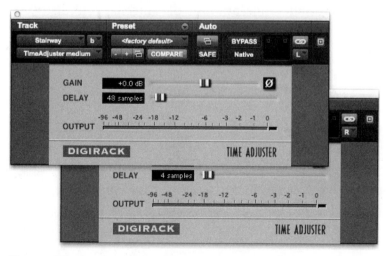

Figure 7.3 At 44.1 kHz, this setup should delay the left channel by about 1 ms.

Listening to the track, you should get the sense that sound is coming more from the right side than the left. Bring the delay up to 92 samples. At 2 ms the sound should swing a little harder to the right. Try 445 samples for about 10 ms difference. How hard the track is pulled to the side by delay will vary based on how wide or narrow the overall stereo mix is. If you try again with a more mono-sounding mix or a mono track, the steering effect should be more obvious. Play with different delay settings for the left channel, and then reset and try the right channel. If one side arrives late, your brain should tell you the signal is arriving from the other side.

We live in a world full of sound energy bouncing around, reflecting off of nearly every surface around us. A friend might say something from across the room, and you imagine the sound is traveling from his mouth to your ear. Really though, that sound is traveling in all directions and bouncing off the floor, the ceiling, the walls, and furniture along the way. Your ears pick up all those sounds, but your brain has learned to ignore any sounds that seem identical if they arrive within about 30–50 ms after the first one. Your brain understands that the first sound to arrive traveled directly to you while the later sounds took a longer path bouncing around the room. It uses that information to tell you where the sound originated as well as where you are located within the room.

After that initial chunk of time, your brain stops ignoring the extra sounds and acknowledges them as distinct events. Depending on the type of sound, that change might happen in as little as 20 ms or as much as 50 ms. Strong, percussive sounds tend to get noticed faster than those with slow attacks. The example many of us are likely to be familiar with is bouncing a basketball near a wall then walking away from the wall. Once you get far enough away, the round-trip distance from ball to wall to your ears takes enough time to start sounding like a distinct echo.

The Creative Side of Delay

All this talk about numbers, timing, frequencies, phasing, and keeping everything lined up doesn't mean these are purely technical utility plug-ins. Delay plays an important part in some of the most popular special effects processor sounds of the last half century. From basic echo to looping, multi-tap delays, artificial stereo effects, reverbs, chorus, and flangers, the basic starting point is delay.

Take an incoming signal, split it, delay one part while the other passes unchanged, and put them together again afterward and you have a basic delay echo. Make the Delay long enough and the result can sound like singing in canon. Think of two children singing Row, Row, Row Your Boat. Feed the delayed signal back into itself at a lower volume and the delayed echo will "ring" several times as it dies away. Feed it back in at full volume and the delay will repeat indefinitely (careful with that one). Set the delay time very, very low, and then slowly adjust the time so the track speeds up and slows down and you get a close approximation of a flanger.

Of course, many of these special effects predate Pro Tools, digital recording, or even multi-track tape recording. Most originated through experimentation (or even mistakes) in the tape-based analog recording studios. The very reason we call the effect a "flanger" is because it was originally created by playing back two copies of the same recording on two different tape machines and gently slowing the timing of one tape reel versus the other by pressing down on the metal flange of the tape reel. That slowed down one copy and created a sweeping comb-filter effect.

So if the humble delay plug-in seems underwhelming at first, or if all these various plug-ins for creating delay seem like overkill, just take a moment to look a little deeper. You might discover some great techniques and familiar sounds that all get their start from arriving late.

When to Reach for Delay Tools

Since delay effects cross the line between being utilities and creative tools, there are many possibilities for when to use these plug-ins. Although whenever there's lots of potential, it can be difficult to know where to start...or stop.

If you are completely new to delay processors, it could be helpful to experiment with some simple tracks just to get a feel for how things work. Clear, percussive sounds are a great way to hear what's happening inside a basic rhythmic delay. Use a simple, single-line melody on a voice or instrument to experiment with a chorus preset. Then use more complex sounds like rhythm guitar chords or an imported CD track to hear what a flanger effect can do.

Use Delay Creatively for Composition and Songwriting

Inspiration comes in many forms and even running a simple delay effect while messing around on a guitar or keyboard can present you with new ideas. Hearing a little mimicking echo after each note can help establish a rhythm, and that rhythm can lead to a groove, and once you're grooving it's hard to stop. Chorus, flange, and other delay-based effects can be inspiring as well, especially for developing tone and timbre. But echoes and loops have an almost magical way of getting ideas moving for some instruments.

Other than the very basic Time Adjuster plug-ins, all of the Pro Tools delay plug-ins have a wet-versus-dry mix control that allows the original signal to be balanced against the repeated delay signal. Hearing both the "dry" attack sound and the "wet" echo sound is the basic starting point of a rhythmic delay. At any setting beyond about 30 ms, the plug-in should create a distinct echo, although clear rhythmic effects need longer times. A delay of 250 ms is equivalent to a 1/8th note at 120 BPM, while it takes a whole 2 seconds of delay to loop one measure of 4/4 time at the same tempo. So if you're aiming to experiment with rhythmic echoes or loops, be sure to run the Long or Extra-Long version of the delay plug-in.

As new ideas come together, try the patterns at slightly longer or shorter delay times. This will change the tempo of the pattern slightly so you can see if it will sound more or less solid when played a little faster or slower. A little tempo change can help the effect match the resonance of your instrument. And, of course, once you start using a rhythmic delay effect as a foundation and groove, the tempo of the song will be dictated by the process. So make sure you've got it where it sounds best.

More than with other plug-in types, when you're using delay and rhythmic effects to inspire and form the foundation for a project, make sure you save all the plug-in settings. Depending on the sounds you're processing, it's not a bad idea to take some extra notes about the setup as well, especially if there are microphones involved. Remember that distance equals time, and if the time is different, the groove may not be quite the same.

Use Delay Cautiously When Tracking or Overdubbing

The same warnings about latency of your audio interface apply here as they do with every plug-in type—maybe even a little more so. Think about it: Delay plug-ins are time-based effects. Any latency introduced by your audio interface will affect the process you hear while recording. Too much latency can throw off the groove in a way you weren't expecting.

It's always a good idea to practice the parts you're going to play before hitting Record, (you knew that already), but if you have to switch off a processor that's helping to create a groove, it can be really hard to maintain the right feel when it's gone. Reducing the level of the processed signal each time you practice can help you disconnect the two parts in your ear and brain. Simply lower the wet-versus-dry mix level in stages until you can barely hear the effect, then bypass the plug-in altogether and record the part. For more complex delay patterns, you can also gradually move the feedback level toward zero. This can help you focus on how the dry signal should fit into place so you can record the part cleanly and then set the controls back where they should be.

If the delay effect is synchronized to a tempo, recording should be much easier since you can activate click track to help keep you in time. You might still feel a little disoriented if the rhythmic pattern drops out abruptly, so it's still a good idea to remove it gradually by lowering the volume. This time, though, as the delay effect slips away you will hear your part against the click taking its place. Best of all, once the track is recorded, there can still be some flexibility in the tempo of the track. Changing the tempo for a section of the song will change the timing on the delay plug-in as well. The audio track won't change, but it's much easier to use a function like Beat Detective or a Time Compression/Expansion plug-in to stretch the audio track so it stays in time. But think of that more as a safety net and aim to get the tempo right before you record.

Use Delay Only to Correct Timing While Editing

When it comes time to do detail editing work on a project, it's important to hear the audio you're working on as accurately as possible. Whether you're trying to line up parts so the whole band sounds a little tighter or compositing a vocal track to make sure each note is in tune and each syllable comes through cleanly, it won't be any easier if you're hearing double. So unless there's a good reason to be running delay effects while you're editing, it's probably best to leave them bypassed.

Reasonable exceptions to this would include using delay plug-ins to create long, rhythmic loops that will form the timing foundation for other tracks, or when processing plug-ins that are available only as off-line, Audio Suite effects. In those cases, the effects really need to be applied before moving into the mixing stage, so fire them up, get things into place, and then get them out of the way to make sure you can hear the detail and timing again.

Use Delay for Mixing

Whether it's time alignment to correct for acoustic delay, a subtle rhythmic effect to add a little interest to a guitar or percussion part, or a thick chorus effect on backing vocal parts to make them seem as though they were double-tracked, delay plug-ins feel right at home in a wide variety of mixing situations. The trick, however, is to stay aware of how each delay effect you add is interacting with other parts or effects in the mix. And that doesn't just mean timing.

By definition, delay processors move things around in time. This can alter the perceived timing of the track, of course, in good ways or bad. Adding a doubling effect to a backing vocal can hide the subtle shifts in timing as notes are sung slightly ahead of, or behind, the lead. But this same effect added to percussion, rhythm guitar, or bass, can make the band seem less tight as every beat is smeared together rather than landing solidly in time.

Many delay effects also bring along more hidden side effects such as tonal shifts and unintended build-up at high or low frequencies. Adding a delay effect to a bright guitar sound can add extra layers of sound at higher frequencies that interfere with the clarity of vocal articulations. Or as various harmonics are boosted or cut due to comb-filtering, instruments or voices can sound brighter or darker; they may even sound out of tune if more dissonant notes are emphasized.

The humble delay plug-in may not be the most obvious culprit as you notice these problems creeping into a mix, so be sure to listen carefully to how each layer of effects interacts with the rest of the mix.

Using Delay for Mastering Isn't so Likely

Using delay for mastering may be unlikely, but that doesn't mean it's not an option. As with everything else, it depends on what kind of material you are working with and how much you would like to change it. Adding a dense multi-tap delay over an entire mix of a loud and busy rock song might lead to a big, steaming pile of rhythmic confusion (careful where you step). But adding that effect to just the last note of the song, or right when the band drops out for an *a cappella* chorus, could really take a mix to the next level.

Remember too that delay is a basic building block of a lot of different sounds and effects including reverb and stereo enhancing techniques. If the mix you're mastering is nearly (or completely) mono and you're trying to widen it, some advanced delay techniques could come in handy. So don't count the delay plug-ins out before getting to know them better.

What's in the Box?

When you first pull down the menu to select a delay plug-in it seems like there are many more options here than in the equalizer, compressor, or reverb plug-in folders. Look more closely though, and you'll see that is somewhat of an illusion. There are multiple versions of the Delay II and Time Adjuster plug-ins that are almost identical. The main difference, as suggested by the name for each different version, is the amount of total delay time available to each plug-in, whether short, medium, long, or extra-long.

The reason for having multiple plug-ins for different delay times, as always, is to help manage system resources. A certain amount of processing power must be available and reserved to delay the audio signal. The longer the signal will be delayed, the more resources the system needs to buffer data and keep track of how and when the audio should finally line up. As with other resource-intensive plug-ins, if you're working on smaller projects and/or more powerful systems, you may never run into an issue. Even so, it's good practice to be efficient with the plug-ins you activate for a track. Use the smallest plug-in available that will still deliver the delay effect you want.

In addition to seeing multiple versions of the same plug-in, you'll also notice there are many similar controls shared across the delay plug-ins. You will see Gain, Phase, and Delay time controls in every plug-in. If the description isn't clear to you when you're reading about a particular plug-in, flip back a few pages and check out another one. The controls may be identical, but none of the descriptions are copied and pasted, so there should be something that makes sense. Of course, each unique plug-in will have some unique controls as well, so those descriptions will be a little more detailed.

Multichannel versus Multi-Mono

With other plug-in types, when you activate a plug-in on a stereo track or bus there is an option to select from either multichannel plug-ins, where one set of controls manages all the channels, or multi-mono versions, where controls for each channel can be adjusted together or separately. However, for all versions of the Time Adjuster and Delay II plug-ins, the interface is effectively Multi-Mono in two different screen layouts. The Multi-Mono instantiation of the plug-ins operate as normal with one set of controls and the typical stereo link controls in the corner (Figure 7.4). The difference is that the Multichannel versions (Figure 7.5) display two sets of controls, one for each channel, with no ability to link the channel controls together.

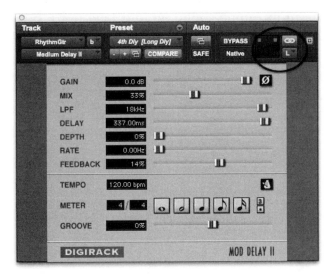

Figure 7.4 A Multi-Mono instance of Delay II has one set of controls with standard link switches.

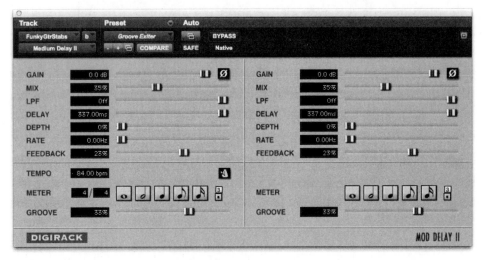

Figure 7.5 A Multichannel instance of Delay II has two sets of controls and no link function.

The only functions that are definitely linked between the channels are the Tempo and Meter controls.

There's nothing at all wrong with this arrangement. None of the controls need to fire both channels from one input like you might expect in a stereo compressor. It's just an unusual design choice. So for these plug-ins, different from the others, the only way to get a linked stereo control of the plug-in is to run the Multi-Mono versions of the plug-ins and keep the link switch enabled. Of course, as with most other plug-ins, for any configuration of three or more channels, Multi-Mono with linked or unlinked controls is all that is available.

Time Adjuster: Short, Medium, or Long

Delay processors are, by definition, designed to catch an incoming sound, hold it back for a brief moment, and then let it pass through unchanged. There isn't a better example of this kind of simplicity than the Time Adjuster plug-in (Figure 7.6). It's designed to be extremely efficient so it can compensate for the delay caused by more complex plug-ins on other tracks, or natural acoustic delays caused by multi-microphone recording setups.

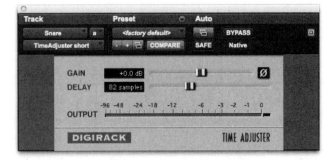

Figure 7.6 Three controls make for a very simple interface.

It could perhaps be simpler if the designers left out the Gain control and the Phase invert switch, but those features are helpful and eliminate the need for pairing this plug-in with another like Trim (Chapter 8) for those basic tasks. The Gain control can cut or boost a signal by as much as 24dB. That huge range provides more boost than even Trim allows, so you could, for example, boost low-level signals to match other tracks so you can hear any phasing issues that may be going on before hitting any other plug-ins.

The Phase invert switch flips the audio signal upside-down so the positive becomes negative and vice versa. Even though most phase-related issues in the recording studio are the result of timing and delay, there are still many places where the signal needs to be inverted as well. Look at the example of how to time-align drum tracks in the "Advanced Techniques" section of this chapter to see that feature in action.

Of course, the main purpose of the Time Adjuster plug-in is to delay the audio track on which it is applied so that track lines up with others that have been delayed because of more complex processors or real-world acoustics. So the Delay control is really the most important, and it quite simply adjusts how long the audio signal is delayed. The control functions the same for each version of the plug-in but the available range changes. That is, the range for Time Adjuster Short is from 4 to 259 samples, for Medium it's from 4 to 2051 samples, and for Long it's from 4 to 8195 samples. It's important to note two things about these values: Remember that it's a measure of samples and not milliseconds, and that these ranges remain the same for any sample rate or bit depth. The table in Figure 7.7 converts from samples to time values at different sample rates.

Samples	Time at 44.1kHz	Time at 48kHz	Time at 88.2kHz	Time at 96kHz
	(all times in milliseconds)			
4	0.09	0.08	0.045	0.042
50	1.13	1.04	0.57	0.52
100	2.27	2.08	1.13	1.04
259	5.87	5.39	2.94	2.69
1000	22.68	20.83	11.34	10.42
2051	46.51	42.73	23.25	21.36
4000	90.7	83.33	45.35	41.66
8195	185.83	170.73	92.91	85.36

Figure 7.7 Converting samples to time values for different sample rates.

The only other controls present on the plug-in are the standard Track, Preset, and Auto controls at the top of the interface window. Most of these operate as normal except for the Bypass control. The control is there and you can switch it on and off to your heart's content, but it just doesn't change anything. That is to say, once you activate the Time Adjuster plug-in for a track, it is on and stays on unless it is removed. There's nothing particularly wrong with that fact, but it's helpful to know. Although if you "print" your effects chain to a new file, move it into place on the track, and bypass all the plug-ins to save processing resources, keep in mind that the Time Adjuster will still be adjusting.

Real-Time Use (RTAS and TDM)

While Time Adjuster is available as a Multichannel and Multi-Mono plug-in for both native and DSP-powered systems, it is available only as a real-time plug-in and has no counterpart in the Audio Suite. This should make sense, considering its function is so simple and tied so intrinsically to real-time playback. So if you need to process a few tracks to save on system resources, you'll have to look at other plug-ins on the chain first.

Usage Example: Time Aligning a Microphone and DI Signal

Whether you're recording acoustic guitar with both a microphone and a DI for the pickup, an electric bass or guitar through an amp and a DI connection, or any other instrument with both a mic and a DI, the two channels may sound a little thinner than you would expect from double the signal. I tend to record a lot of jazz music, and when I have an upright bass in the studio, I usually record it on at least two channels: one or more microphone channels and one direct (DI) signal from the instrument pickup. It's great to have the different sonic options when it comes time to mix, but it can also create a little bit of trouble in the low end. The problem is a difference in timing.

The pickup built into the instrument's body will capture the sound earlier than just about any microphone because it is physically closer to the source of the sound—it's attached to it. So whether the microphone is placed a few inches or a few feet away from the amplifier or the strings, there is likely to be a difference in timing. And a difference in timing means the potential for phase cancellation.

The waveforms shown in Figure 7.8 represent a DI signal from an electric bass and the microphone signal that captured the sound of the bass amplifier. Once it is zoomed in to show the attack of one note, you can see the difference in timing between the two channels.

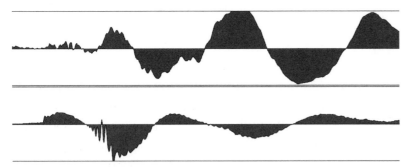

Figure 7.8 Zooming in on one attack shows the timing difference between the mic and DI signals.

Once the energy of the vibrating string hits the pickup in the bass, it's converted to electricity and travels close to the speed of light. That signal is recorded through the DI, but it is also sent to the amp where it is converted back into acoustic energy, and that acoustic energy has to travel a short distance from the speaker to the microphone at the speed of sound. Then it's converted back to electricity and sent on to the recorder. That difference in speed and distance causes the distance you see. Choosing "Samples" as the time display in the Main Counter display at the top of the edit window, and then selecting the audio from the start of the attack on one track to the start on the next should give a count of the timing difference in samples (Figure 7.9), in this case about 100.

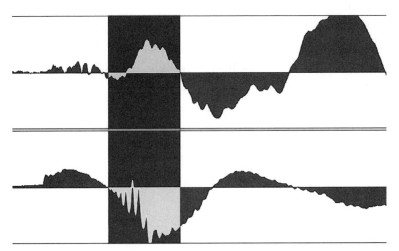

Figure 7.9 Selecting from a 0-crossing point on one track to the matching point on the other track reveals the delay time.

The example was recorded at a sample rate of 88.2 kHz, so the 100 samples of delay represent about 1.13 ms of total delay time. That's equivalent to about 16 inches of distance from the voice coil of the speaker to the microphone, and sounds about right for where I placed the microphone. Don't worry; doing the math isn't at all necessary. The delay is there; I could see it and measure it. It happens to be about half a wavelength of A-440, so it would clearly affect the audible range of the signal. But the two signals are in phase for other frequencies, so inverting isn't the answer.

The solution is to activate a Time Adjuster plug-in on the DI signal that's arriving early, dial in a delay time of 100 samples, and listen to the result of the two tracks together. Depending on the instrument tracks you're listening to, the result will usually sound clearer and more resonant now that the two tracks are working together to reproduce all the frequencies. You can spot check a few other attacks to zero in on an exact timing difference, but since it is caused by the speed of sound, you shouldn't expect to see any change based on the notes being played. Holding down Ctrl (Command on Mac) while adjusting the Delay control will adjust in 1-sample increments. Get as close as you can but don't worry too much about getting things exactly dead-on. At 44.1 kHz, being off by 5 samples would affect frequencies up above 17 kHz, right up at the edge of human hearing.

Delay II: Short, Medium, Long, Extra Long, or Slap

In contrast to the pure utility of the Time Adjuster plug-ins, Delay II, in its numerous forms, adds tools and functions to become a truly artistic tool. You could certainly use the plug-in for basic time alignment, but since delay processors reserve a lot of processing power, it wouldn't be very efficient. Instead, look to the Delay II plug-ins when you're ready to start getting creative.

There are five closely related real-time versions of Delay II and one Audio Suite version that will be covered here. In the plug-in selection pull-down menu, these should appear as Extra-Long Delay II, Long Delay II, Medium Delay II, Short Delay II, and Slap Delay II. That might appear to be a neat and convenient listing by length of available delay time, but it's actually just a coincidence of the alphabetical ordering. Indeed, the Slap Delay II has more available delay time than the Short version and could easily be labeled as "Medium Short Delay II" instead. Taken in ascending (and nearly reverse-alphabetical) order, the various versions provide maximum delay times as follows:

- Short Delay II — up to 43 milliseconds
- Slap Delay II — up to 171 milliseconds
- Medium Delay II — up to 341 milliseconds
- Long Delay II — up to 683 milliseconds
- Extra-Long Delay II — up to 2.73 seconds (2,730 ms)
- Audio Suite Delay II — up to 10.9 seconds (10,918 ms)

These numbers should appear slightly different from the actual numbers you'll see displayed in the plug-in Delay Time control window. That's because these take into account a basic 4 ms delay for simply turning on any real-time version of the plug-in. (The Audio Suite version has no inherent delay since it operates offline.)

All of the real-time Delay II plug-ins can be activated as mono, stereo, and mono-to-stereo versions. There is, however, an interesting quirk about the multichannel version that was explained a few pages back near the beginning of the "What's in the Box?" section of this chapter.

Two additional specialty plug-ins are available under Audio Suite only that look like they should be part of the Delay II package, though they are quite different. The look may be similar, but the procedure is different and control settings cannot be copied and pasted between these and any Delay II plug-in. These are labeled as Multi-Tap Delay and Ping-Pong Delay, and each has its very own listing later in this chapter.

Basic Controls

Starting at the top of the interface window, there are three basic controls to get things started (Figure 7.10): the Gain, Phase, and Mix controls.

Figure 7.10 The Gain, Phase, and Mix controls.

Unfortunately, this means the plug-in interface starts right off with a mislabeled control. The Gain control does not allow for any amount of gain to the incoming signal and should instead be labeled as a "Trim" control. It allows the incoming signal to be reduced by any amount from 0dB to –80dB. That's a handy feature considering that adding extra delayed copies to the original signal is likely to increase the overall level of your track. However, if the incoming signal really is too low, you'll need to pop another plug-in such as Trim (Chapter 8) inline before Delay II.

The Phase control operates exactly as it should, inverting the incoming signal before it is sent into the processor, and it can function independently for the left and right channel. The Mix control also functions as it should, balancing the dry (original) signal against the wet (processed) signal. At 0%, only the original signal is passed through, and at 100%, only the processed signal is passed through. Keep that in mind when you activate any real-time Delay II since the factory default setting comes up as 100% Mix, maximum Delay, and everything else neutral. This means the output will sound exactly like the original except that it will play later in time. Pull the Mix level down to 50% and the effect will be much more obvious. Mix can also be adjusted independently for both left and right channels.

Delay Parameter Controls

The next five controls affect only the "delay," the processed signal (Figure 7.11). These are the Low-Pass filter (LPF) control, Delay, Depth, Rate, and Feedback.

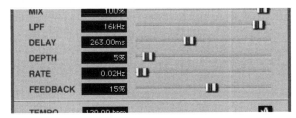

Figure 7.11 LPF, Delay, Depth, Rate, and Feedback affect only the processed signal.

I would prefer to see the Delay control as the first of these controls to eliminate any confusion, but that's not the case, as the LPF control has that top spot. Conceptually though, it makes more sense to explain them the other way. The Delay control has a range from 0 ms to whatever the maximum delay time is for each version. The graphic control doesn't have as detailed a range, but you can type extremely low values into the display window, down to 0.05 ms if you need to.

At a Delay setting of 0 ms, the processed signal should be directly atop the original. At values above that, up to about 30 ms, you may still not hear a distinct echo, although you should hear a timbral change caused by comb filtering. Above roughly 30–50 ms (depending on the sound you are processing), your brain should start to acknowledge the delayed signal as a second, distinct sound.

Once there is a processed delay signal being created by the plug-in, it's time to play with it. The LPF control sets the corner frequency of a low-pass filter that affects only the processed signal. I still prefer to call these "high-cut" filters (see Chapter 4) since they are employed to cut high frequencies out of the signal, but that's more of a semantic argument. This particular filter has a range from 10 Hz all the way up to 20 kHz, with an "Off" setting at the very top.

The filter slope isn't very steep, so it can often be set a little lower then you might expect. It's a helpful tool for taking high-frequency energy out of the delayed signal so articulations aren't as cluttered, and to reduce phase cancellation effects at higher frequencies.

> **Tip** Remember that high-frequency energy is absorbed into the air faster than low-frequency energy in real acoustic environments. So pulling the LPF setting low enough to shave off some of the bright attack on drum sounds, for example, can really help the delay signal sound more like a reflection off a distant wall.

The next two controls, Depth and Rate, are not really delay controls *per se*, although they are necessary to pull off some of the special effects expected from a delay processor. Taken together, these two controls operate an LFO (low-frequency oscillator) that modulates the frequency of the processed signal. That means the delay signal shifts slightly higher and lower in pitch in a very slow cycle (see Figure 7.12). It may seem like a strange feature to introduce regular, repeating variations to delayed signal, but it's essential for creating certain special effects. The aim in a chorus effect, for example, isn't just to make it sound like another voice is sounding slightly late, but to vary the pitch slightly above and below the original to mimic the sound of several voices performing together.

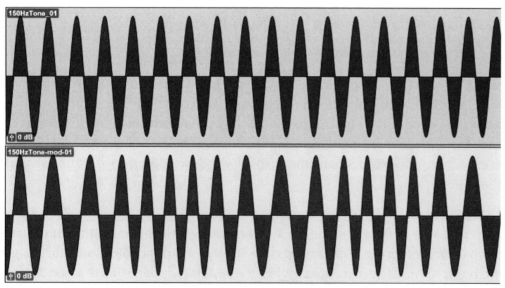

Figure 7.12 A 150 Hz tone (top) is modulated (bottom) at 100% Depth and a Rate of 10.00 Hz.

The Depth control determines the intensity of the modulation and is adjustable from 0% to 100%. Lower settings introduce only slight changes to the pitch. The Rate control adjusts the frequency setting of the LFO and is adjustable in hundredths of a cycle increments from 0.00 to 20.00 Hz. Lower Rate settings can make the effect very subtle and hard to detect. For example, at 0.10 Hz the frequency would shift up and down once every 10 seconds. Faster rates become more audible and produce additional overtones with the audible range.

When one copy of the original audio signal just isn't enough for you, turn to the last control in this section of the interface: the Feedback control. Don't worry though; this isn't the kind of feedback we're always fighting against on stage. This Feedback adds some of the processed delay signal back into the delay processor. This happens after the Mix control, so none of the original dry signal is recycled...only the processed stuff is allowed to go around for another trip.

The Feedback control itself can be a little confusing though, since it runs from –100% through 0% and up to +100%. Think of the percentage as a volume control for the signal being looped back to the beginning. Instead of sending a signal back at full volume, you might only send it back at 50%. On its next trip through, it will be sent back again, but at half level again. And so on, and so on, until the level drops too low to be audible. That means 100% should be a perpetual loop that never goes away...and it is. Be careful with that because it can get stuck. (If it does, just hit Bypass to stop the effect in its tracks.) As for the negative versus positive option, well, that allows the signal to be inverted for the next trip through the plug-in. Since delayed signals can cause phase cancellation and comb filtering, flipping the signal over for each repetition shifts the cancelled frequencies around in the spectrum. Give it a try to hear the difference.

Tempo Sync Controls

For the Medium, Long, Extra-Long, and Audio Suite versions of Delay II, there's an extra set of controls available that allow the delay to be synchronized to tempo and meter selections (Figure 7.13). This section does not appear in the Slap and Short versions of Delay II, because those do not have enough available delay time to make controls relevant.

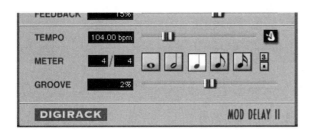

Figure 7.13 Tempo Sync controls.

Most textbooks on mixing or effects processors include a table that converts tempo to delay time in milliseconds, so you can create effects that synchronize with the time and meter of the song. Figure 7.14 shows a very basic formula in case you're interested, although that will only figure the length of one beat in 4/4 time. You'll have to do a little more calculating to subdivide it into eighth notes or sixteenth notes.

60 ÷ BPM × 1,000 = Delay Time
(in milliseconds)

Figure 7.14 Plug in your tempo in BPM to calculate the length of one beat in milliseconds...or just use the plug-in.

For example, that means that for 100 beats per minute you take 60, divide it by 100 BPM, and multiply by 1000 to get 600 milliseconds per beat. Lucky for you, the Delay II plug-in has the conversion process built right in. Dial in your tempo and time signature and it automatically adjusts the delay time. And if that's not enough, you can dial different subdivisions into the left and right channels, and synchronize the whole thing to your tempo track.

Get started by dialing your tempo and time signature into the little display windows labeled Tempo and Meter (Figure 7.15).

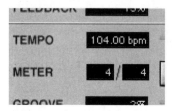

Figure 7.15 Enter the Tempo and Meter of your project here.

If you have set the tempo and meter for the project in the timelines at the top of the Edit window, and especially if you have built tempo or meter changes into the timeline, then it's probably a better idea to Sync to the timeline. The Tempo Sync button (Figure 7.16) is very cleverly unlabeled, but it does have a little drawing meant to look like one of those old-fashioned pendulum metronomes that piano and violin teachers seem to love.

Figure 7.16 This little unlabeled button activates Tempo Sync to lock Delay II to your project tempo.

Whichever way you choose to do it, once you have your Tempo and Meter set, you can move on to the fun part of selecting the rhythmic relationship of your delay. Clicking one of the five Duration buttons (Figure 7.17) allows you to select a whole note, half note, quarter note, eighth note, or sixteenth note value for the delay timing. The very tiny buttons next to the Duration buttons allow you to further select a triplet or dotted value for the delay.

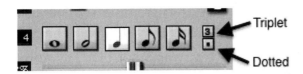

Figure 7.17   Five Duration buttons and the Triplet and Dotted value selectors.

The Duration buttons will highlight as you select a value while automatically changing the Delay time control up above. If you select a particular value and it doesn't highlight, that's probably because you are selecting a value that is too long for the version of the plug-in you have activated. A quarter note at 120 BPM, for example, requires 500 milliseconds of delay time, and that's more than is available in the Medium Delay II plug-in. You should be able to simply activate a longer version of the plug-in to accommodate the delay time, and all of your other settings should migrate over. But for safety's sake, go ahead and copy the plug-in settings before changing over just to be safe.

> **Tip** Making manual adjustments to the main Delay control up above will instantly deselect the Duration buttons below.

The Groove function at the bottom of the Tempo Sync controls is an interesting tool for refining the overall delay timing. After all of the other controls designed to lock the delay timing to the tempo and meter of the track, this function intentionally knocks it back out of sync. The control represents ¼ of a beat (not a quarter note) as 100% variation and provides the ability to shift the delay timing slightly early or late. That means if your project is in 4/4 time, a +10% value would translate to a delay landing too slow by 10% of a sixteenth note (10% of one quarter, of one beat).

The idea of the Groove function is to make the delayed signal land slightly late or early from the exact rhythmic timing. When used effectively, this can create a slight sense of push or pull against the time to make the effect seem to "swing" a little more. Personally, I would like to see a "humanize" function available as well that could move the effect back and forth within a range since real human players tend to drift slightly slower and faster while they play. Conveniently enough, this is a Pro Tools plug-in, and that means every control can be automated. To experiment with this kind of humanizing function, simply activate the plug-in automation for the Groove control. Then draw in some subtle changes in a range from 0% to +10% to create the feel of a player who is "pushing" the time.

Real-Time Use (RTAS & TDM)

The Delay II plug-ins are available for real-time processing in both RTAS and TDM formats for Pro Tools 9 HD and earlier Pro Tools HD systems. On Pro Tools 9 or earlier Pro Tools LE or M-Powered systems, only the RTAS version is available. For Pro Tools 10 systems, all of the Delay II plug-ins are included as RTAS and TDM versions, but they are also joined by the new

Mod Delay III (described next) that runs under either of the new AAX-Native or AAX-DSP versions. Delay plug-ins tend to be resource intensive in general. They only get more power hungry as the delay time increases since the plug-in reserves processing power based on the total delay time available in the plug-in, not how much time you are using. So plan accordingly, and if you are only using a small percentage of the available delay time, look to see if you can step down to the next shorter version of Delay II.

Usage Example: Faking Stereo with Delay and M/S Decoding

So you have a mono track and you wish it was stereo? Whether it's an instrument track, spoken word vocals, or sound effects, it can happen for all kinds of reasons. You may have received tracks from somewhere else. Maybe it sounded all right with just one microphone while recording, but now it seems a little thin. Maybe you ran out of microphones, or input channels, or even cables while recording the original tracks. Whatever the reason, this problem comes up often enough in different recording situations that it's worth looking at a potential solution.

For this solution, we'll use an adaptation of Mid/Side decoding technique. If you aren't familiar with this recording technique, a quick glance at a general recording textbook should fill you in on the details. The general idea (Figure 7.18) is that a single "Mid" microphone, usually a cardioid pattern, is aimed directly at the sound source. A second, figure-eight pattern "Side" microphone is placed as close as possible to the Mid, but turned 90° off-axis from the sound source.

Figure 7.18 A basic Mid/Side microphone pair with cardioid Mid and figure-eight Side.

The on-axis Mid microphone records primarily the direct sound of the source while the Side microphone ignores that sound and captures primarily the reflected sounds bouncing around the room. The mono signal you already have could be considered the Mid microphone in this case. But what is really being captured by the Side? The reflected sound from the room is simply the original sound, bouncing off the walls, floors, and ceiling, and arriving at the microphone a little later. There's more to it than that, of course. The reflected sound will be quieter, but unevenly so, having lost more high frequencies along its journey. There will also be lots of reflections packed somewhat tightly together, which we call "early reflections."

There's also one more step to consider: the decoding process. If you've never worked with a Mid/Side microphone pair, it can seem a strange idea that we might try to get a stereo signal from one microphone facing forward and one facing sideways. I won't go into the details of why the whole thing works (you can find that in a general recording text), but I will explain how it's done because we need to duplicate the procedure.

The Mid/Side decoding process relies on a special property of figure-eight microphones: the fact that material arriving at the front of the microphone is captured in the correct phase relationship to the acoustic sound, while material arriving at the back of the microphone is inverted from the natural acoustic sound. By simply combining the Mid and Side microphone signals, in-phase material is boosted, out-of-phase material is cancelled, and the result is roughly a hypercardioid-shaped pickup pattern aimed about 45° off-axis. By inverting the Side signal and repeating the procedure, the phase relationship is reversed, and a stereo counterpart is derived. The whole process is generally described as in Figure 7.19.

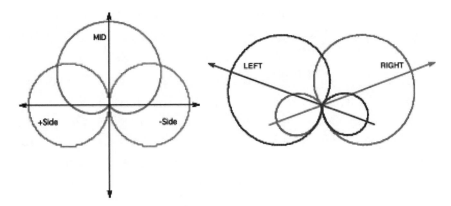

Figure 7.19   Mid + Side = Left and Mid – Side = Right

It may still look a little confusing but the whole technique is time tested and proven, and for our situation, the procedure in Pro Tools is pretty easy. To start, you need two copies of the "Mid" channel, which is the original mono track. Why not simply route the original track to an unused stereo bus? Then that bus will have one copy on the Left side and one on the Right.

Creating a fake "Side" signal is as easy as copying the original signal, lowering the volume level, and creating a somewhat dense and darker-sounding delay effect. So select the track with the original audio, duplicate the track including the audio and routing, and activate a Multichannel, Medium Delay II plug-in on the track. From the default settings, dial in these values for both channels: Gain to –6dB, LPF to 4,000 Hz, Delay to 60 ms, and Feedback to 40%. Then activate the Phase reverse switch for only the right channel. The result should look like Figure 7.20.

The result of all this duplicating and routing should have both mono audio tracks being split into two channels and routed to a stereo bus. The original goes to the bus raw, while the duplicate runs through Delay II and is sent to the bus with one side inverted.

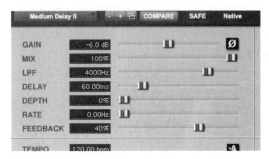

Figure 7.20   Medium Delay II set up to create a fake "Side" signal.

It's likely the fake stereo effect will sound a little tinny and strange at first because the delayed signal will probably be too loud. Try pulling the volume for that track down to about –10dB and listen for whether the sound improves. Also try adjusting some of the parameters on the Delay II plug-in. Shortening the Delay time can create a denser ring, but you'll need a higher Feedback value, and the combination may deliver a ringing and metallic texture, especially if you're working with rhythmic or percussive sounds. You might also try using the modulation functions to give a little more shimmer to the delay signal. Try setting the Depth to 20% and the Rate to 10.00 Hz for both channels as a starting point.

The overall effect of this trick is to spread the various frequencies across the stereo field. Creating a delayed signal to play against the original causes comb filtering as alternating frequency bands are cancelled and boosted. By duplicating the delayed signal and inverting it, the frequencies that are boosted on one side are cancelled on the other and vice versa. This won't really turn a mono sound into a stereo one since there are no references to the original acoustic space, but it can add a sense of width and space to the track. With a little practice, you can develop a more convincing sound for your particular track. Try adding an equalizer plug-in (Chapter 4) before the delay plug-in to help you sculpt the tone of the artificial room sound. Or consider adding a reverb plug-in (Chapter 6) to the auxiliary bus after the whole decoding procedure is finished. That can take the sound even further toward really giving the impression it was recorded in stereo in a nice acoustic space.

Audio Suite Use and an Example of Basic Process Music

Only one version of Delay II appears in the Audio Suite pull-down menu, and it is labeled as "Delay" in the menu, although it is labeled "Mod Delay II" in the plug-in interface window. Don't worry though; this one version covers all of the different setting options for all the real-time versions of Delay II.

This ability to receive the settings from all the real-time versions of Delay II is one of the best features of the Audio Suite version of the plug-in. Delay processors of any type tend to be resource intensive—though they are also time-based effects, which means it's really essential to hear how the process works and develops over time. Using a real-time Delay II plug-in to create an effect or texture is a great starting place, and using the Audio Suite version to print those effects to new files is a great final step in saving system resources as your mix comes together.

Just remember that time-based effects take more time to play out than the original audio you may be processing. This means it's important to select enough time in the timeline to accommodate the entire effect. The track shown in Figure 7.21 is a short drum hit that was rendered with a delay effect that was longer than the amount of time selected in the timeline. The rendered signal was cut off abruptly because Pro Tools will only create an audio file as long as the amount of time you select in the timeline.

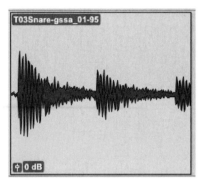

Figure 7.21 Selecting only the audio clip to be rendered didn't leave enough time for the effect to play out.

Always select enough empty time after the audio clip for the effect to play out as intended (Figure 7.22). If the rendered clip runs a little longer than you had intended, you can always undo the effect, adjust the parameters, and try again...or just fade out the new clip to something a little shorter.

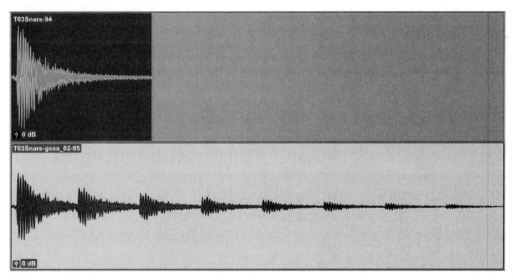

Figure 7.22 Select enough extra time for the rendered effect to play out as intended.

Also remember that at 10.9 seconds, the Audio Suite version of Delay II has far more delay time available than any of its counterpart real-time versions. If you are trying to create truly long delay effects, this may be the only version of the plug-in that's up to the task. This kind of enormous looping delay may fall more into the realm of electronic and experimental music creation, but that may well be an area you are interested in exploring. Try this as an experiment:

1. Record a single short phrase that's about 1.5 to 2 seconds long.

2. Trim the phrase in the Edit window until the selection is exactly 2.0 seconds.

3. Select the audio clip and use the Repeat command in the Edit menu to create nine more copies.

4. Select all 10 copies of the phrase plus an extra 2 minutes or so of time.

5. Open the Audio Suite version of Delay II.

6. Set the Mix to 50%, Delay to 1975 ms, and Feedback to 95%.

7. Render the selection and listen to the result.

There may not be enough time to complete the entire ring out of the delay, but you'll be able to hear the general idea. As one copy of the phrase plays almost all the way through, another starts and layers on top, just slightly out of time. Then another copy joins, and another, and another, and so on. Once all of the copies are playing over each other, the individual syllables will start to smear and turn into rhythmic pulses and textures.

To continue experimenting, try it again with 20 copies of the original phrase, and the texture should end up thick enough that you can't even identify the original words. Then try the same process with a phrase that's only 1.0 second long and set the Delay time to 975 ms. A more energetic phrase should create a more rhythmic texture. This is a rough approximation of what is called Process Music in the experimental music world. If you like it, take a look at some of the music of Steve Reich and other 20th-century writers who pioneered the style.

Mod Delay III (Real-Time AAX and Audio Suite)

The latest update to the Pro Tools plug-in lineup is the third installment of their delay processor that's now actually called Mod Delay III in all of the various pull-down menus. It is included with Pro Tools 10 and is among the first of the new AAX format of plug-ins (Figure 7.23). Although it looks like a fairly substantial piece of software, it is going to get somewhat of a shorter treatment here for two main reasons. The first is simply that it is brand spanking new and I've only just spent a little bit of time working with it to see just what it can do. The second is that it's virtually identical in controls and operation to the Mod Delay II plug-in.

It seems a heck of a thing to start talking about the new sheriff in town by telling you to go back a few pages and read about the old one, but that's exactly what you should do if you haven't yet. Then come back here to read about what's different in the new version. The two are not identical by any means. I tried copying the settings from Delay II to drop into Mod Delay III and they would not take, which is unfortunate but understandable.

Figure 7.23   Mod Delay III sports a new skin and new code but is really quite familiar.

The biggest difference between Mod Delay III and its Delay II predecessors really lies under the hood in the code that runs the new version. As an AAX plug-in, Mod Delay III is built to run on a 64-bit processor. As with the other AAX plug-ins, the native and DSP-powered versions are not labeled as RTAS and TDM anymore, but as AAX-Native and AAX-DSP instead. Other basic and essential Pro Tools plug-ins are sure to follow, but this is simply the first update out of the gate.

Up on the surface, the control window looks radically different. It's a darker, more modern-looking interface with a few more splashes of color. There are meters provided for both the input and the output, and amazingly enough, the layout makes some logical sense. Input meters and Phase switches are on the left, the processing section is in the middle, and the output Gain controls and meters are on the far right. The Gain controls still seem mislabeled in my view since they don't actually provide any boost in audio level (that is what gain is, after all) with a maximum setting of 0dB.

At least in the main control section, things are laid out in a far more logical way (Figure 7.24). Observe that the Delay control stands out as the largest knob, centered, and above the Feedback and LPF controls, with the modulation controls in a separate area alongside.

It has been said that the new layout is intended to make this plug-in easier to operate from a touch-screen control surface. I have always considered a large touch-screen monitor along with Pro Tools keyboard and good trackball mouse to be the ideal control interface for recording and editing in Pro Tools, so hopefully there is more of this kind of redesign coming in the future. Whether or not that is the reasoning, the new interface window is a major improvement.

Only two, very clear, functional differences for Mod Delay III stand out. The first is that since only one version shows up in the pull-down menu, the Delay control sports a huge range from

Figure 7.24 The control layout for Mod Delay III is much more intuitive and well organized than its predecessor.

0.0 up to 5000.0 ms of available delay time. That's double the maximum length of the Extra-Long Delay II plug-in. And Mod Delay III also provides a Link button that quickly locks all of the controls for the left and right channels so they operate in tandem. Activating the Link switch does not automatically push all of the control values from one side over to the other, so you can choose settings that are slightly different between the channels. But as soon as you grab any control on either channel to make a change, the matching control for the other channel jumps into action to match the setting.

Overall, the sonic character of the new Mod Delay III plug-in sounds quite similar to its predecessor, so if there's something different going on in there, it's a very, very subtle change. But the new plug-in also sports a whole new collection of presets to get you started exploring the creative possibilities of this newest delay plug-in.

Multi-Tap Delay (Audio Suite Only)

The Multi-Tap Delay plug-in is an offline only (no real-time application) delay processor designed to allow the addition of short special effect echoes or rhythmic effects of any length to an audio clip. The control interface (Figure 7.25) can look a little intimidating at first, with all the various control sliders and displays. But a closer look reveals that the idea behind this plug-in is to group four simple delay lines into a single processor with just a few extra overall controls at the bottom.

Each individual delay tap has only the basic controls of Gain, Feedback, Pan, and Delay. Taken as a whole, the four sets of controls appear as though they are meant to function independently. For the most part, they do; however, the four taps do operate collectively in a few key areas. Since there is no modulation control or EQ filter within the plug-in, each repeated copy of the

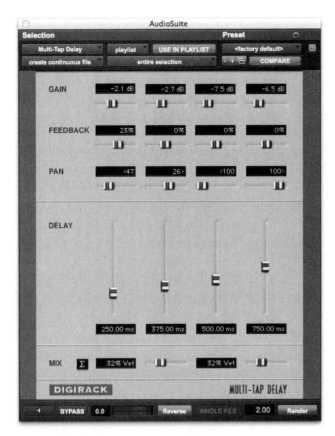

Figure 7.25 The Audio Suite Multi-Tap Delay plug-in control interface.

original should sound identical except for volume or pan position. This means that understanding the relationship of the Gain and Feedback controls (Figure 7.26) in particular is critical to getting the most out of the processor.

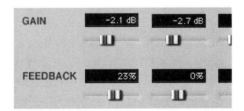

Figure 7.26 It's critical to know how the Gain and Feedback controls relate to each other.

The Gain controls allow individual settings of any value from −96.0dB to +6dB, providing a huge range of adjustment for each delay tap. This makes it easy to create rhythmic patterns of accented and unaccented taps for a more dynamic and varying delay pattern.

Tip Setting one or more of the Gain controls to –INF (all the way off) is the only way to completely remove the tap from the process. One tap may appear inactive if its Delay time is set the same as one of the other taps, but it will still be adding its signal to the overall output.

This Gain control is also unique among the delay plug-ins (and most of the others too) since it remains in the processing chain when a signal is looped back into it. That means when it's used together with the Feedback control, the two can create delay effects that decay very slowly over time, sustain at a consistent level, or even build continuously toward overload until the effect is stopped. Keep that in mind if you boost the gain here since that's the kind of overload that can kill your speakers.

The four Feedback controls are *not* independent for the four delay lines because they do not simply feed each tap back in on itself. If any delay tap is fed back into the processor, its output signal is routed back into the main input and looped through all of the active delay lines again. If you are trying to create a regular, repeating rhythm effect, you may want to loop only one tap back to the beginning. Looping multiple taps means each will start a new pass through all the taps as soon as the signal is sent back. This can quickly turn a cool, syncopated pattern into a machine-gun-like barrage of steadily repeating notes.

The signal levels of the four Feedback controls also happen to be cumulative, meaning they add to each other. Say for example, that the Gain controls for all four delay taps are set to 0.0dB. If the total of all four feedback controls adds up to more than +100%, the repeated signal will grow louder and louder with each tap. Indeed, setting just two of the Feedback controls to +100% would mean the overall feedback is +200%, so the signal strength will double on each pass. This is helpful to know if you are trying to create a particular decay or overload type of effect. Render a short, percussive sound with one delay tap to +100% Feedback with the Gain control set to –1dB and the pattern will repeat for a very long time while slowing losing one decibel on each pass until it is gone.

The Pan control does function independently and allows each delay tap to be placed wherever you would like across the stereo field. Similar to other Pan controls within Pro Tools, each one can be set from <100 (hard left) through 0 (center) to 100> hard right. If a Pan value is set for a delay line that is also being fed back to create a loop effect, the Pan setting does not affect the looped signal, nor is it changed by the Input Sum switch described later. Each tap is returned as a mono signal when fed back through the process.

When it comes to creating stereo or panned effects with Multi-Tap Delay or other plug-ins that are only available under Audio Suite you must select a clip in either a stereo track or two mono tracks to receive the rendered file. If only a mono audio clip is selected, the plug-in will only calculate a mono output file, and any panning effects will be lost.

The four Delay control sliders (Figure 7.27) are the last independent controls for the four delay taps. Each control is entirely independent of the other taps, and can be set to any value from

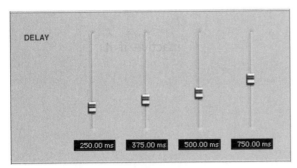

Figure 7.27 The four Delay controls are independent, but arranging them from shortest to longest makes it easier to follow what's happening.

0.00 to 1500 ms (1.50 seconds). To make it easier to understand how you are dialing in rhythms across the four taps, establish a routine for how you arrange the delay times across the taps. Any tap can be set to any value, but it's easier to understand if, for example, the shortest delay is on the left tap and the longest is on the right. This way it's like reading from left to right as the various taps are triggered.

At the bottom of the plug-in window are three more controls that set global parameters for the plug-in. There are two wet-versus-dry Mix controls (Figure 7.28) that allow you to control how much dry (original) signal is balanced against the wet (delayed) signal for the left and right channels independently. Just remember that setting one side too low against the other will undermine any panning effects you have dialed into the delay taps.

Figure 7.28 The wet-versus-dry Mix level can be set independently for the right and left outputs.

The small, Greek, sigma symbol (Figure 7.29) to the left of the two Mix controls is the Input Sum switch. Activating this button will sum the incoming signal to mono before sending it through the plug-in, so the dry signal appears centered in the stereo field.

Figure 7.29 Use the Input Sum switch to sum the incoming signal to mono before rendering.

When the switch is inactive, incoming dry signals play through in their original pan positions. Any delay signals that are fed back into the processor to create a loop are not affected by the Input Sum switch and are sent back as mono signals.

As with all Audio Suite–onlyplug-ins, the Preview button will be especially important to you since Multi-Tap Delay has no real-time counterpart for experimenting. Depending on the kind of effect you want to create, it can be very complicated to dial in the right control values. Using the Preview button for every control adjustment and every audio clip you select will help ensure that you get exactly the sound you're seeking.

Ping-Pong Delay (Audio Suite Only)

In general, a ping-pong delay is an adaptation of a standard stereo delay designed to create more interesting special effects or apparent width. There are many design variations possible, but the most important difference is including the ability for one delay line to feedback into the other, and vice versa. This is the idea behind the Audio Suite Ping-Pong Delay. The plug-in looks deceptively similar (Figure 7.30) to the various Delay II plug-ins, but its various controllers operate more like those found in the Multi-Tap Delay. And don't overlook that extra Cross-Feedback control for each channel.

Figure 7.30 The layout of Ping-Pong Delay looks familiar but behaves a little different.

The first stop for a signal on its way through Ping-Pong Delay is the Gain control for each channel. Separate controls for the left and right channel allow the signal to be cut as low as –96.0dB or boosted as high as +6dB. This allows the audio clip you're rendering to be brought up to match other tracks, down to avoid overload, or whatever your particular need. Although the range is the same as Multi-Tap Delay, this is the only trip the signal will make through the Gain control, so it's not the place to look to create a runaway build-to-overload effect.

In between the two Gain controls, and after them in the signal path, you'll notice a small, Greek sigma symbol on the Input Sum switch (Figure 7.31). When activated, the Input Sum will combine the incoming signal from the left and right channels into a centered, mono signal that will then be split and fed to the two delay taps. If you are rendering a mono audio clip that is residing on only one side of a stereo channel pair, be sure to engage this switch so the signal will be fed to both delay taps…unless you have other plans.

Figure 7.31 The Input Sum switch combines incoming signals to mono before rendering.

Each channel also has its own wet-versus-dry Mix control. As usual, this balances the level of the unprocessed signal against the processed signal, although the signal it considers "dry" has already passed through the Gain and Input Sum functions. Remember also that as with other delay plug-ins, setting the Mix control to 100% means none of the original signal is heard, removing the initial timing reference for the delay.

The remaining controls operate the delay taps for the left and right channel independently (for the most part) and function in much the same way that they do in other delay plug-ins. The two Delay controls operate independently for each channel, and each has a range of 0.00 ms up to 1500 ms (1.50 seconds). There is unfortunately no function for synchronizing the timing of these delay taps to the project tempo. If you want to create rhythmic effects that follow the track timing, activate the real-time, multichannel version of the Extra-Long Delay II plug-in and use the Tempo Sync controls as a calculator. Figure out the delay times there and type them into the Ping-Pong Delay controls.

The Low-Pass Filter control operates the same way as the identical control found in all versions of Delay II. It selects the corner frequency for a basic, High-Cut filter so any material above that frequency corner is reduced or eliminated. High frequencies die out faster than lower ones in real acoustic spaces, so this feature is especially helpful if you're trying to create more realistic-sounding thickener or slap delay effect.

The big difference between Ping-Pong Delay and all of the other delay plug-ins is the doubling up of the Feedback control and the Cross-Feedback control (Figure 7.32).

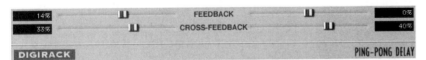

Figure 7.32 Feedback adjusts how much signal is sent in the same delay channel, while Cross-Feedback controls how much is sent across to the other delay channel.

The first Feedback control for each channel operates in exactly the way it would on any other delay plug-in, feeding some of the processed signal back into the plug-in so it can run through the delay process again. Set the control to any value from –100% to +100%, where 0% means no signal is fed back, +100% means the output is fed back at the full output strength, and –100% means the full output signal is inverted and sent back through. Inverting and Feedback signal means that different frequency bands are boosted or cut due to phase cancellation on each pass through the process. Use the Feedback controls to adjust how much signal from each delay is sent back into itself, left to left, and right to right.

The Cross-Feedback control has the same range of available settings and functions almost identically, except that it routes the output of one channel delay to the input of the other, left to right, and right to left. Depending on how you set it, this can create more interesting rhythmic and syncopated rhythmic patterns than a simple stereo delay. Figure 7.33 illustrates how a signal would be repeated with a 500 ms delay in one channel and a 250 ms delay in the other, with feedback in a standard Feedback arrangement, and then a Cross-Feedback effect.

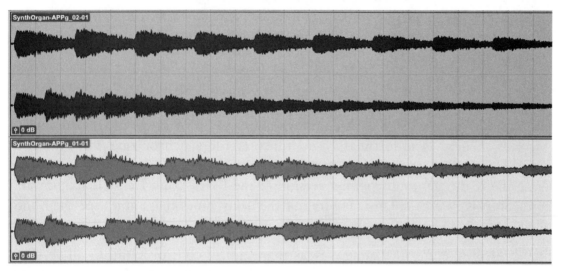

Figure 7.33 A stereo delay through a standard Feedback process (top) and Cross-Feedback (bottom).

Listening to the Preview output of a delay setup in each of these configurations will reveal two distinctly different rhythmic patterns. The first setup will deliver a very strong duple (multiple of 2) pattern and the stereo action will favor one side as the repeated sound plays center, right, center, right, and so on. Using the second setting will deliver a strong triple (multiple of 3) pattern that will also be more active in the stereo field as the repeating elements are played center, left, right, center, left, right, and so on.

Learning to balance the Feedback and Cross-Feedback controls may take some time and practice. But that's really what makes Ping-Pong Delay unique, so that's the key to using this plug-in effectively. Remember that the Feedback control loops a signal back into the same delay tap, while Cross-Feedback loops the signal into the opposite delay tap, and you'll be off to a good start. It's easy to create ping-pong delay effects that sound cool, but end up being too busy for continuous usage on a track. That's not to say you can't use it for a whole track. The more subtle the effect you create with the plug-in, the easier it will be to apply it to larger sections of your track.

Usage Example: Basic 16th Note Ping-Pong
There are only a handful of factory presets for Ping-Pong Delay that give a quick overview of some of the possibilities for the plug-in. If you haven't tried the plug-in before, select a short,

percussive sound and use Preview to hear the sonic effect those settings can provide. Then switch to a vocal or melodic guitar part to hear how those can sound. Scale the Delay times up to slow down the effect, or down to speed it up. Raising the Feedback and Cross-Feedback settings will make the effect ring out longer. Now select a simple audio clip as shown in Figure 7.34 to try this setting.

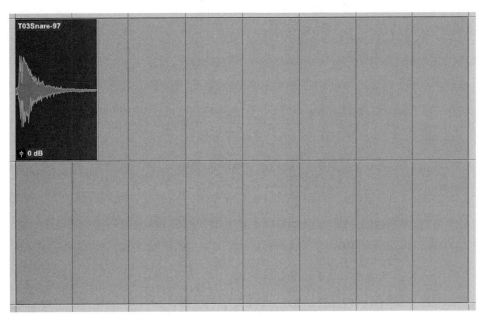

Figure 7.34 The target audio clip is one drum strike, but select two tracks and extra time.

Remember that to render a mono sound with a stereo effect like Ping-Pong Delay, you'll need to select two channels to receive the stereo audio file. And, of course, always select extra time so the effect can play out completely.

The goal of this example is to create a 16th note ping-pong pattern that alternates the repeated sound from left to right. At a tempo of 120 BPM, a quarter note lasts 500 ms, an eighth note lasts 250 ms, and a sixteenth note lasts 125 ms. You'll need to scale up or down for different tempos.

> **Note** Divide 60,000 by the tempo in BPM (beats per minute) to figure out how many milliseconds are in one quarter note of 4/4 time. Then divide that in half for an eighth note, and in half again for a sixteenth note.

Unfortunately, just dialing in a Delay time of 125 ms for each side won't get the result we're after. That would just loop both delays at the same time so the output would sound like it's stuck in the center. Instead, each delay tap needs to loop at 250 ms, the value of one eighth note, but be offset by 125 ms so the two taps are playing at different times. But there's no pre-delay control to offset one tap versus the other, so you'll need another solution. The trick is to use the Feedback control to loop one side of the delay every eighth note, and then use the Cross-Feedback control to send the signal to the other delay that will play a sixteenth note later without looping (Figure 7.35).

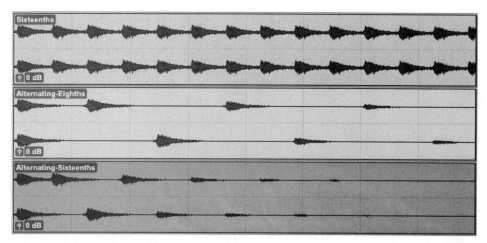

Figure 7.35 Both delays looping 16th notes (top); alternating 8th notes (middle); and looped 8th notes triggering an extra 16th note (bottom).

Luckily, it's a lot harder to describe how this effect works than to actually set it up. Activate the Ping-Pong Delay plug-in, call up the factory-default settings, and adjust a few controls to these values: Input Sum active, Left Delay at 125 ms, Right Delay at 250 ms, Right Feedback at 50%, and Right Cross-Feedback at 75%. The display window should look like Figure 7.36.

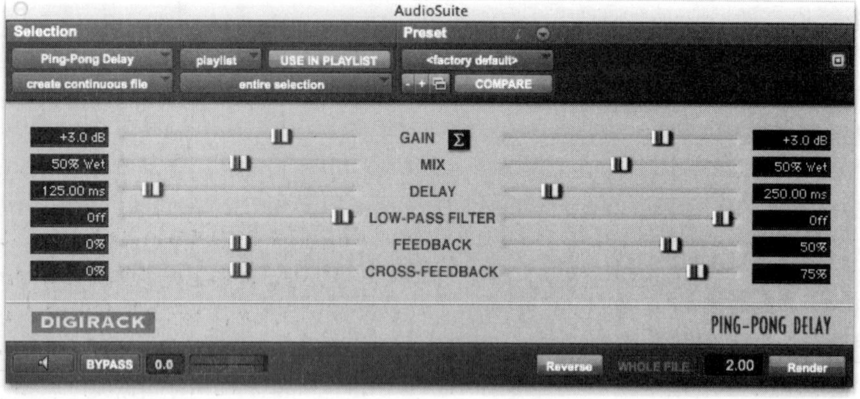

Figure 7.36 Dial these settings into the plug-in.

Now simply click the Preview button to hear the effect. To hear it more clearly, you can set the Low-Pass Filter for both channels to 400 Hz so the rendered signal sounds darker. You should hear the dry signal play in the center, then pass through both delay taps so the 125 ms delay sounds on the left and the 250 ms delay follows on the right. The Left output isn't looped, but the Right output is looped to both delays. That means the looped signal waits another 125 ms before sounding on the left and 250 ms before sounding on the right; and then it's looped again. Each pair of repeats is played lower by 50% until the whole thing is gone. The result is a 16th note ping-pong pattern that decays over about three or four beats.

To modify this effect so it suits your project, try adjusting a few parameters. Set the Feedback lower on the right delay tap so the effect dies out faster, or set it higher so it rings out longer. A 100% feedback setting will ring indefinitely...or at least as long as the audio clip you select to render. Experiment with different rhythmic patterns too. Setting the Left Delay to 375 ms and the Right Delay to 500 ms will deliver a dotted-eighth plus sixteenth pattern similar to a jazz shuffle.

Pro Tools Creative Collection

These last two delay plug-ins are part of the Pro Tools Creative Collection labeled as the AIR plug-ins within your software. They share the familiar look and layout of the other AIR plug-ins as well as some of the quirks, and both are designed for creative applications rather than utility. The AIR Dynamic Delay includes an envelope follower section that allows the processor to automatically adjust the feedback level based on the volume level of the incoming signal. The AIR Multi-Delay provides up to five independent delay taps to create anything from dense short delay stacks to more complex rhythmic patterns. Both plug-ins can be synchronized to a project's tempo track so the delay effects stay in time with the song.

Real-Time Use Only (RTAS)

As with all of the AIR family of plug-ins, the AIR Dynamic Delay and AIR Multi-Delay are only available as real-time plug-ins. It's something to keep in mind while you're working in case you run up against limits of system resources. If you need to conserve processing power, do so by bouncing rendered tracks to disk or by printing your processed channels to new tracks and then disabling the original tracks as described in Chapter 3.

Mono versus Stereo

Both of the AIR Delay plug-ins can be activated as either mono or stereo plug-ins, but like the rest of the AIR family, as of the time of this writing none of them can be started as a mono-to-stereo plug-in (labeled as "Mono/Stereo" within Pro Tools). If you are activating any of them on an auxiliary track, this won't be an issue as you can simply create a stereo aux bus, insert the stereo version of the plug-in, and feed stereo or mono signals to it. However, it's far more likely with delay plug-ins that you would activate the plug-in directly into the chain for a single track or mix bus, so keep this in mind. You can always choose to add only a mono plug-in to a mono track, but some of the features, like the width controls and multi-tap panning, will not function properly. If this is an issue, simply route the track to an unused stereo bus, create a new stereo aux track to catch the signal and route it back to the mix, then activate the delay plug-in there.

This mono-into-stereo issue may be resolved if this group of plug-ins are updated to the new AAX plug-in format for Pro Tools 10, but there is no word yet on whether that is planned or not. But don't worry, the RTAS versions will continue to run in Pro Tools 10 just as they have in earlier versions.

AIR Dynamic Delay

One of the trickiest things about working with delay processors is keeping them under control. When every note played through the plug-in is repeated one or more times, it's easy for things to build up and start to sound cluttered. Rhythm and tempo begin to get smeared, and even harmonies can get lost as notes from one chord ring into the next. One solution is to include some basic automation to the delay processor so it can adjust how it responds to incoming signals. That's precisely what puts the "dynamic" into the AIR Dynamic Delay (Figure 7.37).

Figure 7.37 AIR Dynamic Delay includes an Envelope Follower to adjust how it responds to incoming signals.

To begin with, AIR Dynamic Delay is a fairly comprehensive basic delay processor. Delay time can be set independently or synchronized to the tempo track. Both Low-Cut and High-Cut filters are included to shape the tone of the rendered signal. And there are several stereo balancing features included that aren't available on any other delay plug-in. The key feature that defines this plug-in is the Envelope Modulation section. This function allows the plug-in to adjust two key parameters based on the incoming dry signal. First, though, let's cover the basics.

Basic Controls

The Delay and Sync controls (Figure 7.38) for the AIR Dynamic Delay plug-in operate as a sort of linked pair of controls for setting the overall delay time.

Figure 7.38 The Delay and Sync controls work together to set the overall delay time.

Without the Sync enabled, the Delay control can be set to time-based values from 1 ms (.001 seconds) up to 4000 ms (4.00 seconds). As in other plug-ins, the Delay control determines how long the incoming signal is held back before being sent through the processor. When the Sync switch is activated, the Delay control no longer displays time in milliseconds; rather, it displays note values relative to the project tempo map. The control can be set to the following values:

- 16 = Sixteenth note
- 8T = Eighth-note triplet
- 16D = Dotted eighth note
- 8 = Eighth note
- 4T = Quarter-note triplet
- 8D = Dotted eighth note
- 4 = Quarter note
- 2T = Half-note triplet
- 4D = Dotted quarter note
- 2 = Half note
- 1T = Whole-note triplet
- 3/4 = Three quarter notes (dotted half note)
- 4/4 = Four quarter notes (whole note)
- 5/4 = Five quarter notes
- 6/4 = Six quarter notes (dotted whole note)
- 7/4 = Seven quarter notes
- 8/4 = Eight quarter notes (double whole note)

There is no display for the actual delay time in milliseconds when the Tempo Sync function is enabled, but the plug-in will follow the BPM tempo settings you have placed into the tempo track.

Figure 7.39 The Feedback control adjusts how much output signal is looped back into the processor.

At the bottom left of the plug-in window is the Feedback control (Figure 7.39), which determines how much of the output signal is looped back into the delay processor.

At a setting of 100%, the Feedback function should send the full output signal back through the delay process, creating an infinite loop. This particular plug-in, however, has just a small amount of signal loss built-in so that even at this setting the repeated signal will eventually decay.

At the bottom right corner of the plug-in, the Mix control adjusts the dry (unprocessed) signal against the wet (processed) signal. As with other delay plug-ins, it's possible to set the controls so the dry and wet controls sound identical with the wet signal played slightly later. That also means it's possible to set the Mix control to 100% wet, and hear a signal that sounds exactly like the original—although there's enough going on under the hood of the AIR Dynamic Delay that it's hard to get everything dialed back to that kind of neutral state.

Stereo Effects

Creating more complex and interesting stereo effects with AIR Dynamic Delay is made possible by the addition of three extra stereo functions you won't see on any of the other delay plug-ins. The L/R Ratio and Stereo Width controls are both located under the Delay heading section of the plug-in, while a Feedback Mode selector switch is located in the right sidebar (Figure 7.40).

Figure 7.40 Three extra stereo functions can help create more interesting stereo delay effects.

The Stereo Width control can be set from 0% or mono up to 100% stereo as long as the plug-in is activated on a stereo channel or bus. Most of the other AIR plug-ins that include width controls use a sum and difference matrix, but this plug-in simply pans the outputs from hard left and right in toward the center. So if you are sending a stereo signal into the processor, remember that any setting less than 100% will narrow the imaging of the delayed signal. It won't, however, have any effect on the dry signal.

Whether it's activated as a mono or stereo plug-in, AIR Dynamic Delay has only one overall Delay control. To create different delay times for the left and right channels, use the L/R Ratio control to adjust the relationship between the delay times for each channel. This is an unusual approach to managing delay time, but isn't too hard to understand. Each channel can be set in a range from 50% of the total Delay time to 100%.

When turned hard to the left, the left channel will be 50% of the total while the right is 100%. At the center point both left and right delay taps are at 100% of the Delay setting, and at hard right, the right channel is at 50% of the total time. This does not, however, translate to independence of the two delay taps because that will be determined by the Feedback Mode described below. This limited (and changing) independence of the L/R Ratio can be a little confusing at first, but it can also be very helpful when creating ping-pong delays and staggered stereo effects in Tempo Sync mode. Setting the left side to fire 5% early, for example, can create a subtle left-to-right grace note effect that will automatically adjust with the tempo track.

The Feedback Mode selector switch allows for three different relationships of the output signal as it is looped back into the processor. When set to Mono, the incoming signal is summed to mono, fed equally to both delay taps, and output in stereo.

Any signal looped back into the process by the Feedback function is treated the same way again. This also changes the apparent behavior of the L/R Ratio. Setting that control to a 50% to 100% relationship won't mean the shorter tap will play twice as fast; rather, it will play 50% earlier. The total delay time will remain as set at the Delay control, and the process will loop at that rate with one channel simply playing early. This can deliver a quick and easy ping-pong delay effect where the repeating delay signal seems to bounce from side to side.

When the Feedback Mode selector is set to Stereo, incoming signals are routed through the processor on their appropriate channels, the two delay taps operate independently, and there is no crossing of the signals. This changes the apparent behavior of the L/R Ratio as well since each delay tap now functions on its own. The relationship between the delay time values is still limited to one tap at 100% while the other is set anywhere from 50% to 100% of the Delay setting. Now, however, the slower tap will loop faster. A setting of 100%-50% will mean the right tap is playing twice as fast as the left, while a 75%-100% setting will deliver a true 3-against-4 pattern between the two channels.

With the Feedback Mode selector set to Cross, the AIR Dynamic Delay also functions as two independent delay taps for looped effects, except the output signal of the left delay is fed back to the right channel, and vice versa. It might seem that the only function of this would be to flip the stereo image back and forth on each repeat, but it also changes the apparent behavior of the L/R Ratio function. Now each tap will be delayed for the time value of one channel, then the value of the other, back and forth, again and again. The result is that the overall Delay time for both channels will be the sum of both delay times, as illustrated in Figure 7.41.

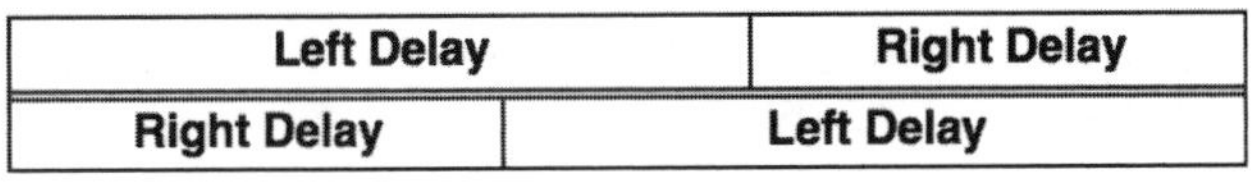

Left Delay	Right Delay
Right Delay	Left Delay

Figure 7.41 The overall delay time becomes the sum of each channel delay tap.

In Cross mode, if the L/R Ratio is set to 100%-100%, the stereo image would simply reverse with each repeat. Any other value will deliver a polyrhythm effect where each repeat sounds at the center, then one side, then the other. A L/R Ratio setting of 100%-50%, for example, won't deliver a 2-to-1 relationship, but rather a 2/3 to 1/3 relationship, resulting in a triplet feel as the repeated taps play back from center, right, left, center, right, left, and so on.

EQ Section

Two basic tone controls are provided in the EQ Section of the AIR Dynamic Delay plug-in: a Low-Cut and High-Cut filter (Figure 7.42).

Figure 7.42 Low-Cut and High-Cut filter controls.

These filters behave exactly as they should, allowing either low-frequency or high-frequency material to be rolled off of the rendered signal. (The dry signal is not affected by these filters in any way.) The Low-Cut filter has a broad range from 20.0 Hz (effectively "off") all the way up to 1.00 kHz. Using this filter to remove some of the low-end of the rendered signal can help keep clarity in bass lines, rhythm guitars, or even vocals as the lower parts are left dry and the higher-frequency parts are processed. In contrast, the High-Cut filter can be set from as high as 20.0 kHz (effectively "off") down to 1.0 kHz. Use this filter to control higher overtones, control some phase cancellation, keep vocal articulations clear, or for other effects.

Envelope Mod (Modulation) Section

The truly unique function within the AIR Dynamic Delay is the envelope follower that can automatically adjust the Feedback and Mix controls in reaction to the incoming audio signal. Three controls are grouped in the Env Mod section of the plug-in: the Rate, Fbk (feedback), and Mix controls (Figure 7.43).

Figure 7.43 Three controls adjust how the plug-in responds to incoming signals.

You can think of an envelope detector as something like a volume level detector. As a signal enters the detector, its overall level is measured to create an envelope, or outline, of the change in level over time. An envelope follower uses that volume measurement to control something else, usually the volume level of some other device. Figure 7.44 shows an audio signal and an envelope that traces the attack, sustain, and release of the signal.

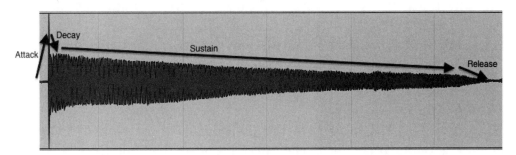

Figure 7.44 An audio signal, in this case a vibraphone note, with its attack envelope outlined.

In the AIR Dynamic Delay, the envelope detector is always actively measuring the level of incoming signals, and the envelope follower can be used to change how the plug-in reacts to changes in signal level. The Rate control allows you to adjust how quickly the envelope follower responds to changes in the signal level. It's adjustable from 10.0 ms to 1.00 seconds. Lower Rate values make the plug-in follow changes in signal level very closely.

The envelope follower can control two key parameters within the AIR Dynamic Delay: the Feedback setting and the wet-versus-dry Mix setting. The controls for these functions are labeled Fbk and Mix, and both have ranges from –100% through 0% to +100%. Dialing either control to 0% means it will not affect the corresponding setting. This is the only way to turn off the envelope follower functions.

At a setting of –100% on either control, the corresponding control value is decreased in proportion to the incoming signal. That probably reads a bit too much like legal-ese, but it's actually a pretty simple idea. If you have the Feedback level set to 50%, then in normal operation the output signal is looped back through the delay process at a 50% lower volume level for each pass. By setting the Fbk control to –100%, if the incoming dry audio signal gets louder, the Feedback level is reduced proportionally. That is, a doubling of the input signal should reduce the Feedback level by half. Use the function this way when you want a dense delay at the ends of notes or phrases, but a shorter, drier effect during louder parts of the original track.

A setting of +100% on either the envelope follower Fbk or Mix control will increase the corresponding control value proportionally to the incoming signal. With the wet-versus-dry Mix level set to 50%, the original dry signal is output at the same volume level as the processed delay signal. By setting the envelope Mix control to +100%, a doubling of the input signal should also double the wet output level. This can create a nice effect for tracks that play at a consistent level except for occasional loud parts—a snare drum track, as a somewhat extreme example. Quieter ghost notes and bleed from other drums would be processed less, while loud drum strikes would have the delay effect intensified.

Like so many other complicated effects, mastering the envelope follower functions of the AIR Dynamic Delay will take some practice and experimentation. The best way to start is actually to set both the envelope follower Fbk and Mix levels to 0%. Then take some time to dial in a nice-sounding delay process for the track you're working on. Once the effect sounds good, think about whether it could sound better by being increased or decreased during louder parts of the track. Set the envelope follower controls as needed and listen to the result. The rest should take care of itself.

Usage Example: Last Word Shimmer

The dynamic part of the AIR Dynamic Delay refers to the ability to have the plug-in change its key settings as the incoming audio signal changes. The effect becomes dynamic...it changes. A common application of this kind of adaptive effect processor is to create a shimmering delay effect that blossoms at the end of each phrase in a lead vocal track.

Shimmery delay effects can sound quite nice on vocals. The trick, however, is to create a nice-sounding effect while still preserving the intelligibility of the vocal track. One solution is to turn off the effect most of the time and only switch it on for the last word of each line, phrase, or verse. But that tends to make the effect more obvious, and can make it seem out of place. You could tediously automate the feedback or wet-versus-dry Mix controller for the track, but that would take a lot of time and effort. Having the plug-in adjust itself is the real key. By reducing the effect while the lyrics are sung, and then returning the effect as the phrase ends, the vocals can stay clear enough to understand while the effect doesn't draw attention to itself by appearing and disappearing abruptly.

Start by activating the AIR Dynamic Delay on the vocal track or bus you want to process. Remember to activate the plug-in on a stereo track if you want to create a stereo delay effect. Then dial in a nice-sounding delay effect. Starting from the factory default settings, I set up the configuration shown in Figure 7.45.

Figure 7.45 Start by setting up a somewhat dramatic vocal delay effect.

Switch off the Tempo Sync switch and set the Delay to 200 ms. Set the Feedback level to 35% and the Feedback Mode selector to Cross. I set the Low-Cut to 105 Hz to remove some breathy sounds and muddiness from my vocal track, and set the High-Cut to 10 kHz to take a little brightness off the rendered signal. You can leave the filters alone, try these settings, or dial in something more appropriate for your particular track. Then set the envelope follower Fbk and Mix controls both to 0% so you can hear the full effect of the delay. Listen to the effect. It should sound a little overwhelming in the middle of phrases, but make sure it sounds nice as it rings out at the ends of each line or phrase. Then dial down the envelope follower settings (Figure 7.46).

Figure 7.46 Set the envelope follower controls to reduce the Feedback and Mix levels.

In the envelope follower section, set the Rate control to 200 ms. That's less time than the effect delay, so the settings will be turned down quick enough at the beginning of any vocal phrases, and it leaves a little time before the effect picks up again at the ends of phrases. Then set the Fbk control to –40%. Reducing the Feedback level will make the effect decay faster while the vocals are loudest. Set the envelope Mix control to –90% so more dry signal will be passed through while the vocals are loudest.

Now listen to the result. This is still a fairly intense vocal delay that will need some adjustments to suit your vocal track, but the effect should be getting out of the way for most of your lyrics. Make some adjustments to the tone and timing of the overall delay process if they are needed, and then adjust the envelope follower controls. Shorten the Rate setting if your track is very staccato so the effect comes back in more cleanly. Adjust the Fbk and envelope Mix settings so the effect is pulled back only as much as necessary.

AIR Multi-Delay

Instead of splitting an incoming signal to pass through dry and be processed by only one or two delays, a multi-tap delay provides more independent delay taps to create more complex rhythmic patterns or realistically dense slap delay effects. The AIR Multi-Delay (Figure 7.47) starts there and goes a step further.

It provides five independent delay taps, each with its own level and pan controls, but also links these to a master delay control that can be synchronized to the project tempo track. And rather than looping all of the delay taps back to the input, AIR Multi-Delay has a selector switch that allows any single delay tap to be routed to the input of any other tap for more rhythmic possibilities. The plug-in window for AIR Multi-Delay can be a little intimidating at first since it has

Figure 7.47 AIR Multi-Delay provides five delay taps linked to a master delay control that can sync to your tempo track.

more knobs than any other AIR plug-in, but a closer look shows a very simple interface that happens to have five copies of the same controls.

Basic Controls

Several basic controls appear in the AIR Multi-Delay interface that are also found on other AIR plug-ins. Use the Mix control to balance the amount of dry (unprocessed) signal output from the plug-in against the wet (processed) signal. At 0%, only dry signal is output, effectively leaving the processor off, although it will still be using system resources to calculate and store all the delays. At 100%, only wet signal is output, so there will be no reference to the original track for timing and that can be important in any delay plug-in.

Above the Mix control are two tone controls, the Low-Cut and High-Cut filters. Use these to shape the sound of the processed signal (they do not affect the dry signal) and control unwanted build-up at the extreme highs and lows. With lots of delay taps bouncing around, it's easy for low frequencies to get muddy or lose definition of the original rhythm. The Low-Cut can be set from 20.0 Hz (effectively "off") to 1.00 kHz to keep the delay effects out of the way of the fundamental range of most any instrument or voice. The High-Cut filter can be set from 20.0 kHz (effectively "off") down to 1.00 kHz, to keep high frequencies under control. All the comb-filtering and other high-frequency build-up can, for example, smear vocal articulation and clarity, even if the delay is placed on other instruments.

Actual control of the delay process begins with a decision about whether to synchronize the delay to the track tempo with the Tempo Sync switch and setting the master Delay time control (Figure 7.48).

Figure 7.48 The Tempo Sync switch changes the range display for the Delay time control.

When the Tempo Sync function is switched off, the master Delay control displays time in a range from 0 ms to 4000 ms (4.00 seconds). With the Tempo Sync function active, AIR Multi-Delay synchronizes to the project tempo track, calculates the value of a 16th note at each tempo, and changes the display of the Delay control to show values from 0.00 16th to 16.00 16th. In either setting, note that unlike all of the other delay plug-ins, this Delay control does not directly control a delay tap. There are five delay taps stacked down the middle of the plug-in window, and the large, main Delay control serves two main functions in managing the individual taps. First, it sets the maximum range for all the taps; no individual time can be set higher than the master Delay control. The second function (that can be both impressive and frustrating) is to scale the timing of all five taps up or down. This allows you to easily spread or contract the overall timing of your multi-tap effect by simply adjusting the master Delay time up or down. (That can be especially cool if you automate the master Delay time.)

Multiple Taps

The large bank of controls down the middle of the AIR Multi-Delay plug-in window may look a little intimidating, but they are simply five copies of the same four controls for each delay tap (Figure 7.49).

Figure 7.49 Each of the five delay taps is controlled by a set of four simple controls.

The first control (which is somewhat easy to overlook) is the On switch that glows green for each tap when it's active. If an individual tap is turned off, it has no effect on the level, timing, or placement of any other tap.

The individual tap Delay time control has a variable range up to whatever maximum value is set by the master control. Time settings will be displayed in portions of a 16th note if the Tempo Sync is engaged and in milliseconds if it is not. It's usually easier to keep track of all your delay tap settings if you organize them from top-to-bottom, shortest-to-longest times, but that isn't a requirement of the plug-in. The taps do not fire from top to bottom, or bottom to top. They fire from first to last based on the individual Delay time, and each tap is independent of the others. So if you have dialed in a cool-sounding effect with the first three delay taps and later decide to slip a fourth tap into an earlier time, there's no need to rearrange or reset any of the taps...unless you really like to stay organized.

Each of the five delay taps also has an independent Level and Pan control. These allow you to create multi-tap effects that move around within the stereo field, build or decay over time, or accent strong beats in a synchronized effect. The Level control operates a trim function that can set the output level of an individual tap anywhere from 0.00dB (no change from the input level) down to –99.9dB, with an –INF (off) setting at the very bottom. Keep in mind that you can only loop the output of one single tap with the Feedback control. The pan position won't affect the looped output, but lowering the volume Level will cause the looped effect to decay faster.

Feedback Routing

AIR Multi-Delay includes a standard Feedback control similar to those found on other delay plug-ins. Adjustable from 0% up to 100%, the Feedback control sets the relative level of the output signal that will be looped back into the processor. A Feedback level setting of 100% means the output signal will be looped back into the processor at its full volume level, which could be used to create infinite loop effects unless the processed signal is reduced somewhere else along the way.

A unique addition to the AIR Multi-Delay that isn't found on any of the other delay plug-ins is the pair of routing switches that allows you to select which delay tap output will be looped back and where it should reenter the sequence (Figure 7.50).

Figure 7.50 Route the output of any delay tap back to any input to repeat all or just some of the effect.

Use the From switch to select the output from one of the five taps. Remember that if the tap you select has its Level control turned down, it will make the overall effect decay faster.

The feedback To selector is intended to select where the looped signal is sent to repeat the delay process, but it feels a little broken until you understand how it's "thinking." So, for example, if you have each of the five delay taps firing a little later than the one before it, and want to repeat only the last tap, it might make sense to loop out From tap 5 and back To tap 5. Try it and you won't hear any continued repeats. This is because the processor does not require that delay times be set from top to bottom; it plays them in order from earliest to latest.

When the output of any tap is fed back into another tap, the sound isn't played immediately as if it arrived at that trigger. Instead, the processor counts the difference in time to the next tap and plays that one. This probably sounds confusing, but it really is a logical (and rather elegant) process.

Say you are using four taps set to 275, 100, 500, and 800 milliseconds (and remember the order doesn't matter). If you route the output of one tap to the input of another, when should it play the sound? It wouldn't exactly be a delay if it played the sound instantly. So the plug-in waits the difference in time until the next tap occurs. That means routing to the 500 ms tap in the above example will make the signal wait 300 ms (the difference in time to the next tap) and play that one. Route the feedback loop into the 275 ms tap and the 500 ms and 800 ms taps will fire, but they will wait only 225 ms and 575 ms, since that's the timing relative to the 275 ms tap. Only routing the feedback To selector to the Input setting will repeat the entire set of taps starting from Time = 0.

Usage Example: Follow the Bouncing Ball

A bouncing ball effect can sound pretty cool if it's spaced right and used creatively in a mix.

Think about what happens when a ball is dropped and it bounces a few times before finally settling down on the ground. Each bounce isn't quite as high as the one before it, so it takes less time to make the trip up from the ground and back down again, and that means the bounces speed up as they go. The diminishing height also makes the sound of each bounce a little quieter. Draw the whole scenario on a graph, and it should look something like Figure 7.51.

The five delay taps in the AIR Multi-Delay aren't quite enough to reproduce the exact physics, but they can create a good approximation. To dial this effect into the plug-in, start with the factory-default settings and make a few key starting adjustments (Figure 7.52). Switch off the Tempo Sync function, set the master Delay to 1.00 seconds, set the Feedback to 60%, set the Mix to 40%, and depending on the sound you're bouncing, set the High-Cut filter as needed.

Next set the individual Delay times for the five delay taps to 275 ms, 505 ms, 670 ms, 810 ms, and 925 ms. Order them from top to bottom to make it easier to follow what's going on, and set the Level of each tap to −1.5dB, −3.0dB, −4.0dB, −5.0dB, and −6.0dB. Setting the Pan placement for each tap is optional but can create some nice effects. If you have a rhythm guitar part panned to the left, try bouncing its last chord from left to right and into the distance.

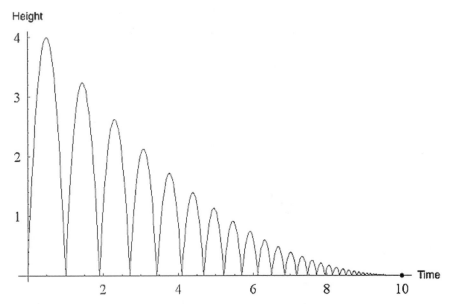

Figure 7.51 The height of a bouncing ball graphed over time.

Figure 7.52 Activate the AIR Multi-Delay and start with these basic settings.

Listen to the effect so far and you'll hear the dry signal followed by five quick bounces that stop a little unnaturally. The last step is to repeat the last bounce. In reality, the bounces should continue to get faster until the ball buzzes into contact with ground, but there aren't enough taps for that. Instead, route the feedback From the output of tap 5 (which should be set to 925 ms and

−6.0dB) back To the input of tap 4 (set to 810 ms). This will loop the last repeating bounce at the difference of 115 ms, with each bounce getting quieter and quieter until the sound is gone. The final settings should look something like Figure 7.53.

Figure 7.53 Other than Pan and filter settings, your display should look something like this.

Depending on the sound you're trying to bounce like a ball, you may need to speed up or slow down the effect a little to make it sound more convincing. But before you moan and reach for all those individual tap Delay settings, remember that the master Delay scales all of those up and down for you. Simply turn the big dial up to 1.5 seconds, and all the individual taps stretch to maintain their relative positions. Very short overall times, below about 250 ms will result in a short buzz similar to a heavy object that doesn't really bounce hitting the ground, like a pipe or a bowling ball. But that can be a handy effect for sound design too. The net result should be a nice approximation of a bouncing ball...or snare drum, guitar chord, primal scream, or whatever your lead actor just dropped off-screen.

Advanced Techniques and Good Practice

Several examples of how to get started using delay effects have already been included among the descriptions for each specific plug-in. Some are clearly separated and labeled as "Usage Examples," while others are simple suggestions that appear while describing a particular function or controller. The following techniques take some ideas a little further to illustrate an advanced technique, while others pull things back to basic to describe good practice.

Time-Aligning Microphone Channels for Drums

Even just saying, "I'm going to time-align the drum tracks" sounds like you're going to be in for a tedious night in front of the computer monitor, and you won't even know if the reward will be worth it until it's all done. Luckily, this is actually a simple task you could get done before you even start recording.

So what is time-aligning, and why should you do it anyway? There's already a lot written in this chapter about timing, delay, and the speed of sound, even in a live acoustic setting like when you're recording drums in a studio. Most people record drums with several microphones. The drum set pictured in Figure 7.54 is ready to be recorded with eight mics total. One is just inside the bass drum. Another is above the snare. There's one each for the three toms, and a trio above to capture the whole thing as a combined instrument (no, those aren't just for cymbals).

Figure 7.54 You might record a typical studio drum set with six, eight, or even more microphones.

The trouble we run into whenever more than one microphone is set up near a sound source is that it takes time for the acoustic sound energy to travel even a short distance. The distance from the snare drum to the snare microphone may be very short, but the distance from the snare to the overhead microphone array, even at only about 4 feet, will take a couple milliseconds to arrive. That timing difference is a delay, and that delay, as you already know, can cause cancellation and comb-filtering effects that undermine the sound.

Many people seem to think this problem can be solved by inverting one or more of the microphone signals, but this problem is caused by timing, so it will take a timing adjustment to fix it. The easiest approach is to delay the microphones that are very close to their sound sources until they line up with the most distant microphones—in this case, the overhead pair.

It sounds difficult but is really an easy procedure. To get started, check the placement and levels on your drum mics, hit Record, and go play some drums. No need to go all crazy on them; that won't help. Just play each drum alone two or three times with some space in between each note. Then back to the control room, hit Stop, and look at the results (Figure 7.55).

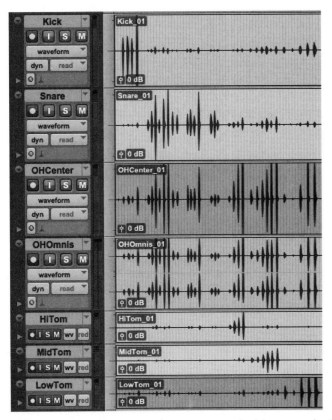

Figure 7.55 Drum samples are recorded into tracks for each microphone.

Each drum note will appear in its close-mic channel as well as the drum overheads, except it will take a little longer to arrive at the overheads. Zooming in very tightly on the snare drum and overhead tracks will show the time discrepancy between the two (Figure 7.56). I set up this kind of modified Decca Tree microphone array for the overheads with a cardioid center mic flanked by a spaced-omni pair. I chose that arrangement because I knew I would record several instrumental jazz tunes during the same session with little chance of resetting the mics, and this would give me a lot of flexibility later on for mixing to either stereo or surround. But it does mean the arrival time between the three overhead mics will be slightly different. Different stereo configurations may have more or less timing difference between left and right, but this is part of the stereo imaging of the pair and shouldn't be changed unless something is seriously wrong—in which case you should probably move the microphones around. My timing reference for the alignment will be the mono, center microphone in the array that's labeled "OHCenter" in the Pro Tools Session.

Now set the main counter window to display time in samples (Figure 7.57). That will make it easier to measure and correct the delay time between the microphones.

Figure 7.56 Zooming in closely shows the discrepancy between the snare and overhead tracks.

Figure 7.57 Set the main counter to display time in samples.

Next, select the time from the first arrival of the sound at the snare drum microphone to the first arrival at the overhead microphones (Figure 7.58). Look for an obvious place where the waveform crosses the 0-line. Often I'll choose the place where the signal crosses the centerline just after the initial attack to account for the difference in transient response between different types of microphones.

Now look at the selection in the numbers displayed in the main counter window to see the Start, End, and Length (in samples) of the selection (Figure 7.59). That Length reading display is the delay time between the two microphones.

You can test again at the other snare drum notes just to confirm the measurement. If they are different, it should only be by a sample or two, so just take an average of them all. If they seem to

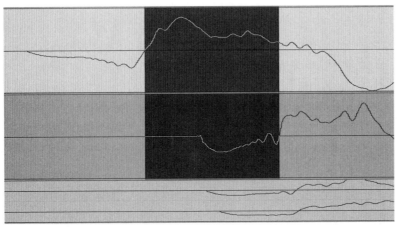

Figure 7.58 Select the time from the start of the note on the close mic to its arrival at the overheads.

Figure 7.59 The main counter displays the Length of the audio you've selected—i.e., the delay time.

be way off from one note to the next, pick a different place in the waveform to measure and match. The waves will look different in each track, since different microphones are capturing the sound in different ways. It can take a little getting used to, looking at waveforms like this. When you have a number that feels solid, activate a Time Adjuster Short plug-in for the snare drum track and dial in the delay time for the track. That track is all set. Well…almost.

You can repeat this process for the high tom and low tom track and they should work out pretty much the same. When you get to the bass drum, however, there will be a difference in how things look (Figure 7.60). The initial attack of the bass drum should appear to be upside-down when compared to the overhead channels.

Think of what is physically happening when the bass drum beater strikes the drum. The drumhead is pressed inward and air is pushed out the front of the drum. That air movement is captured by the microphone as the air pushes the diaphragm in, and the microphone responds to this by sending a positive voltage down the cable. At the same time, air is sucked in toward the drumhead from the player's side. That air movement is captured by the overheads as it sucks the air away from them, and the microphones respond by sending a negative signal down the cable. When considered that way, it should be clear that the same thing happened with all of the other drums, except the close microphones happened to be on the same side of the drumhead.

You can still use the same measuring process to figure out the delay time for the bass drum microphones, only now you'll have to make a decision. The close bass drum mic is out-of-phase with the overheads, but the overheads are the ones that are responding backward. This problem

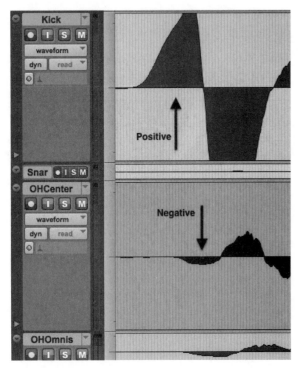

Figure 7.60 When you get to the bass drum track, it should look out-of-phase with the overheads.

is easy enough to fix; you can simply click the Phase Invert switch on the Time Adjuster plug-in and move on. But you are also seeing a demonstration of an issue called "absolute phase."

The first thing that happens when you strike the bass drum is that the drumhead pushes air out the front of the drum. The head then bounces back and vibrates a few times until coming to rest again. If you invert the close bass drum microphone, the first thing your speakers will do when they play the note is to pull back away from the listener. Of course, they will recoil and push forward, and continue to vibrate in analog to the original drum. But is it the same?

This debate has gone on for decades: can we hear the difference in absolute phase. You are free, of course, to believe that humans can or can't. Better still, you can experiment and test the idea. Or you can simply decide to maintain absolute phase because it's as easy as clicking a few buttons in some plug-ins. To maintain the absolute phase, invert the phase on the overhead track instead of the bass drum. Yes, that will throw the overheads out-of-phase with the snare and tom mics, but those are also starting the sonic journey by pulling away from the listener rather than pushing forward. So invert them too.

Regardless of which way you choose to go on the phase of the tracks, it should take only a quick few minutes to time-align all of the close drum microphones to the overheads. The result should be a fuller, more resonant sounding set of drums as all the microphones are working together rather than fighting against each other. Best of all, this setup should stay the same as long as the drums and microphones don't move. You could set this up before you even start recording and stick with it through the whole session. And as an added bonus, you have some convenient drum samples recorded if you need to replace anything when you're editing.

Tempo-Based Delay Effects

Using a delay processor to create a rhythmic echo effect can sound great on an individual instrument, but it can really mess with the timing and rhythm of your song...unless you correlate the delay timing to the tempo.

If you're adjusting the delay time of a plug-in by ear until it seems to fit tightly with the part, then you're probably doing this already without even realizing it. Don't forget that you can automate the delay time of any real-time plug-in in case your song happens to speed up or slow down a bit along the way. On the other hand, synchronizing the delay time to a set meter and tempo or even syncing with the tempo map for the song takes this idea to the next level.

The easiest way to make this work is by recording with a click track. If you're working entirely in-the-box with synthesized instruments, that's an easy task since you already need to set the tempo for the MIDI playback. If you're working with live musicians, set the time signature and tempo in the Edit window, set up an auxiliary track with the "Click" metronome plug-in activated, and send the output to their headphone mix (Figure 7.61).

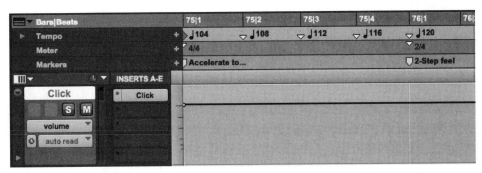

Figure 7.61 Time signature and tempo are set in the timelines, and an aux track is sending the Click output to the headphone mix.

Even if your project has no relation to the time signature or tempo tracks, you can still add tempo markers into the timeline to control delay plug-ins. Instead of automating the delay time for multiple delay plug-ins, set them up to follow the tempo map and simply drop in new tempo markers when you want the effect to change up a little. At a tempo of 120 BPM, a delay plug-in will tap every 500 ms if it's set to quarter notes, and every 250 ms if it's set to eighth notes. Want to change all the delay effects so they ring out 10% faster? Just increase the tempo by 10% to 132 BPM.

If there are holes in the tempo caused by breaks in the music like pauses, fermatas, or out-of-time sections, use automation to get across the gaps. That doesn't simply mean automating the delay time for a plug-in. You can also automate the master bypass control so the delay plug-in is simply switched off, and kicked back on when the music starts moving again.

If you really need to track an accurate tempo map but are working with tracks that were recorded without any kind of click or metronome, try using Beat Detective to map out the tempo. The procedure can be a little slow, but if it's the effect you're looking for, it should be worth the effort.

Start by listening to small sections of the song while counting beats and bars. Along the way, drop markers onto the track every four or eight bars or so. Place them whenever you can say for certain that you're marking a specific measure number. The more markers you place, the more accurate your tempo map will be. Then activate Beat Detective and select the Bar/Beat Marker Generation function (Figure 7.62).

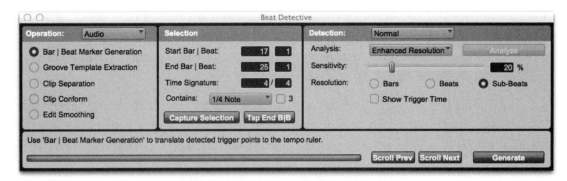

Figure 7.62   Use the Bar/Beat Marker Generation function of Beat Detective to build a tempo map.

Select a section of audio in your timeline from one marker to the next. Tell Beat Detective the bar and beat number for the beginning and ending of your selection as well as the time signature. Then click the Generate button and the software will drop a time signature and tempo marker into the timeline. Repeat this procedure through the end of the song and you'll have built a custom timeline for the song as it was played. It probably won't be accurate enough to add MIDI playback without using some of Beat Detective's other features, but it will certainly get you close enough to create some very cool tempo-based delay effects.

Overuse, Abuse, and Danger Zones

The biggest difficulty in working with delay plug-ins is that the very same principles that make the effects work also make them go haywire.

When a couple of tracks arrive at the recorder slightly out of time due to acoustic delays in the room, you can avoid phase cancellation and comb-filtering by using a delay plug-in to shift things around in time until everything is lined up right. When a backing track sounds a little thin, you can use a delay effect to create extra copies shifted slightly out of time to create phasing and comb-filtering effects.

Phasing and Comb-Filtering

It's been mentioned over and over throughout this chapter, but what is really so bad about a comb-filter anyway?

Since it's a key component of some of the creative uses of delay plug-ins, a comb-filter effect obviously isn't always a bad thing. Just be sure to keep it under control and know what's going on.

Real audio signals tend to contain more than one frequency at a time. Even if an instrument is playing one particular note, the sound of that note is distinct because of the harmonic balance or all the extra multiples of the frequency that are also being produced. When a copy of an audio signal is made and pushed slightly out of time with the original, (Figure 7.63), some parts of the sound line up to work together while others line up to fight each other.

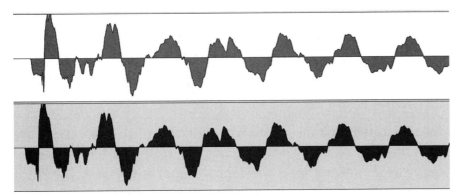

Figure 7.63 Two copies of an audio signal are slightly out of time against each other.

The combining and canceling of signals won't happen at just one frequency. Climbing up the spectrum, the signals will slowly drift out of alignment until one particular frequency where they are exactly out of phase. They then drift slowly back into a brief alignment at a multiple of that frequency, only to drift apart again at another multiple, and then back again, on and on up the audio spectrum. When the two signals are combined in a mix, in-phase portions reinforce each other while the out-of-phase portions cancel. Drawing the result on a graph of amplitude over frequency (Figure 7.64) illustrates where the signal would be boosted and cut, and it happens to look a bit like the teeth of a comb.

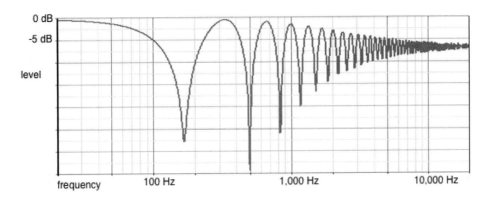

Figure 7.64 A graphic representation of comb-filtering.

The frequencies where this cancellation will occur are predictable based on the speed of sound or the delay time dialed into a plug-in. Take a frequency of 250 Hz (just below Middle C), which completes one full wave cycle every 4 ms, and one half cycle every 2 ms. Copy an audio track and delay it against itself by 2 ms, and the two signals will be pushed out of phase at 250 Hz, back in-phase at 500 Hz, out again at 750 Hz, back in at 1000 Hz, and so on, at multiples of that starting frequency. What happens to the sound of that track includes your lead vocalist singing Middle C.

Remember though that comb-filtering of an audio signal isn't the end of the world. Indeed, it can be the start of some very interesting effects. But it is a fact of the physics of sound so there's no avoiding it as an issue. You can, however, work around it.

One simple workaround is a change in volume. Yes, two identical audio tracks played out of time will cancel some frequencies, but if one of the tracks is played at a lower level, the other track will be stronger so the phase cancellation won't be as severe. So if you're using delay to double a vocal track, turn down the second part a little.

You can also add another delay set to a different time. It seems counterproductive to add more delayed signals and cause more comb-filtering as a way of correcting the problem, but remember that the cancelled frequencies change based on how long the copied signal is delayed. If a third copy is added and delayed by a different amount, it will boost and cancel different frequencies. But when taken on average, at least two of the copies should be closer to being in-phase at any particular frequency, so any cancellation won't be as severe. Adding more delay taps can smooth out this effect even more, but just be careful not to run into the following problem.

Too Many Things Bouncing Around

Delay effects can sound pretty cool on a variety of instruments and sounds, but remember that every time you create an echo of a note for an instrument it will add to the overall texture of the song. That seems like an obvious statement at first glance. Of course there will be more notes playing when they are repeated by the delay plug-in. Even very tightly spaced delay effects used to thicken the sound of an instrument will layer extra attacks on top of the original and smear the sense of time. Once you get too many things playing, echoing, thickening, and bouncing from side-to-side, you run the risk of losing the clarity of the rhythm and beat at the foundation of the track.

Often it becomes hard to discern what is causing this weakening of the rhythm. You might just notice that the track doesn't seem as tight and solid as before. That may lead to pushing up the level on the bass guitar, the snare drum, or other rhythmic foundation. As the volume increases on those, it may start to hide other sounds, and that could lead to increasing the level on something else, and something else, and so on. It's kind of a worst-case scenario, but it does happen. Here are some ideas for preventing this kind of problem before it starts.

- **Listen.** You're working with audio, so everything starts and ends with listening.

- **Analyze.** When you activate a delay effect on a track, listen to how it works at different places throughout the track—at the verse, chorus, bridge, etc.

- **Compare.** It's all right to solo a track to dial in the perfect effect sound, but listen to how it sounds with other tracks. Add one track at a time to hear how this delay sounds against other rhythmic elements. Use Bypass for a before-and-after comparison.

Once you have a better sense of how the track (and the new delay effect, in particular) is blending and balancing with other parts of the mix, some changes may be needed. You want each added layer of sound to improve the mix, not weaken it. If the new effect sounds cool but is undermining something else, make some subtle changes until it works.

- **Adjust.** If the delay effect on one track is competing against rhythms or timing on others, then make some changes. Adjust the delay time to match other rhythms, lower the wet/dry level, or reduce the feedback so it doesn't repeat as much.

- **Switch it off.** If the delay plug-in sounds great for one part of the song but not another, turn it off for that section.

- **Automate.** Using the Bypass may work in some cases, but if the effect needs other adjustments throughout the project then do it. If the tempo, time, or groove changes, make sure the delay effect flexes to fit the new feel.

- **Listen some more.** You won't know how things are fitting together and what may be causing your mix to come apart unless you listen carefully each step of the way.

- **Repeat.** Every time you add another time-based effect—whether it's a delay, reverb, pitch shift, or other plug-in—go through this procedure again. Solid timing relies on every instrument and effect working together.

This is really a good procedure to follow every time you add any plug-in to a mix if you have the time and patience for it. Although especially with delay plug-ins and other time-based effects, it's easy to end up with smeared timing and a weaker foundation before you even realize what happened. So stay on top of things and keep all that bouncing around under control.

Competing with Reverb and Other Effects

Remember that delay and reverb are two very closely related effects. Technically speaking, reverberation is created as a sound source in an enclosed space that causes lots of delayed echoes to build up and slowly decay. That's not to say you have to choose to use one or the other exclusively for any project, or even for any particular sound, voice, or instrument. Just understand that these two related effects share a similar process, and turning up one of them is likely to affect the sound of the other.

Many delay effects can also throw off the tonal balance of a track or a mix as the delayed signals start to cause phase cancellation and comb-filtering. Boosting or cutting different frequency bands can potentially mean boosting or cutting different harmonics of an instrument or different notes in a chord. Changing the harmonic balance of an instrument changes its tone and timbre. It might sound better on its own, but it may not fit with other instruments in quite the same way.

One effective approach to balancing delay processors against reverb is to recognize the two as parts of the same larger effect. Treating delay processors on individual instruments as the "early reflections" component of your overall reverb sound can help you to keep things in balance. The delay effect becomes the sound of the instrument echoing off the closest walls in the imaginary acoustic space of your mix. Then reduce or even eliminate the early reflections from the reverb so that plug-in is handling only the longer reverb tail. The reverb then simply adds extra depth to the space created by the delays.

There are plenty of other possibilities for delay plug-ins to make things sound better...or worse. The best approach, as always, is to listen carefully as each piece of the sonic puzzle drops into its place.

8 Dither, Sound Field, and Other Plug-Ins

More than just the leftovers...

To a plug-in it might seem underwhelming to be lumped into the "other" category, and I'm even including the Dither and Sound Field plug-ins in this chapter too since they are too small a group for their own chapter. At first glance, these plug-ins may seem a little less glamorous, a little less intriguing, and a little less celebrated than the rest of the plug-in suite. But don't let the categorization or plain interfaces fool you: these are some of the most convenient, useful, and even critical tools you may reach for during the recording process.

These plug-ins function more as utilities, measuring devices, and tools rather than creative special effects. Certainly a few tools such as the AIR Stereo Width and the Reverse plug-ins are meant to enhance audio and so fall more into the creative realm. This collection of tools could easily be compared to the basic tape measure, screwdrivers, and hammer of your home toolbox—kind of plain, but absolutely essential.

Refresher

Since the tools covered in this chapter cross several different conceptual areas, a few topics are worth reviewing before diving in and finding out what each plug-in can do. Some of these ideas have already been covered in the Refresher sections of earlier chapters. In particular, go back to read (or review) the discussion of "The Decibel Scale" from Chapter 6 to help understand several of the measurement tools available in the "other" category. Since several of these tools deal with metering and measuring incoming and recorded audio signals, it helps to understand what we are measuring and to remember that wonderful piece of advice the high school shop teacher loved so much: "measure twice and cut once."

Fundamentals

Since they vary so much in form and function, the plug-ins described in this chapter cover a larger range of subjects than those of previous chapters. There isn't one unifying theme that covers all of them, but a few basic ideas and concepts are worth a look before diving in to see what all these goodies can do. These plug-ins deal primarily with measurement, adjusting levels, and stereo balance issues. So let's start with a quick review of some of those concepts.

Measure Twice, Cut Once

Maybe not everyone has taken a wood shop class or done carpentry work at all, but the idea is simple enough and is as much a work ethic as it is a simple bit of shop advice. Measuring the material twice so it only needs to be cut once speaks both to efficiency and to using the available tools. Sure, it's true that cutting too long is relatively safe because the material can always be cut again and shortened to the right length. But that leaves leftover scrap material that is shorter than it could have been and less likely to be useful. That's inefficient use of material. It also means grabbing the tools again and doing the work again. That's inefficient use of your time and wears down the tools more quickly.

Is it really so different in audio production? To be fair, microphones don't go dull like saw blades do, but guitar strings, drum heads, and vocal cords all get worn down a bit every time they are used. A good engineer generally aims to make the most efficient use of those tools. There's never a problem with asking a performer for another take, but it's best to do so because you are looking for a better take, not because the inputs were clipping or the instrument was out of tune. That wastes time, talent, and resources and perhaps allows a truly unique and inspired performance to get away. Reaching for the right measuring tools from this collection of plug-ins throughout the production process helps ensure instruments are in tune, levels aren't too high or low, and multiple channels are in phase.

Of course, mistakes will happen. It might not even be your fault if tracks arrive from another studio with problems that could have been fixed before recording. The measurement tools can help you locate problems that already exist, but it would be just plain rude to leave you with no way of fixing them. That's where the editing plug-ins come into play: they adjust levels, assess tuning, change pitch, change phase, and make sure everything comes out all right in the end. They might not be the most exciting tools in the box, but these little utility plug-ins are session savers. Reach for them often, and they can help you make the most efficient use of your time, talent, and resources.

Clipping

The term clipping seems to come up all the time when discussing recording, editing, processing audio with plug-in effects, measuring audio levels—just about anywhere in audio. Let's take a look at what we are actually talking about. Figure 8.1 shows two waveforms of the same recorded drum strike. The one on the left is clean, but the one on the right has been turned up +6dB to cause the flattened or "clipped" peaks you see in the image.

This type of digital clipping is caused when the signal level is pushed so far that the sampling process simply runs out of digits to represent the number. The system is built around a top and bottom limit where the 16, 20, or 24 bits are either all zeros or all ones, and it simply can't write a bigger number. But binary can be confusing sometimes, so here's a simple example. Instead of a 16-digit number made up of zeros or ones, let's use a 1-digit number.

Consider the number 2, which is a single-digit number. We can multiply 2 times 5, another single-digit number, but to write the result of 10 requires two digits. If we are limited to only a single digit, then we would have to round to the closest number we have available, which would

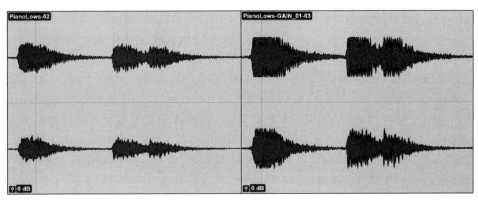

Figure 8.1 A clean recording on the left is turned up +6dB to cause the clipping shown on the right.

be 9. Maybe that doesn't seem like a bad compromise since it's not too far off. But consider a string of numbers, 3, 4, 5, 6, and 7, being multiplied by 2. Start with 2 times 3 becoming 6. No problem. Then 2 times 4 is 8 and again we are all right. We already decided that 2 times 5 will be rounded to 9 as a reasonable compromise. But then 2 times 6 is also rounded down to 9, and 2 times 7 as well. The numbers being dealt with inside the computer are of a somewhat different scale. But whether the maximum number is a 4-digit 9,999 that can't add the fifth digit to make 10,000, or a binary 8-digit number 1111 1111 that can't add another bit, the idea is the same. This is digital clipping, and it's part of the constant struggle that happens inside any digital system.

Clipping does not occur only in digital audio. It occurs anywhere an audio signal reaches the maximum levels a device can handle. From microphone to loudspeaker, there are limits on every piece of equipment. For example, if you place a sensitive microphone in front of a very loud source, it may not matter how low the preamplifier level is set, and you may never see a red line on the meters inside Pro Tools, but the signal may be clipping right at the microphone. Some types of equipment are considered acceptable and even attractive when they are driven hard enough to reach their clipping points because of the harmonic distortion that is added to the signal. Go ahead and try to tell your guitarist to turn down his favorite tube amp but it's unlikely he will. The distorted sound is a critical part of the style and tone, although it's still clipping. Becoming familiar with the look and sound will help you avoid it when you want to or need to.

Sum and Difference Matrixing

When working with microphones, this is called the Mid/Side technique or Mid/Side processing, so if you are already familiar with the concept, it's very much the same. Several of the plug-ins covered in this chapter can be used to manipulate and process audio in this way, such as the Trim, Invert, and AIR Stereo Width processors, and there are several tools for measuring phase relationships between stereo tracks.

A stereo audio signal is made up of two audio components, a left signal and a right signal. Both should contain some identical information, since they are listening to the same source, and some different information since each channel has a slightly different perspective. It's possible then, with a little audio wizardry, to separate out the identical information from the different information, and the process is pretty simple. Take the left and right signals and add them together. The stuff that is the same should be reinforced, and the stuff that is different should be cancelled out. That becomes the "sum channel." Then take a copy of the two original channels, invert the signal for the right channel, and add it to the left channel. Now the stuff that was the same is opposite and cancels out, while the stuff that was different remains. This one becomes the difference channel. We usually write this out to look like a math equation: $L + R = Sum$, and $L - R = Difference$. (Yes, this is exactly the same as Mid/Side encoding.) It's important to note that the volume level will increase since there are multiple copies of the signal being added together, so it is standard to reduce the level on both channels as well—but let's keep this easy for now.

Once we have the left and right stereo signals converted into sum and difference channels, they can be converted back again using the same process. This time adding the sum and difference channels will return the left half of the stereo signal, while inverting the difference channel and adding it to the sum channel will return the right half of the stereo signal. Written as an equation, that's $S + D = L$, and $S - D = R$.

This is where most people cock their heads to the side and wonder why we would go to all this trouble just to end up right back where we started. Well, once we have the stereo signal split into the sum and difference components, we can do some neat things to them. Turn down the volume of the difference channel a bit before decoding, and the resulting stereo signal is narrower and more mono-sounding because there is more of the same stuff and less of the different stuff. Go the other way and turn down the sum channel a bit before decoding, and the stereo signal gets a little wider. Just be careful not to go too far in either direction, as one gets you a mono signal with no stereo activity, and the other gets you an out-of-phase signal that is missing the middle.

It's also possible to use equalizers, compressors, and other processors to enhance what is going on with the sum or difference channels. A common technique for compressing stereo tracks is to convert them to sum and difference channels, compress those, and then convert back again. This way, variations in the left and right channel levels don't shift the stereo image left and right but instead shift it slightly wider and narrower which is much harder to detect. There are many possibilities for applying this technique to your audio productions, and the tools that get you there are described in more detail in the following pages.

When to Reach for These Tools
While these plug-ins are gathered from several different category headings within Pro Tools, they are then divided here into three smaller categories based on how they might be used. Some can be considered effects processors, others are editing tools, and still others can best be described as measurement tools. Since they are mostly a collection of utilities, they can be useful to some extent throughout the audio production process.

During Composition and Songwriting
Most of these plug-ins are not likely to be used often while composing or writing. But as always, that's not to say they are useless or should not even be considered. If a need arises or inspiration

strikes, then that is why any tool exists in the first place. The TL InTune instrument tuner plug-in (Figure 8.2) can be a useful tool throughout several stages of production. It is always a good idea to make sure instruments and voices are hitting the right pitches, even when the material is still being developed.

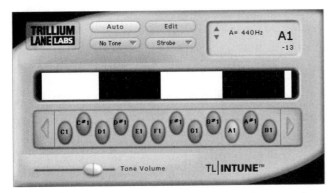

Figure 8.2   Make sure instruments are in tune for every stage of audio production.

TL InTune is likely the only one of the measurement plug-ins that will see regular use during this early stage of pre-production. There also aren't many editing tools likely to be useful while composing since most of them exist only as Audio Suite plug-ins, which means audio will have to be recorded before those can even be applied. If an effect such as reversed vocals will be featured in a song, then there's a plug-in to help you experiment while writing. And since special effects sometimes have a magical way of inspiring an artist and carrying a project in a new direction, it's possible that the TL AutoPan plug-in might be such an inspiration. But, for the most part, expect these plug-ins to be used more often in other stages of production.

During Tracking and Overdubbing

Remember measure twice and cut once? Here is where that analogy applies the most.

As with so many real-time plug-ins, using these tools while recording will be largely dependent on system resources. But the measurement tools described here are part of your protection against cutting bad takes, and, in many cases, they are pretty light on the resource requirements, so use them as much as possible. Get the instruments in tune before recording so they don't have to be cleaned up, edited, or corrected later. Make sure the input levels are set at comfortable levels so great takes aren't lost because of clipping and distortion. Double-check the phase correlation of a stereo microphone pair before it is recorded so any problems can be addressed by adjusting microphones instead of chasing delay or phasing later.

The effects processors covered here aren't likely to see much use while tracking or overdubbing. And the very nature of these editing tools means they won't see much action while recording. But the more your audio signals are observed and measured on the way into the machine, the less they will need to be edited, repaired, or replaced later.

During Editing

The best-laid plans of musicians and engineers often go awry and leave us nothing but grief and pain—or at least a lot of editing work. Maybe that's not quite how the poem goes, but if Burns had been an audio engineer tilling up a field full of clips and clams, then maybe it would have read differently. The point is, however, that no matter how much we plan, measure, and control, there will be times when we have to edit. The fact that some of the plug-ins covered in this chapter are grouped into a category heading of "editing tools" says something about their usefulness. Expect to use Audio Suite editing tools such as Gain, Duplicate, Normalize, or others on a reasonably regular basis; they are simple and fundamental parts of the editing toolkit.

Some of the measurement tools may be useful while editing as well. A real-time meter can warn that some audio levels are a bit higher or lower than the others around them so they can be adjusted. Checking the tuning of an instrument track after it has been recorded can help identify notes that need to be repaired or replaced. Many of the measurement plug-ins will help you zero in on troublesome areas and confirm that any repairs did indeed fix those problems.

During Mixing

There are several special-effects processors that can be applied to individual tracks, sub-mixes, and even full mixes. Tools such as TL AutoPan and AIR Stereo Width (Figure 8.3) are available for this kind of use, and even editing tools such as Reverse can be used to create interesting effects and textures during mixing. And don't forget about adding in those secret messages for all your fans who are willing to take the extra time to listen to your album backward.

Figure 8.3 TL AutoPan and AIR Stereo Width are special-effects plug-ins of this group that might be used in mixing.

As all the parts fall into place, and the tracks are ready to mix, some of the editing tools may logically be put away. However, watching the extra meters at this stage can be critical. There are many measurement tools that are as valuable in mixing as they are in recording—and maybe even more valuable. As tracks are added together, keeping an eye on the overall mix level becomes more important, and assembling a couple of simple meters on your main stereo output (see Figure 8.4) can provide a good view of what is going on as the mix takes shape.

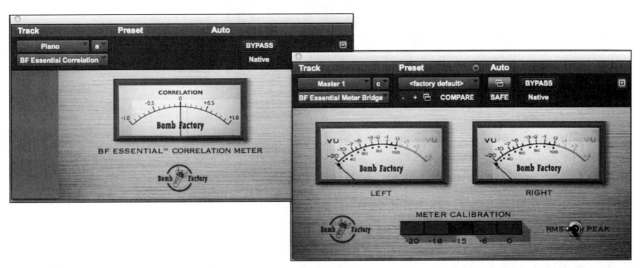

Figure 8.4   Place the BF Essential Meter Bridge and Correlation Meter on the main stereo output to keep a closer eye on the level and phase of the mix.

The plug-ins from this chapter you're most likely to use in mixing are the metering and measurement tools. Remember to measure twice, or maybe even three times, before cutting that final mix.

During Mastering

As I've said before, mastering is more than just a final equalizer or compressor; it's the last chance to catch any mistakes before the project is complete. It is also the point when individual elements of a production are set aside to evaluate the sound of the entire mix and compare it to other final mixes that will be part of the same larger project. How does this song compare to others on the album? How does this scene compare to others in the film?

If the differences between mixes are severe enough, and you also worked on the mixing stages of one or more parts of the final project, consider jumping back a step. A quick remix may be a better option than trying to fix everything in mastering. Of course, it's also possible you may have to master someone else's work and have only finished stereo mixes to work with. In either case, the measuring tools described here, especially tools like Phase Scope and TL Master Meter (Figure 8.5), will be valuable allies.

Measurement is the only function here, however. Basic tools such as Trim are helpful when all a mix needs is a little overall boost or cut. Applying Dither to a final mix before it is torn from the

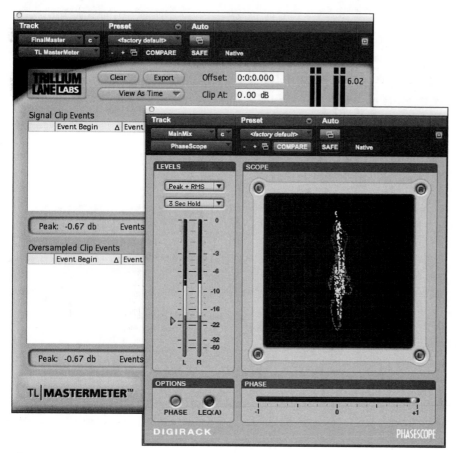

Figure 8.5 Advanced measurement tools such as Phase Scope and TL Master Meter will be especially useful in mastering.

comfortable and spacious 24-bit home inside Pro Tools and sent off into the cold reality of 16-bit CD delivery is an important final step in the process. Whatever the situation, the utilities and processors described here are likely to find routine use when mastering your audio productions.

What's in the Box?

For the sake of organizing ideas and functions together in a way that makes the plug-ins from the "Other" category easier to classify, here they are broken up into three categories.

Dither and Sound Field Plug-Ins

Yes, both Dither and Sound Field are plug-in categories unto themselves but are included here as part of the "Other" category. There are only a couple of tools in each category, and they are primarily utility plug-ins, tools more than effects. So these tools fit well among the other editing and measurement plug-ins described here.

Dither

The DigiRack Dither plug-in (Figure 8.6) operates in real-time only as either a TDM or RTAS plug-in, and can be instantiated as a mono, stereo, or multichannel plug-in. The controls are simple, with one button to select the destination word length and another to select whether noise shaping is switched on or off. Any discussion of this or any other dithering plug-in typically starts with answering the question, "What is dither anyway?"

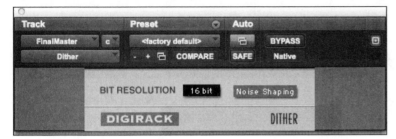

Figure 8.6 Dither plug-in.

To begin with, dither is noise. More specifically, it is noise that is intentionally added to our audio signal. If that doesn't seem like enough of a contradiction of purpose, it is noise that we add intentionally to make the audio signal seem less noisy than it would if it were sent out into the world without dither. And in the end, it's mostly a math problem.

Literally, dither is meant to deal with the mathematical accuracy of our recording system and the various processors we use along the way. Remember that the digital audio we are dealing with consists of samples that are little more than strings of numbers (like a string of 24 ones and zeros) that represent the measurement of an electrical signal (analog audio) that in turn represents changes in air pressure (acoustic sound energy). Those samples have a limitation in their accuracy based on the number of bits used to represent each value, 16 bits, 20 bits, 24 bits, and so on. This creates a few basic math problems similar to the description of clipping in the "Refresher" section of this chapter; but where clipping is an issue for the loudest signals, dither deals with the quietest signals.

Adding, subtracting, multiplying, and dividing numbers sometimes requires more digits than are available. Divide the number 2.5 in half and the result is 1.25, which requires either three digits or chosing how to round the value to only two digits. That's a calculation equivalent to a simple audio process like reducing a signal –20dB; it is simply divided by ten. But to raise a signal +1dB requires multiplying its current value times 1.1220184 (to only eight digits of accuracy). It seems like an unnecessary level of accuracy even at only eight digits, but that accuracy translates into clean-sounding audio signals, smooth fades, and quiet details in audio like the ambience and space around your sounds.

For more on decibel values, check out the "Refresher" section of Chapter 5, "Dynamics Processors."

To maintain mathematical accuracy, digital processors typically calculate at higher bit depths with the main Pro Tools mix bus operating at 48-bit resolution to maintain low-level accuracy and detail. But no matter how accurate the processor may be, the processed files will eventually be stored as 16-bit or 24-bit data. The system adds dither at nearly every processor along the way to help with these rounding errors and other rendering artifacts. But if that's the case, why is there a Dither plug-in?

The Dither plug-in is intended for use when you know your 24-bit resolution audio is headed for a 16-, 18-, or 20-bit digital destination and provides two main advantages. When added to the master fader of your final mix output, Dither will add a small amount of very quiet random noise to the signal, just enough to account for the last 4, 6, or 8 "least significant bits" that will be lost when converting away from 24-bit. You can think of these as random numbers added in to each sample. The random numbers increase the value of whatever information is down in those low-level depths just enough to push it up to the range of the shorter word length. When the audio signal is converted down to 16 bits and the least significant bits are discarded, most of that low-level detail is preserved.

The other effect of this low-level noise is to hide some of the more random noises that might be present as artifacts from processing. The random noise creates a masking effect that tames some unwanted noise in a way similar to how a restaurant uses background music to subdue sudden outbursts from the different conversations in the room. So two benefits from the added random noise are that low-level wanted signals are pushed up past the least significant bit of the shorter word length, and more random low-level noises and artifacts are subdued.

Even this low-level noise can be audible, but you can take a couple of steps to minimize its presence. First is the noise-shaping switch in the plug-in. This is a simple on/off switch that changes the type of random noise from a broad, even noise across the spectrum to something tailored to the human ear. This is basically an equalizer circuit that reduces the level of the noise at the most sensitive ranges of our hearing (around 4 kHz) and leaves it a little stronger at the extremes where we can't easily detect that kind of low-level sound. The second is a caution not to overuse the plug-in. While Dither helps reduce some noises and artifacts, it is a cumulative process—each successive layer of dither adds to the last layer. The plug-in itself is limited to eight simultaneous channels of "uncorrelated" noise, meaning that the same noise signal will be applied to multiple tracks if more than eight are processed at the same time. That may seem unlikely at first glance, but if you happen to be working on surround mixes, a single output bus may require six or more channels of dithering noise. A more likely scenario for most users though is that since so many audio processors need to apply some amount of dithering, that's a lot of layered noise that can pile up. The Dither plug-in is really intended to be the last stop, and isn't even a necessary stop if your final destination is a 24-bit file, 24-bit digital audio output, or a 24-bit digital-to-analog converter.

Pow-R Dither

The best way to understand the Pow-R Dither plug-in is to understand what dithering is as a general concept. And conveniently enough there is already a description of that in the previous section of this chapter that describes the "Dither" plug-in. So if you aren't already familiar with what dither is all about, start there.

Pow-R Dither (Figure 8.7) basically picks up where the standard Dither plug-in leaves off. It is also a real-time plug-in that can run in TDM or RTAS, but it is only available to Pro Tools HD and LE systems. The controls are just as simple to operate and understand as Dither with a selector for the output destination word length that now chooses only between 16 and 20 bits, and a noise-shaping selector that now selects between three different curves labeled as Type 1, Type 2, and Type 3.

Figure 8.7 Pow-R Dither plug-in, left, and its expanded pull-down control options, right.

As with any dithering plug-in, it is best to use Pow-R Dither as the last insert of a signal chain or final mix before it is truncated to a smaller word length. Select between 16-bit or 20-bit output format based on the target destination. The biggest difference in the Pow-R Dither plug-in is that the noise applied to the audio is always shaped by one of three more advanced curves.

Type 1 noise shaping has the flattest frequency spectrum across the audible range, with a slight increase at the very highest frequencies allowed by the sample rate. This places the noise as far up in the human range of hearing as possible, where it is least likely to be noticed. It is ideal for exposed recordings, such as solo instruments. Think of it as the kind of noise shaping to use for a violin sonata, or samples for an instrument or sound-effects library.

Type 2 noise shaping applies a simple equalizer curve to reduce the noise level in the midrange and leave it higher at the extreme high and low ends of the spectrum. It is ideal for material with a lot of stereo complexity, or for more dense materials. Think of it as the noise shaping to use for a typical rock mix or an involved action scene in a film or video soundtrack.

Type 3 noise shaping applies a more complex, high-order filter to the noise to more accurately mimic the sensitivity of human hearing. This allows the maximum amount of noise to be applied in the dithering process while keeping as much as possible away from the listener's attention. It is ideal for wide-spectrum material with a lot of ambient detail. Think of this as the noise shaping to use for a symphony orchestra or other larger acoustic ensemble recording.

Overall, the usual warnings apply to not overuse dithering since the noise will accumulate as more layers are added. Dithering should be the last stop on the way out to a lower-word-length, digital destination. When choosing the right noise-shaping option, don't let the choices scare you: there's no wrong answer for most applications. It's best, however, to set up the Pow-R Dither plug-in as the last insert of your master fader and listen carefully while clicking through the options. Choose the setting with the least coloration or noticeable effect on the quietest details of your audio.

TL AutoPan

AutoPan and all the Trillium Lane Labs plug-ins stand out from the rest of the plug-ins included with Pro Tools in that they already include good documentation. Abundant documentation, really—more than seems necessary for such simple processors. That doesn't mean they are not worth mentioning here, although I will keep these descriptions to only the most essential functions.

The TL AutoPan plug-in is a special-effects processor that, as the name implies, automatically pans your audio signal across the stereo sound field. The effect can be implemented in several ways that should be clear when you take a closer look at the plug-in interface window (Figure 8.8). The overall window is divided into three main sections to manage the intensity of the effect, the shape and speed of the effect, and whether it is triggered from another source.

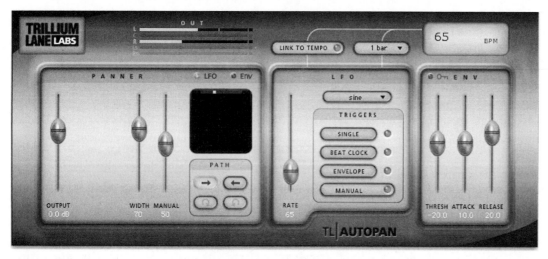

Figure 8.8 AutoPan controls are divided into three main sections to adjust the Panner, LFO, and Envelope.

The Panner control section handles the basic settings that determine the intensity of the auto-panning effect. At the top, you'll see two small indicators that let you know (and change) whether the process is being controlled by the low-frequency oscillator (LFO) or by the envelope trigger. The Width control allows you to adjust how wide the panning effect will swing, from hard left to hard right at 100%, to anything narrower, and down to nothing at all. At any Width setting below 100%, the Manual control allows you to automate the movement or assign it to an external control. The Path switches allow you to choose whether the panner will swing from left to right, right to left, or even clockwise versus counter-clockwise when you're mixing in surround.

Extra controls labeled Angle, Spread, and Place appear when you are running the AutoPan plug-in in a surround mixing environment. Angle allows you to change the orientation of the pan from a left-to-right to a front-to-rear arrangement. Place allows you to place the left-to-right panning plane forward or back in the surround-sound field. And the Spread control widens or narrows the panning field when a circular pattern is chosen in a mono-to-surround configuration.

The LFO controls at the center of the plug-in window allow you to adjust the speed and shape of the effect (Figure 8.9). These allow you to fine-tune the panning effect from something very subtle to something quite intense to best suit your project.

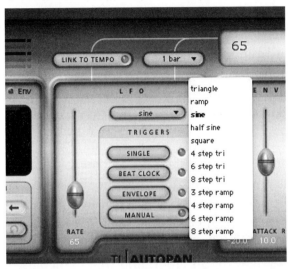

Figure 8.9   The LFO section allows you to adjust the speed and shape of the AutoPan effect.

If you are using the LFO, then the Rate control will help you adjust how quickly the sound is moved around, from a rate of 0.01 cycles per unit (with the units adjusted at the tempo controller just above) to 500 times per unit. The pull-down menu allows you to change the shape of the LFO wave so the movement appears more or less smooth. And the Trigger controls allow you to activate the panning effect from the beat clock, envelope generator, or even manually.

The last control section allows you to adjust the attack envelope so the plug-in can respond to the output of another channel or bus through a side-chain key input. For more information on side-chain connections, revisit Chapter 5, where those connections are much more common. The general idea is that you can select a Key Input, in the form of another input or bus, that will trigger the AutoPan effect to start. This can be especially effective if you have the Trigger control set for Single, although that's not necessary. Each time a signal arrives at the side-chain input that is loud enough to cross the Threshold setting, the AutoPan effect will activate in the time set at the Attack control and stop in the time set by the Release control. That probably sounds complicated, but the upshot is that one sound triggers the movement of another. For example, you might have a big snare drum hit during the bridge of your song trigger the snare reverb on an auxiliary bus to bounce from left to right and back. Or perhaps the loudest peaks of the lead vocal track will cause the bright synth pad to wobble in a tight back-and-forth movement as if they are shimmering in sync to the voice. You can imagine the possibilities.

The last stop through the plug-in is, of course, the first control on the left. The Output control provides a way to adjust the overall output level after the effect is applied, which can be helpful since the panning effect is based on changing the signal level being sent to either the right or left (or surround) busses. It's easy to push the level a little too high on one side and risk clipping the signal at your mix bus, so that's a good safety net.

AIR Stereo Width

Before digging too deeply into what a width processor is, how to apply one, and what's going on with this particular plug-in, keep a couple of key ideas in mind: First, remember that adjusting the stereo width means manipulating audio signals based on how human ears localize sound. Our brains analyze the differences in volume, timbre, and timing of sounds arriving at each ear to tell us what direction a sound is coming from. A quick look at the "Refresher" sections of Chapters 4 and 7 will help you understand that concept (and this plug-in). Second, remember that a stereo-width processor doesn't exist for the sole purpose of making sounds seem wider; it can also create tighter and more focused sounds.

Changing the apparent width of an audio signal is generally accomplished by adjusting the timing or volume relationships between the left and right signals. If you add a slight difference in the timing between the left and right audio channels, a sound will appear to move or widen slightly as the apparent source of the sound moves away from the delayed channel. When working with a stereo sound, you can use a sum and difference matrix to change the volume level of the signals that are the same in both channels versus those that are different, and that can change the perceived width. AIR Stereo Width (Figure 8.10) incorporates both of these principles along with the ability to make different spectral adjustments so the effect is applied to varying degrees based on frequency.

Figure 8.10   AIR Stereo Width can use volume or timing variations to change the apparent width of a sound.

A quick look at the controls reveals the familiar look of the AIR plug-in family. Unfortunately, the layout doesn't provide a clear view of the signal path through the processor, and that path is important to know for this kind of plug-in. As the signal enters the plug-in, the first step along the way is the "Process" control section (Figure 8.11), which has three control knobs for Low-, Mid-, and High-frequency adjustments, and a Mode selector switch that places this section into one of three modes.

Figure 8.11 Mode selector switch and Process control section of AIR Stereo Width.

The mode selector switches AIR Stereo Width into three different operational modes that change the way audio is processed by the plug-in as well as the behavior of the process knobs. Those will be described in more detail in the "Operational Modes" section for this plug-in. The signal then continues through the remaining controls (see Figure 8.12), starting with the Width control, followed by Delay (for two of the three modes), then a last stop at the Trim section before heading out of the processor.

Figure 8.12 After the Process section, audio passes through the Width, Delay, and Trim section controls.

The function of the Width and Delay controls varies with the various processing modes. The controls under the Trim section are consistent throughout all of the modes, and all of them are described in more detail in the "Other Controls" section.

Operational Modes

In Adjust mode, the plug-in applies a standard sum-and-difference matrix to the incoming audio signal, and then passes the difference (Side component) audio through the process controls that are set to run as a three-band equalizer. The signal is then sent through another sum-and-difference matrix and returned to a left-and-right stereo format. Instead of displaying a decibel scale for the boost and cut levels, the process controls display a percentage value that represents the amount of apparent width added or removed from each frequency range. When the Low, Mid, or High controls are centered, they read 100%, which signifies no change, or 100% of the original width. Turn a control to the left (down) and the display descends toward 0%, where all of the difference information is removed, leaving a mono signal in that band. Turn a control to the right (up) and the display ascends toward 200%, where the difference information is doubled, leaving a wider-sounding stereo image in that band. For this mode, the Width control operates similarly to the Process section controls, adjusting the entire difference channel from 0% through 200% before the audio is returned to stereo format. Adjust is the most subtle of the mode settings and the one most suitable for more complex stereo material like full mixes.

When set to Comb mode, the AIR Stereo Width plug-in again applies a sum-and-difference matrix to the incoming audio signal, but it also applies a delay to the sum channel. The delay causes some frequencies to shift out of phase with the difference components and results in a comb-filtering effect that shifts some information toward the left and some toward the right. Since the difference-channel components arrive slightly earlier than the sum-channel components, the brain interprets the source of the sound as moving outward, away from the center. The Low, Mid, and High controls of the Process section still control the amount of the effect that is applied to the various frequency ranges. However, the Delay and Width controls change function for Comb mode. Delay becomes an overall control for the Process section that appears before the Width control. And although the label doesn't change, the Width control becomes more of a "process amount," or "wet/dry" controller. At 0% the original dry signal is passed through; at the 100% point the dry signal is reduced by 6dB while the processed signal is added in to compensate; and at the 200% point the dry signal is reduced by 12dB. The Trim section continues to function as the last step before leaving the processor. This mode has one problem: Incorporating timing and phase elements to the normal volume changes of a standard sum-and-difference matrix delivers a more dramatic effect that can be hard to control.

In Phase mode the AIR Stereo Width plug-in puts aside the sum-and-difference matrix to process the signal with delay and phase alone. The Low, Mid, and High controls of the Process section change their labels from percentage to frequency to control the center point of three phase shifters. The Width control moves back to the position between the Process section and Delay control although it again operates as a mislabeled "wet/dry" controller. This mode can create a more dramatic effect than the basic sum-and-difference matrix of Adjust mode or a more subtle widening effect than Comb mode. It still, however, introduces more out-of-phase material that may be too intense for all but the slightest use on dense stereo tracks or full mixes.

Other Controls

In addition to the Mode selector switch and Process controls already described, the AIR Stereo Width plug-in has four more specialized controls, Width, Delay, Level, and Pan. Width acts as an overall amount-of-process control, although it does act a little differently for each mode. When the plug-in is set to the Adjust mode, the Width control adjusts the balance between the sum and difference components before the two channels are decoded back to left and right stereo. At 0% the difference component is removed entirely; at 100% the sum and difference channels are equal; and at 200% the difference channel is 6dB higher than the sum channel. For the remaining two modes, Comb and Phase, the Width control acts as an overall amount-of-process or wet/dry control. For these modes, the display for Width is confusing since it still reads from 0% to 200%. At 0% the original signal passes through without any processed signal added. Moving up the control, the dry signal is reduced –6dB at the midway point of 100% and then

−12dB at the 200% marking, while an equivalent amount of processed signal is added to make up the level difference.

The Delay control also changes function slightly based on the operational mode of the plug-in. When running in the Adjust or Phase modes, Delay appears after the Width control and before the Trim section controls. In this position, Delay adds a slight signal delay to the right channel of the processed stereo signal. The human brain interprets the earlier arrival of the sound at the left ear to mean that the sound source is located to the left, a phenomenon referred to as either the Haas Effect or Precedence Effect. When the plug-in is running in Comb mode, the Delay control changes its function to become an overall delay control for the Low, Mid, and High controls of the Process section.

Although it is labeled as a "Trim" section rather than a "makeup gain" section, the Level and Pan controls of AIR Stereo Width operate as the last step before the audio signal departs the plug-in. If indeed your incoming signal is too loud and distorts the processor, you will need to use another plug-in to reduce the level before it arrives at the input to AIR Stereo Width. The Level control acts as a master fader for the outgoing signal, allowing it to be cut all the way down to − ∞dB and boosted as much as +12dB. The Pan control is designed to function as a stereo balance control where the left and right channels are both shifted to either side until a mono signal at the extreme left or right. In the mono instantiation of the plug-in, the Pan control has no effect at all.

Applications

As of this printing, the AIR Stereo Width plug-in doesn't ship with a Mono/Stereo (mono input to stereo output) instantiation, which limits its use for widening the stereo presence of mono audio tracks as described in the Pro Tools Creative Collection Guide. The mono version of the plug-in processes the incoming audio signals as well as it can, but without a stereo output the processed audio is summed to mono on the way out of the processor. Tracks can emerge with a slightly phased and mechanical sound but without any increase in apparent width since the output is mono.

The easiest way to process mono tracks with the plug-in's configurations is to route your mono tracks to an available stereo bus, set up a stereo Aux Input track to receive that bus, and then activate a stereo version of AIR Stereo Width on the auxiliary track (Figure 8.13). Since sum-and-difference matrix processing has no effect on mono tracks, you won't get much stereo action from the Adjust mode, but the delay and phasing effects of the Comb and Phase modes can create some interesting effects.

This is a great way to use a setting like the "Haas Guitar Doubler" preset. This effect uses a slight delay on the right channel to create a sense that a rhythm guitar part was played twice and is panned wide across the stereo output. For a more dramatic effect on strummed acoustic guitar chords, start with this preset and then shift into Phase mode and dial the Low, Mid, and High controls to about 150 Hz, 450 Hz, and 1.8 kHz as shown in Figure 8.14. A little fine-tuning of the Delay time and the Pan control should get you to a nice effect that is wider but still quite comfortably in-phase. As always, use the Bypass button to hear the difference between the dry and processed track more clearly.

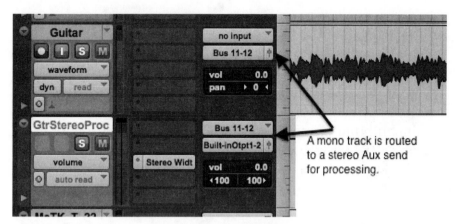

Figure 8.13 Process a mono track by sending it to a stereo aux track that has AIR Stereo Width active.

Figure 8.14 Starting from the Hass Guitar Doubler preset, dial in these settings for a dramatic effect for doubling acoustic guitar.

The AIR Stereo Width plug-in really shines in processing stereo tracks. Almost any stereo track, bus, or mix can be processed, although, as with any effect, try not to overdo it. Keep the effect subtle when the track is complex or exposed. Also be careful about using delay effects too heavily on a track that is rhythmic and percussive such as drum overheads or a rhythm guitar part. Unless, of course, that's the effect you're after. Stereo tracks with a wide frequency range like piano or acoustic guitar can be widened very nicely with either the Adjust or Phase modes, leaving a cozy spot in the middle to nestle in the lead vocals.

To get a feel for using AIR Stereo Width, load up a few stereo mixes and run them through the processor. These could be your own mixes or imported tracks from commercial CDs, but try to get a few different kinds of mixes. Pull up something dense and heavy, something light and spacious, and something in between. Put them all up on one stereo track, activate an AIR Stereo Width plug-in, and also activate and open a Phase Scope plug-in to get a visual sense of what is happening with the tracks. Then start at the factory default presets and listen to the effect as you turn the Width control down to 0% and back through 100% to the 200% setting. Then do that again while watching the display on the Phase Scope.

This very basic, subtle effect also works well when mastering stereo mixes. The ability of Adjust mode to act as a spectral width control, widening some frequency bands while narrowing others, can be very powerful. Start with settings like the ones shown in Figure 8.15 on a basic rock mix.

Figure 8.15 Try these settings as a starting point for a subtle widening effect for mastering.

The plug-in is set to run in Adjust mode; the Low, Mid, and High controls are set to 40%, 80%, and 150% respectively; and the overall Width control is set to 150%. This starting point tightens the low frequency so the bass guitar and kick drum sound more focused, leaves the midrange relatively unchanged so the vocals and lead instruments stay in the center, and then spreads the high frequencies wider to give a sense of ambience and space. Obviously, much of the effect depends on the kind of material you are processing. Try fine-tuning the controls a bit to suit the song you are listening to. Then make a CD of the original track and the processed track and listen to them both on your favorite car stereo. Tighter bass with more ambient space up top may be just the right sound for your car stereo. It will take some getting used to the controls and modes, but this can be a good starting point to experiment with using AIR Stereo Width as a mixing and mastering tool.

Editing Tools

The following plug-ins appear under the "Other" category; only Trim appears as both a real-time and Audio Suite plug-in. The rest are true editing tools that only appear in the Audio Suite realm.

Of course, calling them editing tools doesn't mean they cannot be used to create interesting effects as well. But they will most often be used to fix small problems during editing more than any other part of your recording process. Indeed, the Audio Suite–only plug-ins listed won't be very useful at all during other phases of production.

Trim

Trim, an oddity among the plug-in suite, can be confusing to some users because it seems like a redundancy. The Trim plug-in (Figure 8.16) includes several tools that are already included within every audio track, aux bus, and mix bus within Pro Tools.

Figure 8.16 The Trim plug-in includes Gain, Mute, and Phase Invert controls.

It has a Gain (volume) control, a Mute switch, an output meter, and, at first glance, only seems to add a Phase Invert switch. That additional Phase Invert switch is enough to make Trim a useful tool, but if that were the only useful feature, it could just as easily drop the other features and simply have a real-time Invert plug-in. Likewise, Trim doesn't appear among the Audio Suite plug-ins because the Gain and Invert plug-ins cover the bases for non-real-time applications.

The real usefulness of the Trim plug-in becomes obvious when you remember that the plug-in chain for any given track or buss follows an order of operations from top to bottom (Figure 8.17). And especially when you remember that the track or buss Volume and Mute controls come at the end of that chain.

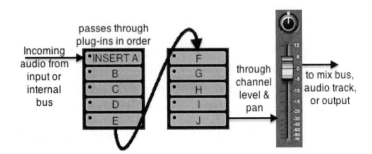

Figure 8.17 A flow chart of the order of operations for a track or buss within Pro Tools.

Trim really shows its strength when we realize that its typical place in that chain is among the first one or two insert slots. You may often run into tracks that were recorded too soft or too loud. A track that is too soft may not trigger certain plug-ins the way you would like. For example, if a live track were recorded with an average level around –24dB and peaks that only reach as high as –18dB, it may be worth increasing the level of that track +6dB with the Trim plug-in before passing the signal into a Reverb plug-in so the level can adequately trigger the reverb to blend with the rest of the mix. Or, as is much more often the case, an audio track may have been recorded too loud, which may cause the signal to peak (overload) a plug-in like an equalizer. Here, Trim can be useful to reduce the level of the signal before it hits (and overloads) the equalizer plug-in.

A new feature of Pro Tools 10 called Clip Gain allows you to apply an independent level control to each individual audio clip within your session. This feature does offer the same kind of level control at the beginning of the signal path, but it doesn't completely replace the Trim plug-in. If you're working on a track with lots of clips, it's a lot easier to adjust one Trim plug-in instead of lots of individual Clip Gain settings. Trim also allows for automation, and it can be placed in between other plug-ins in the chain.

The Multi-Mono Trim plug-in is an extremely useful tool when dealing with stereo or multi-channel audio tracks or busses. Despite our best efforts, we will often encounter stereo tracks that hang a little louder on one side versus the other. You might run into a stereo recording of an acoustic guitar that is a little louder on the body of the instrument versus the fret board, or a piano that is a little louder toward the low end of the instrument, or a drum overhead track that leans toward the hi-hat side during the verse and then toward the ride cymbal during the chorus. Using a Multi-Mono Trim plug-in (Figure 8.18) and separating the controls for the Left and Right channels will allow you to even up the levels between the two sides of the stereo track before they trigger compressors, add reverb, or throw off the balance of your overall mix.

Figure 8.18 A Multi-Mono Trim plug-in can be split to control the Left and Right channels independently.

Gain

Moving into the Audio Suite editing tools, we find under the Other category, it seems logical to first look at Gain for its similarity to Trim and for its obvious simplicity. The Gain plug-in (Figure 8.19) has a very simple and straightforward function. It writes a new file for the selected audio clip that is either louder or quieter than the original.

Figure 8.19 The Gain plug-in is an Audio Suite tool for boosting or reducing the level of an audio clip.

So why do we need a plug-in that can grab an audio clip and increase or decrease the overall volume? This is actually why Gain is included here under the heading of "Editing Tools." When cutting together various parts of tracks and takes you will often encounter parts that are a little louder or softer and don't fit as smoothly together as you might hope (Figure 8.20). For example, if the singer took three takes of a particular line and you want to move one word from the third take into the first, but the third take was sung a little louder overall.

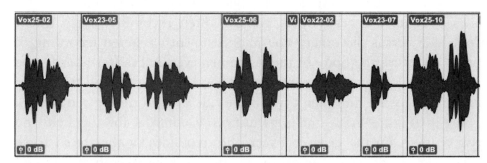

Figure 8.20 A composite vocal take like this one would require automation to even out the levels.

You could certainly just make the edit and then automate the volume control for the track to balance the volume...although it is important remember again that the volume control comes at the end of your processing chain. And, of course, there's the new feature for Pro Tools 10, the Clip Gain control, that allows you to adjust the individual gain of each clip right on the timeline. But this is an example of how to use the Gain plug-in, so let's stick with that.

Using Gain to reduce the level of the audio clip that is a little too loud before it is cut together with the other take means your new composite take will already be at an even level (Figure 8.21).

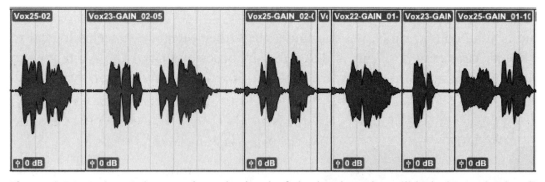

Figure 8.21 Using Gain to reduce the level of the louder take will help keep the levels even.

As always, there are several ways to approach this situation. If the third take is simply louder overall, you might consider selecting the entire take and reducing the level by a few decibels to even it up with the other takes. But if only a small section, like one particular word or phrase, is louder, then it is better to select a slightly larger region than just the clip you need to change and adjust the level for just that section.

Of course, a closer look at Gain shows a few extra tools beyond the simple function of increasing or decreasing the level, and it's important to know about these. Included with the plug-in is a set of measurement tools that will scan the audio clip you have selected to measure the average or highest peak levels. These are managed with three controls (Figure 8.22).

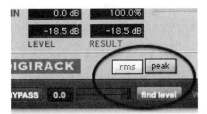

Figure 8.22 Switch between "rms" (average) and "peak" measurement, and then click the "find level" button to scan the selected clip.

The "rms" and "peak" buttons switch measurement modes so the plug-in will scan for the average level ("rms," or root-mean-square) or the highest peak level. Once you have decided what to measure, clicking the "find level" button will run the scan, and the resulting levels will be displayed in the window. In an editing example like the one already mentioned, measuring the average levels of the audio clip before and after the edit point, and of course the new clip to be cut in, should show how much you need to increase or decrease the signal before making the edit.

One catch to the Gain plug-in is that it will not tell you where it found the highest peak within an audio clip. For that, you must rely on what you see in the edit window, or you can select smaller portions of a larger clip to see what the peak level is for each section. Of course, you can similarly measure smaller portions of a larger clip for average level. And knowing that Gain has this quick measurement feature can be very handy if you are working on the mastering phase of your production and trying to see how the average levels balance out from one song to the next.

Invert

The Invert plug-in is one of the delightfully simple processors to explain in terms of operation, although it is worth spending a little time explaining some examples of when to use it. The controls are simple enough: There is one button called Render. Click that, and the selected audio clip is written upside-down into a new file. And of course, by upside down, we mean that where the wave swings positive it will now swing negative, and vice versa (Figure 8.23).

The process of inverting the audio signal is easy enough to understand, but when to use it is another question. And as it happens, the preceding example also illustrates part of an ongoing debate among audio engineers, audiophiles, and others about the importance of something called absolute phase. Consider the implication that when the audio signal depicted on the screen swings positive (upward above the centerline), that signal should eventually arrive at the speakers and "push" the speaker cone outward toward the listener. And, of course, when the signal swings negative, the speaker cone "pulls" back away from the listener. Some would argue that it doesn't matter if a signal like a snare drum hit is presented in its original (absolute) phase or

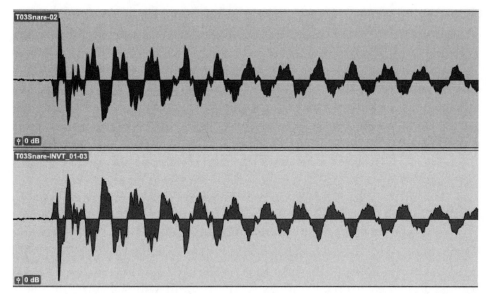

Figure 8.23 The top image is a single snare drum hit. The bottom image is the same signal inverted.

not. Others would argue that the first thing the wave should do is "push" the speaker toward the listener to give the impression of the impact of the drum being struck.

I won't try to place such a value judgment on absolute phase; that is for you to decide. But I will offer a couple of interesting examples of odd scenarios where the Invert plug-in has been helpful. The first is an interesting situation that arose during a recording session for a jazz big band. I had three tenor trombones among the horns and placed the same model of ribbon microphone in front of each of them. Six of the microphones had only just arrived a week or so earlier, and these three were seeing their first studio session. Trombones and trumpets both have a very distinctive waveform in that there is considerably more positive energy than negative. The screen shots in Figure 8.24 show the three trombone tracks.

Notice that one of the audio tracks appears to be flipped the wrong way. Of course, this didn't show up during setup or the sound check where we set the recording levels. It needed to be recorded before the problem was revealed. As it turned out, the culprit was actually a microphone that was incorrectly wired at the factory, but it still left me with an audio track that was inverted from its natural state and that needed repair. A quick render with the Invert plug-in fixed the issue.

The second example is a very unusual application, but one of those that just can't really be made up—and that's always kind of cool. While recording a country/bluegrass group, we ran into a sustained note at the end of a fiddle take where the player made it about halfway through the note on a down-bow, but then reversed to up-bow to continue the note. While recording the track, the change wasn't really noticed, but while cutting together the final fiddle track, the hole in the middle of the note and the slight timbre change were both a little too noticeable. When I zoomed in (Figure 8.25) and saw the problem up close, the shape of the waveform suggested that I could flip the second half of the note over, pull the note in a little closer, and cross-fade the two halves into a single note.

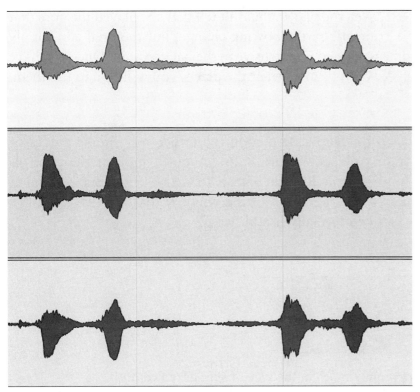

Figure 8.24 Three trombones playing into three of the same ribbon microphones with one microphone wired incorrectly.

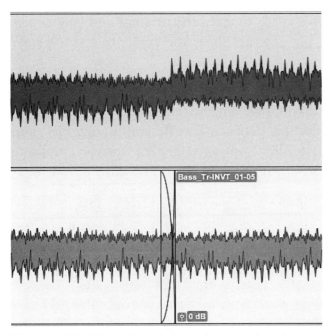

Figure 8.25 The original down-bow and up-bow waveform (top), and the finished edit (bottom).

When the rendering and edit was complete, even the player couldn't tell that she played the note that long. Certainly the original take wasn't "ruined" by the bowing change, but the final edit simply sounded cleaner and assured that the fiddle remained unobtrusive in the background. Once you have these tools incorporated into your arsenal, you'll be amazed at the places you will find to use them.

Duplicate

Not to be outdone for apparent simplicity, the Duplicate plug-in is another very simple processor that can also seem a bit redundant at first glance (Figure 8.26). A quick look at the controls shows another plug-in with nothing more than a Render button to make it go. But remember some of the common features with the buttons at the top of the window that are seen on all of the Audio Suite plug-ins, because they can be especially useful here.

Figure 8.26 The Duplicate plug-in doesn't require much in the way of specialized control.

So why use the Duplicate plug-in at all versus simply using the Ctrl-D (Cmd-D for Mac) duplicate function? The Duplicate plug-in differs from the Edit menu function in that it writes a new file for the audio clip being duplicated. This is a particularly important feature if you are planning additional processing for the original or duplicated clips, as it will preserve the original audio clip. As always, this does mean more hard-drive space to store the original and new copies of the audio files, but that's why you're using that big external drive for your projects anyway, right?

As mentioned, another way the Duplicate plug-in can be a handy tool is when we remember those extra control buttons at the top of the control window. On the left side of the controls at the top is the pull-down menu that allows for a selection between "create continuous file" and "create individual files" (Figure 8.27). The "overwrite files" option is grayed out for Duplicate because, after all, it would kind of defeat the purpose of duplicating the audio clips if you overwrite the originals.

Figure 8.27 The pull-down menu for Duplicate can help determine how the plug-in will handle multiple audio clips.

Why is this feature such a big deal here? Well, sometimes an audio track can become so fragmented that it begins to slow down or glitch the system during playback because the hard drive cannot read all the various portions of information fast enough. And remember, this is compounded with every track that is similarly diced into little pieces. Certain styles of electronic music run into this issue very quickly during production. Selecting a portion of an audio track where many small clips are separated from one another, and choosing the "create continuous file" option can consolidate those little clips into one continuous file that will be read (ideally) from a more continuous set of sectors on your hard drive. It's true that there is also a "Consolidate" function listed under the Edit menu pull-down as well; however, using the Duplicate plug-in also allows you to steer the new files in a direction of your choosing. The "USE IN PLAYLIST" button allows the option to immediately put the new duplicate file into the selected track and time position, or to drop the newly written file into the Clip List for placement as you choose.

Reverse

The Reverse plug-in is another fantastically simple interface with a single button to "Render" the selected audio clip(s) and write a new file of the same material played backward (Figure 8.28). The interface looks remarkably similar to Invert or Duplicate, and the same rules apply regarding how the processor handles the newly written files and their placement into the Playlist or Clip List.

Figure 8.28   The Reverse plug-in also doesn't require much in the way of specialized control.

One particularly important thing to keep in mind when using the reverse plug-in is that the system simply reverses the selected audio clip(s) and, assuming you have selected the "USE IN PLAYLIST" option, drops the new file into the same segment of time occupied by the original clips. If you have selected a segment of time that corresponds to say, a whole measure of a drum set part, that measure will be reversed from beginning to end, so that beat 4 will be played backward in the place of beat 1, beat 3 will be played backward in the place of beat 2, and so on (Figure 8.29).

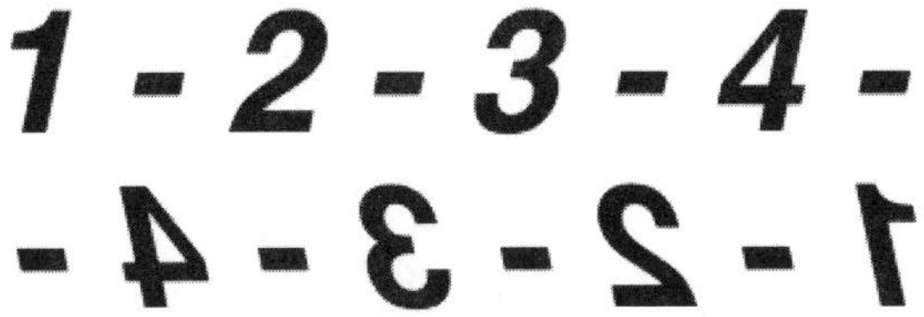

1 - 2 - 3 - 4 -
- 4 - 3 - 2 - 1

Figure 8.29   Imagine that a four-beat measure (top) rendered by Reverse as a continuous file will play back as shown.

However, if you split up the audio clip into one-beat segments and choose the "clip by clip" option, each individual beat will be reversed. So beat 1 will play backward in the place of beat 1, beat 2 will play backward in the place of beat 2, and so on (Figure 8.30).

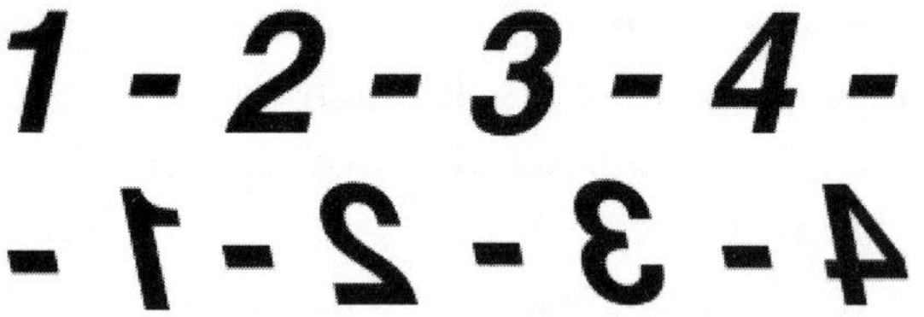

1 - 2 - 3 - 4 -
4 - 3 - 2 - 1 -

Figure 8.30 Imagine a four-beat measure rendered "clip by clip" by Reverse playing back like this.

Remember that as these audio clips are reversed, regardless of whether you select to render the "entire selection" or "clip by clip," they are simply played from the end to the beginning in time. The processor makes no allowances for landing these backward sounds on the beats. This means that if you are hoping to create an effect such as reversing the snare drum notes for a drum beat, you can break up the notes into individual clips and reverse each clip in its own time, but the processor will not place the impact of the notes on the appropriate beats to line up with the rest of the drum part. Figure 8.31 shows the audio clips for bass drum and snare drum both before and after the snare drum part is Reversed.

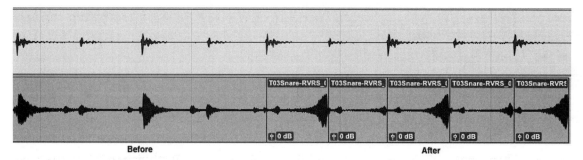

Figure 8.31 The bass and snare drum notes are shown before and with the snare drum reversed.

The effect seems somewhat lost since it places the impact of the snare drum note at the end of beats 2 and 4, closer to beats 3 and 1. But simply selecting the newly reversed snare drum notes and slipping them back in time until the impact is once again aligned with beats 2 and 4 delivers the effect as intended (Figure 8.32).

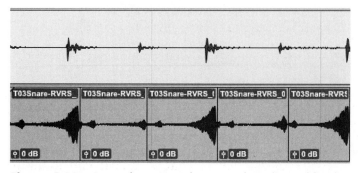

Figure 8.32 Once the snare drum track is slipped backward in time, the effect is heard as intended.

As with so many of the plug-ins we have explored, the process itself is simple enough to understand. How you choose to use this tool in your own production, and what sorts of odd situations might develop, will depend entirely on how you use this as a creative tool.

Normalize

The Normalize plug-in, and the normalizing of audio tracks in general, can be slightly confusing at first glance (Figure 8.33). Like many other tools, the basic concept seems simple enough.

Figure 8.33   The Normalize plug-in.

The Normalize processor scans the selected audio clips, finds the loudest peak, and then renders the entire track by boosting or cutting the level in order to move that loudest peak up or down to match a level you choose. Sometimes an explanation doesn't always read as easily as an example, so let's say that you recorded a 32-measure piano solo for a jazz tune. A stereo pair of microphones was placed reasonably well, and the levels were set so the average level landed around –18dB and the loudest peak hit just shy of –6dB. Jazz musicians being how they are, the word "compressor" frightens them, yet the piano track needs to come up a bit to be the star of the show for that part of the tune. And to be fair, it might be nice to keep the full dynamic range of the original performance and simply set the track a bit louder in the mix without distorting on any of the loudest peaks. By selecting the audio clip, activating the Normalize plug-in, and setting the Level to a maximum peak at, say, –2.0dB, the processor will scan the track, find the loudest peak, and adjust the entire track up in volume until that peak reaches –2.0dB.

If you have been paying attention along the way, you're wondering what is so special about that. After all, the Gain plug-in has a "find peak" option that scans the selected audio clips and can then boost or cut the whole selection until the peak level lands at a chosen level.

Here is where Normalize has a few extra surprises under the hood that can give a little more than just simple level adjustment.

Let's say that stereo recording of the piano solo happened to be slightly louder in one channel versus the other—say the bass was a little stronger than the treble. Normalize can be set to find the loudest peak across all of the selected channels, or it can find the loudest peak within each channel and adjust each independently to match the output level. That means it can actually boost one side of a stereo pair to match your maximum level, and if necessary, it can cut the other side to bring it down to your maximum level. Think of it as a kind of "smart" gain control.

Here's another quick example we will look at with some screenshots. Let's say you have a drummer whose left hand was a little less consistent on the snare drum than you were hoping for. (We drummers like to call that "dynamic range," but some people just don't seem to approve of such musical sensitivity.) Figure 8.34 shows the foolish ways of one such "sensitive" jazz drummer.

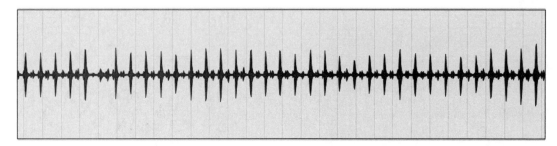

Figure 8.34 Unforgivably inconsistent snare drum notes across several measures.

Here's where the Normalize function can act a lot like a compressor, except that instead of slowly varying the volume level up and down to even out the overall level (and at the same time changing the attack envelope of the notes), Normalize can be set to "clip by clip" mode to adjust the level of each note up or down. The overall level of each clip may change, but within each clip, the level change will be consistent and not variable. So if we split the clip up into pieces as seen in Figure 8.35 we can set the Normalize plug-in to a single output level of perhaps –6.0dB, and the "clip-by-clip" setting as in Figure 8.36. And then the Normalize processor will set about analyzing, and then boosting or cutting each audio clip so the resulting snare drum track delivers every note at the same peak volume level of –6.0dB (Figure 8.37).

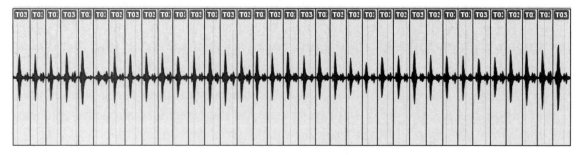

Figure 8.35 Snare drum track split into single-note clips.

Now that's a pretty severe example of a way to use the Normalize plug-in. And, of course, real instruments will have a different timbre when played loudly or softly, so the resulting audio track will sound like the volume has been turned up and down on an instrument that has been

Figure 8.36 Normalize set to −6.0dB and "clip by clip" mode.

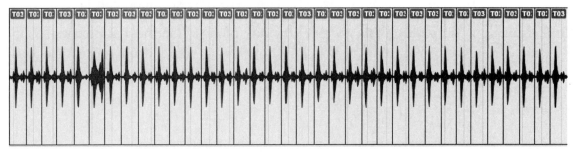

Figure 8.37 Processed snare drum track with nearly any hint of dynamic range removed.

played loudly and softly. But as always, when working on your own productions, you will find ways to apply the ideas and concepts to your own, real-world situations.

BF Essential Clip Remover

If you keep running into situations where the BF Essential Clip Remover has been a necessary tool to repair your clipped audio signals, then your first stop should probably be a visit to the section in Chapter 2 about "Setting Levels and the Myth of Using Every Bit." Although, realistically, there will be lots of times that you encounter clipped audio signals. You might deal with tracks coming from someone who is not as careful about setting levels on the way in, or might have a musician who gets a little more enthusiastic about his performance after the sound check. Whatever the reason, it is good to know that the BF Essential Clip Remover (Figure 8.38) is available, but also good to know about its limitations.

Figure 8.38 BF Essential Clip Remover.

The general idea of the clip removal process is fairly straightforward and can actually be done "manually" as well with some careful use of the Gain plug-in and the Pencil tool. The first step is to scan the audio clip to find the places where the signal has been clipped. Then reduce the overall level of the segment of audio (usually a single note or syllable) by an amount that leaves some room to repair the clip without substantially changing the level—often between –3db and –6db. Then attempt to redraw the peak of the waveform to smooth out the audio signal. The BF Essential Clip Remover does this automatically, and much faster than you might do it by hand.

The limits, however, are that the processor is trying to recreate information that has been lost when the signal was clipped. So, naturally, if the clipped section is small enough, the process can be very effective. But if the signal was very severely damaged, only so much can be done.

Figures 8.39–8.42 provide a simple example to give an idea of how far the BF Essential Clip Remover plug-in can be pushed. The first audio clip shown is a snare drum note that was recorded through a compressor onto tape, and then transferred into Pro Tools on a mono audio track (Figure 8.39). The original peak level measured –2.0dB.

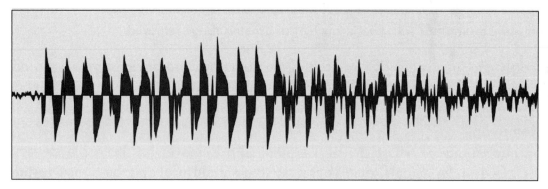

Figure 8.39 Original snare drum note with a peak level at –2.0dB.

Two copies of the original audio clip were made, and the Gain plug-in was used to boost the level of one clip +4dB (Figure 8.40) and the other by +8dB (Figure 8.41) to push both waveforms into clipping.

Then I used the Gain plug-in one last time to turn the clip back down –3dB to provide a little headroom, and, of course, the BF Essential Clip Remover was applied to each audio clip so it could attempt to repair the clipped peaks (Figure 8.42).

You can see from the close-up image of Figure 8.42 that while this plug-in makes a strong attempt at correcting the clipped audio signal, it has some limitations based on how severely clipped the audio signal is. So set good levels that provide at least some extra space before clipping and watch to see if the musicians are getting a little too enthusiastic. But if you happen to run into clipped audio, having this tool handy can help you to reduce a little stress along the way.

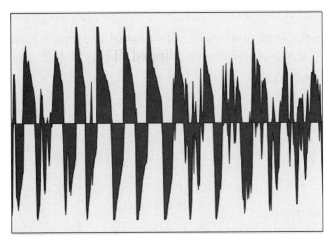

Figure 8.40 The preceding audio signal was increased +4dB with some minor clipping on a few peaks.

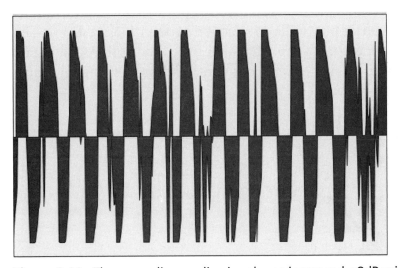

Figure 8.41 The preceding audio signal was increased +8dB with more severe clipping.

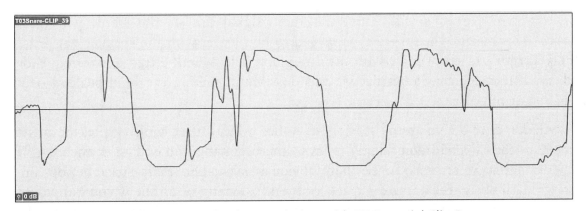

Figure 8.42 Clipped audio signals after rendering with BF Essential Clip Remover.

DC Offset Removal

The DC Offset Removal plug-in is another very simple tool, and probably one of the more rare tools you might ever need to use (Figure 8.43). The processor scans an audio clip to detect any possible DC Offset and applies a filter algorithm to remove it.

Figure 8.43 DC Offset Removal tool with its single control button.

A DC offset is an unusual artifact for Pro Tools that is sometimes caused by the analog-to-digital conversion process. It is visually apparent when the entire audio signal is set slightly above or below the 0 line in the middle of the waveform graph. That zero-line represents 0 volts of alternating current (A/C), and it is often good to imagine the graph we see on the computer screen as it relates to a loudspeaker at the eventual end of our audio production process (Figure 8.44). The 0 Volts line represents the driver "at rest" where it is simply hanging freely and still. As the signal swings positive (upward on the graph), the speaker pushes outward, and as it swings negative (downward on the graph) the driver is pulled inward.

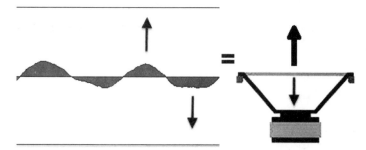

Figure 8.44 An audio waveform is a graphic representation of how a loudspeaker will move.

A small amount of direct current injected into the audio signal can set the whole waveform slightly off balance. This means when there is supposed to be silence, with the speaker "at rest," it is instead being slightly pushed or pulled and held in place. The overall effect is low-frequency distortion of the audio signal being reproduced, and possibly damaging the loudspeakers over time.

Should you ever encounter one, you are most likely to notice a DC Offset while editing the offset track if you cut the audio clips and don't apply fades to the beginning and ending of each cut. If the cuts were made in a place that should be quite obviously silent but small clicks or pops are audible, there may be an offset. Enlarging the track view and zooming in on the waveform would reveal a waveform sitting slightly above or below the 0 line. When cut, that signal would enter the mix like the front half of a square wave and be audible very briefly as a click or pop sound.

Measurement Tools

It's fine to talk about measuring audio signals as they go flying by, but that requires a good measuring stick. All the tools in this group are designed to provide some kind of numerical or visual feedback on the condition of your audio signals while recording or playing back. They are also exclusively real-time plug-ins since it doesn't really make sense to run a visual meter in anything but real-time.

The basic channel meters in Pro Tools provide one particular view of what is happening with the audio signals. The vertical bars light up in a way that mimics LED meters on outboard equipment, and are calibrated so the red line at the top of the meter represents 0dBFS, the maximum possible digital recording level. The ballistics (how the meters respond) are set to display the peaks of the audio signal so you know when they are getting close to clipping. Peak meters like these are designed to respond very quickly on the way up and fallback more slowly to keep the motion smooth. This is a great meter arrangement for basic metering and watching to keep levels within bounds, and that's the reason why it's the basic meter display for the system. Sometimes, however, it helps to get a different perspective on what's going on in there or to measure something other than the peak signal level. This is where that measuring stick gets swapped out for a nice tape measure, bubble-level, or protractor.

BF Essential Meter Bridge

At first glance, the BF Essential Meter Bridge (Figure 8.45) can seem like an odd extra plug-in that might have been thrown in to give a "vintage" look. Once you understand how the BF Essential Meter Bridge operates, its value as a measurement tool should be more obvious. It's designed to display the average signal level rather than momentary peaks to represent the overall perceived loudness.

Figure 8.45 The BF Essential Meter Bridge is designed to display the average signal level like a classic VU meter.

The plug-in displays a classic VU meter (which stands for "volume units") with a range of –20dB to +3dB, which means that right off the bat it's important to know what's going on with that scale. All of the standard meters in Pro Tools display 0dBFS as the highest possible signal because that is the point where all the little bits are either ones or zeros and can't possibly go any further. This one shows +3dB at the top mostly to match the appearance of classic analog VU meters, but also because that is kind of the point of the tool. This is not a meter designed to show absolute levels; rather, it is designed to show the level relative to a value that you select. So 0dB in this case means "on target" for whichever calibration level you happen to choose, and the relatively large display covers a very small volume range to give a clearer view of the action. There are five calibration buttons below the meters (Figure 8.46) that allow you to select how the meter translates to the standard full-scale displays.

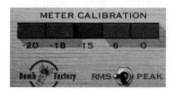

Figure 8.46   Five calibration buttons control how 0dBVU relates to various dBFS values.

The five calibration modes allow the 0dB point on the VU meter to correspond with –20, –18, –15, –6, or 0 decibels full-scale. Once that selection is made, the scale of the VU meter should make a lot more sense. As an example, if you are aiming to record a track with an average level of –18dBFS, then choose the –18 calibration setting. When the needle is at 0, the signal level is on target, and if the needle starts wandering higher or lower, it's clear the level is drifting off of that target. There is also a switch that allows the BF Essential Meter Bridge to change between a Peak mode and its standard RMS average mode. This allows for quick comparisons between the two modes, though it still responds a little slower than the standard bar graph meters.

The basic Pro Tools channel meter is set to react quickly to display the peak levels of an audio signal so you know whether they are approaching the system limitations. A classic VU meter takes a little more time so it can display the average signal level, usually over a period of about 300 milliseconds. This idea usually stirs up the question of why anyone would ever want to look at things moving more slowly to see their average. (That is exactly what you were thinking, right?) A simple answer is that sounds don't simply sit at their peak levels. They change over time, tending to peak but then sustain at a lower level, and it's the average of the changing levels that we perceive as loudness.

Think about two different instruments that are common and essential to a typical rock band recording: a snare drum and an electric bass guitar. When the drummer plays the snare drum, there is a brief and intense peak of audio energy that dies down quickly and is gone. When the bassist plucks a string and lets it ring, the initial peak may be intense, but the sustained note is quite a bit softer. Figure 8.47 shows a typical waveform of a snare drum and an electric bass where both instruments have a peak level of about –3dBFS.

From the perspective of a peak meter, both instruments peak at about –3dBFS, and then the snare drum drops off quickly while the bass sustains for a while. Measuring a typical 2 and 4, backbeat snare drum with an averaging meter is actually kind of silly, because the instrument

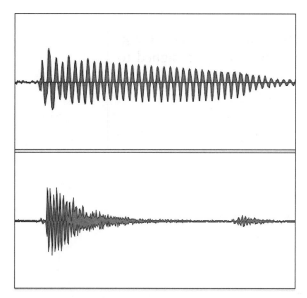

Figure 8.47 Waveforms of a typical electric bass note (top) and snare drum note (bottom).

can't really sustain unless the player strikes the drum again and really it is far more important to watch those almost instantaneous peaks. For the bass, however, the peak meter is only showing half the story. Using the BF Essential Meter Bridge for the electric bass should show that the average level of the sustained notes is lower than the peak levels, or even the sustained level shown by the peak meter. This kind of discrepancy can be frustrating for those just getting started in audio production because they see the levels are pushed up to the point of peaking, but may not hear the instrument as being "loud enough" for the mix. (For more on how to overcome that problem, jump back to Chapter 5 and read about compressors.)

Even if the signal levels aren't being troublesome right now, plug a BF Essential Meter Bridge into a track or two while recording or working through a mix. Since the basic channel meter doesn't go away, it's easy to compare how the level is displayed differently by the two meters. It's a different way of measuring, a different way of viewing, and one more tool for watching what's going on while recording and mixing.

BF Essential Noise Meter

While the BF Essential Meter Bridge provides a narrow-range VU meter to help get a better view of what's going on at the top of the signal level, the BF Essential Noise Meter (Figure 8.48) displays a 100dB wide view to better see what is going on at the bottom of the scale. When first opened up, the plug-in is set to act like a standard VU meter with a range set from −100dBFS to 0dBFS.

From this basic starting position, the BF Essential Noise Meter can provide perspective on the average levels of tracks while recording or mixing. A switch allows the meter to be switched between RMS average and peak modes for quick reference back and forth. It also makes for a convenient noise meter, and that is, after all, what the plug-in is called. In Figure 8.48, the meter

Figure 8.48 The BF Essential Noise Meter is a VU meter with a 100dB wide range.

is shown with no signal passing through it, so the needles are sitting motionless at the bottom of the scale. But in Figure 8.49, the BF Essential Noise Meter is plugged into an audio track with the input set to "In 1-2" from an Mbox 2 Mini. Nothing is plugged into the input connections on the Mbox 2, but the gain control for both channels is turned up to about 2 o'clock. The track is record enabled, and you can see the meter showing a small amount of signal level.

Figure 8.49 A small amount of system noise is revealed by the BF Essential Noise Meter.

That display is showing the system noise of the input preamplifier, analog-to-digital converter, and any radio or electrical interference that might be present. That's before any microphone or instrument is even connected, but don't take it as some kind of statement against the quality of the equipment. All audio equipment has some amount of system noise present; that's just the nature of our world. Take a closer look at Figure 8.49 and notice the noise level is lower than –85dBFS. That's lower than the noise-floor of a typical 16-bit CD player, and it doesn't even register on the standard peak meter for the track. Plug an average studio condenser microphone into that input with the gain set so high and the noise of the room, ventilation, computer fans, traffic outside, and the musicians breathing will register much higher on the meter.

The whole point of this application of the BF Essential Noise Meter is to give a visual display of the noise that may be present on any particular audio track. But noise can be a relative concept. There are noises present in an audio system that are not immediately obvious to the listener simply because of how our ears respond to sound. We are extra sensitive to certain frequency bands and less responsive to more extreme high and low frequencies. Real people will perceive real noise to be louder or softer based on what frequencies are present in the noise. So it is perfectly normal to reduce the level of some of the very high and very low frequencies before measuring the overall signal level to provide a better sense of overall loudness.

The BF Essential Noise Meter has three filter setting buttons below the meters, labeled "A," "R-D," and "None." In "A" mode, the plug-in applies an A-weighting curve similar to that used in standard audio equipment measurement and low-level sound pressure level measurement. The filter drops off some of the high- and low-frequency content before measuring to mimic the human ear's response to those frequencies at lower volume levels. In "R-D" mode, the plug-in applies a Robinson-Dadson equal-loudness curve instead. This filter attempts to more closely model the sensitivity of the human ear to give a better representation of the perceived overall noise level.

Overall, the BF Essential Noise Meter is useful as a general noise meter for assessing system noise, verifying that channels are routed properly and receiving signal, and as a broad-range VU meter to see the average levels of your tracks.

BF Essential Correlation Meter

It's more than likely that if you are working on music production (or any other kind of audio production) you will be working in stereo. It might start right at the beginning with a stereo pair of microphones recording a live performance, an acoustic instrument, or some other kind of sound. Or perhaps the stereo imaging won't start until all of those mono tracks are panned across the stereo field, or when a little reverb is added to give your dry sounds a better sense of space. Either way, the most likely destination for your audio will be a left/right stereo output. Whether it is stereo on the way in, on the way out, or both, it is important to know how the left and right channels of any stereo pair relate to one another. Are they both moving in roughly the same direction at the same time? That's where the BF Essential Correlation Meter (Figure 8.50) comes in handy.

Figure 8.50 The BF Essential Correlation Meter lets you know if both L and R channels are moving in the same direction.

Remember that when the audio signal swings up toward positive it will eventually translate to a speaker pushing air outward toward the listener, while a swing downward toward negative will translate to a speaker pulling air back away from the listener. When the speakers move back and forth at exactly the same time, they are simply playing in mono. When they are moving back and forth exactly opposite each other, they are perfectly out-of-phase, or inverted. Normal stereo playback lives somewhere in between those two extremes, though usually closer to the mono side. We want to have the speakers moving in roughly the same direction, but with the little variations that place sounds more to the left or right, or that help give us a sense of space.

The BF Essential Correlation Meter uses a single needle display to show the relationship between the left and right channels in a stereo track, bus, or mix. At rest, the needle sits at the neutral point in the center. As the meter detects a signal that is in-phase, it swings toward the +1.0 marker on the right, while out-of-phase signals pull the needle to the left. If the meter were set to respond too quickly, the meter would quite literally spend most of its time zipping from side-to-side. Instead, the ballistics are set to respond like a peak program meter with a quick rise time and slow fallback. But in an odd reverse of the peak-versus-average situation with signal levels (see the previous BF Essential Meter Bridge description), it quickly finds its way toward the right or left to show the average phase correlation, and the slow fallback time means that brief discrepancies won't register across the meter.

You can use the BF Essential Correlation Meter on audio tracks to see if incoming stereo signals are in phase, or use it on stereo busses or outputs to make sure your stereo mixes have stayed in phase. It's a great idea to use the plug-in while setting up stereo microphone pairs to check that they are generally in phase before you start recording. When there are two microphones on a solo acoustic guitar, a piano, or even a small ensemble, plug the Correlation Meter into the audio track for each to make sure the microphones are set up well and catching the instrument in phase throughout its frequency range. You can even use it to check unpaired microphones that might still affect each other, such as when you are recording an acoustic guitar and vocal at the same time. Briefly patch the pair of mono microphones into the meter to see if they are complementing or fighting each other when only the guitar or voice is going. Even though both microphones will eventually be combined and panned dead center, if they are tending toward being out of phase it is much easier to adjust the microphone positioning than to chase down the problem when you get to mixing.

One thing to keep in mind while doing this kind of testing during setup is that the speed of the meter won't show short deviations in phase very clearly. For example, if there is a cowbell positioned on a drum set in a way that causes it to be out-of-phase with the drum overheads, one stray note on it here and there may not be enough to move the needle of the Correlation Meter. If you're using the plug-in like this on the drum overheads track, be sure to spend a little time playing each individual instrument around the kit a few times. Or for material that is far more complex than a single instrument, consider moving on to the Phase Scope to get an even better view of how your left and right tracks are getting along.

SignalTools: Phase Scope and Surround Scope

Calling these plug-ins the ultimate in metering may be a bit of an overstatement. There are still other metering plug-ins that add even more features. However, recommending that no more mixes leave your Pro Tools system without first watching them on this display at least once seems like a reasonable suggestion. The Phase Scope and Surround Scope plug-ins are described here together because they represent different versions of what is effectively the same plug-in. The Phase Scope plug-in (Figure 8.51) is designed to run on stereo tracks and provides meters similar to the kinds described in the preceding three BF Essential plug-ins. The Surround Scope is the multi-channel instantiation of this metering plug-in designed to display anywhere from 3 channels (LCR) to 8 channels (7.1 Surround).

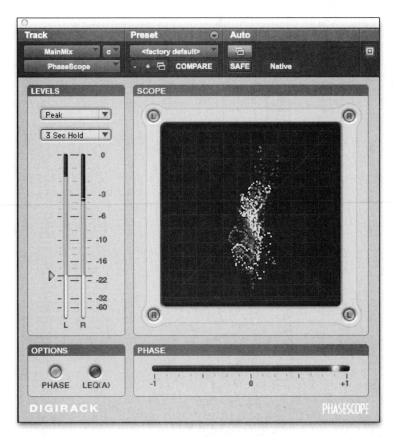

Figure 8.51 Phase Scope combines peak meters, a correlation meter, and a Lissajous meter in a single display.

Several tools are common to both plug-ins, starting with the peak meters. The Levels section at the left side of the plug-in display (Figure 8.52) shows output peak meters for each channel of the stereo or surround track. The meter display starts in the same Peak mode used throughout Pro Tools and the other Digidesign plug-ins, but different meter ballistics are selectable from the pull-down menu at the top of the display.

The available meter ballistics include several common types that also appear in other measurement plug-ins.

■ **Peak** is the default meter type used throughout Pro Tools and the other Digidesign plug-ins.

■ **RMS** is a root-mean-square meter that shows the average signal level.

- **VU** is a volume unit meter following the AES standard.

- **Peak + RMS** is a very useful mode that displays both a Peak meter in green and yellow along with an RMS meter in blue.

- **BBC** is a peak program meter following the IEC-IIa standard.

- **Nordic** is a peak program meter following the IEC Type I standards.

- **DIN** is a peak program meter following the IEC Type I standards.

- **Venue** is a peak meter that follows the calibration of the Digidesign Venue family of live-sound mixing consoles.

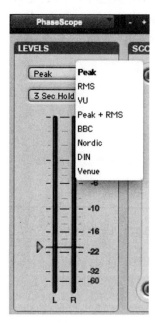

Figure 8.52 The peak meters for Phase Scope and Surround Scope and pull-down menu to select the meter ballistics.

For most audio production needs, the Peak, RMS, or Peak + RMS modes will likely be sufficient. However, if you need to comply with standards for radio or television broadcast in the United States or Europe, consult the DigiRack Plug-Ins Guide for the exact calibrations of these meters. All of the meter ballistic settings can be made to hold or release peak displays with the Peak Hold selector just below the Meter Type selector.

At the bottom-left corner of both the Phase Scope and Surround Scope plug-ins is the Options section that allows you to select from two different meters available on the bottom right. When set to the LEQ(A) mode (Figure 8.53), the LEQ(A) meter appears in the bottom right of the plug-in display.

Figure 8.53 The LEQ(A) meter shows the true A-weighted average of the power level sent to any channel.

The LEQ(A) meter shows the true, A-weighted average power level being sent to any single channel or combination of channels. A-weighted averaging is standard for low-level sound pressure level measurement. It applies an equalization filter that drops off some of the high- and low-frequency content before measuring the level to mimic the human ear's response to those frequencies at lower volume levels. The Window pull-down menu sets the length of time the signal is measured before an average level is displayed. It can be set to various increments from 1 second to 2 minutes or to the somewhat deceptively labeled "infinite" setting, which displays a real-time moving average. Two latching buttons set the behavior of the LEQ(A) when starting and stopping playback. The Auto Reset button resets the average power level display every time playback starts while the Hold On Stop button pauses the timer while playback is stopped. The non-latching Reset button clears the average to start a fresh measurement. To select the channel or channels measured by the LEQ(A) meter, click the green channel buttons (Figure 8.54) around the display in the Scope section of either the Phase Scope or Surround Scope version of the plug-in.

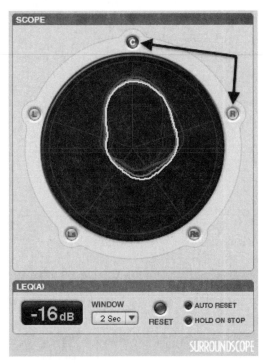

Figure 8.54 The green channel select buttons in the Scope section select which channel(s) are measured for the LEQ(A) average display.

Selecting the Phase mode from the Options section activates and displays a correlation meter in the lower right of the plug-in display (see Figure 8.55). Except for using a simulated LED display instead of a needle, this meter functions in the same way as the BF Essential Correlation Meter described earlier in this chapter. At the center position of 0, the left and right signals are in a fairly consistent stereo balance. At the +1 position to the far right, the stereo pair is in phase, approaching mono. At the –1 position to the far left, the pair is completely out of phase.

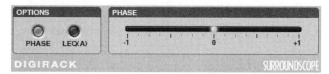

Figure 8.55 Selecting the Phase mode displays a correlation meter in the lower right of the plug-in.

The Phase Scope version of the plug-in always displays the correlation of the left and right channels in this meter. For the Surround Scope version, any two channels can be fed to the correlation meter by selecting the blue channel buttons in the Scope section of the plug-in, just as you would to select which channels feed the LEQ(A) meter.

The place where the two plug-in versions take a more dramatic turn from one another is in the Scope display section. In Phase Scope, this display is a Lissajous meter that compares the level and phase relationship between the left and right channels in a stereo signal. Figure 8.56 below shows a mono signal panned center and displayed in the meter to illustrate how a mono signal should look.

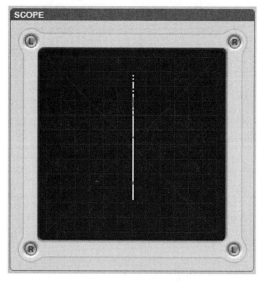

Figure 8.56 The Lissajous meter in Phase Scope displaying a mono signal panned center and in phase.

The sharp, straight line is a dead giveaway that the signal being metered is in mono. Mono signals are exactly the same in the right and left channels, so both the left and right busses would be moving up and down, from positive to negative, together. On the other hand, Figure 8.57 shows a mono signal panned center (equal strength to both left and right channels). The signal is being fed to the bus out of phase, meaning that the signal being sent to one channel is being inverted along the way. The same sharp line now appears horizontal in the display.

The graph is literally showing you that when the right channel moves toward the positive, the left moves toward the negative, and vice versa. Those images both show mono signals in the display

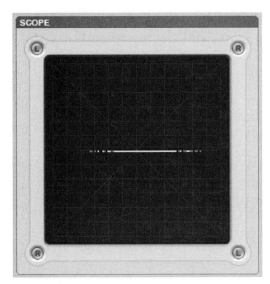

Figure 8.57 The Lissajous meter in Phase Scope displaying a center-panned mono signal that is out of phase.

but provide a good reference for what direction things should be pointing. Stereo displays will look more like the little blobs of green dots shown in the display in Figure 8.58. To effectively use the meter to determine whether your stereo tracks, channels, or mixes are in phase, watch to make sure the dots appear primarily between the upper and lower quadrants. Out-of-phase signals will group horizontally between the left and right quadrants.

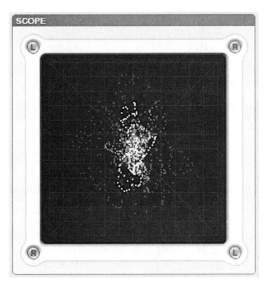

Figure 8.58 A typical in-phase stereo signal will be displayed as a collection of green dots mostly grouped vertically between the upper and lower quadrants.

For the Surround Scope version of the plug-in, the display in the Scope section is a surround level scope that displays relative signal levels from each channel in the multichannel group. Silence would display as a single dot in the center of the scope. An audio signal arriving at roughly the same strength from all directions will be displayed as a circle (Figure 8.59), and if the signal arrives at a stronger level from any particular channel, the shape will deform slightly to point toward that channel marker.

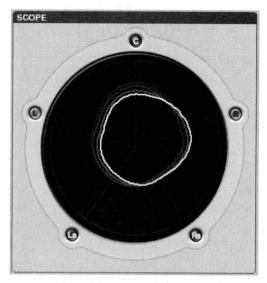

Figure 8.59 The Surround Scope shows that signals are arriving at almost equal strength from all channels with a little extra from the right front.

Whether working in stereo or surround, Phase Scope and Surround Scope provide a consolidated set of meters that display peak channel levels, phase relationships, and average power levels in a large and easy-to-read display. It can be a lot of information to display on every channel, but it can be used to get the best view possible of what is happening on any stereo or multichannel track, channel, or mix. It can be helpful to see what is happening before tracks are recorded, to watch what is going on while mixing, and to make sure everything is all right before final mixes are printed. Truly, no finished audio should leave your Pro Tools system without being viewed through one of these SignalTools plug-ins.

TL InTune

As with the Trillium Lane Labs AutoPan plug-in covered earlier in this chapter, the TL InTune plug-in has very good documentation included with ProTools. It's covered there in far more depth than you might expect for a simple tuner. That doesn't mean I will leave it out here, but it's reasonable to give just a basic overview of the functions here since there is much more detail already available if you need it.

The first thing to realize about TL InTune (Figure 8.60) is that it is not an automatic pitch correction plug-in. It is a measurement tool. That's precisely why I included it here. It is a plug-in for measuring how close (or far) your instruments are from being in tune.

Now that's not to suggest that InTune isn't a very useful plug-in or that it can't help you to correct pitch issues if you happen to record them despite your best efforts.

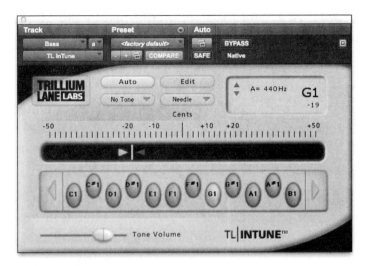

Figure 8.60 TL InTune is a measurement tool that allows you to see whether you are in tune. It's not a pitch correction program.

There are a few ways you can use InTune to get your instruments aimed in the right direction *before* you record, instead of chasing down pitch problems afterward. First, InTune can act as a tone generator. Activate the plug-in on an auxiliary bus like your monitor feed, or directly on a channel. Then use the Tone pull-down menu to switch from No Tone to another setting such as Sine or Triangle. Those different wave shapes change the timbre of the tone being played. Then select a note and InTune will play the pitch so you can tune to it.

When tuning to a tone, it's usually best to listen through headphones, particularly when tuning string instruments like guitar or bass. Listening through speakers can cause sympathetic vibrations of the strings that can make it hard to get yourself properly tuned up.

You can select the pitches you'd like to tune each string to yourself, or you can use one of the presets in the pull-down menu (Figure 8.61). This menu includes presets for all kinds of string

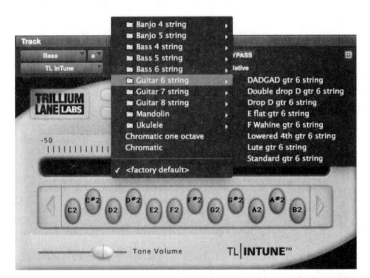

Figure 8.61 InTune has an extensive selection of presets for tuning up string instruments.

instruments that might show up in a pop, rock, folk, or bluegrass session, and blanks out all the unused notes from the scale so as not to confuse.

The other option for tuning up your instrument is to play the notes, with or without a tone playing along, and feed the microphone or direct signal into the ProTools channel that has the plug-in running. You can either use a Needle display or rock it old-school style with a simulated Strobe tuner (just like the high school band teacher used to have!). Either approach will show you if your instrument is leaning a little flat (low) or sharp (high) so that you know whether to tune up or down until you're right on the money.

While it isn't an automatic pitch corrector, InTune does have a button labeled Auto that can be very helpful during the editing stage of your project if somebody drifted away from being in tune with the rest of the band. By switching to Auto mode, the tuner will try to identify what note is being played and show how far off it is from the target.

This can be a very handy feature when you hear that something isn't quite matching in your track, but you're not sure what direction to go. You can measure what note each instrument is playing and then tune the one that is furthest out down to match the others. Remember, though, that it's not always best to simply pull each note to the exact right pitch. Real musicians tend to wander off the pitch center as a group and find a place that works for them. A band might play an entire song, even an entire session amazingly well even though they are all playing 10 cents sharp. In those cases you might still have an out-of-tune note you can hear, and it might even measure as dead on for what it's supposed to be, while still not matching the others. Always measure a few different notes and instruments before making any changes, and then reach for the Pitch plug-in to shift things around to where they need to be.

TL Master Meter

The TL Master Meter (Figure 8.62) is kind of unique among the Pro Tools metering plug-ins in that it isn't able to be configured for different views and perspectives on your audio. Instead, it is designed for one primary purpose: to let you know when your signal will go over the limit during digital-to-analog conversion.

Remember that PCM (pulse-code modulation) digital audio streams are made up of samples, and those samples are really just lots and lots of measurements. At a sample rate of 44,100 samples per second (44.1 kHz), your analog audio signal will be measured 44,100 times each second. Each measurement will be represented by a number of ones and zeros, the binary code that your computer understands and can process. I know that seems oversimplified, but stick with me.

After your audio signal is chopped into bits (literally) and equalized, compressed, summed, differenced, bent, cracked, broken, frayed, frozen, and fried, it will eventually need to be returned to the land of the living. That is, it will need to be reconverted to analog. In your studio, that might happen only when the playback finally leaves the computer, soundcard, or I/O interface on its way to the speakers or headphones. It might even stay digital all the way to the client's car, or to the final customer's house. But at some point, the digital data will be turned back into analog audio voltages. At that point, there's some number crunching to do.

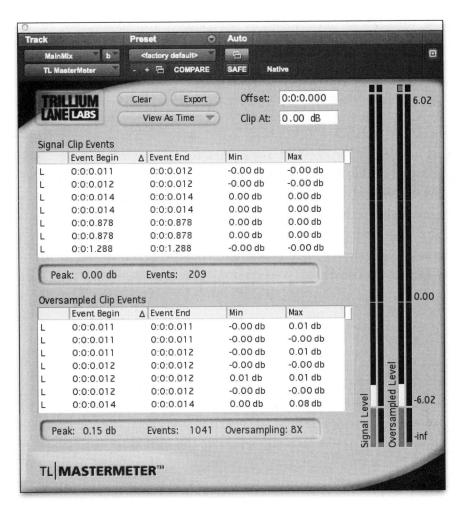

Figure 8.62   TL Master Meter tells you if your tracks will clip later on, during D-to-A conversion.

Simply setting each digital value to an analog voltage value for the brief length of time each sample represents creates an audio signal that isn't as smooth as a natural analog waveform. The wave can be slightly jagged and inaccurate to the original analog sound. So digital-to-analog converters use something called oversampling to try to smooth the curves of the analog wave form by trying to determine what values should appear between each of the given samples. If a wave seemed to be moving upward and then seems to plateau between two samples, it may have originally curved upward with a peak that occurred just between the two.

That's what TL Master Meter is looking for. It's built to watch for all the times that your audio signal may look (to a computer) like the signal is within limits, while it's really destined to cross over that 0dBFS absolute threshold once it's really being converted back to an analog audio signal. The plug-in logs all such events so you know where they occur, and makes them available in a format that can be exported and sent to your mastering and/or duplication facility. If either destination encounters digital overages or distortion, they can refer to the exported document to know if you were aware of the issue and sent the material forward to them anyway. It's a rather specialized meter that can be a little difficult to understand at first, but if you're sending any of your material on to mastering, duplication, or even just making a bunch of copies to send or sell on your own, you should keep TL Master Meter in mind as your last best hope at keeping your final client-side D-to-A conversion sounding just as good as it's supposed to.

Advanced Techniques and Good Practice

Are there really advanced techniques or special tricks when it comes to using the editing or measurement tools described in this chapter? Maybe not anything as flashy as some of the other plug-in categories, but there are some tools that might be worth a little more time and exploration. Where the editing tools such as Gain or Normalize are concerned, the best approach is to become comfortable with the basic functions of each plug-in and then learn when to use the clip-by-clip mode for batch rendering. That was already described in some detail in the Normalize section above, but can be applied to almost all of Audio Suite plug-ins. But here are a few more ideas to peruse and ponder.

Throw It in Reverse

There is at least one technique that seems to show up on the creative landscape at some point in every engineer's experience, and that is playing with backward vocals, also known as "backmasking." The Reverse plug-in makes experimenting with this technique far easier than it ever was with analog tape machines, and the flexibility of moving audio around within Pro Tools means that timing phrases with beats is easier as well. Whether the aim is to use backward vocals as an audible effect, or a secret hidden message, or even some kind of attempt at subliminal suggestion, the technique begins with selecting an audio clip, reversing it, and listening to the results.

The usefulness, truthfulness, and effectiveness of backmasking have all been the subject of controversy over the years. People may claim to hear hidden messages in places where the artists never actually placed them. Others may claim those hidden messages must then be a window into the subconscious of the artists. Meanwhile, some recordings really do contain intentional backward vocals with some meant to be heard audibly during forward playback and others meant to be hidden. A quick search around the Internet for "backward vocals" or "backmasking" can help as a guide toward some of the history and possibilities for the technique. Whether the messages have been intentional or imagined, there are many stories, many believers, and many skeptics.

About the only consistent, current use of backward vocals is the intentional reversing of obscenities in lead vocal parts. Radio edits of the past often simply removed an offensive word from the vocal track, leaving a rather obvious, gaping hole in the middle of the lyrics. A more popular trend for the last decade or so has been to create a copy of the vocal track, select the individual word, and reverse that small audio clip. The musical result is that a word like "shit" sounds like "ish" in the recording. But the somewhat more humorous cultural result is that the word "ish" has become a common slang replacement in normal speech as well.

Regardless of how backward vocals or backmasking might be incorporated into your audio productions, remember that the reversed words will not usually sound like what they look like spelled backward. When the audio clip is reversed, the sound of each phonetic component of the word is reversed and our ears may often hear the new sounds as entirely different phonemes and syllables. A simple test is to pick a few random words, speak them into a microphone, record them, reverse them, and listen. Try a word like "pizza" as a good starter. Looking at the letters would suggest the reverse to sound like "a zip" or something close to that. But if you say the word at all close to the way I do, it may sound a lot more like "asleep" with a very short and hard "p" at the end.

...But I Love to Watch You Go

Good metering, and paying close attention to what is going on as far as levels and phase isn't something that ends at tracking, editing, or even mixing. With memory and processing resources at a premium, it may not always be possible to run all of the metering and measurement tools throughout your entire production process. But with the end drawing near, it's a good idea to plug those tools back in and see exactly what kind of product you will be delivering. Some tools, like the TL MasterMeter, are specifically designed to provide that last and final assessment of your mix. But setting up a parallel bus with a couple of measurement plug-ins engaged to analyze the final mix is a great way to make sure the project is truly complete.

Depending on your mix destination, the final mono, stereo, or surround mix may be routed to physical outputs or internal busses for recording the final mix, and then eventually to physical busses for monitoring. Select the last stop before the final mix is recorded as the spot to measure. The example below (Figure 8.63) has several tracks being mixed to Bus 1-2 (Stereo), which is controlled by a master fader, then picked up as an input to a stereo audio track where the final mix will be recorded, and subsequently routed to the Out 1-2 (Stereo) output of an Mbox 2 for monitoring.

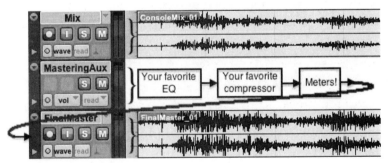

Figure 8.63 Several audio tracks are routed through an internal bus to an audio track that will record the final master.

You can set the extra meters in the signal path where they are labeled above, or optionally you could create an additional auxiliary bus just for metering. From this setup, you could also add an extra stereo Aux Track that draws its input from the main stereo mix on Bus 1-2 (Stereo) and send its output to an unused destination. This would set up a parallel destination for the final mix to be monitored visually through a few plug-ins, but this extra copy doesn't need to be recorded or sent to a physical output for audio monitoring. Remember that a secondary Master Fader cannot be used here because any bus or output can only be controlled by a single Master Fader.

From this configuration, it is easy to assign a couple of metering and measurement plug-ins to get a good last look at the condition of the final mix. Consider assigning the BF Essential Meter Bridge, Phase Scope, or TL MasterMeter plug-ins to the inserts on the new monitoring Aux Track and opening the windows for all three measurement tools (Figure 8.64).

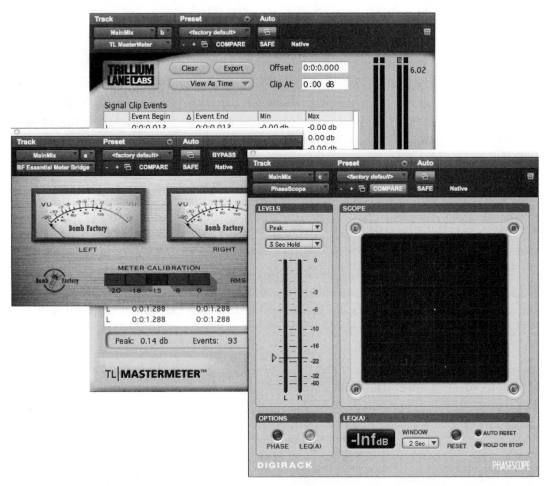

Figure 8.64 A collection of measurement tools gives one last view of the mix as it heads for the door.

If your system has the resources to run all these measurement tools while the final mix is being recorded, then do it! However, the beauty of arranging all of these on an Aux Track in this way is that the track can be selected and made active or inactive with one or two clicks of the mouse. This saves on resources as necessary to stay out of the way of the audible real-time plug-ins that may be running, but keeps the tools setup handy for checking on things along the way.

Overuse, Abuse, and Danger Zones

Is it even possible to measure something too much? Well, yes...kind of.

While it's always a great idea to have a good grasp of what is going on with all the tracks, busses, instruments, sounds, and mixes throughout production, there are times when watching the meters too closely can make us lose sight of the goal. What's really important in all of this is making great-sounding recordings and productions. The meters and measurement tools are there to help keep things within certain boundaries and provide some reassurance that our tracks and mixes are in-tune, in-phase, and at consistent volume levels. But the meters don't test for quality of performance or creativity of material. They can tell how in-tune each individual bass guitar note might be, but not how funky that bass line really is. They can tell you when one take is louder than another, but not when it is better, and that's a very important distinction.

There is a lot of talk and writing throughout the audio world that describes the "loudness wars" of both CD mastering and FM radio. Radio stations need to compete for the attention of the potential listener while he is spinning the radio dial. A louder station will capture the listener's attention by default, and is likely to be perceived to sound better than other stations. The practice isn't much different with CD mastering, where the average level of the program material on one album is pushed slightly louder than its competitors to make that album stand out from the rest. In small doses, people will almost always pick the louder sound as the better sound. And just to complicate things a little more, sometimes the louder one really is better. But the idea is to separate the measurement of how loud your material is from the assessment of how good it is.

This balance doesn't apply exclusively to peak and average levels either. It can apply to tuning, phase correlation, or almost anything that can be measured. Yes, it is important to watch for phase problems with stereo tracks and final mixes. We might hope that our music will be played back only on properly configured stereo systems, but the real world is full of lots of mono clock radios, background music systems, and AM radio stations. To obsess too much about the phase correlation might simply mean narrowing the entire recording down to mono. Sure, that will guarantee that no phase problems will be sent out into the world, but it also means there will be no stereo movement or sense of space around the material. The point of a tape measure isn't to ensure that every piece of wood you cut is the same length. The point is to make sure every cut is the right length.

In the end, it's best to remember that the metering and measurement tools are there for measuring quantity and not quality. They can help to provide a framework and reference of how your tracks and mixes compare to one another and to other material out there in the world.

Index

Like the Book?

Let us know on Facebook or Twitter!

facebook.com/courseptr

twitter.com/courseptr

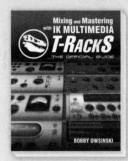